RETAIL BUYING

AND

MERCHANDISING

MILTON L. SHUCH, Director

Prince Program in Retailing Management
Simmons College

PRENTICE HALL, ENGLEWOOD CLIFFS, NJ 07632

Library of Congress Cataloging-in-Publication Data

Shuch, Milton L.
    Retaiil buying and merchandising.

    Includes index.
    1. Purchasing.   2. Merchandising.   3. Retail trade.
I. Tiitle.
HF5437.S49   1988   658.8'7   87-25923
ISBN   0-13-775222-9

Editorial/production supervision and interior design: Maureen Wilson
Cover design: George Cornell
Manufacturing buyer: Barbara Kittle

 © 1988 by Prentice-Hall, Inc.
A Division of Simon & Schuster
Englewood Cliffs, New Jersey 07632

Printed in the United States of America

10   9   8   7   6   5   4   3   2   1

ISBN 0-13-775222-9   01

PRENTICE-HALL INTERNATIONAL (UK) LIMITED, *London*
PRENTICE-HALL OF AUSTRALIA PTY. LIMITED, *Sydney*
PRENTICE-HALL CANADA INC., *Toronto*
PRENTICE-HALL HISPANOAMERICANA, S.A., *Mexico*
PRENTICE-HALL OF INDIA PRIVATE LIMITED, *New Delhi*
PRENTICE-HALL OF JAPAN, INC., *Tokyo*
PRENTICE-HALL OF SOUTHEAST ASIA PTE. LTD., *Singapore*
EDITORA PRENTICE-HALL DO BRASIL, LTDA., *Rio de Janeiro*

To my wife, Sheila,
to our children,
and to all people
who have not found numbers to be their friends.

Contents

8 REPRICING 150

9 THE MERCHANDISE BUDGET 167

10 PURCHASE PLANNING AND CONTROL 188

11 MEASURING AND EVALUATING SALES RESULTS 214

12 MERCHANDISING AND SALES-RELATED REPORTS 238

13 SALES ASSOCIATE SCHEDULING AND PRODUCTIVITY ANALYSIS 260

Preface

During the eighteen years that I spent as a retailer, growing from the owner of a single store to the operator of a small chain of stores, many of the principles and techniques described in this book evolved. Some of these were outgrowths of my formal undergraduate education, but many developed from "street sense" and my recognition of the urgency of retailing and my priority to be better than my competitors.

After deciding to put my practical experience to use as a teacher, I learned, during graduate work, to analyze broad concepts and structure them into small teachable units. Therefore, one of my goals in assembling this text was to present practical information concisely in a relatively noncomplex format.

While earlier editions of this book have gained many supporters from people already in the field, the intent is to produce a text that can serve novices in entry-level positions, satisfying their immediate needs while providing a background that will assist them in reaching subsequently higher levels of retailing management.

The total role a buyer fills within a retail organization is seldom fully appreciated and understood by students. I know that executive trainees will not become involved, early on, with six-month buying plans, vendor analysis, and day-to-day pressure of "beating last year," but the more learners see of the buyer's job, the better they will comprehend the qualities they must have if they aspire to become buyers.

This book is written for the person who has acquired a basic knowledge of retailing through work experience, by successfully completing introductory retailing classes, or both. Each topic has been explained and those which are computational have been illustrated with step-by-step examples followed by problems that reinforce the learning. Summary problems are provided, where appropriate, at the end of each chapter, requiring students to use information taught in prior chapters as well as from the unit they have just completed. In addition, situational case problems have been included that assist the student in understanding the context in which a particular topic must be viewed and to sharpen their analytical skills.

The appendices, which contain a condensation of federal legislation affecting retailers; forms used in buyer evaluation; a glossary of terms; and a formula summary indexed to the text, should be viewed by both the instructor and student as valuable adjuncts to the learning process.

Overall, it is my desire to assist in some small way those who strive to become the retailing professionals of tomorrow.

ACKNOWLEDGMENTS

I wish to extend my thanks to the following members of the Prince Program in Retailing Management's Advisory Committee who, with many members of their organizations, have provided me with counsel, advice, and assistance for my students and with the writing of this text:

- Angel Algeri, President
  David Banash and Son, Inc., Boston, MA
- Virginia Caillouette, Vice President
  Macy's, New York, NY
- M. Kaminstein, President and CEO
  J. Bildner & Sons, Boston, MA
- Maurice Segall, Chairman of the Executive Committee
  Zayre Corporation, Framingham, MA
- Jerry M. Socol, Chairman of the Board
  Filene's, Boston, MA
- Elliot Stone, Chairman of the Board
  Jordan Marsh, Boston, MA

My gratitude is extended to my friend and colleague, Norma Rusbar, whose knowledge of the field and commitment to excellence in retailing education provided me with added impetus to write this text.

I am also indebted to William J. Holmes, Jr., president of Simmons College, who has provided me with a fertile environment, encouragement, and opportunities for personal and professional growth.

While Dr. Karen Gillespie of New York University is always satisfied with a sincere thank you, it will not suffice here for the support, counsel, and patience she has given me as advisor, teacher, and friend. As a master teacher,

Karen has successfully launched many of us into careers in education and business. I, as well as many others, am fortunate to have benefited from her wisdom.

Although many people have contributed to my practical retailing background, my uncle, Benjamin Spector, taught me the value of ethics, kindness, and generosity. He was a giant in retailing in terms of human relations, and his presence in the market was always enthusiastically acknowledged by vendors and fellow retailers, great and small, who sought his advice.

Humble thanks go also to my father, Harry Shuch, who was a man of endless patience and structured my practical retailing learning from porter-stock boy to chainstore owner, so that I would know every job and fully appreciate what each person who did the work had to endure and enjoy.

I must also give recognition and thanks to all of my former students who have taught me as they tolerated and, hopefully, learned in my class and to the following people for their helpful comments while I was preparing the manuscript: Carole Lissy, William Rainey Harper College, Judith Paul, University of Wisconsin—Platteville, Jerome Greenberg, Rutgers University, John L. Roman, Rochester Institute of Technology, and Ray Tewell, American River College.

The greatest gift I could give my secretary, Gail Christine, would be to stop writing, which I will, after I formally say thank you. She has typed, retyped, spaced, made divisions, and produced countless other word processing maneuvers to give the manuscript of this book continuity and a professional appearance. No author could ask for more. Thank you, Gail.

M. L. SHUCH
Boston, Massachusetts

The Buyer's Environment

1

MACRO-CONSIDERATIONS

To many students of retailing, as well as to a large number of people in the general population, the title of "buyer" conjures up visions of individuals who are wined and dined by vendors, live elegant and privileged lives, and fill their days with visits to fashion shows and unpressured decision making.

The truth, however, is that buyers are often fortunate to find time for lunch, for they work intensely, making many of their decisions under "pressure-cooker" circumstances. Nor are buyers often located in luxurious quarters; their offices may be tucked away in a stockroom area or under noisy air-conditioning equipment.

Why, then, do so many people aspire to become buyers? Because buying is where the "action" is. No one believes that the sales force is unimportant or that Personnel or the Control Division is nonessential, but it is the buyer who projects the image of the store and whose taste in merchandise may please (or displease) hosts of customers.

If they are to be successful, however, buyers must understand the climate within which they work. This environment consists of four components: customers; types of retailers; the strategic planning process, which combines the first two and develops a format for profitable operation; and the organization within which the buyer operates.

Buying is obviously not a job for the timid; it also requires stamina and organization. The basic principles of buying can be mastered, particularly the general knowledge needed by all buyers in their day-to-day activities. You will see how the application of these principles is the variable you must consider as you move from one classification of merchandise to another in your job as a buyer.

Buyers are not selling agents for vendors but rather purchasing agents for their customers.

This statement, more than any other, provides definition to the role retailers and buyers must fill. It indicates that the format for retailing success is one of customer orientation and, more specifically, of understanding and providing merchandise and services which will generate consumer satisfaction.

Every day the ranks of retailers increase; each retailer with its own formula for attracting customers, which will hopefully generate profits. Unfortunately, the great majority will not succeed, due to poor managerial ability. This includes their failure to know their customers, as well as their lack of buying competence.

The next section of this chapter will be devoted to highlighting the criteria used by customers in their retailer selection process; setting forth basic standards which will assist you to identify and categorize various types of retailers; introducing strategic planning; and finally, discussing the role a buyer has in the retail organization.

CONSUMER ORIENTATION

Given the large numbers of retailers striving to attract customers, people have become astute shoppers, measuring the offerings of each store against their own personal standards and rewarding the retailer who best meets these criteria by purchasing from that store. Generally, these criteria include

1. Store location
2. Merchandise assortment
3. Individual attention
4. Services offered
5. Pricing
6. Store image

Each of these criteria will have different levels of significance to individual customers; these will also vary for different purchases. As an example, customers may elect to purchase their designer clothing from I. Magnin or Neiman-Marcus but will buy gasoline for their cars at a discount service station selling unbranded fuel.

Store location. For certain types of purchases, customers will not object to traveling some distance or shopping in a low-rent area. Other items, however, which are needed quickly, are bought from local merchants. Convenience stores, such as 7-ELEVEN and Lil Peach, are prime examples of retailers who are filling consumers' needs by virtue of their neighborhood locations.

Merchandise assortment.   The assortment of merchandise carried by a store can be described (besides its styling) in terms of breadth and depth of lines,[1] where breadth indicates the diversification of merchandise and depth refers to the quantity carried within each line. It can also apply to the numbers of styles carried within a line (breadth) and the assortment of colors or range of sizes (depth) stocked. (See Fig. 1–1)

Figure 1–1 illustrates an assortment which has a breadth of seven merchandise lines; line four having the greatest depth.

In a practical sense, you could observe that a small-electrics department carries seven lines of toasters, with line four represented by four styles.

A specialty store or boutique would have a narrow assortment of lines of merchandise, but customers should find considerable depth; conversely, a convenience store carries a broad and shallow assortment compared with a supermarket.

Individual attention.   Personalization has been the mainstay of many retailers, particularly small independents. Many customers enjoy receiving the individual attention of a store owner; being addressed by name; having their preferences in colors and styles noted; and subsequently receiving calls when "just the right item" has come in. Large stores and chains attempt to emulate this personalization via sales training programs and by encouraging their sales associates to develop customer reference files.

Services offered.   A list of general services which may be offered to customers could easily fill many pages and is covered effectively in numerous introductory retailing texts. There are several that are most directly related to the buyer, however. These include special orders for sizes, colors, and styles (or locating comparable merchandise) not carried in your normal assortments but available from your regular vendors; a reasonable customer return and replacement policy for defective goods; warranty and repair support; and proper instructions and assistance for assembly and operation. The latter service is most often a function of your sales staff, and the training for your sales associates can be pro-

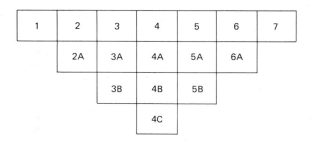

Figure 1–1 Breadth and Depth in Inventory

vided by vendors or their representatives. This instruction can be a basis for negotiations between the buyer and vendor.[2]

Pricing.   A buyer employed by a large organization is seldom able to establish a pricing policy; that is, conventional markup and prices or discount pricing. This is not true for the independent retailer, who has the latitude to control the markup and retail price for each item carried in stock.

Price is, nevertheless, a store selection factor for customers and is most often addressed as a strategy by a retailer attempting to maximize profits through either conventional pricing (thus permitting increases in the availability of the other criteria) or discount pricing, which generates profits through a higher volume of sales per item than can be attained through the customary method.

Store image.   The projected image of a store is a combination of all the criteria previously listed, as well as others such as promotion, merchandise arrangement, decor, and appearance of staff. Image should be portrayed as a cohesive appeal. It is often ego-satisfying, attracting shoppers who desire chic surroundings in which to purchase their elegant fashions or, at the opposite end of the scale, those whose egos are rewarded more by the value they are receiving for their money than by the splendor of the environment in which the merchandise is set.

TYPES OF RETAILERS

Retailers must strive to be different from their rivals if they are to survive in a highly competitive environment.

From the preceding statement, you might conclude that successful retailers are so different from each other that they cannot be segmented into limited classifications. If finite typifications were attempted, this would be true; however, certain broad measures can be used to provide useful definition to the retailing setting. (See Fig. 1–2)

The basic standards are

1. Location
2. Sales strategy
3. Size of store(s)
4. Variety of merchandise lines

Location.   Stores are classified according to the physical site they occupy. The most venerable of these is the downtown, or main street, store. Although the status of stores located in a central business district has varied considerably since the 1950's, "downtown" continues to remain an important location. In many cities, such as New York, Boston, Chicago, Detroit, and St. Louis, busi-

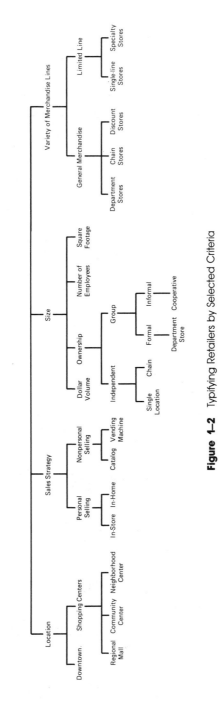

Figure 1-2 Typifying Retailers by Selected Criteria

ness property developers and government have teamed up to rejuvenate areas that had become shoddy and unattractive to shoppers. This has been accomplished through improvement of buildings currently occupied; creating pedestrian malls by prohibiting vehicular traffic; rebuilding and remodeling old unoccupied buildings, creating new shopping centers in downtown locations; or building vertical malls which contain several levels of retail space followed by floors designed for office occupancy and apartments or as a hotel site.

Shopping centers came onto the retailing scene as our population began to migrate to suburban areas after World War II. These are segmented into (a) regional malls, which have one or more major department stores as their "anchor stores" and upwards of 50 smaller shops (see Figs. 1–3, 1–4); (b) community shopping centers, which usually have a single department store or a smaller modified department store as their main customer attraction, accompanied by 20 or more smaller stores; and (c) neighborhood centers, those with a large supermarket as their principle tenant, complemented by a drugstore, dry cleaning establishment, and/or other personal service stores.

Figure 1–3 Regional Mall Overview

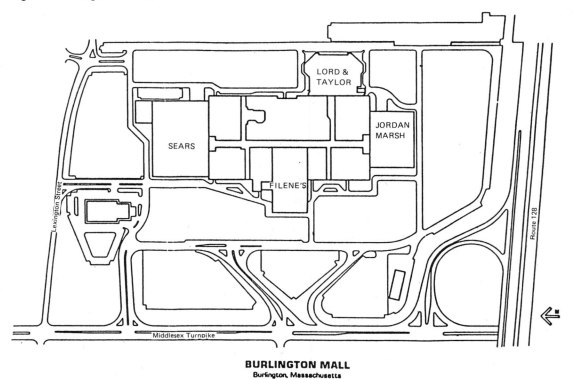

BURLINGTON MALL
Burlington, Massachusetts
Site Plan

SOURCE: Reprinted courtesy of Burlington Mall Management, Burlington, MA.

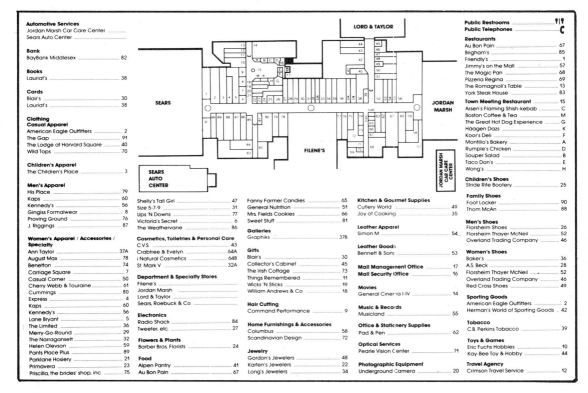

Figure 1-4 Regional Mall Tenant Listing

SOURCE: Reprinted courtesy of Burlington Mall Management, Burlington, MA.

Sales strategy.   Retailing has been defined as the sale of goods and/or services to an ultimate consumer. Therefore, the selling methods employed to convey these goods and services become a system to identify one retailer from another. They are separated into two broad categories: personal and nonpersonal selling.

The most common form of personal selling is the sales associate within a store. In addition, another type is the in-home salesperson who accomplishes selling by door-to-door techniques with merchandise such as cosmetics, home-care products and newspaper delivery. Also included in the in-home category are sales of services such as lawn maintenance and snow removal, as are purchases arranged by telephone solicitations.

Nonpersonal selling, that is, selling without personal contact between customer and retailer, includes catalog or mail-order selling and vending machines. The former category is commonly associated with Sears, Montgomery Ward, and J. C. Penney, although many smaller firms and individuals have entered into the catalog market, some selling very narrow lines of merchandise, such as Christmas decorations or greeting cards, while others list clothing for men, women, or children as their product offerings.

Vending or merchandise machines distribute a wide range of goods, including food and general merchandise. They are also used in a service orientation selling airline tickets at busy airports for commuter or shuttle flights, as are Eastern Airlines' machines in Boston, New York, and Washington; and used by banks to facilitate a wide variety of transactions.

Size of store.   The use of "size" as a descriptor is the most fundamental identifying characteristic and can be represented in terms of dollar volume, ownership, numbers of employees, and square footage. It is also common practice to combine several of these characteristics to produce other distinguishing traits, as well as measures of productivity such as dollar sales per square foot (dollar sales ÷ square feet) or dollar sales per employee (dollar sales ÷ numbers of employees).

DOLLAR VOLUME.   Describing a store by its dollar volume is stating only the total sales without regard to whether the retailer sells 100 units at $15,000 each (automobiles) for a total of $1,500,000 or thousands of items to reach the same volume. Therefore, this criterion, like others, must match up similar retailers for any comparisons to be valid.

OWNERSHIP.   The size of a retailing firm is also expressed by indicating if the organization is owned independently, that is, one which is not affiliated with any other, or if it is a division of an ownership group. An independent retailing firm can be one which operates from a single location, or it can be a chain such as Sears and J. C. Penney. Many formerly independent firms, particularly department stores, have merged or have been absorbed into ownership groups.

The impact of ownership size is that certain economies of scale can be gained. As an example, buyers can write orders for ten stores as easily as for one store, assuming the customer profiles for all stores are the same; and in ownership groups centralized data processing and policy planning are common. Each division of a group buys merchandise for its own stores and continues to set standards for its own image depending upon its customers. The ownership group may, however, establish buyers' committees to share information and also develop exclusive merchandise for the group as a whole.

Unaffiliated stores may also join together and form cooperatives or, as many independent grocery retailers do, organize voluntary wholesale groups. Many of the same economies of scale attained by chains and ownership groups are thus available to smaller organizations.

NUMBER OF EMPLOYEES.   The size of a firm is also gauged by numbers of employees. Many stores have one or two paid employees. A typical "Mom and Pop" store would have no paid employees, as Mom and Pop are the owner-operators. At the other end of the scale, major department stores employ thousands of workers under one roof.

SQUARE FOOTAGE.   Square footage refers to the space occupied by the store. This can range from a few square feet, as typified by a newsstand or kiosk such as those occupied by Fotomat, to over two million square feet as represented by Macy's Herald Square store in mid-town Manhattan.

Variety of merchandise lines.   Retailers are characterized according to the number of different merchandise classifications (breadth) carried in their inventories and to the extent (depth) each is stocked. There are two major categories which encompass the retail environment: general merchandise stores and limited-line stores.

GENERAL MERCHANDISE RETAILERS.   This category of retailer carries the broadest assortment of merchandise classifications, including apparel and accessories for all members of the family; furniture, home furnishings, small and large appliances; hardware; and food.

Department stores are identified with this variety of goods. The department store category is itself separated into three headings: the traditional department store typified by Jordan Marsh, Macy's, or J. W. Robinsons; the chain store such as Sears; and the discount or mass merchandising chain, which would include Zayre and Kmart.

LIMITED-LINE RETAILERS.   Limited-line retailers are either single-line stores or specialty shops. The former are stores which carry one or relatively few major lines of merchandise, but carry them in substantive depth. Hardware stores, paint and wallpaper centers, and grocery and produce stores are examples.

Specialty shops are those whose breadth of merchandise is made up of one major classification. Greeting card shops, bookstores or stores catering to customers with special clothing size requirements (petite, full figure, or extra sizes) fall into this classification. These stores, like single-line stores, have considerable depth of stock to attract customers.

STRATEGIC PLANNING PROCESS

The core responsibility for you as a buyer is to purchase merchandise that will sell and generate a profit for your organization.

In a single word, the most important, difficult, and time-consuming task for a buyer is PLANNING. You must plan for the proportions of the various lines of merchandise you are to buy; plan for the breadth and depth of assortments within each classification and subclassification; plan floor layouts and plan to work with your department managers to implement them; plan when to peak your stock levels; plan special events and advertising; plan for your market visits; and plan to evaluate your results.

The actual process of selecting merchandise will require you to combine your understanding of the stores' customer and your "taste" for merchandise. It becomes a function of the strategy you (and others in your organization) have developed.

During the strategic development process[3], you must not forget that the ultimate goal of the strategy is to provide your firm with competitive advantages over its rival stores. These advantages will originate from your customers' superior satisfaction with your merchandise and service offerings compared with those of your competitors. A state of equality exists between you and your competitors when neither of you has a competitive advantage over the other. This can be seen algebraically as

Customer Perceptions (of all similar stores) =
Customer Expectations → Customer Satisfactions

However, as you attain competitive advantages,

Customer Perceptions (of your store) >
Customer Expectations → Superior Satisfactions

The use of a clearly defined development process minimizes the potential for failure and assures realization of differentially perceived competitive superiority by your customer against your competitors. Ultimately, these advantages will produce repeat customer purchases, increased sales, and market share growth.

The strategic planning process involves six factors (see Fig. 1-5):

1. Assessment
2. Core customer
3. Core competition

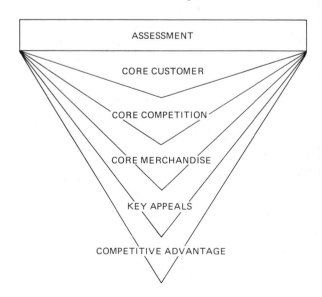

Figure 1-5 Strategic Development Process
SOURCE: Copyright © by *Management Horizons,* A Division of Price Waterhouse.

4. Core merchandise
5. Key appeals
6. Competitive advantage

ASSESSMENT.   Assessment takes place as a store-wide project to provide a wide overview and is accomplished subsequently down to the department level. This appraisal is designed to survey the company's monetary and personnel resources and capabilities, evaluate all environmental forces impacting on the firm, and establish short- and long-term objectives for its strategy.

A strategic assessment could produce analyses which would aid in formulating plans to add other store locations, remodel a whole store or selected departments, increase (or decrease) merchandise lines, or render a decision to alter pricing policies. All of the foregoing determinations, in addition to many others, impact on buyers.

CORE CUSTOMER.   Identification and selection of core customers results from the assessment process. (The balance of the steps in the strategy development process will hinge upon your core customer, given your stores' commitment to a consumer orientation.) The core customer is one whose characteristics, orientation, and expectations are known and understood by the retailer. Core customers are then the target market for the company; as their purchasing power and habits (which have been learned) will generate a profit; show an identifiable positive response to your total retailing strategy; are accessible to the store via advertising; and have (public or private) transportation available.

CORE COMPETITION.   Core competitors are those whose merchandise and service offerings match or closely approximate the expectations of your stores' core customers. The ways and means through which these competitors are able to provide customer satisfaction are either known or can be assessed by you and your firm.

CORE MERCHANDISE.   Any merchandise carried in the proper breadth and depth and priced appropriately to provide satisfaction for your core customer is core merchandise.

KEY APPEALS.   Defining your key appeals requires analyzing those elements of your business which will best satisfy the tangible and intangible aspects of your core customers' needs. These would include providing (or not) specific services, at a specific level, such as gift-wrapping, using simple boxes or ornate coverings; the general ambience of the store; try-on rooms; and so on.

COMPETITIVE ADVANTAGES.   Competitive advantages are those aspects of your business that will be performed in a superior fashion, compared with your core competition, to clearly position the store uniquely. This could mean extending the breadth or depth of merchandise classifications, providing extra hours for shopping, or presenting goods more conveniently so that core customers can touch or try them before making their selections.

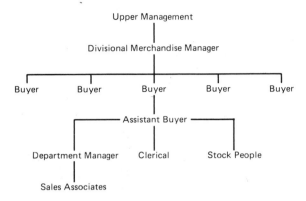

Figure 1-6 Modified Buying Line Organizational Chart

THE BUYER'S ROLE IN THE ORGANIZATION

As you have just learned, buyers must be aware of myriad external variables in their environment if they are to be successful. There are also internal forces to be considered, which exist as a result of the organization within the retail firm.

The simplest type of organization is the owner-operated single store, wherein the owner is the buyer, manager, head of receiving and marking, and probably the bookkeeper who draws the checks to pay bills and payroll. Here owner-operators are responsible to themselves for all decisions.

In larger firms, the organizational structure becomes more complex. It would be useless to attempt to generalize with a "typical" chart delineating who is responsible to whom and for what because, as you have seen, retailers are constantly striving to improve their competitive advantages by, among other ways, amending their organizational chart to improve efficiency.

One fact remains constant in large firms: Buyers are responsible to some higher authority, such as a divisional merchandise manager (DMM), and may have subordinates that could include assistant buyers, clericals, department managers, sales associates, and stock people.

The executive to whom a buyer is responsible will have other buyers who are similarly accountable. These executives are answerable to upper levels of management and must carry out the strategic plan developed for the firm through their personnel, which would include you. (See Fig. 1-6)

They have been buyers previously, succeeding to their current positions after demonstrating strong merchandising ability, competently working with vendors, and building a team with their peers and subordinates.

A buyer's role, whether or not the buyer aspires to higher levels of management, is to acquire the attributes of his or her superiors: merchandising capability—planning and buying, good vendor relationships, and team building. Therefore, it is with good reason that buyers are often seen as the critical factor in the success or failure of a retail firm, because if they do not fulfill their role the organization will fail.

THE BUYER'S QUALIFICATIONS

What are the qualities you will need if you aspire to a buying line position? The list is a long one reflecting the prestigiousness of the title "buyer."[4]

Personal qualifications.   The personal qualities you must have are

1. **Ethics and Loyalty.**   Be ethical in your relationships with vendors and associates and loyal to your organization, always working to insure that your store and all of its employees receive the maximum benefits of your efforts.
2. **Assertiveness.**   Have the ability to "sell" your point of view and obtain the best advantages for your company.
3. **Goal-Setting Ability.**   Given the store's goals and an understanding of your own capabilities, be able to set a path towards their attainment. This will require that you prioritize your time and energy, motivate yourself, and have high expectations for achievement. You must also be self-confident and, above all, realistic.
4. **Decision-Making Skills.**   Be prepared and able to say yes or no and accept the responsibility for these decisions.
5. **Ability to Work Well Under Pressure.**   Buyers are under pressure almost every moment of every working day; they must meet deadlines for plans and buying decisions constantly, and no sooner have they completed one task than there will be a host of others waiting for their attention.

Interpersonal qualifications.   Buyers never work in a vacuum, and must therefore have the following qualities:

1. **Team Builder.**   Develop an esprit de corps with your immediate staff, such as clericals and assistant buyers, as well as with others in the store including department managers, receiving personnel, and staff departments such as display and advertising. You must also accept responsibility for all decisions made by your immediate team and be certain that recognition is given to those who have done their work well.
2. **Trainer.**   Work to develop others in the organization, sharing your skills, helping others to attain their highest level of achievement.
3. **Communicator.**   Be able to speak and write clearly and concisely so that your ideas are understood and can be carried out accurately and without delay.

Merchandising qualifications.   These qualities are the most obvious to your superiors:

1. **Understanding the Store's Customers.**   Here you must interpret the needs and wants of your core customers and provide an appropriate selection of core merchandise to satisfy these customers' requirements, generating a profit for your store.
2. **Product Knowledge.**   Have the ability and stamina to learn the construction materials and techniques of manufacturing which impact on the price and desirability of the products you buy.
      If you are moved from one classification of merchandise to another, this will mean considerable work for you. Consider, however, that as you broaden your base of product knowledge you become more important to the company and are better prepared for promotion.

In addition, when you can recognize the value of individual pieces of merchandise, you will be in a better position to negotiate with vendors, as your knowledge of their costs will bring reality to any negotiating session. (See Chapter Four.)

3. **Arithmetic Competency.**   As a buyer you must be able to perform many computational tasks; over time, they become almost routine. Accuracy is essential; an improperly placed decimal point or an incorrect computation may cost dollars. Develop the habit of checking your work to avoid monetary catastrophes.

CASE STUDY

THE MOUSE TRAP

After working four years as a buyer for a specialty store chain, you have decided to open a shop of your own called "The Mouse Trap," taken from the nickname given you by your family.

Your preliminary plans call for a unisex boutique carrying casual clothing such as sweat shirts and pants, and tee tops and jeans. Decals of various kinds will be available, as will lettering for those customers who want personalized clothing.

Two locations are available: one in a community shopping center anchored by a modified version of a statewide department store chain; the other on the main street in a small town which has a prominent ski slope as its principal winter attraction and continues to draw customers during the nonski season by providing summer theater and arts and crafts shops, coupled with camping and hiking in the scenic mountains. You want to provide yourself with a detailed strategy before you make any commitment.

Given that you can afford to open a shop in either location, develop a strategy to follow for each site and raise questions; indicate the sources you will pursue to find the answers.

NOTES

[1]Breadth and depth are discussed further on in this chapter in the context of describing retail organization.
[2]Chapter Four is devoted to the development and use of negotiating skills.
[3]Adapted from material developed by Management Horizons, a division of Price Waterhouse, and reprinted with permission.
[4]Refer to Chapter Fourteen for an explanation of buyer productivity evaluation.

The Buying Function

2

PRODUCT LIFE CYCLE

All merchandise classifications share one common descriptor—the **Product Life Cycle**; that is, the period of time over which a particular item, classification, fabric, color, style, and so on will sell well enough to provide the retailer with a profit. Graphically, the product life cycle is represented in Fig. 2–1.

As the merchandise may vary from a new kind of socket wrench or nail polish to a differently styled jacket, there are no easy rules to apply as to which stores are more, or less, affected by the cycle. During each phase, however, three factors will change: price, numbers of manufacturers, and the product itself.

Introduction.   During this phase, the price may be very low to penetrate the market, particularly if the product is one which must force existing items off the shelf, or it could be high if it is unique and nothing else competes with it. There may be one or very few suppliers of the merchandise, and distribution may be very limited. The product itself may be one basic model with little, if any, variation available.

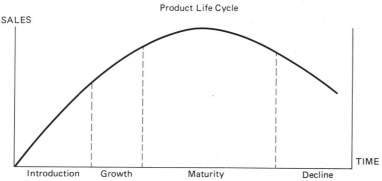

Product Life Cycle

Figure 2-1 Product Life Cycle

Growth. As the product's popularity increases, the price range will broaden to attract a larger consumer market. Many more manufacturers will be producing the merchandise, with commensurately wider distribution. Similarly, the basic product will be available with modifications.

Maturity. This phase will see the broadest range of prices, but they will begin to concentrate at the lower end. The numbers of producers will also begin to taper off, although the item itself will be available in the greatest variety.

Decline. In this period, prices will fall off markedly as vendors attempt to clear their inventories, and only those whose prices were initially low will continue to manufacture the goods. Similarly, the numbers of variations of the product will shrink.

There are variations to the basic product life cycle, such as one for fad items, which show a sharp incline in the introductory stage but do not sustain, and die as rapidly as they are born. Other types of merchandise, such as seasonal goods, have repetitive product life cycles, their rise and fall coinciding with the beginning and ending of their particular season.

During which period of the cycle you buy a particular product will depend upon the image of your store held by your core customers. If you are perceived as an innovative retailer, you will buy in the introductory stage. Conversely, if you are seen as a discounter, the merchandise will show up in your stock late in the maturity phase or early in the decline phase.

BUYING FOR DIFFERENT TYPES OF STORES

As you have seen in Chapter One, stores are not the same. These macro-differences and the following micro-distinctions will impact on the buyer. We will now consider

1. The area of the store or department within which the merchandise is presented
2. The buying cycle

3. Purchasing brand name, private label, generic and/or national (manufacturer) brands

Area of the store.   General merchandise stores differ from limited-line stores (see Fig. 1–2) in that they occupy broad expanses of floor space. This is especially true of department stores, which often have multilevel operations. These types of retailers subdivide their selling areas into units that are manageable for both the customers' orientation and the buying function.

Purchasing merchandise for stores of this size requires not only harmonizing goods within the department but coordinating the overall presentation of the department with adjoining areas and the store as a whole in order to offer a cohesive presentation to customers.

Limited-line stores, particularly specialty shops, present a total appearance to the consumer by virtue of their combined merchandise offering. Therefore, your buying requires coordinating those elements of your lines, such as color, to show your customer a satisfying picture.

Fixturing and aisle space are also a function of overall store size. General merchandise stores, with their greater space, tend to have more flexibility than limited-line stores and can expand or shrink departments overnight. Buyers must be conscious of their fixturing limitations so as not to overcrowd or sparsely present merchandise, or to order merchandise that cannot be properly displayed without concurrently arranging for the appropriate fixturing.

Floor space also places limitations on the quantities you buy and have present at any given time. This may place restrictions on the number of merchandise lines and the depth and breadth of your assortments, although the overall strategic planning process and the resulting buying plans can accomplish the same result.

The buying cycle.   Broadly stated, the buying cycle consists of[1]

1. Planning
2. Viewing vendor offerings and order writing
3. Evaluating sales and either continuing or discontinuing merchandise
4. Final evaluation

PLANNING.   The finite planning for your purchases, regardless of the type of store, will take place months before you actually set foot in a vendor's showroom. Your plan will include both the numbers of units you are to purchase in each merchandise category and the dollar investment required to support these quantities.

VIEWING VENDOR OFFERINGS AND ORDER WRITING.   For chain and department store buyers, the timing for the viewing and order writing process begins much earlier than for other store types. This is necessary because of the relatively large size of the organization, particularly the national chain, where the logistics of receiving, checking, marking and, when necessary, delivery to individual stores consumes a considerable amount of time. Discount store buyers also buy early in an attempt to find brand names of merchandise which can be promoted as having high quality with a relatively low price. The discount buyer also scours the market during the season for advantageous purchases, which may be merchandise discontinued by vendors early enough in the season to still be acceptable to customers at bargain prices.

Specialty store buyers normally follow the "heavies" into the market. This is not necessarily a disadvantage. Understandably, vendors are anxious to have orders from large retailers as early as possible. This gives them information so that they may time their production and shipping, while also supplying them with solid knowledge of which of their styles are "hot" and which are "dogs." Therefore, a manufacturer's line, after the large retailers have been through it, usually represents an edited version. This is not to say that each remaining style is "hot," or for your customer, but many items have been edited from the presentation. The relationship you have (or have not) with the manufacturer's sales representative will count heavily towards your selection process, as this person can guide you towards or away from individual styles.

EVALUATING SALES AND EITHER CONTINUING OR DISCONTINUING MERCHANDISE. Regardless of store type, the buyer begins to evaluate sales as soon as possible after the merchandise is arranged on the selling floor; and if your buying responsibility includes purchasing staple or basic items, which are stocked continuously, your reorders are ongoing.

For chain and discount store buyers of seasonal merchandise, reorders may not be possible, owing to the limitations expressed previously. Their decision, based upon sales analyses, will be how to discontinue the merchandise; that is, to either allow it to sell down priced as is if sales have been good-to-modest, or to reduce the price in an attempt to accelerate sales.

Department store, and particularly specialty store, buyers have greater opportunities to reorder goods than have other types of retailers; hence their sales-analyses-generated decisions could be to continue items via reorder or replacement with similar items or to discontinue, using the same rationale and methods mentioned previously for chain and discount stores.

Specialty store buyers are in a more unusual position for reorders than other buyers in that many of their purchases are made from manufacturers who have limited production, and they are therefore unable to sell large-volume stores. Those vendors who realize their retailer market is the specialty store will have reorderable merchandise and may also continuously introduce new items which will enable the specialty store to have an ongoing fresh look.

PURCHASING BRAND NAME, PRIVATE LABEL, GENERIC, AND/OR NATIONAL (MANUFACTURER) BRANDS. Traditional price line retailers purchase brand name merchandise for their stores. Many chains and department stores have set aside areas within selected departments or have established boutiques devoted exclusively to a particular brand such as Espirit or Ralph Lauren. Discount stores do not attempt to project an image of exclusivity, hence the use of a high-fashion brand name would be counter to their strategy. Specialty store buyers purchase brand name goods; however, their space and budget limitations permit relatively small amounts of this kind of merchandise in their stock.

The use of private label merchandise is usually restricted to those retailers who can buy in large quantities. Chains such as J. C. Penney and Sears, as well as department stores like Macy's, have developed their own private labels. Private brands are more profitable for the retailer and provide customers with an opportunity to purchase quality merchandise at a price less than that of comparable national (manufacturer) brand goods. Retailers must, however, make a substantive investment to develop their own brands and assume dollar and image risks for defective or shoddy goods. Small specialty stores seldom venture into private label development, owing to the investment requirement.

Generic merchandise is unbranded and carries no label other than an identification of the product contained in the package. This type of merchandise is popular with supermarket and pharmaceutical buyers, regardless of the size of the organization.

National, or manufacturer's, brand merchandise is purchased by buyers from large stores to round out their stocks.

FINAL EVALUATION.   Buyers for all types of retail organizations accumulate sales and stock level data at the end of each season as a measure of their success and to provide background information for future periods. This data, coupled with input from a bookkeeper, accountant or, in large firms, the Accounts Payable Department, will generate an analysis of each vendor from whom the buyer has purchased merchandise.

METHODS OF BUYING

Buying as a responsibility can be accomplished in several different ways, and at times it can be performed as a combination of three separate methods.

Individual buying.   Individual buyers have the authority to visit the marketplace and to view vendor presentations in their offices or in the vendor showrooms. They select merchandise based on their own criteria and knowledge of the market, as these best satisfy the needs of their customers. The most important advantage of this method is that decisions can be made with great speed, which is often very critical.

The most obvious disadvantage is that the total responsibility for buying has been placed with a single individual, whose permanence with the organization is uncertain. This is why many small shops owned and operated by one person go out of business after the retirement or death of the principal owner.

Committee buying.   In committee buying, a number of people from within the store or company make the purchasing decisions together. Some organizations require that all of the buyers, regardless of their specialization, constitute the committee, whereas other stores organize the buying committees to include only buyers and assistants in related merchandise areas.

No matter which method is used to form the team, the rationale for using a committee is that the team members have a better overall perspective of the goals and makeup of the store than any one individual would have. The buying process under these circumstances is clearly slow, and as a result some advantageous purchases may be missed.

Group buying.   Group buying is done either informally or through a formal organization known as a **resident buying office (R.B.O.).**

INFORMAL GROUPS.   As you travel through the market, it is not uncommon to find another buyer who works for a noncompeting store, perhaps in a different town or city, who is visiting many of the same vendors you are. Through conversation, you may both decide to visit showrooms together and share opinions and ideas. You have just formed an informal buying group. As time passes on, other buyers may join you. While the initial purpose of your group may have been to discuss negative and positive aspects of merchandise lines, the next logical step would be joint negotiations with vendors for better delivery, terms of sale, and so on. Your group would be capitalizing on the strength of the total numbers in the group. The larger the membership, the greater the impact. Informal groups of this kind are common and continue to operate in the market based upon the trust and respect each buyer has for the others.

RESIDENT BUYING OFFICES.   R.B.O.s are formal organizations located in major market centers. They are either *INDEPENDENT* (privately owned by individuals who at one time may have been buyers, divisional, or general merchandise managers); or *STORE-OWNED*. Their clients (retailers) are non-competing and include stores with a wide range of sales volume. Many relatively low-volume stores engage the services of an R.B.O. (see Fig. 2-2) to take advantage of the many services the office can provide. The people who work in a resident buying office are essentially researchers and advisers to their member stores' buyers. Except for the buyers in central buying offices, the employees of a resident buying office seldom purchase merchandise for their clients, although they may have special arrangements with one or more of the stores they represent. They should be more properly referred to as market representatives or merchandisers.

INDEPENDENT offices are of two types: the salary, or fee, office and the merchandise broker, or commission agent. The *salary, or fee, office* is paid by the retailers who affiliate with the office. The payment for the services of this agency is usually a percentage of the sales from the previous year, ranging, for example, from one half to one percent. *Merchandise brokers, or commission agents,* are paid by the vendors they represent. Their fee is a percentage of the dollar value of the orders placed with each vendor by retailers who have been brought into the showroom, or who have permitted the broker/agent to write an order.

NEW YORK NY
MACY'S NEW YORK (Continued)
Small Electrics...................Heidi Hamilton
Personal Care......................Laura Colletti
Ceiling Fans.......................RaeAnn Larato
STEPHEN CONSIDINE....MA Electronics A:
Televisions........................J P Le Deur
VCRs..............................Sanford Perlman
Telecommunications.................Rick Posti
Radios, Cassettes & Phonos........Anthony Barbaccia
LARRY MEADS....MA Electronics B:
Stereo Components & Accesories....Randy Scalise
Typewriters & Computers...........Ruth Summers
Cameras, Projectors & Film........Gerald Fengel
JOSEPH PENNACCHIO....VP - MA Domestics A:
Blankets & Comforters.............Bill Buczak
Pillows, Bedding Accessories......Paul Callaro
Comforters........................Larry Scott
Private Lives, Ralph Lauren.......Joe Gordon
Sheets............................Harvey Sukman
Bedspreads & Sleep Sets...........Robert Stark
BARBARA PARASCO....MA Domestics "B," Curtain &
  Draperies:
Towels............................Amy Slaff
Table Cloths & Accessories,
  Kitchen Linens...................Jeff Goldberg
Bath Shop, Bath Rugs..............Janet Solomon
Draperies.........................Jeff Vaughn
Curtains, Closet Shop.............Franne Manne
Window Tretments, Decorative
  Pillows.........................Donna Vance
JACK B LANDOVITZ....VP - Administrator of Leased
  Departments and Director of Consumer Affairs

MARTHA INC   **(WSS)**
475 Park Avenue
NEW YORK   NY   10022
  Ph: 212-753-1511
  Branches: Bal Harbour & Palm Beach FL; and
    Trump Tower in New York
  MARTHA R PHILLIPS.....Chairman - Buyer
  LYNN P MANULIS........President - Buyer
  J RAYMOND BARTOW......VP - C O O
  ANDREW P BURNSTINE....VP - Genl Mgr Bal Harbour
    Oscar Ilson.........Controller
Couture Coats Suits Dresses Sportswear and
Accessories

MARWEN STORES (Vaughn Co)   **(FCSC)**
1594 York Avenue
NEW YORK   NY   10028
  Ph: 212-288-3644 (Five Stores
    NY Res Buyers, Henry Doneger Assocs Inc, Mens
    Fashion Guild and Youth Fashion Guild
  HENRY FELENSTEIN.......Chairman
  MARSHALL E FELENSTEIN...President
  HARVEY L HARLOW........General Merchandise Mgr
Coats Suits Dresses Sportswear
  Lingerie Robes Foundations
  Accessories.......................Robert Garber
Toddlers & Infants Wear..............Carol Hamilton
Mens & Boys Sportswear...............Robert Walsh

I MILLER   **(WSSC)**
730 Fifth Avenue
NEW YORK   NY   10019
  Ph: 212-586-5525 Annual Volume: $50,000,000
  53 Womens Shoe Stores and Leased Depts
  EDWARD RAYNE........Chairman
  FRED MONGELUZZI.....Exec Vice President
  PATRICIA KALBERER...Treasurer
  Buyers of Womens Shoes and Handbags:
I Miller Stores..................Pat Webb
Bonwit Teller, New York NY.......Robert Bauman

NEW YORK NY
I MILLER (Continued)
Frost Bros, San Antonio TX.......Philip Bencivenga
Delman(Bergdorf Goodman), NY N Y..Michael Garrett
Garfinckels, Washington DC.......Paul Trusen
Delman Out of Town Stores........Hank Greenwood

MR EPHRAM INC   **(WSSC)**
1796 Broadway
NEW YORK   NY   10019
  Ph: 212-247-7640 Annual Volume: $2,000,000
  (Three Stores)
  NY Res Buyers, O P'S Only
  JOSEPH SETTON.......General Merchandise Mgr
  Alvin Drucker......Display Manager
  Sara Landa.........Store Supplies & Fixtures
Coats Suits Dresses Blouses
Sportswear Sweaters...............Joseph Setton

MODELL'S
280 Broadway
NEW YORK   NY   10007
  Ph: 212-962-6200 Annual Volume: $50,000,000
  (19 Stores)
  Member Natl Buying Syndicate, Ft Worth TX
  WILLIAM MODELL.......President
  MARCUS FISH.........Exec Vice President
  MITCHELL MODELL.....VP - Closeouts
  IRWIN GOODMAN.......General Manager
  MICHAEL S MODELL....General Counsel
  MICHAEL McCOURT.....Advertising Mgr
  LEONARD STIGLITZ....Display Manager
  RAY LOCH............Security Director
Mens & Boys Furnishings & Sptswr...E Figler
Mens & Boys Clothing & Shoes.......H J Weiss
Sporting Goods, Sundries..........Peter Lindenbaum

MONTALDO'S   **(WSSC)**
1450 Broadway
NEW YORK   NY   10018
  Ph: 212-840-1616
  12 Stores: Colorado Springs & Denver(2) CO; St
    Louis MO; Charlotte(2), Durham, Greensboro,
    Raleigh & Winston-Salem NC; Upper
    Arlington OH; and Richmond VA
  BARBARA SHAW.........Chairman and C E O
  MENELAOS G RIZOULIS...President and C O O
  JACK REED............VP - Operations
  JOHN CLANCEY.........Treasurer
  GENE BOLGER..........Advertising Director
  HEATHER ROSS TRAENDLY...MM Cosmetics & Fragrances
  MIRIAM WHITMORE STONE...MM Coats & Suits, Moderate
    & Better Dresses, Junior, Bridal
  MARCIA LAPHAM..........MM Sportswear
  WILLIAM BEAL..........MM Shoes
Better Coats & Suits.............Mary Murphy
Couture Dresses..................Sarah Selsavage
Bridal...........................Susan Wells
Misses Dresses...................Lee Lewis
Contemporary Sportswear..........Vivian Goodstein
Designer & Misses Sportswear.....Cathy Couture
Junior Coats Suits Dresses,
  After 5 Dressing...............Simone Klein
Junior Sportswear................Vivian Kyriazis
Jewelry Handbags Boutique Items
  Umbrellas Hats & Hosiery.......Linda Killion

MOTHERCARE STORES INC   **(W&CSSC)**
529 Fifth Avenue
NEW YORK   NY   10017
  Ph: 212-557-9400
  (200 MOTHERCARE, MOTHER TO BE and
    MATERNITY MODES Shops)

Figure 2-2 Selected List of Resident Buying Offices in New York City
SOURCE: Reprinted with permission of Phelon, Sheldon & Marsar, Inc.

STORE-OWNED OFFICES are identified as either private, corporate, or cooperative. A *private office* serves a single store or chain organization. An office of this type is used by Neiman-Marcus. These offices function much the same as independent offices, except that their work is exclusively for the parent organization. A private office may also function as a central buying office if the buyers in the office have been given authority to place orders and have limited or extensive control of the inventory and the amount of dollars spent for merchandise. In a central buying office, the buyers for an organization have been grouped in a market city and may be geographically away from the actual physical locations of the stores they represent.

A *corporate, or syndicated, office* is a resident office owned and operated for the benefit of all the stores that belong to a particular corporation. Macy's corporate buying office services Macy's New York and the other members of the Macy's Corporation, such as Macy's California.

The *cooperative, or associated, office* is owned by their member stores, who are otherwise nonaffiliated. The Associated Merchandising Corporation (A.M.C.) is a buying office of this type. Although it is owned by some of the stores that are part of the Federated Department Stores, Inc., such as Filene's in Boston and Abraham and Straus in New York, A.M.C. also represents Strawbridge & Clothier in Philadelphia, an independently-owned organization of department stores.

UTILIZATION OF THE RESIDENT BUYING OFFICE

Depending on their type and size, resident buying offices offer a variety of services to buyers. Certainly the most important function of merchandisers, however, is to research thoroughly the markets for which they are responsible, accumulating data on styles, size ranges, colors, fabrics, or other materials; identifying trends; ascertaining delivery dates and shipping information; and locating new and outstanding vendors.

The buying office makes this information available to its members through newsletters (see Fig. 2-3), market reports, vendor lists, and similar kinds of reports. In addition, buying office merchandisers are available to answer specific questions about merchandise availability for reorders and also for replacement, if necessary.

Representatives of the buying office also handle many tasks that are of a more routine nature, such as placing reorders and following them up, making inquiries about adjustments and complaints, arranging for returns to vendors, and placing special orders.

Under certain circumstances, after you have become a buyer, you may give your office merchandiser permission to write original orders or sample orders. This authority, which is called **open-to-buy (O.T.B.)**, should be conferred cautiously, as an overzealous merchandiser can easily involve you with many new items or lines, infringing or expanding upon your planned assortment and

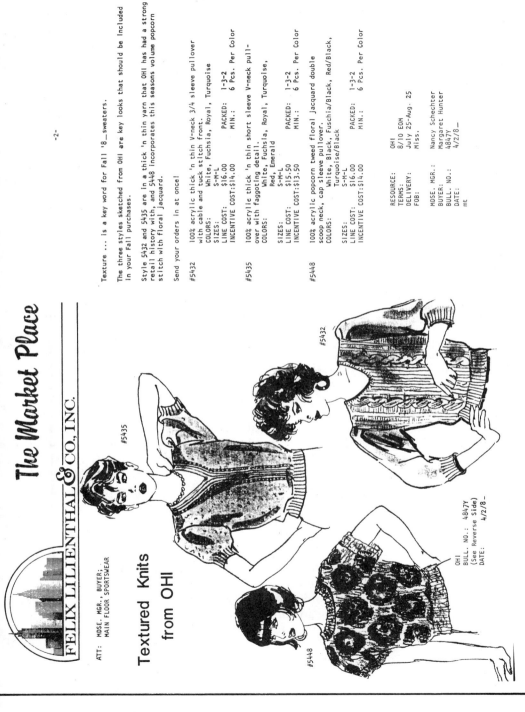

Figure 2-3 Buying Office Fashion Bulletin

SOURCE: Reprinted with permission of Felix Lilienthal & Co., Inc., 417 Fifth Avenue, New York, NY 10016.

price lines. The advantage you may gain by permitting the market representative to write orders is that occasionally new merchandise with high sales potential may become available when you may not be able to visit the market soon enough to place an order. Your buying office merchandiser can then do this for you.

Certain general services that are available from many offices are

1. Arranging hotel accommodations and transportation
2. Providing office space for you to work and see vendor sales representatives
3. Placing advertisements in trade papers to notify vendors of your arrival
4. Accompanying you to the market, having researched, scheduled, and carefully listed the vendors you are to visit
5. Negotiating price concessions, terms, and so on from vendors, based upon the size of the orders placed by you and the other members of the office

A number of larger offices are able to offer their members a range of administrative services, such as

1. Providing information on the most recent developments in data accumulation and systems
2. Compiling financial data in an anonymous fashion from the member stores, which would allow you, as well as the other buyers, the opportunity to measure your performance against norms for a relatively homogeneous group
3. Organizing purchasing of basic store supplies to obtain price concessions as a result of large orders
4. Performing marketing research to help the members learn more about the demographic features of their core customers, identifying trends of all kinds, and possibly assisting them with site selection

Centralized buying. Multi-unit retailers, particularly those with locations across the country, develop variations of centralized buying. The principal difference between modified central buying and the others previously mentioned is that some of the purchasing and reordering is done at the individual store level, either by the store manager or in combination with department managers.

The primary advantage of centralized buying is that it promotes a relatively homogeneous merchandise presentation for all stores, regardless of their geographical location. Visit a Zayre, Kmart, or Sears, as examples, in many cities and see how closely the stock in one location will resemble that of another.

You should also note that any form of centralized buying which prohibits store-site management from buying merchandise required by core customers in their area will certainly inhibit profitability. While this argument may appear inconsistent with the primary advantage of centralized buying, it demonstrates that flexibility and responsiveness to core customers' wants and needs are the driving forces in retailing.

Centralized buying is accomplished through any of the following systems alone, or by linking two or more together:

1. Automatic open-to-buy

2. Opening stock distribution
3. Price agreement and listing
4. Warehousing and requisition

AUTOMATIC OPEN-TO-BUY.   With this plan, the buyers in the central office are given a limited dollar amount of a store's open-to-buy. This money is usually invested in new styles or lines. The balance of the purchasing is done by store personnel and is generally accomplished in conjunction with the opening stock distribution plan.

OPENING STOCK DISTRIBUTION.   This method requires the central buyer to establish a plan which represents all of the styles (both new and continuing) each store should carry. These styles are rank-ordered in terms of their overall sales potential; each store is then ranked according to its dollar volume; central buyers then assign the styles to each store so that the higher-volume stores will receive all styles in quantity, while the smaller units are sent only the better styles in lesser amounts. The opening stock distribution system is also success-fully combined with the price agreement and listing method.

PRICE AGREEMENT AND LISTING.   To accomplish the listing method, central buyers provide store managers with approved lists of vendors and of the particular styles each can provide. Each store manager then orders directly from each supplier according to stock needs. Staple and basic goods are commonly purchased through the price agreement and listing method. Vendors are willing to assume the cost of stocking and warehousing this kind of merchandise, as its selling life is long and sales are relatively steady.

WAREHOUSING AND REQUISITION.   Retailers who use this central buy-ing plan for their stores limit the control their managers have over the makeup of their stock; managers do, however, adjust the depth of their inventory by requi-sitioning fill-ins from inventory in a central warehouse. Store managers are pro-vided with a basic stock list and must compare their physical inventories to this list at regular intervals, ordering enough merchandise to bring their stock up to the assigned level and providing enough goods to carry them through the next reorder-delivery period. Similarly, the central buyers must keep the warehouse levels high enough to resupply the stores, making allowances for their own reorder-delivery time frame from suppliers. Supermarket and drugstore chains use this method, particularly for staple lines, where a large variety of steadily selling merchandise is required to be on hand.

THE MARKETPLACE

Markets are divided into two classifications: DOMESTIC, composed of local and central markets, and FOREIGN.

Domestic markets.   *Local markets* are close to, or in, the city in which your store is situated. They are used by merchants such as food retailers, who try to buy their fruits and vegetables from local farmers to obtain the freshest merchandise quickly. In some cities, Boston and Atlanta, for example, many clothing manufacturers maintain small sales offices operated by their local sales representatives who combine office time with traveling through their territory making on-site calls to their accounts.

Central markets contain the widest possible range of vendors or manufacturers for a particular type of merchandise. For example, New York City has long been considered the fashion clothing capital for men, women, and children. If your store were located in this metropolitan area, the central market would also be your local market.

TYPES OF RESOURCES.   There are three basic kinds of suppliers from whom you may buy: farmers, middlemen, and manufacturers. Basic retailing and marketing courses and texts list in detail the services each of them offers. They are listed here for reference purposes and are further explained in the glossary.

Merchandise Resources:

1. Farmers
2. Middlemen
   (a) Service and limited-function wholesalers
   (b) Rack jobbers
   (c) Brokers
   (d) Commission houses
   (e) Selling agents
   (f) Auctioneers
3. Manufacturers

LOCATING RESOURCES.   Becoming acquainted with the *vendors* who service your particular merchandise area is accomplished in two ways: Either they find you or you locate them. After you acquire buying responsibility, your name finds its way into directories of various kinds that vendors and their representatives use with great frequency. (See Fig. 2–4) If you work for a large chain or department store, your name and merchandise classifications become known very quickly through vendor inquiries at your office. In addition, most sales representatives travel throughout their territory on a regular basis, and they routinely stop in to see you. If you are concerned about becoming known after opening your own shop, this latter point should put you at ease.

The other method of finding vendors depends upon you for its success. Prime among these procedures is relying on your past experience. If you bought a particular classification of merchandise previously, you should have developed a resource file or book to track down and rate various vendors. Later in this chapter and also in Chapter Fourteen, you will learn about the type of information and the data you should consider developing for each vendor.

Another way of locating suppliers is through your market representative. If you or your store is a member of a buying office or has its own office, the

EVANS INC   333 Seventh Avenue   (BO)
  Ph: 212-947-3000   10001
        BUYING OFFICE FOR SELF-OWNED FUR STORES,
        WOMENS SPECIALTY STORES & LEASED FUR DEPTS
  BARRY NOVICK.....Vice President
  Paul Becker.......Merchandise Manager
  Pat Mechanic........Genl Mdse Mgr Ready-to-Wear
  Barry Novick, Paul Becker, Byron Brown,
     Peter Capozzi & Thomas Pacilio..............Furs
  CAESARS PALACE FUR STORE, Las Vegas NV
  EVANS FUR CO, Chicago IL
  KOSLOW'S, Fort Worth & Dallas TX
  KOSLOW'S, New Orleans LA
  KOSLOW'S, Oklahoma City OK
  MGM FUR STORE, Las Vegas NV
  ROSENDORF/EVANS, Washington DC
  21 Lease Fur Depts in Other Stores

JOANNE EVANS INC   159 Madison Avenue   (RB)
  Ph: 212-686-4322   10016
        BUYS FOR WOMENS SPECIALTY STORES
  Joanne Evans.....Sportswear
  Lori Gershon.....Coats, Swimwear, Accessories
  Donna S Cowhig...Designer Dresses & Sportswear
  Silvia DiGrande..Weekendwear
  ABERSONS ALLEY, Tulsa OK
  APPLE TREE, E Stroudsburg PA
  BALCONY, THE, Jackson MS
  BEARD, LEE, Oklahoma City OK
  BLOOMINGALS, Bellevue WA
  BRITTONS, Columbia SC
  CADEAU, THE, Austin TX
  CHASE, KRISTIN, New Orleans LA
  CHEMIN DE FER, OakhurstNJ
  CHWATSKY, Oceanside NY
  COCO, Nashville TN
  COLLECTIONS, Columbus MS
  COUSINS, Little Rock AR
  DEAN'S TOWN & COUNTRY, Columbia MO
  DIMENSIONS (Kel Inc), Houston TX
  EXPRESSIONS, Burlington VT
  FENZI, Brooklyn NY
  GABRIELLA, Indianapolis IN
  GAZEBO, THE, Montgomery AL
  GENTLEMENS QUARTER, New Orleans LA
  HANDS ALL AROUND, Mystic CT
  HANNAH, Aurora CO
  IVY SHOPS, Worcester MA
  JAZ, Pittsburgh PA
  JONES, ALEX, Lake Charles LA
  KATZ, BARBARA, Miami FL
  KENT, DEBORAH, Tampa FL
  LEEDS, Boston MA
  LINDISSIMA, San Juan PR
  LOOOIE'S, Margate NJ
  MICHELLE'S, Highland Park IL
  PORCUPINE, Hilton Head SC
  PRINCE, BETSY, Birmingham AL
  R F D INC, Baton Rouge LA
  SHERRE'S CLOTHING, Scottsdale AZ
  SIDESTREET, Atlanta GA
  SMITH, M C, Minnetonka MN
  WESTBROOKS INC, Tupelo MS
  WRIGHT, FRANCES, Memphis TN

EXTRA TOUCH BUYING SERVICE   488 Seventh Ave (RB)
  Ph: 212-279-0772   10018
        BUYS FOR LARGE SIZE WOMENS SPECIALTY STORES
  Judy Zajicek, Arlene Birnbaum & William Zajicek...
  ...Upper Moderate To Better Large Size Coats,
  Suits, Dresses, Sportswear, Intimate Apparel and
  Accessories
  ALEXANDRA, Miami FL
  ANNETTE'S ARMOIRE, Chicago IL
  APROPOS, Bangore ME
  ASHANTI, New York NY

EXTRA TOUCH (Continued)
  BROOKS, ANN, Niles IL
  DESIGNS LARGESSE, Phoenix AX
  CLASSIQUE BOUTIQUE, Matawan NJ
  DEANE, T, Wellesley MA
  DU BARRY'S, Overland Park KS
  ELEGANT WOMEN, Greenwich CT
  ELEGANT WOMEN, West Orange NJ
  ELOISE, Los Angeles CA
  FILLY'S, Brooklyn NY
  GRANDE, DONNA, Seattle WA
  GREATER NEW YORK WOMEN, New York NY
  HARRINGTON'S, London, England
  JULEE'S, Beachwood OH
  LA GRANDE DAME, Charlottesville VA
  LAUREN LTD, ANNE, Framingham MA
  LAWRENCE, NANCY, Edina MN
  LEE'S, ANNETTE, Stony Brook NY
  LYLE, B, Sarasota FL
  MAGNIFIQUE, Great Neck NY
  MORE TO LOVE, Colonia NJ
  NEW DEH, A, Flemington NJ
  PANACHE, Colorado Springs CO
  PARAGON WOMAN, DaytonOH
  PLUS WOMAN, Philadelphia PA
  PLUS WOMAN, St George's, Bermuda
  ROSEMARY'S REALITY, Montclair NJ
  ROYAL WOMAN, New York NY
  RUBENESQUE, Baldwin NY
  SKINNY MINNY'S BOUTIQUE, Boca Raton FL
  STARR, ABIGAIL, Lahaska PA
  TOY WYNN, Dallas TX
  VALENTINE'S, Southfield MI
  WOMEN AT LARGE, Farmington Hills MI
  WOMENS CORNER, Merrick NY

FASHION BUYING SERVICE   225 West 34th St   (RB)
  Ph: 212-244-1360   10122
        BUYS FOR WOMENS SPECIALTY STORES
  MARVIN ADELGLASS.......Genl Mdse Mgr
  Marvin Adelglass....Better, Missy & Contempo Sptswr,
     Jr & Missy Knitwear, Jr Sportswear
  Jules Nathanson.....Coats Suits Carcoats Raincoats
  Charlotte Gold......Dresses
  Natalie Adel.......Lingerie & Robes, Accessories
  B J'S CLOSET, Birmingham MI
  BAILEY'S, Vidalia GA
  BUTENSKY'S, Lakewood NJ
  CLAUDIA SHOP, Glen Cove NY
  DARLING SHOP, Corona NY
  ETHEL'S, Hallandale FL
  FACTORY PANTS STORES, Chattanooga TN
  FASHION CORNER, Los Angeles CA
  FASHION SCENE, Miami FL
  FELDMAN'S DEPT STORE, Newton MS
  FREDERICK CLOTHIER, Frederick MD
  GOLDEN'S, Marlboro MA
  HANDEL & CO, Pennsauken NJ
  HOPKINS, BOB, Rockville Centre NY
  HURST DEPT STORE, Spur & Muleshoe TX
  ICI PARIS, North Miami FL
  JAIZ, New Hyde Park NY
  KLEIMAN'S, Philadelphia PA
  KORNBLUT'S, Latta SC
  KOVEL'S, Norridge IL
  LA FASHION (Frazier & Assoc), Evansville IN
  LYNNS, Oneida NY
  MARLENE SPORT SHOP, Irvington NJ
  MELANGE, West Orange NJ
  MILGRE SHOP, Brooklyn NY
  NADON'S, Southfield MI
  NEWMAN'S, Bronx NY
  PATLEN'S,Chatham NY
  RALLS & CO, Austin TX

Figure 2-4   List of Selected Buyers within New York City

SOURCE: Reprinted with permission of Phelon, Sheldon & Marsar, Inc.

merchandisers in the office have, as indicated earlier, the task of researching the market and notifying you of the available opportunities.

Manufacturers' sales representatives can also be very helpful in recommending vendors to you. They travel the marketplace and generally pride themselves on their knowledge of who carries what. They are understandably reluctant to disclose the names of their competitors, but you can usually obtain a variety of names of vendors with whom they do not compete.

You should also learn to "shop" core competitors (known as **shopping the competitor's market**) as a means of identifying resources. Buyers from these stores are very likely visiting you, and there is nothing you can do about it. In a broader sense, you should evaluate your core competitors for a variety of reasons other than to locate vendors; this, too, is certainly a professionally acceptable practice.

Buyers from noncompeting stores are also good sources of information. You may, as previously mentioned, develop a working relationship with many of them and not only trade buying information but also exchange sales promotion ideas, floor layout suggestions, and similar information.

Shopping the market is certainly a worthwhile activity. In many central markets, entire buildings are devoted to a single type of merchandise. Without a doubt you could spend many hours going in and out of showrooms making rapid mental and written notes about each vendor.

In a similar fashion, you should plan to visit the *market shows* for your merchandise, which are well advertised to buyers through the mail and trade papers. These shows occur at regular intervals each year in central market cities and involve a respectable selection of vendors displaying their merchandise in hotels, exhibition halls, or auditoriums.

The final source of information can be generally classified as publications. Included are trade papers and magazines, direct mail sent out by the vendors, and trade and building directories, which are available from a variety of sources.

CHOOSING RESOURCES.   Depending upon your merchandise classification and the marketplace, your major decisions will be confined to selecting vendors from the list you have previously identified as possible resources. Two general areas that will require your attention are whether you should buy from a relatively small number of suppliers, as opposed to dispersing your orders among many resources, and whether you should purchase from large or small manufacturers.

If you place the bulk of your orders with a small number of vendors, it is reasonable to feel that you will be considered a very important client. As such, you should have first call on off-price merchandise, prompt or early delivery of goods, and fast service on reorders and claim adjustments. You will also save yourself time in the marketplace.

By spreading your merchandise dollars to more vendors, however, you have the opportunity to bring diversity to your merchandise assortment and also minimize the risk of having your supply of goods curtailed because of fires, strikes, or transportation problems that may affect the vendor with whom you have written a very large order.

The decision to use large, as opposed to small, suppliers hinges upon the answers to the following questions: Do you believe in featuring unusual items of merchandise instead of entire lines? Are well-known, nationally advertised brands important to you?

In addition to these factors, another very important consideration for vendor selection would certainly be the result of your evaluation of the merchandise you see and of the management policies of the supplier. The merchandise should be appropriate for your customer in terms of styling and price, and it should also provide your department with a distinctive, cohesive appearance.

The management policies that are of concern to you include advertising and promotion allowances; terms of sales, such as dating, freight prepayment, and cash and quantity discounts; adherence to strict manufacturing standards; distribution policies as they are legally permitted; timely delivery; and general dependability.

It is also appropriate to determine the financial soundness of your vendors (they will undoubtedly want that kind of information about you), and you should try to ascertain how aggressive the owner(s) of the firm is in promoting its business and yours, thereby helping both to grow.

VISITING THE DOMESTIC MARKET. Regardless of the merchandise you buy, your preparation for visits to the marketplace must be extensive and thorough. As you will learn, time is your most valuable commodity, and for a buyer to waste it in the market is inexcusable, as it will only require spending more hours trying to accomplish what could have been completed earlier.

To optimize your time, there are a number of essential steps you must take before, during, and after your trips to the market. You will very likely develop a great deal of sophistication as you sharpen your buying skills, and you may find that some of the following procedures can be modified to suit your style and the needs of the store. As a novice, however, you should not underestimate their value to your future as a highly efficient and productive buyer.

Review of current business. The first concern must be with your *core customer* and to determine if there has been any kind of change that would have an impact on your business. Fluctuations such as changes in disposable income, growth or decline in the population, or dispersion of the populace over a wide geographical area can affect your buying.

Generally, you should be aware of the development of trends in your average consumer's behavior. Many times these changes occur over a period of time and can only be identified if you are regularly attuned to their presence. As an example, changes in the hours of shopping by your typical core customer may mean that shoppers will have more, or less, time to spend examining merchandise. This may cause you to offer goods in packages for the purchasers who are on a tight schedule. You may also recognize the need for various types of selling aids or point-of-purchase displays, which are offered by vendors, that you previously thought were not important.

Review of your merchandise. Another area of concern is the current status of your stock and how opportunities for growth can be found. Expansion of your business can take place through a variety of strategies, some of which are broadening or narrowing the scope of your merchandise assortment, increasing or decreasing the depth of the stock, and varying the price lines. Later in this text, you will learn some of the quantitative methods that can assist you in making the kinds of decisions required of merchants.

Preparing buying plans. Your buying plans are blueprints that you–and if you are in a large organization your superiors—have prepared, reviewed, modified, and finally accepted as workable and having the potential to produce a profit.

The plans are of two types: the *six-month merchandise plan*, which is involved with dollar values, and the *unit classification plan*, which is concerned with merchandise assortments and quantities. You will become familiar with both of these plans in succeeding chapters.

TYPES OF MARKET VISITS. Each visit you make to the market may be for a different reason, and you should set your goals accordingly. Do not permit yourself to become diverted from your original purpose, or you will find yourself back in your office frustrated because of the lack of complete information.

The overview visit. This kind of trip occurs at the beginning of the buying season. Depending on the classifications of merchandise you buy, these visits may be required two, three, or four times each year.

The purpose of this visit to the market is to give you the opportunity to see a broad overview of merchandise offerings without concentrating on individual styles, materials, or deliveries but rather to get a sense of what the coming season will bring. You can accomplish this yourself by making rapid visits to showrooms and by consulting buying office representatives and the other sources mentioned earlier.

Follow-up visit. This type of visit is usually equal in number to the overview visit. During the follow-up visit, you will spend time with your key resources, making major buying commitments and filling in the balance of your needs with merchandise from secondary resources.

Some buyers prefer not to write initial orders in the market but instead very carefully take notes on merchandise they find attractive, and armed with this information, complete their orders after they return to the quiet of their hotel rooms or offices.

There are valid arguments for following this procedure. In this way, you will have time to think and review your notes from each vendor before writing any orders. It will help to eliminate unnecessary duplication of inventory. You will also be away from the pressure of sales representatives who are naturally concerned with the size of the order you leave, as their income depends upon the volume of business they write. If you do decide to write your orders in a showroom, however, you have the advantage of being able to see the merchandise again as well as being able to use the sales representative as a consultant.

Figure 2-5 A Buyer Completing a Purchase Order
SOURCE: Courtesy of Thomas J. DiGiovanna, buyer—Jordan Marsh, and John
Corcoran, salesman—Karastan.

Specific needs visits.   Visits of this type may occur six or more times each
year. The purposes for this kind of trip are diverse, including placing reorders
for fast sellers, locating replacement merchandise if reorders are unavailable,
and seeking solutions to problems that you may have encountered, such as returns to a vendor or delivery difficulties.

Foreign markets.   **Foreign markets** are any located outside the United States.
Many countries and cities have developed industries to produce limited
classifications of merchandise, such as leather goods from Spain and Italy, a variety of woven and knitted items from Hong Kong, and electronic and photo
equipment from Japan.

WHY BUY MERCHANDISE OVERSEAS?   There are three basic reasons why
you would want to buy merchandise abroad:

1. It would be your expectation that the total cost of the merchandise delivered to
    your door (landed cost) would be less than the cost of comparable domestic
    goods; hence, you could add on a larger-than-usual markup, which would help
    to offset the risks and costs of importing and also provide a higher level of profit.
2. The merchandise would be unique, unusual, or perhaps manufactured to your

specifications, thus giving you a strong competitive advantage over other retailers.

3. There is a limited prestige factor associated with goods carrying a foreign country of origin label, which would generate still another type of competitive advantage.

DIFFICULTIES INVOLVED WITH OVERSEAS BUYING. The number of problems buyers may encounter as they plan to travel abroad and visit foreign markets are numerous; some are easily overcome, while others are considerably more troublesome. The list includes the following:

1. Taking the time to accomplish an overseas visit may be difficult or impossible. Many of the largest retailers are restricting buyers' overseas trips and, in some cases, limiting these visits to personnel at the divisional merchandise manager level or higher. Given the rapidity with which data is accumulated, due to computerization, and the commensurate speed with which buying decisions must be made, it is ineffective for buyers to be away from their offices for long periods of time.

2. The dollar expense of travel, as well as the cost of telex, cable, mail, and telephone, are not to be underestimated as deterrents to importing.

3. Language differences are another barrier, as they can lead to confusion. In attempting to clarify the fine points of a purchase, you may have to spend an inordinate amount of time, thus returning to the difficulties mentioned in points 1 and 2.

4. Your ability to work through monetary problems quickly and accurately requires the ability to do rapid conversion of pesetas, yen, or other currency to dollars and some knowledge of the economic climate so as to be able to project future monetary value.

5. You must understand the complexities of bringing merchandise to your receiving door in the United States. These include using letters of credit to pay for goods, arranging transportation, and the payment of duties and other fees, combined with anxieties about late deliveries, with subsequent undue markdowns.

6. You must find manufacturers and vendors with appropriate goods who produce merchandise sized to an American consumer; manufacture their product to last in the American climate (glues used in wooden furniture that will not soften under conditions of high humidity, as an illustration); and label the items in conformity with United States laws, which include the Textile Fiber Products Identification Act. (See Appendix A for other relevant laws.)

7. You must be able to plan ahead for purchases which will have to be made, in many cases, a full year in advance. This means anticipating styles, colors, prices, quantities, and so on and making early commitments of your open-to-buy dollars.

8. Finally, you will encounter problems when much of your overseas purchased goods cannot be reordered, leaving you with poor size or color assortments and, worse, unhappy customers.

OVERCOMING OVERSEAS BUYING DIFFICULTIES. The small retailer, particularly, may overcome the foregoing problems by finding domestic importers or wholesalers who carry the appropriate lines of goods and purchasing from them. The prices paid will include a markup for this intermediary, reducing extra markup and consequently profit dollars, but the advantages of exclusivity and prestige will remain.

Other alternatives are to join a buying office which either has overseas offices or is itself affiliated with a larger buying office with foreign branches, to whom you would pay a fee assessed as a percent of the dollar purchases made for your store; or use a commissionaire who acts as your general representative much the same as an expert merchandiser in a resident buying office.

Commissionaires may cover more than one exporting country and have expertise with several merchandise lines. Their services continue after you have departed, providing follow-up on the orders you have placed, in terms of inspection of the goods, to assure conformity with your specifications and quality requirements; and assisting with financial arrangements and shipping. Fees for a commissionaire's services are negotiable and depend on the volume of your orders, the type of merchandise, and the complexities of the purchase.

Buying offices abroad furnish their clients with many of the services associated with domestic resident buying offices. In addition, they also must provide their members with assistance, such as

1. Searching out reliable manufacturers who will produce to the specifications of a buyer or who will fabricate a style as an exclusive for a retailer.
2. Arranging for bulk or full container size shipments of merchandise to the United States by combining orders from several retailers. This saves transportation charges for each client.
3. Combining orders from several retailers to a single manufacturer and subsequently obtaining quantity discounts on the sum of the total purchases.
4. Researching and accumulating data on economic and monetary trends.
5. Arranging meetings with other buyers to show new merchandise; linking up buyers directly with vendors; organizing shows where merchandise from many resources are displayed. A cautionary note, however, is that no pricing discussions should be held between buyers from competing stores as they may be held in violation of federal legislation.
6. Establishing an in-house record-keeping system of payments to vendors, letters of credit, vendor rebates, and so on; notifying both vendors and clients of their account balances.
7. Checking merchandise for quality control and conformance to labeling requirements.
8. Negotiating with vendors for sales promotion money and for rebates to offset losses due to defective or poorly manufactured merchandise.
9. Providing multilingual merchandisers who will facilitate the work of a U.S. buyer in a foreign country.

CUSTOMS BROKERS. Customs brokers act as your agent to facilitate the movement of the store's merchandise through United States Customs. They are licensed by the Treasury Department to perform their specific tasks. These include

1. Preparing and filing the required customs forms.
2. Arranging for appraisal of the goods and payment of customs charges.
3. Acting to have your merchandise released from custody.
4. Organizing with freight carriers to have the goods delivered to you.

Fees charged by customs brokers depend upon a variety of factors, such as the number of invoices covering the shipment, the value of the goods, and the intricacies of the brokers' involvement in clearing the shipment.

LANDED COST. Total landed cost is the dollar expenditure to have imported merchandise delivered to your door. It includes the cost of the merchandise itself; commissionaire, broker, or buying office fees; foreign packing and shipping charges to the point of exit; surface or air freight to the United States; entry, storage and duty charges; and appraiser's and customs broker fees.

The following example illustrates the necessary computations to arrive at a dollar value for each unit of merchandise purchased overseas:

Country of Origin: Italy	Exchange Rate: 1,523 lire per dollar
First cost, 100 handbags @ 20,000, lire	2,000,000
Packing (in lire)	10,000
	2,010,000
8% Commissionaire's fee (in lire)	160,800
Shipping (in lire)	100,000
Cost in lire	2,270,800
1,523 lire per dollar (2,270,800 lire/1,523)	US $1,491.00
Shipping and insurances to United States	150.00
Entry and storage fees	30.00
25% duty on 2,000,000 lire (500,000 lire/1,523)	328.30
Customs broker fee	100.00
Transportation to store	35.00
Total landed cost	US $2,134.30
Delivered cost per handbag: ($2,134.30/100)	$21.34
First cost per handbag: (2,000,000 lire/1,523)	$13.13

While foreign buying is considerably more involved than domestic purchasing, it is a way of retailing life that is becoming more prevalent.

CASE STUDY

The Elegant House

When you launched "The Elegant House," a home furnishings shop catering to an affluent clientele, it was your intention to eventually open a Trim-a-Tree Department for the Christmas shopping season. After two years, you feel that you have developed the customer loyalty and the reserve of cash necessary for buying this classification of merchandise.

Your resident buying office, Consolidated Atlas-Hall, has been helpful in providing you with the following useful information:

1. Buying Christmas tree ornaments and related goods must be done at least a year in advance (you still have time to accomplish this work).
2. The central market for this merchandise is in the area served by Consolidated, but there are also excellent resources abroad with which the office has no connection.

You realize that, since it is now mid-September, if you are going to proceed with your plan to start this department next year, you must move ahead rapidly.

How will you plan the strategy for this new department?

SUPPLEMENTARY CASE STUDY

BRISTOL'S—PART I

Bristol's Department Store has been owned and operated by a family organization since it first opened its doors at the turn of the century. As the size of the city increased, Bristol's followed suit. First, a third floor was added onto the original building, and then a large section of the basement was converted to a selling floor for specially purchased merchandise. Finally, the family rented adjoining buildings, breaking through walls and constructing underground and overhead walkways to connect the various structures.

The store continued to show a profit. Over the years, however, more than one member of the staff, as well as numerous customers, were overheard saying that a road map was necessary to go through the store to locate various departments. It was also rumored that no one really knew how many departments existed and what was being sold.

From a buyer's point of view, it had become increasingly difficult to work in the marketplace, as Bristol's was located several hundred miles from any central market city. The Bristol family also refused to engage a resident buying office or even to consider any form of computer system.

During the preceding year, the last member of the Bristol family involved in the business sold the business to a non-retailing corporation seeking to diversify its interests. The new ownership installed its own management team and, after six months of intensive research and study, produced a strategic plan for change.

The first step was to close down the operations in the adjoining buildings. Although these structures accounted for about 30 percent of the total floor area, the investigations showed that the main building was underutilized and contained much wasted space. Concurrently, the main building was slated to undergo extensive remodeling to gain more selling room and to update the interior. The architects estimated that the net difference in space would be about a 10 percent loss of square footage, but the new fixturing would permit approximately 5 percent more merchandise in forward stock. This alteration would take about eighteen months to complete.

The second phase of the strategy involved opening branch stores and boutiques that would quadruple the selling area of the rejuvenated flagship store within a five-year period.

While you and the other buyers are very excited about the long-term prospects, you are all apprehensive about the next eighteen months. You have been told initially to cut back your buying by 40 percent, owing to reduced floor space during alterations, and to find and purchase about 50 percent of the inventory for promotional purposes.

You have historically bought about 80 percent of your goods from 10 percent of the vendors with whom you do business. The reason for this is that your department has relied heavily on national brands. Among the difficulties you expect to encounter: These large vendors are able to offer you promotional merchandise only twice each year, and the amount of off-price goods you are able to buy is based on a percentage of your total regular purchases.

Next Monday, you are going to have a meeting with your new divisional merchandise manager (DMM) to discuss the buying plans during the alteration period. The DMM indicated on the first day you met that adherence to dollar plan was the road to success in retailing and that you and the other buyers, although skilled in buying, should learn to ". . . stick to the merchandise expenditures that were assigned to you . . ."

How will you approach this meeting in terms of setting forth your buying plans with current vendors and new suppliers and proposing a post-alteration strategy to feed into the expansion plans for Bristol's?

NOTE

[1]These topics are presented in detail in later chapters as a process and are included here to emphasize the differences and similarities between types of retailers.

The Buyer
in the Marketplace

3

Whether you as a buyer represent your own firm or are employed by an office or store, you will be judged and experience success or failure essentially because of two qualities: astutely knowing and practicing the "corrects of buying" and your professional behavior.

The **corrects of buying** are having the *correct merchandise* at the *correct time*, in the *correct place*, at the *correct price*, in the *correct quantities*, and *correctly promoted*. Some of these factors are discussed in this text, whereas others you will learn about in other courses. Needless to say, all of them will be brought sharply into focus through your experiences in the field.

Your professional behavior as a buyer is another issue, and it is dealt with now and further along as part of an ongoing process. Simply stated, *your ethics should always place you above reproach*. Some may say you do not know your merchandise, and this can be true. Not even the best and greatest of all merchants would hold themselves up as omniscient about all kinds of goods; in a larger sense, neither could they apply the corrects of buying in a flawless manner every time. But truly professional buyers always behave so that no one can raise a single doubt about their ethics.

You may be a buyer with relatively small buying power, but if you have maintained a "squeaky clean" reputation, you will be welcomed and respected by everyone. Similarly, if you buy for a large organization, your name is what you can always trade upon. Although you may be catered to and fawned over by vendors and their representatives, they are in fact attempting to ingratiate themselves with you because of the organization you represent, the size of the purchases that may result, or both. If you allow yourself to accept gifts or favors, your "popularity" will be in direct proportion to the size of your orders. Not only is this highly unflattering, but it is also extremely dangerous. If your store experiences setbacks, or if you leave one organization and find yourself with another company with less buying power, your former "friends" will very quickly show you their backs, which you will have earned and deserve.

What are considered gifts or favors? They are defined as any goods or services of value received at prices less than generally available to the public or to all employees on an equal basis. The use of cars, boats, airplanes, and escort services, and also meetings at a nonbusiness type of hotel or resort location, are also certainly highly suspicious, and you should vigorously avoid them. Accepting a gift of cash is obviously an improper act. Conducting business with relatives or companies with which you have a personal interest of any kind is another doubtful practice, and it should be avoided to prevent conflict of interest charges.

The foregoing is not intended to exclude business lunches, provided that they are freely offered and that you do not just show up in time for lunch. In addition, you must reciprocate. A word of caution is extended here to the social drinker: Do not imbibe before either driving or writing orders. More than one buyer has returned to the office and, upon reviewing the recently made purchases, found that one or two of them were unaccountably large. Your crystal clear mind is your best asset in the marketplace. If you find your thinking becoming hazy because of weariness or illness, stop working.

THE ITINERARY

Planning the visit.   Your visits to the market must be well organized in advance of your arrival to avoid spending precious time on details that should have been attended to before you left the office. You should expend your energies in the market on merchandise-related problems and not on details such as finding street addresses or phone and suite numbers of vendors. This means planning thoroughly well ahead of your visit. If you work with a buying office representative, this person will do some of the work for you, provided that you have communicated your wishes well enough in advance of your trip.

The initial step in planning a market visit is to determine which classification of merchandise you wish to review. If you buy dinnerware, for example, list the vendors who sell fine china, then compose another list for earthenware suppliers, and continue in a similar manner for all of your merchandise. You should keep yourself on a schedule that permits examining similar lines in sequence. This allows you to make mental comparisons and notes as you move along, rather than requiring you to attempt to sort out your information and thoughts when the day has ended, after you will undoubtedly have seen dozens of items, groups, and sets. When you have concluded examining one classification of merchandise, go on to the next category in the same fashion.

Once you have established whom you want to see, organize your visit by location. In many markets, over a period of time it has evolved that vendors have clustered together in several buildings close to each other. Visiting these vendors will reduce your travel time, but even so, your appointments should begin in one building and then move to the next, rather than skipping from one building to another and then back again. If the suppliers are located in various parts of a city, you must systematize your showroom calls so that you do not cross your own trail unnecessarily; do not run uptown, downtown, crosstown, uptown, and so on.

Simultaneously, when setting up your visits by location, write out the full address of the vendor, including the floor and suite number, phone number, and the name of the person you wish to see. You are now prepared to phone each vendor and request specific dates and times. If you are making an *overview market* visit, inquire about the length of time your representative feels is adequate to review the line. This will keep you from running over into another appointment or wasting time because your estimate was for a longer time than was actually needed. Figure 3-1 illustrates a completed schedule. As a professional courtesy, you should call as early as possible to cancel an appointment or to notify the vendor that you will be late; you should also inquire whether your late arrival will be inconvenient.

Your visit to the market should not only allow you time to see your regular vendors but also permit you to explore new resources and to shop lines used by your core competitors.

The last item of information you will need is an analysis of each vendor you plan to visit with whom you have done business or are currently doing business (a discussion of the qualitative analysis of resources is covered later in this chapter, and the quantitative aspects are explained in Chapter Fourteen). The vendor analyses should be taken with you to the market, and thus you can free your mind to concentrate on merchandise and not be concerned with trying to recall specific details about the vendors.

Reviewing the plans.   It is always prudent to spend time examining the proposal for your planned market trip. If you are employed by a chain or department store, it may be mandatory that you meet with your *divisional merchandise manager* to review your visit to the market. Regardless of whether you are employed by someone else or are a sole proprietor, you should learn to be objective in evaluating your plans.

You should have clearly defined the purpose of the market trip—overview, follow-up, or specific needs. Be sure that you know how much money *(open-to-buy)* you are prepared to spend for initial purchases and for off-price merchandise, and the sum you will hold back for reorders. These amounts should be divided by classification, and a reserve should be included for new items that you may become aware of as you move through the marketplace.

MARKET VISIT ITINERARY

Date(s) of Visit __10/13, 10/14__ Merchandise Classification(s) __Sweaters__ Phone __212-555-6397__ Buyer __Kendall__

Buying Office Location __1430 Bway, 9th Floor__ Phone __212-555-6397__ Representative __Green__

Hotel-Location __Sheraton, 34th St and 6th Ave__ Phone __212-555-4900__

Time		Monday	Tuesday 10/13	Wednesday 10/14	Thursday	Friday
9:00	Vendor		Bloomin' Knit	Tee Tops		
	Address		1407 Bway, Rm 994	1411 Bway, Rm 2602		
	Phone		212-555-9400	212-555-4243		
	Rep.		Burg	Wells		
10:00	Vendor		Sensational	Knits Ltd.		
	Address		1407 Bway, Rm 1016	1411 Bway, Rm 3814		
	Phone		212-555-1100	212-555-8900		
	Rep.		Sanders	Silver		
11:00	Vendor		QT	Intarsia, Inc.		
	Address		1407 Bway, Rm 1104	1411 Bway, Rm 3806		
	Phone		212-555-6390	212-555-8056		
	Rep.		Edwards			
12:00	Vendor			Le Sex		
	Address			1411 Bway, Rm 4726		
	Phone		LUNCH	212-555-9088		
	Rep.			Carroll		
1:00	Vendor		Fireside			
	Address		1407 Bway, Rm 1631			
	Phone		212-555-4100	LUNCH		
	Rep.		Evans			
2:00	Vendor		Softee Knits	Carry-On		
	Address		1407 Bway, Rm 2703	1410 Bway, Rm 932		
	Phone		212-555-2310	212-555-5651		
	Rep.		Marlns	Dammes		
3:00	Vendor		Plush Top			
	Address		1407 Bway, Rm 3222	Buying Office		
	Phone		212-555-3000	For		
	Rep.		Frankenheim	Reviews		
4:00	Vendor		Zip Top			
	Address		1411 Bway, Rm 812			
	Phone		212-555-4269			
	Rep.		Adler			
5:00	Vendor		Tastee			
	Address		1411 Bway, Rm 619			
	Phone		212-555-7136			
	Rep.		Wright			

Airline __Eastern__ Flt. __631__ Depart __7:15 AM__ Arrive __9:30 AM__ Date __10/12__

Airline __Eastern__ Flt. __624__ Depart __6:20 PM__ Arrive __8:35 PM__ Date __10/14__

NOTES:

Figure 3-1 Completed Market Visit Itinerary

Your itinerary should be scrutinized to be certain that priorities have been set for visiting your major resources while also leaving time for secondary vendors. In addition, ask yourself if you have carefully examined market reports, trade journals, and other publications that may identify new and rising manufacturers whom you should visit.

After your itinerary is established, be sure to leave copies of it with superiors, assistants, and anyone else who might need to communicate with you. It is also a good practice to establish a regular call-in time, for then your messages and any problems that require your attention can be relayed to you quickly, rather than keeping you waiting on the phone while this information is assembled.

THE VENDOR-BUYER RELATIONSHIP

Who is the vendor?   There is always a first visit to any vendor. This supplier may become a major resource or be useful only occasionally or perhaps even only once. You have no way of predicting the outcome of your relationship, even if the vendor is someone you may have inherited from a predecessor. You should always identify the names of the key executives with whom you come in contact. These people are the owner, sales manager, Shipping Department head, and of course the sales representative whom you will deal with both in the showroom and in your own store when he calls upon you; if they are different people, get to know all of them.

Learn to work with the people who best suit your needs. If the vice president of sales normally helps you in the showroom, and this time you need only a single item on a special order that can be attended to by anyone in the vendor's office, do not waste your time, or the vice president's time, waiting for her or him to help you with a relatively simple matter.

If you have a problem with a vendor, such as the need to return merchandise, be sure to see the most appropriate person. As a matter of practice, any discussion involving a substantial problem should be directly with the person or persons who are able to make the corrective decision, not with someone who can only transmit the information to the decision maker. It is too easy to have your problem "forgotten" or misinterpreted. You should also develop the habit of writing out the problem and its resolution, for both you and the vendor, to avoid a misunderstanding sometime later.

How to work with resources.   All vendors from whom you buy must understand that you view the relationship as a *partnership* between them and you. The profitability of your department or store hinges upon the success of your vendors, and if the association is to be continuous, it must be mutually satisfying.

The development of alliances between you and your resources usually depends on your ability to communicate this idea to them. After the idea of an alliance has been accepted, it requires honesty and frankness on the part of both parties. You and your vendors must be *constructively* critical and help each other grow in your business relationship.

Although this goal may seem very idealistic, it will work if each of you respects the professionalism and integrity of the other. Ethics play a large part in this kind of relationship, particularly the recognition and adoption of the concept that each party can and must help the other in achieving profitability.

Information gathering in the showroom.   The common thread that will run through all of your work as a buyer is *organization*. Nowhere is it of greater importance than during your showroom visits. To facilitate your working quickly and efficiently with vendors, you must identify the information you will need to write your order, particularly if you write it after leaving the showroom.

The type of information you will require varies to some extent from one classification to another; four areas are common, however.

MERCHANDISE.   It is obviously impractical to pick up a sample of each item you may consider including in your order. The next best procedure is to develop a system of note taking that permits you to "picture" each item. This could mean providing a form with a general silhouette of the merchandise, such as that of a blouse, with a blank area next to each outline allowing you to record the style number; sleeve and collar type; form of closing; fabric content; colors available; cost at wholesale, as well as the planned retail price; and room for general comments about outstanding and distinctive features.

Many vendors supply prepared description sheets for their merchandise that sometimes include sketches or photographs. These forms (see Fig. 3-2) can simplify your work. Just make certain that the information you require for each style that interests you is complete.

DELIVERY.   It is important to learn when the manufacturer will be ready to ship the merchandise. Do not assume that all styles from a particular vendor will have the same delivery date. In addition, ask the vendor when the delivery for each style will be complete, if reorders will be available, and through what date you can reasonably expect to receive them.

TERMS.   You should inquire about and make note of discounts, as well as anticipation, dating, shipping point, and delivery arrangements (these topics are covered in Chapter Six).

VENDOR SERVICES.   Services offered to retailers by vendors are seldom "free"; that is, the costs of these services are normally included in the purchase price of the merchandise. In compliance with the Robinson-Patman Act of 1936[1], it is lawful for vendors to provide services to buyers if they do so on a proportionately equal basis. Similarly, suppliers can pay retailers for services the retailers perform if such payment is offered to all retailers on a proportionate basis.

As an example, a vendor may offer to reimburse retailers on a matching basis for 50 percent of the cost of advertising the vendor's merchandise. This repayment may be limited to a maximum of 10 percent of the purchases made by retailers during the season or year.

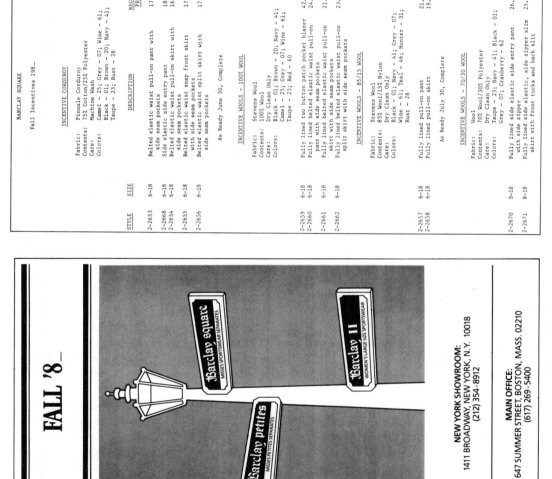

BARCLAY SQUARE
Fall Incentives 198_

STYLE	SIZE	DESCRIPTION	REGULAR PRICE	INCENTIVE PRICE
		INCENTIVE CORDUROY		
		Fabric: Pinwale Corduroy		
		Contents: 75% Cotton/25% Polyester		
		Care: Machine Wash		
		Colors: Camel - 25; Grey - 07; Wine - 61; Black - 01; Brown - 20; Navy - 41; Taupe - 23; Rust - 28		
2-2653	6-18	Belted elastic waist pull-on pant with side seam pockets	17.00	13.00
2-2668	6-18	Side elastic side entry pant	18.00	14.00
2-2654	6-18	Belted elastic waist pull-on skirt with side seam pockets	16.00	11.00
2-2655	6-18	Belted elastic waist snap front skirt with side seam pockets	17.00	13.00
2-2656	6-18	Belted elastic waist split skirt with side seam pockets	17.00	13.00
		As Ready June 30, Complete		
		INCENTIVE WOOLS - 100% WOOL		
		Fabric: Stevens Wool		
		Contents: 100% Wool		
		Care: Dry Clean Only		
		Colors: Black - 01; Brown - 20; Navy - 41; Camel - 25; Grey - 07; Wine - 61; Taupe - 23; Red - 60		
2-2659	6-18	Fully lined two button patch pocket blazer	42.00	36.00
2-2660	6-18	Fully lined belted elastic waist pull-on pant with side seam pockets	24.00	19.00
2-2661	6-18	Fully lined belted elastic waist pull-on skirt with side seam pockets	21.00	17.00
2-2662	6-18	Fully lined belted elastic waist pull-on split skirt with side seam pockets	23.00	18.00
		INCENTIVE WOOLS - 85/15 WOOL		
		Fabric: Stevens Wool		
		Contents: 85% Wool/15% Nylon		
		Care: Dry Clean Only		
		Colors: Black - 01; Navy - 41; Grey - 07; Wine - 61; Teal - 46; Hunter - 31; Rust - 28		
2-2657	6-18	Fully lined pull-on pant	21.00	16.50
2-2658	6-18	Fully lined pull-on skirt	19.00	14.50
		As Ready July 30, Complete		
		INCENTIVE WOOLS - 70/30 WOOL		
		Fabric: Wool		
		Contents: 70% Wool/30% Polyester		
		Care: Dry Clean Only		
		Colors: Taupe - 23; Navy - 41; Black - 01; Grey - 07; Cranberry - 62		
2-2670	9-18	Fully lined side elastic side entry pant with side zipper	26.00	19.50
2-2671	8-18	Fully lined side elastic, side zipper slim skirt with front tucks and back slit	25.00	18.50

FALL '8_

Barclay square
MISSES SPORTSWEAR SEPARATES

Barclay petites
MISSES PETITES SEPARATES

Barclay II
WOMEN'S LARGE SIZE SPORTSWEAR

NEW YORK SHOWROOM:
1411 BROADWAY, NEW YORK, N.Y. 10018
(212) 354-8912

MAIN OFFICE:
647 SUMMER STREET, BOSTON, MASS. 02210
(617) 269-5400

Figure 3-2 Vendor's Descriptive Sheet.

SOURCE: Reprinted with permission of Barclay Square.

If you were to purchase $5000 worth of merchandise from this vendor, for example, you would be entitled to receive a maximum of $500 ($5000 x 10%) for advertising, provided that you spent a similar amount. Meanwhile, if your competitor were to buy $10,000 worth of goods, this retailer would then be entitled to receive up to $1000 ($10,000 x 10%) if the store's advertising expenditure reached this limit.

While keeping this information in mind, you should ask yourself if any of the services offered by the vendors are important for your store, and if not you should inquire if it is the practice of the manufacturer to reduce the cost of the merchandise to compensate for the value of the services you do not wish to accept.

You should understand, of course, that vendors are trying to sell more merchandise to you than their competitors do. Therefore, your first concern in considering whether to accept certain services is to think through whether the vendor's aids will help you in increasing your business overall or merely move your customers from one item of merchandise to another.

There are also a variety of promotional aids that suppliers may be able to provide, such as counter cards, posters, fixtures, window units, "stuffers" for inclusion with packages and monthly statements to customers, radio and television scripts, advertising mats for newspapers and magazines, trainers for your sales staff, and demonstrators. Any or all of these aids may be important for you; however, you should also consider the possibility that you and your organization may be in a better position to develop them at less cost and to better advantage for the store than your vendors would be able to do.

Some suppliers may extend credit for your purchases, as well as offer you merchandise on consignment or indicate that they will either share or wholly absorb your markdowns. Although these forms of risk absorption by vendors are desirable, they are expensive, and the costs are passed on to you in terms of higher unit prices for the merchandise.

Manufacturers may also offer to preticket your merchandise, either with tags you supply to them or with their own tags which would be compatible with your inventory control system.

Vendors may also be willing to "drop-ship" goods to various branches of your store if you have provided them with the appropriate information about distribution for the merchandise.

In these cases, you need to know if the expense to the supplier (which you will ultimately absorb) is less than what it would cost you to mark the merchandise, or if the time needed by the vendor to preticket or distribute the merchandise is less or greater than the time you would need to perform similar work.

Negotiations.[2]   Bargaining is a way of life for buyers and sellers. In a professional setting, it is governed by the underlying principle that both parties must come away from the "table" knowing that each has won. You as a buyer should recognize that your competitors, not your vendors, are your adversaries. What you are attempting to accomplish through negotiations with your suppliers are advantages that will permit you to make a better profit, faster and easier, than other merchants.

As indicated earlier, services and terms of sale obtained from vendors may increase your profitability. The greatest opportunity for making a profit, however, is in purchasing the merchandise at a good price. While buying in the beginning of a season or purchasing staple merchandise usually means a fixed price from vendors, you should be alert to quantity discounts, or reductions in price if orders are placed early. This latter situation is advantageous to manufacturers as it permits them to keep their factories operating during slack periods and gives them an early sense of what the demand is for their merchandise. Vendors may also be able to offer price concessions if you are prepared to buy substantial amounts of merchandise that they develop exclusively for you.

Certainly the most lucrative area of price negotiations involves entering the marketplace in search of off-price merchandise. Other than knowing accurately your own stock position, promotional plans, and anticipated rate of sale for your classifications of goods, you should have an acute awareness of conditions in the market.

Information such as the manufacturing costs for the merchandise you buy helps you identify the bottom-line price for various items. In addition, a knowledge of the amount and suitability of merchandise available is important in order to press for lower costs. If there is a glut on the market of merchandise you wish to purchase, you should have more and better opportunities to purchase off-price goods than if the stock you are searching for is in short supply.

Many large vendors set their closeout prices and tie them into the purchase of established "packages," involving a combination of random assortments and fixed quantities. Small manufacturers may be able to offer you greater flexibility in the goods you wish to buy. Theatrics may play an important part in this kind of bargaining. Learn to maintain an unruffled appearance; do not give away your purchasing limits in terms of price and quantities of goods; and try to "read" the face of the vendor for hints of anxiousness to sell.

While terms of sale and conditions of delivery, as well as price, are negotiable, attempt to resolve each of these issues separately to avoid confusion.

ORDER WRITING

The most important point that you must remember about an order, domestic or foreign, is that once it has been accepted by you and the seller, it becomes a binding contract that is enforceable in court. When you are writing your orders, therefore, great care must be exercised.

Order forms are standard in every vendor's showroom and every sales representative's briefcase. These forms are designed primarily to suit the needs of the vendor and not the buyer, however. In many instances the form contains information in fine print that is meant to protect the vendor, but at the same time it may place the buyer at a disadvantage. It is a common practice for large-scale retailers to develop their own order sheets, and merchants of small or modest size should also design and print their own forms, which is a relatively inexpensive investment.

The advantages of using your own order pads include the following factors: uniformity in size and shape for easy storage and identification of information; certainty that all information you consider to be standard, such as delivery point and terms of sale, is included; adequate space provided for you to write descriptions of the merchandise, retail prices for each style of merchandise, coding to appear on unit control tickets, and an area that you can use to write in the total cost and retail value of the order. This latter point is particularly important, as including this information allows you to review the expenditure and is also useful in computing the balance of purchases that remains. In addition, on foreign orders, if your purchase is intended for men, women, boys, or girls, be sure to indicate the gender of the intended customers, such as "men's casual slacks." For knit goods, the exact specifications of the gauge of the knitting equipment and yarn to be used must be shown, as with woven fabric you should list the yarn count; and for any product with color, the methods of color application and the type of dye, stain, or glaze should be specified.

Figure 3-3 is a form designed by a small retailer that effectively meets the needs of the store; Figure 3-4 is a copy of an order supplied by a vendor; and Figure 3-5 is an order form used by a leading multi-unit department store.

As a buyer, you must discipline yourself to write out orders completely for the quantities being purchased, no matter whether it is for one piece of merchandise or thousands of pieces. Although many vendors may tentatively accept phone orders to facilitate your request for merchandise ahead of other orders they receive from your competitors, they normally insist on obtaining written confirmation by mail before they actually ship the goods.

The number of copies of your orders may vary from two upward, depending upon the systems to which you are committed. Usually the original form remains with the vendor, and a second copy is retained by the buyer. Other copies of the order may go to your Accounting Department, where the dollar amount of your open-to-buy is updated; another copy may go to the Receiving Department so that they will know if arriving shipments are authorized. Your Ticketing Department may also require a copy to permit it to prepare tags for the incoming merchandise. Finally, you may feel that a copy should be filed with an assistant who can accumulate data on your purchases by classification, colors, sizes, or whatever categories you find important to help you perform your work. The assistant would also be responsible for keeping you informed about what merchandise has been received, what is outstanding, and which orders are beyond the delivery date you have established and require either follow-up calls or cancellation.

YOUR STORE
7504 Main Street
Cincinnati, OH 45202
(513) 555-1071

DATE ___ / ___ / ___

ORDERED FROM _____

_____

_____

Ship To: 278 Fulton Ave.
         Toledo, OH 43606

RETURNS TO _____

	30	32	34	36	38	40	42
A	30	32	34	36	38	40	42
B	6	8	10	12	14	16	18
C	5	7	9	11	13	15	
D	XS	S	M	L	XL		
E	8½	9	9½	10	10½	11	
F	6	6½	7	7½	8		
G							
H							

MU%	TOTAL OF ORDER—RET.	ORDER NO. 02492	SALESMAN	TERMS: AS OF /

DELIVERY START	COMPLETE	SHIPPING INSTRUCTIONS BEST WAY ☐ AS HAD ☐	SPECIAL SHIPPING INSTRUCTIONS ☐

STYLE NO.	QUANTITY	WHOLESALE PRICE	RETAIL PRICE	COST TOTAL	DESCRIPTION	CODE	COLOR

POSTIVELY NO BROKEN SIZES SHIPPED AND NO SUBSTITUTIONS OF STYLES, SIZES OR COLOR, UNLESS PERMISSION
IS OBTAINED. MDSE. RECEIVED AFTER 20th OF MONTH PAYABLE AS OF THE 25th.
MDSE. SHIPPED AFTER COMPLETION DATE, SUBJECT TO RETURN AT BUYER'S DISCRETION.

Figure 3-3 Purchase Order Form for an Independent Retailer

Barclay square **BARCLAY SQUARE**
BOSTON HARBOR INDUSTRIAL PARK
647 SUMMER STREET
BOSTON, MA 02210

TELEPHONE: (617) 269-5400

Date ____________

DEPT. NO. ____________
CUSTOMER'S ORDER NO. ____________
START DATE ____________
COMPLETE DATE ____________
SHIP VIA ____________
SALESMAN ____________
TERMS: 8/10 E.O.M. F.O.B. BOSTON, MASS.

BILL TO:
Name ____________
Address ____________

SHIP TO:
Name ____________
Address ____________

ACCOUNT NUMBER | STORE BRANCH CODE | CUSTOMER TELEPHONE ( ) —

	STYLE	QTY.	DESCRIPTION & COLORS	COLOR CODE			S		M		L		XL		PRICE	TOTAL
							30	32	34	36	38	40				
							36	38	40	42	44	46				
					1	3	5	7	9	11	13	15	17	19		
					2	4	6	8	10	12	14	16	18	20		
1																
2																
3																
4																
5																
6																
7																
8																
9																
10																
11																
12																
13																
14																
15																
16																
17																
18																
19																
20																
21																
22																
23																
24																
25																
26																
27																
28																
29																
30																
31																
32																
33																
34																
35																
36																

THIS ORDER IS NOT SUBJECT TO CANCELLATION

____________ Buyer

The acceptance of Copy of Order makes this a Binding Contract. The Delivery of these Goods is subject to Labor Strikes, Accidents by Fire or any causes beyond our control. No returns accepted without authorization sticker.

Figure 3-4 Vendor's Purchase Order Form

SOURCE: Reprinted with permission of Barclay Square.

ALL PACKAGES AND INVOICES MUST BE MARKED WITH OUR DEPT. NO. & ORDER NO.

DEPT. NO.	ORDER NO. 705371
A/P VENDOR NO.	MR/ HOUSE NO.
VENDOR NAME	
STREET	
CITY, STATE & ZIP	

jordan marsh BOSTON, MASSACHUSETTS 02107

UNIT OF ALLIED STORES CORP

VENDOR COPY

INVOICE INSTRUCTIONS

1. Submit separate invoice for each store. Invoice must show appropriate store code, order number and department number. When shipping merchandise for more than one purchase order, please submit separate invoices by purchase order per store. Bill of Lading must accompany invoice.
2. On each invoice, itemize color and size as well as store name to which merchandise was shipped.
3. Invoice must accompany shipments in an envelope attached to the lead carton, marked "Invoice enclosed". When this is not possible, a packing slip must accompany the shipment and the Invoice air mailed (the same day shipment is made) to the Invoice Order Department, Jordan Marsh Company, P.O. Box C2506, Boston, Mass. 02205.
4. All invoices, packing slips and correspondence must show our complete order number, store code, date shipped, number of cartons, total weight, shipper's name and complete routing.

PACKING AND SHIPPING

1. Pack merchandise separately per store distribution code with individual packing slip.
2. Mark each carton or container with a) STORE CODE b) DEPARTMENT NUMBER and ORDER NUMBER(S) c) NUMBER OF CARTONS IN SHIPMENT (i.e. 1 of 3, 2 of 3, etc. . .)
3. Consolidate all cartons or containers for a department, on one Bill of Lading and route per guide instruction applicable to total weight. DO NOT include more than one department per Bill of Lading.
4. Ship complete unless otherwise instructed. If this order is not shipped complete, all freight charges on subsequent shipments must be prepaid.
5. We encourage the use of the NRMA approved swivel neck plastic hangers.
6. Failure to comply with the invoice, packing, shipping, and routing instructions on this Purchase Order will result in our chargeback to your firm for additional handling and transportation expense incurred.

DATE OF ORDER	MDSE. TO BE SHIPPED ON BUT NOT BEFORE:
F.O.B. CITY/STATE	CANCELLATION DATE WILL NOT ACCEPT RECEIPT AFTER ______
WHO PAYS FREIGHT ☐ VENDOR ____ % ☐ STORE ____ %	TERMS

CANCELLATION POLICY

Any or all of this order not received on or before the cancellation date is automatically cancelled. Merchandise will be returned at your risk and expense and you will be billed for handling charges.

PURCHASE ORDER SUBJECT TO THE TERMS AND CONDITIONS ON THE FRONT AND REVERSE SIDE OF THIS SHEET

SHIP ALL MERCHANDISE TO: DISTRIBUTION CENTER 500 COMMANDER SHEA BLVD. NO. QUINCY, MASSACHUSETTS 02171

BUYER INDICATE RECEIVING LOCATION ☐ NORTH ☐ SOUTH ☐ OTHER

MARK EACH PACKAGE WITH ORDER & DEPARTMENT NUMBER & STORE CODE BELOW.

CLASS	STYLE	SKU/DESCRIPTION	COLOR CODE	COLOR	SIZE	BOJ 1	FOJ 2	POJ 4	NHJ 5	BRJ 6	BUJ 7	MEJ 8	RWJ 9	WOJ 10	LWJ 11	MTJ 12	BWJ 13	CCJ 14	SMJ 15	NEJ 16	HAJ 17	WFJ 18	ALJ 19	XSJ 80	ORDERED QTY.	ORDERED TYPE OF UNIT	COST UNIT	COST TOTAL

SPECIAL INSTRUCTIONS	BUYER SIG. DATE
	MDSE. MGR. SIG. DATE
	COUNTER SIG. / OTHER

For shipments originating within the Greater New York City area, deliver all weights F.O.B. Regional Imp. & Ext. Trucking, 115 Paterson Ave. Hoboken, New Jersey.

All excess charges will be deducted.

Where rates are dependent on value, forward shipments at · MINIMUM VALUATION.

ROUTING INSTRUCTIONS

Unless otherwise specified herein, ship per instructions in Allied Stores Routing Guide (if you do no have a guide, immediately contact Allied Stores, Traffic Dept., 1114 Avenue of the Americas, N.Y., N.Y. 10036.)

TOTAL ORDER AMOUNT AT COST	
TRADE DISC. %	
NET ORDER AMOUNT	

(2-82)

Figure 3-5 Department Store Purchase Order Form

SOURCE: Reprinted with permission of Jordan Marsh, Boston, MA.

ORDER FOLLOW-UP

The act of placing an order with a vendor begins a chain of events that should culminate in the satisfaction of particular needs or desires for your customers. The road toward this fulfillment, however, is an arduous one for you, the retailer.

Although vendors can be held legally responsible for shipping the merchandise you have ordered, there are a host of reasons that may preclude this from happening. Acts of God, strikes, and transportation delays are only a few of the legitimate reasons that will be encountered.

Once your orders are placed, therefore, you should not simply sit back and wait. The wisest practice is to develop a "tickler" file, arranging your orders by date of completion, and, depending on the particular market conditions for your classifications of merchandise, you should plan to call or visit vendors who have not shipped or completely shipped the items you have ordered by the specified time.

Placing an order is a commitment of your funds, and it represents a need for merchandise. If the goods are not received on time, sales that cannot be recaptured will be lost. In addition, if stock is received late into a season, you will not have a complete selling period, and unnecessary markdowns will result.

Figure 3-6 Buyer and Assistant Recording Purchase Order Data
SOURCE: Courtesy of Jill Kamen and Elizabeth Filardi, ass't buyers—Filene's.

Many vendors, both large and small, arrange orders received from buyers in chronological sequence and fill them as the goods become available, without regard to the importance of the purchase. Manufacturers and suppliers of this type are highly respected for providing equal opportunities for all retailers.

Unfortunately, there are also sellers who cater to the "squeaky wheel" or the "biggest wheel," thus filling orders for their loudest or most important clients. Some vendors even permit buyers to "visit" the factory or warehouse and pick up their orders on site. Suppliers of this type are the prostitutes of the marketplace and, although it may be to your advantage to buy from them if your order is sizable, you will soon learn to shun them, for their behavior will ultimately work against you.

You always have the right to cancel orders for merchandise not shipped by your completion date. If the goods are badly needed, however, it is far more important to receive the goods than to cancel them. Some vendors, after receiving a follow-up call from you in advance of the completion date, may explain that the merchandise has been shipped. Under these circumstances, you should obtain the name of the freight carrier and a receipt number for the shipment so that you can trace the goods to determine the approximate date of delivery.

The frustration of not receiving merchandise you have expended time, energy, and expense to order is insignificant compared to the frustration of being unable to meet your planned sales figures. You should, therefore, view order follow-up as a critical part of your work.

VENDOR ANALYSIS: QUALITATIVE CONSIDERATIONS

Qualitative assessments of a person or an item are particularly difficult to accomplish because, although the criteria may be clearly defined, the ratings are produced by human beings and no two of us usually see the same thing in an identical manner. This phenomenon is the problem you will face as you attempt to evaluate your vendors. How you *qualitatively* view a supplier may be completely different from the perception of another buyer. As you must learn to rate different merchandise offerings, however, you must also develop the sophistication needed to appraise vendors.

In Chapter Fourteen you will learn the criteria and mathematical computations used for evaluating vendors *quantitatively*. The following information is listed here as a guide for you to use when considering the conditions that require you to rate suppliers *qualitatively*.

Essentially, you should develop a system with a rating scale, either using numbers (for example, 1 to 10, with 1 representing the lowest evaluation); or words (poor, fair, and so on to excellent); or letter grades (A through F). Regardless of the method used, it will serve you better if you can define in writing what a "6" or "fair" or a "C" represents. Forcing yourself to think about your system will undoubtedly result in a better system than if you just plod along expecting to remember next season the values of your ratings.

Merchandise. The most important aspect to consider when evaluating your vendors is their merchandise. Specifically, your concern should be with the styling, distinctiveness, and quality of the goods. The importance of each of these categories varies from retailer to retailer, and for this reason they are presented here in random order.

STYLING. Does the vendor produce originals, copies of originals, or less expensive copies of copies; and how good are they? Is the merchandise available for your viewing early in the buying season?

DISTINCTIVENESS. Is the merchandise different, and are the variations (if it is a copy) major or of little consequence?

QUALITY. Are the goods, when delivered, similar to or better than the sample you viewed before ordering; is the merchandise of consistent grade? If there are industry or statutory standards, how does the product measure up?

Vendor policies. The policies of your suppliers greatly affect your profitability. Although it is likely that most vendors will tend to be consistent in the categories described below, it is not uncommon for a change to occur when the manufacturer hires a new shipping director or traffic or sales manager. A cautious procedure is to review your vendor's nonmerchandising behavior regularly.

DELIVERY. Are shipments of orders received when promised? Has the merchandise been packed as prearranged (on hangers, flat, boxed, crated, etc.)? Are reorders and special orders attended to in a comparable or better manner?

ADHERENCE TO THE ORDER. Has the vendor strictly followed your order by shipping only the styles, colors, and size assortments you indicated, or have substitutions been made without your permission? Have the proper quantities been shipped? If the merchandise was to have been grouped and delivered as sets, has this been done?

OFF-PRICE OFFERINGS. Does the vendor or representative offer you off-price buys as soon as they become available, or are you further down on the list, getting the "leftovers"? When off-price merchandise is available, does the vendor price the goods to you realistically so that you, the vendor, and your customer can all benefit?

RETURN POLICY. Will the vendor "work with you" on merchandise that does not sell up to expectations, providing full return, partial return, or markdown allowances? Are completely justifiable returns, such as defective goods or merchandise that you have not ordered, accepted back quickly? Does the vendor issue merchandise credits, which compel you to buy other goods to get your money back, or are checks issued to clear balances?

Vendor services. The last category to review for each supplier is the list of services provided. Many of these services were discussed earlier in this chapter. Generally, however, they fall into three categories: promotional assistance;

financing and risk assumption; and inventory aid. Your evaluation of these services has to be based upon your need and use of the particular service as related to the quantity and quality of the assistance.

CASE STUDY_____

SEAM SCENES

The new merchandiser in the store's buying office in New York, L. Sanders, is a real go-getter. Although you have not met, you've spoken on the phone many times and "Sandy" has sent you many pages of handwritten notes on new goods and suppliers for the coming season.

You routinely gave the buying office a list of vendors you wanted to see for your upcoming market trip, identifying the Monday-through-Thursday period you would use for initial viewing, with Monday morning reserved for working in the office. Sandy sent back your itinerary within days, with all of your visits confirmed.

Admittedly, it looked a bit more hectic than you would have liked, but there were several new suppliers listed, and you were pleased about this. There was even a 12:30 luncheon visit with one of them, "Seam Scenes," for Monday. What struck you as odd was that this visit was the only one in which the showroom location was omitted from the plan.

As it was the Saturday prior to your market trip before you realized this, however, it was too late to change it. But as you walk toward Sandy's office, you make a mental note to ask about it.

Sandy is a great match for the market—neat, well-groomed, friendly, and, from the way the vendors' samples are hung and folded in the confined space of the office, this merchandiser appears to be very well organized. A good beginning.

As you begin to talk, you also realize that Sandy has done a great deal of homework about you, your buying habits, and the store. You're very flattered and impressed.

The morning progresses rapidly, with Sandy moving quickly and efficiently through the prearranged merchandise. Sandy has pointed out many items you feel have merit for your department and, similarly, has indicated a larger number of styles that you both agree are of marginal value. You like the way Sandy thinks.

Finally, Sandy moves with obvious pleasure to a small group of articles folded on the edge of the desk and with some flourish announces, "Seam Scenes."

As Sandy shows you each piece of merchandise, the presentation becomes more professional, and you wonder if Sandy could visit the store to train your sales people, because you're ready to order every style.

Sandy glances at the wall clock and announces that you're both due to meet the sales manager of "Seam Scenes," Jackie, at the "Market Pub" for lunch.

The sales manager is also a good market type—neat, sharp, and aggressive—but no more so than you're accustomed to working with.

Seam Scenes is new; this is their first line. The firm is composed of bright young people who have invested their money and everything they can borrow to start properly. They need and want your order. You can have 15 percent of your purchases as an advertising allowance and you have to spend only 25 percent of the sum, with Seam Scenes paying the balance. You're told that this is because you're a "preferred" customer; all other customers get 10 percent of their orders on a 50-50 matching basis. Besides, Seam Scenes will give you a 5 percent markdown allowance on your total order, which is also only for you as a "preferred" customer. The dating and shipping terms are the same as are common in the market for the season.

As your host signs the check, you do some fast mental computations about the size of the order you plan to write, based on the samples you saw in the buying office. You picture a very profitable relationship.

The sales manager signs for the luncheon, "J. Sanders."

1. How do you feel about "preferred customer" status?
2. Are there any implications that your office merchandiser is L. Sanders and the sales manager of Seam Scenes is J. Sanders? What will you do?

SUPPLEMENTARY CASE STUDY_____

BRISTOL'S—PART II

Note: Bristol's–Part I, which can be found at the end of Chapter 2, should be read for background.

Your meeting with the divisional merchandise manager last week produced several changes, the most important of which is that you have been moved to buying different classifications of merchandise within the division. The previous buyer has left Bristol's, and no explanation has been advanced. You suspect that the circumstances were somewhat less than pleasant, based on the fact that neither you nor the former buyer's assistants can locate any vendor analysis records; the sales reports indicate that the department has failed to meet its planned sales figures for almost a year; and the markdowns have been excessive.

Although the divisional merchandise manager was very enthusiastic about your new assignment, the phrase, "stick to your buying plan and sales will take care of themselves," rings in your ears. The problem now seems to be that in the absence of vendor records, and with a mandate to reduce purchases by 40 percent and buy about 50 percent of the stock as promotional goods, you have a lot of research to do before your upcoming visit to the market.

Fortunately, a buyer's guide is available, and you have done much reading in it in preparation for your trip.

You have been able to identify five wholesalers who carry a broad range of merchandise appropriate for your department, two of whom have price lines that are in the promotional range for Bristol's. There are also twenty-three nationally-known vendors and sixteen others with merchandise either priced at your regular levels or priced to sell below.

As market week for your classifications of goods is almost a month away, what will you do to meet the challenge of your new position?

NOTES

[1]Appendix A contains a brief summary of the most important federal legislation affecting retailers.
[2]This topic is covered in detail in Chapter Four.

Negotiating

4

WHAT IS NEGOTIATING?_____

Negotiating techniques are skills which most of us learn early in life and use frequently without a thought given to the process. Day-to-day examples of negotiating are: convincing the owner of the family car that you should be allowed to use it; swaying a companion to go with you to a concert rather than a movie; or persuading a teacher to extend the due date for an assignment, to name but a few.

As a buyer, you will have many opportunities to use negotiating skills with vendors and their representatives, as many conditions and terms relating to the purchase of merchandise (and, at times, the product itself) are negotiable.

The sequence of activities which involves give-and-take by all parties to reach a common, mutually acceptable objective (usually profit, in retailing), is known as negotiating.

The most frequent view of the individuals and issues in a negotiating session is that of adversaries pitted against each other in mortal combat. While there are many instances to support this picture, your future as a successful buyer will hinge upon your ability to arrive at best possible agreements, leaving you and your vendors satisfied that each will be profitable. This is a "Win (vendor)/Win (buyer)" outcome; both parties have emerged as winners.

DESIRED OUTCOMES OF NEGOTIATION

In Chapter Three, a reference is made to the relationship you as a buyer should maintain with your suppliers; that is, a long-term partnership wherein you and your vendors see that mutual profitability is the most desirable state. Hence the posture you assume as a negotiator will impact on the balance of this partnership.

There are essentially two concerns which are important to a long-term partnership between you, as a buyer, and your vendors; they are person-to-person relationships between you, built upon mutual respect which will provide longevity; and the concern each of you demonstrates for specific issues, that is, discussions referring to merchandise, terms, and other conditions.

A word of caution is appropriate here to those of you who find yourselves working for retailers of considerable importance, who have strengths by virtue of their purchasing power: Do not abuse vendors with your employer's clout. Historically, almost all retailers have experienced lean times; and furthermore, what certainty is there that you will always be employed by a powerful retailer? Just as everyone else, vendors do not like to be abused, and they have long memories about who their tormentors have been.

TYPES OF NEGOTIATORS

It is important that you recognize the different personality characteristics of the people with whom you will come in contact during negotiations. You should also identify those traits which match your own personality. Equipped with the foregoing, you will be in a better position to understand statements made by vendors and be prepared to counter with meaningful and acceptable solutions.

People who are involved in negotiations assume one of the following "C" general postures:

1. Combatant
2. Conceder
3. Compromiser
4. Conciliator
5. Collaborator

At various times during discussions, their positions may switch to a back-up position, but in a final evaluation they feel most comfortable with one style.

Combatant.   Lose/Win. The combative negotiator is one who is not concerned with a person-to-person relationship or its longevity. The goal is total victory at any cost, using power, threats, deception, insults, and abuse.

Figure 4-1 Vendor, Divisional Merchandise Manager, and Buyer Negotiating a Promotion Agreement

SOURCE: Courtesy of Lee Bor, terr. manager—Jacqueline Cochran, Inc., Leonard Ichton, divisional merchandise manager—Filene's, and William Marcus, buyer—Filene's.

Conceder.   Lose/Lose. The negotiator who concedes on every issue—people, merchandise, terms, and so on—is going through the motions, feeling that whatever he or she can get or is given should be accepted. The goal is to maintain a low profile and avoid any form of confrontation. The conceder negotiator is the direct opposite of the combatant negotiator.

Compromiser.   0/0. A compromising negotiator is one who demonstrates concern for both issues and person-to-person relationships. However, these persons readily look for and/or accept a reasonable middle-of-the-road solution, rather than pursuing an agreement which would produce optimum results. They are concerned with each party going away with something, regardless of how minimal, so that no one has given up anything without getting something in return.

Conciliator.   Win/Lose. The concern of the conciliatory negotiator is towards development of person-to-person relationships, in the hope that this kinship will lead to the solution of all problems. Confrontations are avoided. Peace, happiness, and tranquility are foremost. Naively, this type of negotiator reveals all of his or her information as a sign of trust, demonstrating a complete lack of negotiating sophistication.

Collaborator.   Win/Win. A negotiator who is a collaborator moves to preserve and improve both person-to-person relationships and the buyer-vendor position on the issue under discussion. These negotiators accomplish their goals through a problem-solving approach involving all parties, wherein each participant views issues as mutual problems which can be resolved with mutual gains. Discussions are constructively directed towards the issues and not destructively at the personalities of the participants.

Figure 4-2 and Table 4-1 illustrate and summarize the effects of each of the five types of negotiators.

The negotiating style which has the most advantages for all parties is that practiced by the collaborator negotiator. This assures a Win/Win outcome.

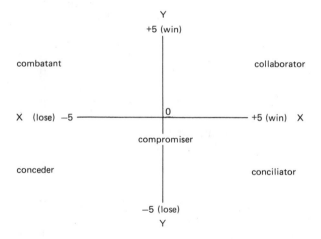

X Axis = Person-to-person values
Y Axis = Issues Values

Figure 4-2 Negotiating Styles and Their Results

Table 4—1 End Results of Negotiating Styles

Negotiator Style	Person-to-Person	Issues	Total
Combatant	−5	+5	0
Conceder	−5	−5	−10
Compromiser	0	0	0
Conciliator	+5	−5	0
Collaborator	+5	+5	+10

WIN/WIN SKILLS

There are learnable skills connected with successful negotiating. Some of these you may have acquired; the others can be learned through practice.

The following are the broad Win/Win skills, as they are used in negotiating:

1. Communication
2. Problem solving
3. Convincing

Communication.   The process of communication involves speaking, active listening, clarifying specific points, and summarizing.

SPEAKING.   When you are presenting your ideas to a vendor, your message is conveyed both by *WHAT* you say and *HOW* you say it. (The *HOW* will be discussed later in the chapter.) *WHAT* you say should be presented clearly, in an organized fashion. If necessary, refer to notes to be sure that all facets of your message have been presented.

ACTIVE LISTENING.   Active listening is a communication skill you will use to convince vendors that you have *REALLY* heard what they have to say. It is a two-step process. The first step is to *LISTEN WITHOUT INTERRUPTING*; then, in your own words, *SUMMARIZE AND STATE THE MESSAGE BACK* to the vendor. This serves to tell the vendor that you have been listening, and, at the same time, that you have understood what the message means.

As a negotiating tool, your active listening provides vendors with the means to verbalize their feelings, and will often lead to a stronger feeling of trust than can otherwise be established.

CLARIFYING SPECIFIC POINTS.   Many times vendors will attempt to speak in broad generalities such as "Don't worry about it; I'll take care of it later on." You must obtain the specifics about what kind of "care," and when is "later on."

Clarifying specific points will help you make decisions and avoid future misunderstandings.

SUMMARIZING.   Summarizing during negotiations is critical to avoid misunderstandings at later stages in the process. You should verbally bring together all of the salient points in the discussion without injecting editorial comments. One such statement could be: "The points we've covered so far are that if I will buy 25 dozen of style 1812 and 20 dozen of style 1963, you will give me a markdown allowance of 5 percent overall. Is that correct?"

A mid-discussion summary is also a good way to slow the talk down and allow you to regroup your thoughts without appearing confused.

Problem-solving.   A problem exists when either the parties involved see the facts of the situation differently, or one party believes or insists that there is only one best solution for all concerned.

Clarification of facts is the first step towards reaching an agreement. Once this is accomplished, you can proceed to find a solution to the problem.

VENDOR-GENERATED SOLUTION. Asking the vendor for a solution accomplishes several things: It gives the vendor a sense of importance (which is as it should be), continuing to build upon the "partnership" concept; the vendor may offer ideas or alternatives that you have not been aware of; and, if the problem is truly a vendor-oriented problem, who is better able to address the issue than the vendor?

DETERMINE THE VENDOR'S NEEDS THROUGH QUESTIONS. The information you develop through questioning vendors about their needs will prove useful in making proposals to resolve the current problem. For example, you might say: "You've said you are overstocked on styles 610, 711, and 861. If I order 5 dozen of each style, will you give me a 20 percent markdown allowance on 4 dozen of style 531?"

In this instance, you have offered to assist the vendor with a problem if the vendor will, in turn, help you with yours.

GENERATE ALTERNATIVE SOLUTIONS. An alternative solution is one which is not all of what you are asking for, nor is it one which is all the vendor is asking for. It is a settlement based upon the facts and information agreed to as accurate by all concerned.

One way to arrive at an alternative solution is to list all the points of agreement, then list unresolved issues and mutually decide which items can be balanced off against which others. Any remaining points are more easily addressed, and the following technique is used:

This technique involves "giving ground" from an original stated position to one which you have planned to be acceptable. A vendor viewing your movement will usually give ground to a point within an area which you mutually find agreeable. (See Fig. 4–3)

The key to finding a solution via this route is that your *stated position*, while being one which you can move from, must be realistic. If the position is unrealistic, it will be assumed that you either do not know your business or that you *do* have another position. Where the latter is true, you will undoubtedly give ground sooner than you should and subsequently fail to attain your planned acceptable position.

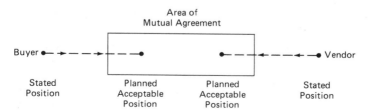

Figure 4-3 Developing an Alternate Solution

Convincing.   Convincing vendors to move towards your position as opposed to remaining firm with theirs requires several skills.

BE ASSERTIVE.   Assertive behavior requires that you ask for what you want, honestly and in a straightforward manner, without intimidating the vendor. It is the technique which will generate the long-term goal of a relationship while accomplishing the immediate task of resolving a problem. It differs from aggressive behavior, as indicated earlier in this chapter, in that it avoids hurting others to reach objectives.

Assertiveness is a sophisticated approach involving choices of words and their use in statements and body language.

Words and statements.   Assertive words and statements are those which are positive and active, omitting unnecessary self-demeaning phrases. A good assertive statement would be: "We will have style 1620 ready for return before 10:00 a.m. Please notify your Receiving Department to expect the shipment. Thank you for your help." Conversely, the same situation could be poorly stated as: "I *think* we can have style 1620 ready for return *sometime* tomorrow morning. I'd *really appreciate* your notifying your Receiving Department to expect the shipment. Thank you for *all* your help."

You should also learn to deliver your assertive message at a more rapid speed than you use in normal speech. The sentences should be complete and said without pauses, unless these are required for effect.

Body language.   Much has been written about the signals we transmit via our physical presentation. This certainly applies in the area of negotiations.

Make comfortable eye contact; avert your eyes occasionally to avoid staring or glaring.

Stand or sit erect, but not stiffly. Avoid slouching or a lounging appearance.

Gesturing at people by pointing your finger into their faces or slapping or pounding a table is aggressive, not assertive, behavior. Similarly, your facial expressions can be either those of a concerned, interested buyer or of an angry, snarling, out-of-control person.

Remember, your body language and words and statements reinforce each other and can either get your message across clearly or present a very confused story, hence a confused "you," to a vendor.

SELL BENEFITS.   Relating the benefits of your position to the vendor's needs is the key to arriving at a rapid and satisfactory agreement.

As your needs are different for each negotiating situation, so, too, are those of your vendor. Therefore, if you are to successfully sell a vendor on the benefits of a particular solution, you must know and understand the vendor's needs. Some may be vendor-specific, such as an overstocked situation; others may be industry-related, as the case might be when ". . . sweaters aren't selling this season. . . ."

Presenting only those benefits which are of greatest importance to the vendor will emphasize your concern and also condense negotiating time. Avoid saying what is obvious, but be absolutely certain that what you believe is apparent is clear to everyone else.

OVERCOME OBJECTIONS.   An objection from a vendor is a sign of interest in your proposal. It is not a rejection which indicates no interest.

Objections should be responded to as they arise, or if a vendor presents several at once they should be addressed after you have evaluated them and mentally organized them into a list reflecting their importance to the problem.

The process you should use to deal with objections includes two of the basic communication skills described earlier—active listening and summarizing. The next step is to emphasize facts as they have been introduced and re-present or present the benefits of your proposal.

The final phase is to ask if there are any questions about your response to the objection. If there are, better to get them at that moment than having to return at a later time and rehash the whole issue.

PLANNING FOR NEGOTIATION

Knowing the techniques of negotiating is only a part of your job. The planning homework you do prior to negotiations will usually determine how well you will do.

Gathering data.   There are three areas about which you should acquire information. These are: (1) the situation, (2) the vendor, and (3) the bottom line.

THE SITUATION.   Be sure you have clearly defined the real problem. If the difficulty is that the merchandise has not sold, is it because it has not been promoted; does it require a demonstrator; do your sales associates need special training or instruction; or is it overpriced? After you have determined the *real problem*, prepare yourself with relevant facts or substantively supported assumptions. Know your stock position, the profit margin with this vendor, and the current market trends with similar merchandise. You will not be able to convince a vendor to provide support in this situation unless you can show that the merchandise is not selling and that you have the documentation to prove it.

THE VENDOR.   Find out from reliable sources, such as buyers from noncompeting stores or your resident buying office, what is the status of the vendor—profits, salability of current merchandise, prospects for the future, and so on. This will give you some idea about the vendor's possible objectives during negotiations. If the business is doing well, the vendor may be generous. Conversely, the vendor may need to get rid of goods via special prices or exchange if the season has been poor.

You should also attempt to ascertain the vendor's style of negotiating. Which of the five "C's" mentioned earlier does he or she project? How will you counter or react to this posture?

THE BOTTOM LINE.   Understanding in advance what it is that you will minimally accept in negotiations is an important step in planning. You should also make note of what it is that you will trade off for what. As an example, if you had a bottom line of "5 percent of the total order for sales promotion," and the vendor has offered ". . . 3 percent, but I'll give 6 percent on the next order . . . ," you should have preplanned your response(s).

Given the preceding illustration, observe that a bottom line is not a fixed, single objective. It is one which is determined by balancing the components (or objectives) and trade-offs. This concept is illustrated in Figure 4-4.

Establishing objectives.   Establishing your objectives and goals is part of the overall planning process. These should be set so as to be *measurable*; thus providing feedback, fixing accountability, and establishing a basis for evaluation. When objectives are clearly stated, so that they are measurable, they are also effective in improving your performance. A measurable objective statement includes a "what" and "when," such as "to increase markup by 1.2 percent [what] by February 17 [when]."

In setting out your objectives, be certain to include both your long-term and short-term goals, as well as those (as you may know or perceive them) of your vendor.

List your highest-priority objective first and any trade-offs you will accept to reach a bottom line. Also, tabulate the data and skills you will use to support your objective.

Don't be afraid to set your goals and objectives high. When you aim at the top, your bottom line will be closer to that point than if you are only looking to achieve the middle.

Dr. Bernard Rosenbaum, president of Management of Human Resources Development, Inc. (MOHR), Stamford, Connecticut, has developed a *Retail Negotiation Skills* training program which employs, in part, the forms illustrated in Figures 4-5, 6, & 7. You should consider using planning tools such as these, regardless of whether you are a new buyer or one who has many negotiating sessions as seasoning. Their use will insure that your goals and strategies for obtaining objectives are carefully thought through, thereby increasing your possibilities for success.

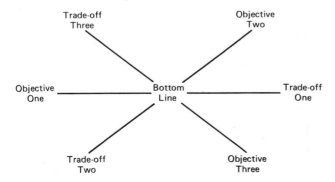

Figure 4-4 The Bottom Line

NEGOTIATION PLANNER — NEEDS

	SHORT TERM (THIS BUY)	LONG TERM (LONG TERM RELATIONSHIP WITH VENDOR/BUYER)
BUYER NEEDS	1. _____ 2. _____ 3. _____	1. _____ 2. _____ 3. _____
VENDOR NEEDS	1. _____ 2. _____ 3. _____	1. _____ 2. _____ 3. _____
DATA TO SUPPORT ASSUMPTIONS OF VENDOR NEEDS	1. _____ 2. _____ 3. _____	1. _____ 2. _____ 3. _____
	• LIST THE NEEDS THAT EACH PARTY WILL ATTEMPT TO FULFILL DURING THE NEGOTIATION. • LIST THE LONG-TERM NEEDS THAT EACH WANTS TO FULFILL DURING THE BUYER/VENDOR RELATIONSHIP.	• LIST THE NEEDS FROM MOST IMPORTANT TO LEAST IMPORTANT TO MEET • WHAT DATA SUPPORTS YOUR ASSUMPTIONS REGARDING VENDOR NEEDS.

© MOHR DEVELOPMENT, INC. STAMFORD, CT.

Figure 4-5 Planning—Needs

SOURCE: Reprinted with permission, Management of Human Resources, Stamford, CT.

THE NEGOTIATING MEETING

Any negotiating meeting should be approached as a furthering of mutual interests and relationships. It should also be one you are fully prepared for. If you are, you will be comfortable and confident about your preparation and the anticipated outcome.

To whom do you talk?   In Chapter Three, reference was made to which person you would normally work with; that is, the person who is the decision maker. Many times your ongoing contact will be with a sales representative. Certainly, as a courtesy to this individual, your problems should be discussed with her or him. If this person says no to something, however, don't give up.

NEGOTIATION PLANNER — SHORT TERM OBJECTIVES

VENDOR

SHORT TERM (THIS BUY)

1.

LEAST DIFFICULT TO ACHIEVE

2.

SOMEWHAT DIFFICULT TO ACHIEVE

3.

MOST DIFFICULT TO ACHIEVE

• WRITE OBJECTIVES YOU THINK THE VENDOR WILL TRY TO ACHIEVE DURING THIS NEGOTIATION.

BUYER

SHORT TERM (THIS BUY)

1.

LEAST DIFFICULT TO ACHIEVE

2.

SOMEWHAT DIFFICULT TO ACHIEVE

3.

MOST DIFFICULT TO ACHIEVE

PREPLANNED LIMITS:

1. MAXIMUM

MINIMUM

2. MAXIMUM

MINIMUM

3. MAXIMUM

MINIMUM

• WRITE OBJECTIVES THAT WILL MEET YOUR NEEDS IF YOU ATTAIN THEM DURING THIS NEGOTIATION.
• PREPARE FOR THE MAXIMUM LIMITS YOU WOULD LIKE TO ACHIEVE AND FOR THE MINIMUM LIMITS YOU WILL ACCEPT FOR EACH OBJECTIVE THAT YOU LIST.

HIP POCKET CONCESSIONS

• FOR EACH OBJECTIVE, LIST A HIP POCKET CONCESSION TO USE AS A CONTINGENCY.

Figure 4-6 Planning—Short-term Objectives

SOURCE: Reprinted with permission, Management of Human Resources, Stamford, CT.

NEGOTIATION PLANNER — LONG TERM OBJECTIVES

VENDOR

BUYER

LONG TERM (LONG TERM RELATIONSHIP WITH VENDOR/BUYER)	LONG TERM (LONG TERM RELATIONSHIP WITH VENDOR/BUYER)	PREPLANNED LIMITS:	HIP POCKET CONCESSIONS
LEAST DIFFICULT TO ACHIEVE 1. _____	1. _____	1. MAXIMUM _____ MINIMUM _____	_____
SOMEWHAT DIFFICULT TO ACHIEVE 2. _____	2. _____	2. MAXIMUM _____ MINIMUM _____	_____
MOST DIFFICULT TO ACHIEVE 3. _____	3. _____	3. MAXIMUM _____ MINIMUM _____	_____

- WRITE THE OBJECTIVES YOU THINK THE VENDOR WANTS TO ACHIEVE DURING YOUR LONG-TERM RELATIONSHIP AS BUYER AND VENDOR.

- WRITE OBJECTIVES THAT YOU WOULD LIKE TO ACHIEVE DURING THE COURSE OF THE LONG-TERM RELATIONSHIP BETWEEN BUYER AND VENDOR.

- PREPARE FOR THE MAXIMUM LIMITS YOU WOULD LIKE TO ACHIEVE AND FOR THE MINIMUM LIMITS YOU WILL ACCEPT FOR EACH OBJECTIVE THAT YOU LIST.

- FOR EACH OBJECTIVE, LIST A HIP POCKET CONCESSION TO USE AS A CONTINGENCY.

Figure 4-7 Planning—Long-term Objectives

SOURCE: Reprinted with permission, Management of Human Resources, Stamford, CT.

Quite often the vendor's district sales manager or national sales manager, as well as the vendor, will be able to assist. Ask to speak with each of these in turn.

If the retail organization you work for is a large one, involve your divisional or general merchandise manager. They are there to assist you and, by virtue of their positions, have acquired considerable negotiating skill.

Similarly, if your store belongs to a buying office, a representative may be of assistance.

When do you talk to them?   Ideally, the time to conduct negotiations is before you have placed an order. The vendor will be anxious to speak with you and resolve any differences in anticipation of your placing an order or increasing the size of an order you are expected to write.

If you decide to wait, or circumstances compel you to wait, until the middle or the end of a season, the vendor may not be in a position to help you, because other buyers may have preceded you and "the well is dry."

What do you talk about?   Buyers buy "terms" and "conditions" (known as vendor services) as well as merchandise. The negotiating process begins as you view a vendor's line and are mentally selecting items. Your decision to choose one style over another may be made as a result of promised delivery, promotional allowance, or discounts.

Your responsibility as a buyer is to insure that your store receives every service to which it is entitled. This is not as easy as it appears. You may not *know* what services are available, as they may have increased (or decreased) since you last visited the vendor. You may have to originate a service the vendor has hitherto not offered, or you may have to suggest changes or improvements to existing services.

You must never be afraid to ask about what services are available. Use a checklist of possibilities, if necessary, and don't be afraid to negotiate.

The following list is by no means complete; its inclusion is to illustrate to you the wide variety of possible topics, many of which can be combined during negotiations either as objectives or as trade-off positions.[1]

Negotiation Checklist

1. Price
    (a) Guaranteed margin (guaranteed markup for a defined period of time)
    (b) Rebates
    (c) Reorder pricing (lower price on reorders)
    (d) Buying as a "house" account (the store avoids a sales representative's commission)
    (e) Price-decline guarantees (if the vendor's price declines after you have ordered, your price is adjusted)
2. Delivery
    (a) Freight charges
    (b) Timing of delivery
    (c) Cancellation agreements

3. Allowances
   (a) Advertising
   (b) Sales promotion (use of demonstrators)
   (c) Markdown money
4. Return Privileges
   (a) Exchange (the vendor will exchange nonselling merchandise for items that are selling)
   (b) Damaged goods (merchandise which arrives at the store in defective condition)
5. Dating of Invoices
   Ordinary; advanced; E.O.M.; extra; regular; R.O.G.; anticipation
6. Special Terms
   Consignment; memorandum
7. Discounts
   Quantity; trade; cash; seasonal or early bird (buying early and getting a special price)
8. New Item Introductions
   Promotions (such as fashion events, trunk shows, visiting fashion experts, models)
9. Exclusives
   Merchandise carried in your store only
10. Off Price
11. Style Modifications
    Changes to your specifications
12. Private Label
13. Vendor Support
    (a) Sales associates
    (b) Stock count and stock control assistance
    (c) Source marking
    (d) Sales staff training
14. Unique Packaging
    Different or better graphics; new materials; improved package design—openings or closings

---

CASE STUDY_____

L'CLAIR CRYSTAL

Today, September 16, was a day you were dreading. As you sat at your desk reviewing the L'Clair order and letter folder, your mind wandered back to August 1 when, as the new buyer for china and crystal, you had begun to review the memos on your desk.

Among them had been one upon which the previous buyer had written "Important." It was from the United States sales manager for L'Clair Crystal, dated 1 July 198__. It read as follows:

TO: All U.S. Buyers of L'Clair
FROM: D. Stein, U.S. Sales Manager

Please be advised that as of 1 August 198__, the cost price for all L'Clair merchandise will increase by 25 percent. A similar increase at retail will take place on 1 September 198__.

Between now and 1 August, you may make a single purchase for any and all of our merchandise at the old cost price. However, as of 1 September, you will be expected to reprice your goods to reflect the new retail.

Obviously, you will be able to make increased profits on all merchandise you own at our old cost after 1 September, and I encourage you to increase your purchases (even to anticipating Christmas).

I am pleased to offer you this opportunity for increased markup and trust that in the interest of maintaining the high level of worldwide prestige for L'Clair Crystal and your own stature as a prominent retailer, you will adhere to the new price schedule on the appointed date.

This memo had been initialed by both the former buyer and D. Stein.

You had hastened to examine the L'Clair open order file. With much relief, you had seen a very large order with a note handwritten directly on the order copy and signed by the former buyer to indicate that the merchandise had been purchased at the old cost and this, as well as old stock, was to be sold as per the memo from D. Stein.

Another memo you had found that day was from the store president indicating that on September 9 the store would have its annual three-day fall sale. The memo had been accompanied by a schedule to indicate when the sale items were to be given to the Sales Promotion Department for newspaper, radio, and in-store advertising planning.

As a new buyer, you had decided to build your in-house prestige by running L'Clair on promotion; selling it at the old retail, even though all stores and national advertising by L'Clair would have the new price. You would still make your regular full markup but give your customers 25 percent off the retail price everyone else was charging.

The sale had been a rousing success. Your DMM and GMM and the store president had sent notes of commendation. Your rise in the store's organization had seemed off to a good start.

All of this was history. The note you had received from D. Stein dated September 11 was brief and to the point. It read, in part:

". . . You have chosen to violate our price structure, even though your predecessor had written that your store would comply. I have been instructed by L'Clair, Paris, to do the following:

1. Discontinue all shipments and business with you and your store at once.
2. Buy back all inventory remaining in your stock at its cost value. Your failure to

return these goods will compel me to instruct our attorneys to commence legal action for contract violation.

If you wish, you may call upon me in my office on September 16, with your inventory list . . .''

Stein was a tough but honest and reputable person. How will you negotiate yourself through this problem when you cannot afford to lose the L'Clair merchandise from your department?

SUPPLEMENTARY CASE STUDY

BRISTOL'S—PART III

Note: Bristol's—Parts I and II can be found at the end of Chapters Two and Three and must be read for background.

As market week approached, you decided to call first upon nationally-known vendors. This decision was made after you evaluated Bristol's long-term goal of developing a boutique look and carrying recognized brands. It had been your expectation that some of these vendors would expect to either remain or become key resources for Bristol's.

Several vendors had interesting programs, but none were unique except Samantha's.

The district sales manager at Samantha heard your requirements for buying over the next eighteen months and conferred privately with the national sales manager and returned with the following offer:

1. Guaranteed minimum purchases (by Bristol's) of $185,000 per year for the first two years; 15 percent increase each year for each of the following three years
2. Prominent displays in all stores each season
3. 50 percent of all merchandise to be selected by representatives of Samantha
4. Samantha will supply 50 percent discount off-price packages amounting to 35 percent of total purchases for the first two years and 30 percent of total purchases for the following three years
5. Samantha will give 10 percent of total purchases each of the five years as markdown contribution
6. Samantha will give 1½ percent of total purchases each of the five years as promotional money

You have told the sales manager you would think about this program and get back to him.

All of the above would have to be committed to writing and your divisional merchandise manager would be required to approve and sign.

Your problem is your DMM. You know the Samantha merchandise has had confirmed customer acceptance at Bristol's for years and, as a manufacturer, the company has incomparable stature in the industry.

Notes:

1. $185,000 is almost 20 percent of your total open-to-buy
2. Displays have to be negotiated with each store and department manager
3. The DMM will not like having 50 percent of all merchandise from Samantha selected by their representatives
4. Items 5 and 6 of Samantha's offer will probably be acceptable to your DMM
5. The off-price offer is less than what your DMM told you to obtain

In preparation for your meeting with your DMM, plan your strategy.

NOTE_____

[1]The more important points are explained in other parts of the text. Those not addressed elsewhere are briefly covered here.

Managing
Incoming Merchandise
and Data Movement

5

Understandably, buyers are anxious to see the merchandise they purchased out on the selling floor and moving into the hands of delighted shoppers. This total activity is gratifying to buyers both from the standpoint of financial remuneration and for satisfaction of their egos.

Our profit-making society, in which rewards go to the successful, is readily accepted by those of us involved in the system. It does, however, tend to make us more aggressive, anxious, and impatient with others who do not move at a similar pace, and whose goals and priorities appear at variance with our own. Nowhere is this difficulty more apparent for a buyer than during the period that begins with the delivery of merchandise to the store or receiving point and concludes with its appearance on the selling floor.

It is clear that time must elapse as the goods move through the various stages of preparation for sale. In a relatively small store, the preparation can be finished in minutes, but in a multi-unit store with a large central receiving warehouse, several days would be a more realistic estimate of the lead time needed. Your understanding of the purpose of the transition process and the steps and details required will help you respect and be thankful to the people who are assisting you in making a profit.

For purposes of illustration, we will consider the problems and decisions to be faced during one season in a multi-unit system, as opposed to a small organization. Making a shift from a complex situation to one that is less complicated can be accomplished with relative ease; the reverse is not necessarily true, however.

You must also recognize that as one phase of a season is underway it will overlap with other phases of preceding and following seasons.

CONTROL

All of the time, effort, and expense involved in receiving, checking, marking, and inventory record keeping are done in the interest of *control*. These necessary aspects of retailing life, which are accomplished in a monetary as well as a physical and inventory sense, are achieved concurrently with each other and also mutually support each other.

Figure 5-1 illustrates the types of control required, as well as the office or department responsible during each of the four phases of merchandise and data movement. Arrows indicate transmittal of information from one area of control to another during any phase.

PHASE I: ORDER PROCESSING

This phase of your retail operation is still concerned with paperwork, even though it is beyond the point at which you have placed your orders with the vendors. You and the store organization are now prepared to receive the merchandise.

Figure 5-1 Merchandise and Data Movement

Phase	Monetary Control	Inventory Control	Physical Control
I. Order Processing	Accounting ⟶	Buying	Receiving
II. Merchandise Handling	Accounting	Buying ⟵	Receiving
		⟵	Checking
		⟶	Marking
			Distributing
III. Merchandise on the Selling Floor	Accounting	Buying ⟵	Store or Department
		⟵	
IV. Merchandise Sold	Accounting	Buying ⟵	Store or Department
		⟵	

Accounting responsibility. The Accounting Department reviews each order you have written. Their responsibilities include tabulating the planned expenditures for each, which in many cases means checking work that you have already done; computing the markup in percentages and dollars for each order; making estimates of the discounts and dates of payment; and providing you with an update of the amount of money you have left to spend for merchandise.

This department may also combine the values of the orders you have placed with individual vendors, thereby furnishing you with a historical record of the planned purchases for each supplier. Information of this type is extremely valuable when you assess the importance to your store of any manufacturer, as you will want to know how much merchandise of the amount ordered a seller actually ships to you. Ultimately, the Accounting Department will also be able to give you the dollar amount of payments made to each vendor, as well as additional information. Chapters Twelve and Fourteen will illustrate the use of these data.

Buying responsibility. During the first buying phase, your office is concerned with a variety of tasks. One of the first tasks has to be tabulating the numbers of units of merchandise you have ordered in each of the classifications for which you are responsible. This information is then compared with your

Figure 5-2 Processing Orders in the Accounting Department

Source: Courtesy of Judith A. Malone, Jordan Marsh.

original buying plans. These reports are as detailed as your inventory record-keeping system requires.

To illustrate, if you are a buyer of men's shirts, your buying plan might require knowledge of the following specifications from your orders:

1. Number of dress shirts and sport shirts, respectively
2. Quantities in each color—for example, solids, prints, stripes, or patterned
3. Sleeve length, short or long, and inch length
4. Overall size, by neck size and shirt size, such as extra small, small, medium, large, and extra large
5. Fabrics
6. Quantities purchased in each price line

Abstracting this information from your order sheets is obviously a tedious task, and it certainly requires that you write your orders in sufficient detail to allow this work to be accomplished accurately. This labor should not be viewed by you or your subordinates as "busy work." As you may recall from Chapter Three, one of the "corrects of buying" is quantity, and the purpose of this seemingly routine procedure is to help you ascertain that you have purchased the proper quantity of goods.

After these tasks have been completed you can, by simply subtracting these figures from your original buying plan figures, determine how many units of merchandise you have left to purchase. As a final step during this phase, to facilitate follow-up calls and visits, your orders should be placed or listed in sequence of the due dates for receiving the various merchandise. The use of a tickler file was discussed in Chapter Three.

Receiving responsibility.　After receiving copies of your orders, the receiving and marking personnel must prepare to manage your merchandise physically when it arrives. So that the Receiving Department employees can properly discharge their responsibility, they must know and list, from your order forms, the names of the vendors from whom you have purchased goods and their respective order numbers. In this way, the incoming shipments can be verified. Organizations with computers have this information programmed into the memory of the computer, and the data can be referred to in the receiving area as shipments are delivered by freight carriers.

To some extent, checking incoming shipments prevents the acceptance of goods that have not been ordered. Occasionally, however, vendors ship merchandise that has been purchased, but the buyer's order has not yet been processed, and the employees in the Receiving Department are unaware that the shipment is bona fide. This situation might occur if a vendor sent goods before the buyer had returned to the store from a market trip. It might also occur if a buyer was careless in handling copies of the order. Most stores establish a holding room or perhaps even allow processing of such merchandise pending official word from the buyer.

You should be extremely careful to avoid these kinds of situations. For example, you could phone your office from the market if you believe a shipment might arrive before your return. Buyers who fail to make official notification of their purchases are often accused by their superiors of attempting to circumvent the accounting system from keeping track of their dollar purchases, which is designed to prevent overbuying.

Another problem that you may encounter arises from dealing with unscrupulous suppliers who detect a measure of laxity in your system and consequently ship unordered merchandise. They may feel that once you have received their goods, you will probably keep them rather than doing the work required to arrange for their return. Vendors who do this must be "educated" after the first offense to know that you will not tolerate their preempting of your authority to make the buying decision.

Another operation that can sometimes be arranged for during the first phase of merchandise and data movement is the printing of the inventory control tickets from your order and setting them aside pending the arrival of the merchandise. This may not always be possible, but when it is it saves time in moving the merchandise from the receiving and marking area to the selling floor.

PHASE II: MERCHANDISE HANDLING

This stage of merchandise and data movement begins with the goods being presented for receiving at your store or warehouse and concludes with the merchandise being ready for the selling floor. Again, if you are the owner of your own shop, you will undoubtedly perform many of these tasks yourself. The size of the store alters only the number of people involved, not the actual work.

Receiving, checking, marking, and distributing responsibility.   Accepting merchandise from freight carriers and preparing it for sale involves three operations. Each operation is then divided and subdivided into a series of steps to insure that the control exerted provides you and personnel from the other concerned offices in the store with valuable and necessary data while at the same time protecting your investment in the stock.

RECEIVING.   Merchandise may be delivered in cartons, crates, or other containers; or it many arrive loose, as on hangers. The responsibilities involved in receiving goods are as follows:

1. Inspecting the shipping containers for any signs of damage, such as breaks or tears in the wrapping, which may or may not have been repaired; evidence of water or other potentially damaging stains; or broken and replaced security tapes

2. Verifying that the number of cartons or pieces of merchandise (if they are shipped loose) matches exactly the quantity called for on the freight bill

3. Weighing incoming shipments in the receiving area (which is a common practice) to

(a) Verify the amount charged for the shipment (as freight charges are usually related to weight)
(b) Serve as a form of evidence if merchandise is missing

If there are any discrepancies between the amount of merchandise listed on the freight bill and the amount or condition of the merchandise delivered, these differences should be clearly indicated on the carrier's freight bill *before* the receipt for the goods is signed. Failure to notify the vendor of these conditions makes the store clearly responsible for losses of and damage to the merchandise in the shipment.

Once the merchandise has been accepted, by signature, forms known as the **key receiving sheet (key rec.)** and the "apron" are prepared to record that the merchandise has been received. A copy of the apron is attached to the purchase order; these forms accompany the merchandise throughout the receiving process to the selling floor.

At the time the key receiving sheet is being prepared, you should be notified that the merchandise has arrived. In this way, you will be prepared to participate in the checking activity.

CHECKING. The checking process involves the following four functions:

Figure 5—3 Checking an Incoming Shipment for Agreement with Its Purchase Order

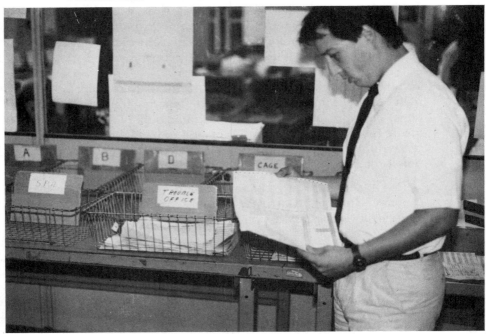

SOURCE: Courtesy of Robert McManus, Jordan Marsh.

1. *Checking the manufacturer's invoice* against your purchase order to insure that
   (a) The styles (or descriptions), quantities shipped, and cost prices of the merchandise match
   (b) The terms of sale are identical

   The presumption is that the vendor has mailed the invoice to you before the shipment arrives, the invoice is attached to the outside of the carton, or a duplicate invoice or packing slip can be found with the merchandise.

   If the vendor has failed to do any of these things, the usual practice is to prepare a receiving form that indicates no invoice has been received and that lists the description of the goods, as well as the terms of the sale. This document follows the merchandise throughout steps 2 and 3.

2. *Unpacking and sorting* the merchandise according to the specifications on your order. This may mean simply separating one style from another, or it may require that the goods be arranged by style, color, size, or any other subdivisions that you have specified.

3. *Checking quantity* is the next step. It involves verifying the actual number of pieces of merchandise received against the figures indicated on the invoice. This work can be done in either of the following ways or by a combination of both methods:
   (a) The *direct check* is the most commonly used method; it involves comparing the amount of merchandise physically present with the amount listed on the invoice or on the form developed as a substitute. While this is the most rapid way to confirm quantities, it is also the most error prone, as people tend to "see" and "count" the quantity of merchandise that the invoice indicates should be there, even though the actual physical count may differ from that recorded on the bill. This technique may also encourage employee theft. Occasionally vendors bill for less merchandise than they have shipped, and their own system picks up this error at a later date. They then mail you a corrected invoice for the increased amount. If your employees have failed to notify you of the extra merchandise, you and your vendor may become engaged in lengthy communications. The exchange may be an exercise in futility for the vendor, but it will do little to maintain your good relationship with this supplier.
   (b) When a *blind check* is used, the checkers are not supplied with an invoice; instead they fill out another form upon which they record the vendor's name, style numbers, and quantities received. This method is generally more accurate, and it is not hampered by the absence of an invoice. It is much slower than the direct check, however.
   (c) The *semiblind* or *combination check* is a system of checking that provides the employee with a form identifying the vendor and style numbers. The checker must then note the amounts of merchandise physically counted. Although the semiblind check is faster than the blind check and is perhaps more accurate than the direct check, time is lost while the form upon which the checkers will list the merchandise received is prepared from the invoice.

4. *Checking quality* is the last step before the merchandise is marked. This is the only part of the merchandise verification process that involves you, the buyer. Your responsibility here is singular, for as you were the person who bought the goods, presumably you are the only one who can attest to its authenticity. You may have some assistance if your purchases required that certain specifications be adhered to and your store has access to a testing laboratory, or if the manufacturer certifies that standards conforming to those of the National Bureau of Standards were met. In the final analysis, however, it is your opinion that counts.

When the checking process is completed, this department supplies you with the "counts" of the merchandise as outlined in step 3. The Accounting Department simultaneously receives notification of the shipment by way of the approved invoice (or form), which has accompanied the merchandise since its receipt.

MARKING.   There are two basic goals to be accomplished by placing tickets on merchandise. The first is to provide information to your customers that will assist them in their buying decisions. The data must not only be easily understood and placed on the ticket in an obvious position, but it also must not be redundant with information that is easily discernible by the shopper. You have undoubtedly observed illustrations of this latter point on tickets that label an obviously green garment "green" or a sweater "sweater." This practice is useless to the customer, and it also takes time for the merchandise marker to place this information on the ticket.

The second reason for marking merchandise is to provide data to assist you in tracking each article under your control. Toward this end, a coding system can be used that allows you to retrieve all necessary information from the ticket stubs, which are removed as the merchandise is sold. Figure 5-4 illustrates a two-part ticket, the upper portion of which remains with the merchandise when it is sold to facilitate a return or adjustment. The lower portion is removed as the item is sold and sent to the buyer's office or to whichever department is concerned with inventory record keeping. Three- or four-part tickets are used in many stores to facilitate returning merchandise to the selling floor without reticketing if the goods are brought back by customers and as an aid to taking a physical inventory, when a stub will be removed.

The Marking Department is responsible for producing and affixing tickets to your merchandise in keeping with the two priorities indicated above.

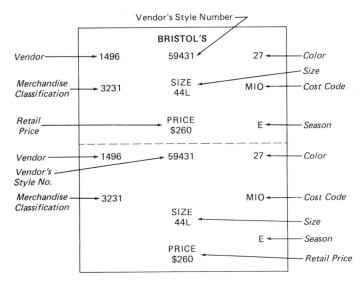

Figure 5-4   Unit Control (Inventory) Ticket

Care should be taken to insure that tickets or labels are legible, and attached securely in consistently obvious positions on the goods, and that when removed by the customer after purchasing they leave the item undamaged.

Because the incidence of price alteration by dishonest employees and customers has been increasing, you may find it necessary to pursue more stringent rules about the manner in which the price portion of a ticket is changed. In some cases, new tickets should be attached, or the original price should be covered over by specially printed gummed labels. Many other methods are also available; your attention is directed to this unfortunate problem, which requires constant review.

A parallel problem is shoplifting. All sizes and types of stores have been compelled to resort to various forms of security tags and merchandise enclosures that, if not removed at the time of sale, cause an alarm to go off as the merchandise is moved from one floor to another or through a street exit. Your employees must be carefully instructed about how to remove these special tags and labels to avoid embarrassing situations for legitimate customers, as well as for the store itself.

Your responsibility during the marking process is confined to supplying the necessary information for coding the tickets. This may include providing all the data, as shown in Figure 5-4, or it may be limited to indicating the retail price.

Figure 5-5   Attaching a Ticket to Newly Arrived Merchandise

Source: Courtesy of Margaret Maloney, Jordan Marsh.

Many stores and buyers practice preretailing; that is, they write the retail price for items bought directly on the purchase order. This procedure was indicated in Chapter Three, and if it is done it helps the marking staff to move the merchandise rapidly. In Chapter Three, *vendor* or *source marking* was also mentioned; this service eliminates the need for this step to be performed in your store.

Some organizations have arranged with freight carriers to mark their merchandise while the goods are in transit. If this practice is used, time can be saved by eliminating the ticketing process in the store. If all goods carried in the store can be marked in this way, the space and personnel for this task can be eliminated, with commensurate savings in expense to the retailer, of course.

A system of source marking known as the **Uniform Product Code (U.P.C.)** has been developed, which is a series of thick and thin lines printed onto labels and packages. These markings are "read" by optical scanning equipment at cashier and checkout counters and translated by the store's computer into **alpha-numeric symbols** (words and prices) visible to the customer on a display screen, while simultaneously updating the store's inventory records.

When this system was first introduced, there was concern that customers would react negatively to the lack of traditional pricing. U.P.C. was first adopted by supermarkets, drugstores, and mass merchandisers to facilitate customer checkout and improve inventory record keeping. Through this widespread exposure to U.P.C., consumers' attitudes toward bar coding have changed from skepticism to acceptance.

The National Retail Merchants Assn. (NRMA) has formally recommended bar code labeling for vendor marking of retail goods, including apparel. This endorsement by the 4100-member organization, operating 55,000 retail stores in the United States and overseas, has great implications for buyers of fashion merchandise. Other than the possible saving of time and expense in store marking (as mentioned previously), the use of optical scanning devices with bar codes and computers will provide more accurate information on sales and stock faster than was previously possible. This will accelerate the turnaround time from merchandise receipt to decision making for reorder or discontinuance.

DISTRIBUTING. Sending merchandise to the appropriate store, floor, or department should not be left to chance. In many large organizations, the buyer's purchase order (see Fig. 3-5 in Chapter Three) provides space for the buyer to indicate which store is supposed to receive the stock. Even so, when writing the order you may feel that the distribution decision can be better made when the merchandise is ready to leave the marking room.

You might decide that your merchandise would sell well in more than one department ("correct place"). In a large organization, this decision would undoubtedly have to be made in conjunction with your divisional merchandise manager and other buyers or department heads.

You might also find it necessary to hold the merchandise in reserve stock for a variety of reasons, such as waiting for coordinating pieces; accumulating the stock for a planned advertisement or other promotion; allowing inventory currently on the floor to sell down; or because the items are for a coming season, and their presence on the floor at this time would produce more clutter and confusion than sales (''correct time''). Although the responsibility for channeling and moving the merchandise rests with the employees in the distributing area, it is your job, nevertheless, to instruct them about the precise location(s).

Buying responsibility.   During this phase of merchandise and data movement, you have been involved with checking, marking, and distributing the goods. At the same time, however, two departments have been communicating information to your office that must be attended to.

The receiving and checking departments have transmitted the names of vendors, styles and quantities of merchandise received, and, as necessary, a breakdown of each style by color, size, and so on. Several activities are set in motion with this information. The first task is to determine if the merchandise has been shipped exactly as ordered; that is, to verify that the quantities in each size, color, and style conform exactly with the quantities on your purchase order.

Figure 5-6 illustrates an order that has been checked. The encircled quantities indicate goods that have been actually received. There are discrepancies between the merchandise ordered and the merchandise received in several sizes in colors 23 and 29, and you will have to decide if replacements should be obtained from the vendor. You will be guided by such factors as the minimum number of pieces in each style you need to distribute to each store (if you have more than one location to service) as well as whether the quantities received generate an imbalance in your stock based upon your anticipated sales in each size. If colors, sizes, or styles that were not ordered have been shipped, it will be easier to decide what to do.

The second task is to transfer the merchandise information to the inventory record-keeping system. The methods of unit control vary widely, ranging from a simple procedure in which the stock on hand is determined by a stock count or ''eyeballing'' of the goods, to a complex method in which an inventory card for each style of merchandise is prepared. These controls are segmented to reflect quantities in reserve and also in each store, by both color and size. This latter form of control is updated from unit control stubs (see Fig. 5-4), either daily or at another practical time interval. The use of a computer system is obviously easier and faster for the more complex types of inventory control systems.

Accounting responsibility.   After the Accounting Department receives the approved invoices from the Checking Department, it verifies the billed amounts and the terms. As this process is completed, the Accounting Department produces a new statement of your open-to-buy dollars and then processes the bill for payment according to the date indicated by the terms, minus any appropriate discounts.

			DATE	9/19/8-

ORDERED FROM **Green Apples**   Vendor No. 2361
350 - 5th Ave
N.Y., N.Y. 1001   212-563-2700
RETURNS TO Ruleville, Miss.

		30	32	34	36	38	40	42
A		30	32	34	36	38	40	42
B		6	8	10	12	14	16	18
C		5	7	9	11	13	15	
D		XS	S	M	L	XL		
E		8½	9	9½	10	10½	11	
F		6	6½	7	7½	8		
G								
H								

MU%	TOTAL OF ORDER—RET.	ORDER NO.	SALESMAN	TERMS: Less 1%
53.1%	$23,040.00	02492	Phil	AS OF 11/25 no Ant.

DELIVERY START	COMPLETE	SHIPPING INSTRUCTIONS BEST WAY ☐ AS HAD ☐	SPECIAL SHIPPING INSTRUCTIONS ☒
As Ready	Nov. 15	Inter Coastal Freight	

STYLE NO.	QUANTITY	WHOLESALE PRICE	RETAIL PRICE	COST TOTAL	DESCRIPTION	CODE	COLOR		A	B	C	D	E	F
62910	16 -	18 75ea	40.00	3600.00	St. Lg. Den. Zip Fr. 1341	23	B		24	36	47 48	47 48	24	12
"	16 -	18 75ea	40.00	3600.00	"	29	B		23 24 35 36		50 48	47 48	24	12
"	16 -	18 75ea	40.00	3600.00	"	36	B		24	36	48	48	24	12
				10,800 00										

POSTIVELY NO BROKEN SIZES SHIPPED AND NO SUBSTITUTIONS OF STYLES, SIZES OR COLOR, UNLESS PERMISSION IS OBTAINED. MDSE. RECEIVED AFTER 20th OF MONTH PAYABLE AS OF THE 25th. MDSE. SHIPPED AFTER COMPLETION DATE, SUBJECT TO RETURN AT BUYER'S DISCRETION.

Figure 5—6 Checked Purchase Order

PHASE III: MERCHANDISE ON THE SELLING FLOOR

Store/department responsibility.   At this point the merchandise has been distributed to the appropriate selling area in accordance with your instructions. Some inventory and accounting systems require that the goods be checked against the distribution slip before being placed into stock, to insure that the department receives the exact quantity specified, in the correct styles, colors, and sizes. Occasionally, merchandise meant for one store or department finds its way to the wrong department or store because of an error in distribution or delivery. Employee theft is another difficulty that you will encounter, and frequently items "disappear" as they are being transported. A verification procedure assures that both the records you have established during the preceding phase and the dollar value of the inventory are correct.

Once merchandise reaches the selling floor, the department manager and the sales staff are responsible for maintaining the correct tickets on the stock (some tickets may be detached by customers or fall off because of careless handling). They must also make sure that stubs are removed, or read by the optical scanning equipment, as sales are made.

Another important function performed by the Selling Department for you and the Accounting Department is the maintenance of accurate records of price changes. These alterations to the original selling price are done at your direction.

Finally, the department must furnish accounting personnel with its gross sales figures and the amount of any refunds to customers, if this function is performed within the department rather than in a central customer service area.

Buying responsibility.   When the merchandise is placed on the selling floor, the accumulation of sales data in the form of ticket stubs, stock counts, computer printouts, or whatever form of inventory record keeping your store follows, begins. Regardless of the method employed, you are involved in the following kinds of decisions: whether to continue the merchandise through reorders; whether to reduce the price; and whether to consolidate your stock to fewer locations.

REORDERING.   If your classification of merchandise is considered a staple, reordering is required; it is usually done on an almost automatic basis (Chapter Ten covers this procedure in detail). If the goods you are responsible for are fashion or similarly seasonal merchandise, however, the determination to reorder is based on tangible factors, such as the availability of the merchandise from the respective vendors and whether you have money left with which to buy. Without purchasing power, you obviously will be unable to reorder merchandise that is selling, although you may be able to "find" cash by either canceling other orders (if this is possible) or by going to your divisional merchandise manager and presenting strong arguments for additional dollars of open-to-buy.

With money available, you must contact the vendors and determine if the items you want are available and, if so, when they can be shipped. In most instances, reorders are needed "yesterday" or as soon as possible. The timing of additional merchandise is critical. It is not uncommon for "fad" items to sell at an extremely high rate and then stop suddenly, as if a faucet had been shut off. Only experience and courage can provide you with the background to know when and how much to reorder.

An additional problem may crop up if you do decide to reorder merchandise and then find that the items are not available from the vendor. Before you discontinue the styles, consider making a trip to the market or placing a call to your resident buying office and finding out if similar goods are available from other resources. You might also review your notes from earlier visits to the market to see if perhaps another manufacturer may have merchandise that resembles what you need.

If merchandise has been reordered, your sales force should be informed, to permit them to take orders or promise to call interested customers. It must be pointed out, however, that arguments have been presented against the advisability of this practice. They are based upon the assumption that salespeople tend to follow the course of least resistance with customers and show them merchandise that has proven easy to sell. Although there may be some validity to this proposition, many customers will not accept promises of reorders, preferring to select items that are on hand, which gains the sale immediately for the store.

In a larger sense, this same argument can be made for reordering merchandise generally. As is the case with the prior example, there is a measure of truth here. But customers enjoy a variety of offerings; all of them do not want to be identical, and what may be desirable to many will be unattractive to others.

DISCONTINUING. All nonstaple merchandise is discontinued at some time (staples are also discontinued as new and better products become available). The usual reasons for dropping merchandise are either inability to reorder or poor sales performance. The items in question should be flagged on your unit-control records and noted or listed in an organized manner so that they can be readily identified.

If discontinuance occurs early in the season, it may be possible in limited situations for you to consolidate the stock through merchandise transfers, thereby providing fewer stores with a more complete assortment of colors, sizes, and coordinating pieces than would be available if the merchandise were left as originally distributed. Some large chains and multi-unit department stores have eliminated this practice, arguing that sales lost during the time required for physical transfer from one store to another, coupled with damage to the merchandise and employee pilferage, have made consolidation of merchandise too costly.

Regardless of whether you can reassemble the stock, you will have to consider when and how much to reduce the price of the merchandise to clear your inventory. Here again timing is most important. If the merchandise is not selling because, by comparison with similar merchandise, it is overpriced, or because you have marked the goods higher than your competitors, you must authorize an immediate markdown, notifying the Selling Department of your decision. If the merchandise is selling at a normal rate, however, you will probably wait until your regular department clearance sale begins and then reduce the price in accordance with your general price-reduction policy.

Accounting responsibility.   The Accounting Department, which has been receiving data about sales and customer refunds from the sales floor daily, will generate "flash," or audited, sales reports for you. This information shows the actual net sales for your department, segmented by store. By comparing these actual sales figures with your planned sales figures, you will have an accurate, up-to-date indication of your success as a buyer.

   The Selling Department will also send to the Accounting Department the dollar value of all price changes which, together with the sales figures and charges for new merchandise received, will permit computation of the retail dollar value of the inventory. This information is also sent to you for comparison with planned stock figures.

PHASE IV: MERCHANDISE SOLD

As in Phase I, the work to be accomplished in this phase is essentially record keeping.

Store/department responsibility.   The department manager is responsible for continuing to record price changes accurately and for notifying you of any problems that may arise during the final sale period, such as customer complaints about your competitors' having lower prices.

   The sales force can be extremely useful to buyers by providing information about merchandise that may not be apparent from the ticket stubs. For example, the sales force can communicate with the buyer customer comments about fit, usability, construction, and durability, which are only a few of the areas that are very helpful in evaluating vendors and particular types of merchandise.

   The final step for the Selling Department is to return any unsold merchandise to a central stockroom, where it may be either combined with the returns from the other stores, inventoried and packed for storage, or sold through brokers or auctioneers, thereby keeping the store in a liquid dollar condition.

Buying responsibility.   Your office will finish gathering data on the sales for each location and then analyze the results. Information should also be assembled on the activities of each vendor and recorded by you for future use.

   Similarly, after the last step on the selling floor has been completed, the inventories of merchandise remaining and the markdown records should be carefully reviewed with an eye toward changing vendors, price lines, or size assortments, and also possibly either discontinuing or increasing the purchase of various classifications of merchandise.

Accounting responsibility.   The Accounting Department will complete the work of dollar inventory control for the season and provide you with dollar-activity information about each vendor for future reference.

CASE STUDY_____

GROWING PAINS

When you opened the door to your own store, it was a banner day. You felt prepared for whatever lay ahead, having worked for a multi-unit store. You began as an executive trainee and ended your employment with three successful years as a buyer.

You have worked very hard since opening day, performing the day-to-day accounting work, buying, taking care of receiving and marking, and doing the inventory record keeping. You did all of this while keeping a watchful eye on the selling floor.

It hasn't been easy, but it's been rewarding. The sales volume has increased to such an extent that you are now faced with the problem of "what should I do first?" The buying must be attended to, and because of the higher sales volume, you need more time in the market. The accounting work has grown measurably more strenuous; as the numbers of vendor orders increase, so do the invoices and the paperwork required to evaluate each source of supply. Similarly, it has become more difficult to find time for handling the incoming merchandise.

Your only alternative seems to be to find help and to determine which responsibilities you should relinquish.

What alternatives will you pursue?

SUPPLEMENTARY CASE STUDY_____

SUNDANCE ORIGINALS

As your assistant hands you the phone, you can see from the concerned expression of her normally placid face that this call is not going to be easy to deal with.

You recognize the voice on the other end of the line as that of the head of the Receiving Department who, in a matter-of-fact fashion, tells you that your anxiously awaited shipment from Sundance Originals is arriving, but five of the forty-two cartons are missing.

The voice seems to fade away as you recall the events leading up to this minute. You remember the countless seasons when you looked hungrily at the "Sundance" line, hoping that this might be the season that the limited production of this company—one of the most respected manufacturers in the business—could accommodate you.

Finally, it happened: Sundance accepted your order. Although it was far from easy to convince your divisional merchandise manager that a commitment of such a large portion of your open-to-buy to one vendor was like money in the bank, and that even though the terms required payment ten days after delivery, it was a good investment because of the prestige offered by this merchandise and its high customer acceptability.

You had even scheduled two newspaper advertisements and had included some of the pieces in the store's catalog, which was to be mailed soon.

If you refused the shipment, you might never be able to set foot in the Sundance showroom again. If you accepted the thirty-seven cartons, what merchandise assortments would you have? Could any of the items be sent out as sets and groups to the stores, and if so, to how many stores?

The voice on the other end of the line came back, rather loudly, saying, "Look, we can't tie up the receiving area forever with this truck, and the driver wants to get moving. What do you want to do?"

What will you do?

Invoice Mathematics

6

The primary goal of a retailer is to sell goods and/or services to an ultimate consumer, generating a profit. Therefore, a merchant must have money in order to purchase and pay for these goods and/or services. It follows that wherever a retailer can save money by practicing expense control; developing long-term plans for cash expenditures, thereby minimizing loans which cost money in terms of interest; or reducing outward cash flow in ways such as gaining advantageous terms of sale, there will be additional funds available to buy goods or services for resale.

As indicated in the Negotiation Checklist in Chapter Four, delivery, discounts, and dating are subjects that should be considered for negotiations, particularly since they are commonly indicated on order forms and your ability to secure the best terms will impact on your store's cash position.

THE INVOICE

An invoice is a bill from a supplier to a retailer for goods sold and shipped to the retailer. This document is usually prepared when the merchandise is ready for shipping; hence it should accurately represent the contents of the shipment. Some vendors choose to mail invoices rather than include them with the shipment, and in this case a *packing slip* may accompany the merchandise. Care should be taken to insure that shipments are properly identified by an invoice number that appears on the invoice and the packing slip.

Although an invoice appears to be a simple piece of data on the surface, several factors can cause it to be confusing. Any errors that may result can be expensive. The invoice should reflect exactly the styles, quantities, prices, and terms of the buyer's order. Inaccuracies can lead to incorrect pricing of goods, acceptance of merchandise not ordered, or paying the vendor sooner or more than is due.

Analysis of an invoice reveals that this document refers to the following areas: *merchandise, payment,* and *shipping.* Refer to Figure 6-1 for a typical invoice that has been labeled to show the various elements and subelements. There are an infinite number of variations that can occur between the terms. An understanding of the individual items, however, is easily acquired; this knowledge will help you to master the invoice.

Merchandise.   The elements of an invoice that we consider first are related to merchandise (see Fig. 6-1). The beginning paragraph in this section indicated that the invoice should be an accurate representation of the merchandise contained in the shipment. The document of origin for the shipment is the order written by the buyer, however. Therefore, before any computational work is done, the information related to the merchandise must be verified.

Verification begins with the style numbers and descriptions of each item. These numbers should match the numbers on the copy of the original order. Similarly, the quantities ordered and the prices for each style should coincide. If there are any discrepancies in this information, they should be called to the attention of the buyer, who must then decide either to keep the merchandise or to return it. In any event, differences between what was ordered and what was billed and shipped must be communicated to the vendor. If circumstances require that the merchandise be returned, undoubtedly the vendor's prior approval will be required. The vendor may also send out a special label to be affixed to the outside of the package indicating that the return is authorized (see Fig. 6-2).

If the merchandise information is accurate, the terms for payment and shipping should next be verified as correct. If there are differences between the order and the bill, the buyer should be notified; the buyer can then contact the vendor.

Payment terms.   Payment terms are separated into two groups: discount, or the amount of the payment; and time and dating, or the time by which the invoice is to be paid.

Discounts. There are four kinds of discounts common to retailing: quantity, trade, net, and cash; each will be discussed separately. A *quantity discount* is a discount offered by vendors in which the cost is reduced in order to induce retailers to purchase larger quantities (larger quantities can be defined here as

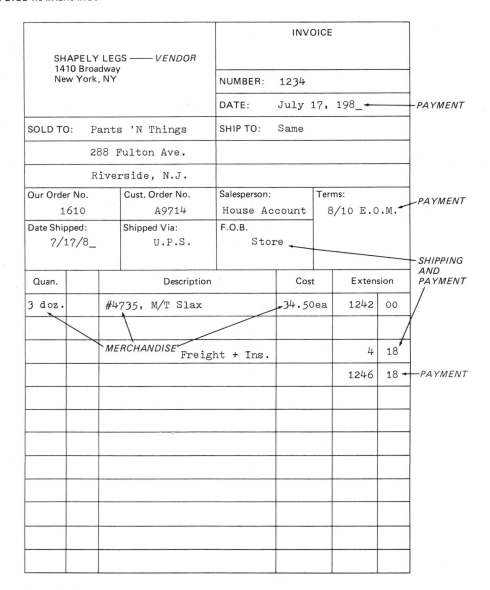

Figure 6-1

more units or more dollars). This kind of discount depends on the size of the order and should be deducted automatically. You would be well advised to remember that the size (units or dollars) of your order has to be justified by your retailing plans, and you should not permit a larger discount to influence you in purchasing beyond your open-to-buy.

Quantity discounts are expressed as either *straight line* or *stepped* dis-

RETURN AUTHORIZATION

BOSTON HARBOR INDUSTRIAL PARK
647 SUMMER ST. • BOSTON, MA 02210

THIS NUMBER MUST APPEAR ON
YOUR REMITTANCE DEDUCTIONS

CUSTOMER NO.   SLM

DATE

AUTHORIZED
BY

STYLE NO.	QTY

REASON FOR RETURN

FROM:

TO:

  BOSTON HARBOR INDUSTRIAL PARK
  647 SUMMER STREET
  BOSTON, MA 02210

☐ DAMAGE ☐ LATE DELIVERY ☐ WRONG STYLE SIZE COLOR ☐ OTHER (EXPLAIN)

SOURCE: Reprinted with permission of Barclay Square.

Figure 6-2

counts. The straight line discount is one wherein the same percentage of discount is offered for all merchandise above a certain base quantity. The stepped discount indicates that different percentages of discounts, usually increasing as quantity increases, are offered above a certain base amount. The base quantity is a lower limit established to ensure to the vendor that a minimum amount will be purchased before a buyer's purchases can qualify for a discount. As an example:

QUANTITIES	DISCOUNT
51–100	3.0%
51–150 but greater than 100	3.5
51 to more than 150	4.0

Here the discount schedule indicates that a base quantity (minimum amount) of 50 units must be purchased before any quantity discount can be taken.

Therefore, for an order of 75, you would take a discount of 3.0% on 25 (75–50); an order for 140 would qualify you to take a 3.5% discount on 90 (140–50); and for 250, 200 (250–50) would be discounted at 4.0%.

The stepped quantity discount establishes plateaus such as

QUANTITIES	DISCOUNT
51–100	3.0%
101–150	3.5
151 and over	4.0

An order for 250 units would be calculated as follows:
(*Note*: The first unit at each step is to be included for the discount; therefore, your computation would be: Upper limit − Lower limit + 1).

FOR QUANTITIES BETWEEN
100 − 51 = 49 + 1 = 50
150 − 101 = 49 + 1 = 50
250 − 151 = 99 + 1 = 100

In both illustrations, the first 50 do not qualify for a quantity discount.

Examples 6-1 and 6-2, followed by Problems 6-1 and 6-2, are representative of straight line quantity discount computations.

• *EXAMPLE 6-1*

A vendor of toasters offers the small appliance buyer the following straight line quantity discounts:

5–10 units	4% off total price
5–30 units but greater than 10	5% off total price
5 to more than 30 units	6% off total price

If the cost price of a single toaster is $12, determine the net price and dollar discount of each toaster at each discount level, assuming the buyer purchases within the specified ranges.

$$\text{Cost price\%} - \text{Discount\%} = \text{Net price\%}$$

where cost price% is allowed to equal 100%; for 4% discount it is then

$$100\% - 4\% = 96\%$$

and

$$\$\text{Cost price} \times \text{Net price\%} = \$\text{Net price}$$

then

$$\$12.00 \times .96 = \$11.52$$

and

$$\$\text{Discount} = \$\text{Gross cost} - \text{Net cost}$$
$$= \$12.00 - \$11.52$$
$$= \$.48$$

Similarly for 5%:

$$100\% - 5\% = 95\% = .95$$

and

$$\$12.00 \times .95 = \$11.40$$
$$\$Discount = \$12.00 - \$11.40 = \$.60$$

And for 6.0%:

$$100\% - 6\% = 94\% = .94$$

and

$$\$12.00 \times .94 = \$11.28$$
$$\$Discount = \$12.00 - \$11.28 = \$.72$$

• *EXAMPLE 6-2*

A vendor offers a buyer the following straight line quantity discounts:

For orders between $500 and $1000	4.0% discount
For orders between $500 and $3000 but greater than $1000	5.5% discount
For orders of at least $500 and over $3000	6.5% discount

If the buyer's open-to-buy and buying plan permit purchases at $900, $1800, or $3600, calculate the net cost and dollar discount that will result, if cost is permitted to equal 100 percent.
For $900 with a 4% discount:

$$Discount\% \times \$Discountable\ amount = \$Discount$$
$$.04 \times (\$900 - \$500) = \$16$$

and

$$\$Total\ purchase - \$Discount = \$Net\ cost$$
$$\$900 - \$16 = \$884$$

Similarly, for $1800.00 with a 5.5% discount

$$.055 \times (\$1800.00 - \$500.00) = \$71.50$$
$$\$1800.00 - \$71.50 = \$1728.50$$

And for $3600.00 with a 6.5% discount

$$.065 \times (\$3600.00 - \$500.00) = \$201.50$$
$$\$3600.00 - \$201.50 = \$3398.50$$

• *PROBLEM 6-1*

A buyer is offered straight line discounts on sets of dishes as follows:

6–12 sets	3.0%
6–24 sets but greater than 12 sets	3.5
6 to more than 24 sets	4.75

If the cost for each set is $119, determine the discount amount and the net price for each set if the buyer orders 18 sets.

• *PROBLEM 6-2*

A buyer is offered the following straight line quantity discounts:

For orders between $250 and $500	2.5%
For orders between $250 and $1000 but greater than $500	3.75
For orders of at least $250 and over $1000	4.75

If the buyer contemplates placing an order for $862, determine the net cost for the order and the discount amount.

Examples 6-3 and 6-4, with Problems 6-3 and 6-4, illustrate stepped quantity discounts.

• *EXAMPLE 6-3*

A buyer is offered stepped quantity discounts on purchases as follows:

49–96 units	2.5%
97–144 units	4.0
145 units and over	5.5

If each unit costs $15 and the order is for 180 units, calculate the dollar discount and net cost of the order.

Compute the number of units, dollar cost, and dollar discount at each step:

$$96 - 49 \text{ units} = 47 + 1 = 48 \times \$15 = \$720 \times .025 = \$18.00$$
$$144 - 97 \text{ units} = 47 + 1 = 48 \times \$15 = \$720 \times .04 = \$28.80$$
$$180 - 145 \text{ units} = 35 + 1 = 36 \times \$15 = \$540 \times .055 = \$29.70$$

$$\overline{\hspace{2cm}}$$
$$\$76.50 \text{ Discount}$$

and

$$\text{Total order} = 180 \text{ units} \times \$15 = \$2700$$

then

$$\text{Net cost} = \$2700.00 - \$76.50 = \$2623.50$$

• *EXAMPLE 6-4*

A buyer is offered stepped quantity discounts as follows:

For amounts between $501 and $1000	1.5%
For amounts between $1001 and $1500	2.0
For amounts of $1501 and above	3.0

Calculate the dollar discount and net cost for an order of $2250.

$$\$1000 - \$ 501 = \$499 + \$1 = \$500 \times .015 = \$ 7.50$$
$$\$1500 - \$1001 = \$499 + \$1 = \$500 \times .02 = \$10.00$$
$$\$2250 - \$1501 = \$749 + \$1 = \$750 \times .03 = \$22.50$$
$$\overline{\$40.00}$$

$$\text{Net cost} = \$2250 - \$40 = \$2210$$

• PROBLEM 6-3

A shoe buyer is offered stepped quantity discounts as follows:

73– 96 pairs	3.0%
97–120 pairs	3.5
121 pairs and over	5.0

If each pair of shoes costs $30 and the order is for 144 pairs, calculate the dollar discount and net cost of the order.

• PROBLEM 6-4

A small electric appliance buyer is offered the following stepped quantity discounts:

For amounts between $5001 and $7500	4.0%
For amounts between $7501 and $10,000	5.5
For amounts of $10,001 and above	7.0

Calculate the dollar discount and net cost for an order of $16,500.

The second kind of discount we consider is the **trade discount**. This discount is offered by vendors to members of the trade, certain buyers, or other middlemen, and it is offered for their performance of services such as warehousing and distribution. The discount is taken from a retail price or list price that is quoted to the public as well as to retailers. The discount percentage is known only by the trade. This form of retailing may be carried out by using catalogs from which customers select merchandise that is subsequently ordered for them by the retailer.

• EXAMPLE 6-5

A customer looks through the catalog in the local Save-All store and selects a lamp with a list price of $38. The retailer consults the trade discount chart and determines that the discount on this item is 36 percent. Find the retailer's net price and the discount amount.

$$\$\text{List price} \times \text{Discount\%} = \$\text{Discount}$$
$$\$38.00 \times .36 = \$13.68$$
$$\$\text{List price} - \$\text{Discount} = \$\text{Net price}$$
$$\$38.00 - \$13.68 = \$24.32$$

• PROBLEM 6-5

The list price in Kenyon's catalog for a television set is $269. Your trade discount is 24.5 percent. Determine your net price and the discount amount.

Trade discounts are often offered as a series of discounts, such as 40 percent, 30 percent, 20 percent. This system may be devised to coax buyers to purchase inventories for their customers, rather than relying on the manufacturer to warehouse the merchandise. The trade discount thus becomes a series of quantity discounts. The net price for the merchandise can be found by multiplying together the complements of each discount and then multiplying the resulting value against the list price. To find the discount amount, the net price is subtracted from the list price.

• *EXAMPLE 6-6*

A buyer is offered a trade discount as a series of discounts. These discounts are 28 percent, 18 percent, and 6 percent. Find the net price and discount amount for a radio with a catalog list price of $49.95.
Determine the complements of each discount.

$$100\% - 28\% = 72\% = .72$$
$$100\% - 18\% = 82\% = .82$$
$$100\% - 6\% = 94\% = .94$$

Multiply the complements:

$$.72 \times .82 \times .94 = .5549$$

Determine the net price in dollars:

$$\$List\ price \times Complements\ of\ discounts\% = \$Net\ price$$
$$\$49.95 \times .5549 = \$27.717 = \$27.72$$

Determine the dollar discount:

$$\$List\ price - \$Net\ price = \$Discount$$
$$\$49.95 - \$27.72 = \$22.23$$

• *PROBLEM 6-6*

A series discount of 36 percent, 27 percent, 7 percent is offered to a retailer. An item is selected from the catalog with a list price of $62.50. Determine the dollar discount amount and the net price to the retailer.

Both trade and quantity discounts may be offered to buyers. When this occurs, the trade discount must be deducted first, as this discount reduces what is a retail or list price (see pp. 97-98) to a cost price. To illustrate:

• *EXAMPLE 6-7*

A buyer purchases merchandise amounting to $1000 subject to a trade discount of 40 percent. The vendor also offers stepped quantity discounts as follows:

For amounts between $251 and $500	2.0%
For amounts between $501 and $750	3.0
For amounts of $751 and above	4.0

Determine and deduct the trade discount first.

$$\$1000 \times .40 \quad = \$400 \text{ Trade Discount}$$
$$\$1000 - \$400 = \$600 \text{ Base Cost}$$

Now determine and deduct the stepped quantity discounts from the remainder

$$\$500 - \$251 = \$249 + \$1 = \$250 \times .02 = \$5.00$$
$$\$600 - \$501 = \quad 99 + \$1 = \$100 \times .03 = \$3.00$$

Total quantity discount $\$8.00$

$$\$600 - \$8.00 = \$592 \text{ Net Cost}$$

• *PROBLEM 6-7*

A buyer decides to write a purchase order amounting to $5000. The vendor offers a trade discount of 25 percent and straight line quantity discounts as follows:

For orders between $1500 and $2500	3.5%
For orders between $1500 and $4000 but greater than $2500	5.0
For orders of at least $1500 and over $4000	6.5

The next discount we consider involves no discount at all and is called either **net** or **net billing**. In this instance, the price quoted by the vendor to the retailer is the cost price, and it must be paid as such within the payment period. To illustrate, a manufacturer quotes a price of $3.45 net each for a particular style of hand towel. This price, $3.45, multiplied by the quantity ordered, must be paid by the retailer. If the retailer orders one dozen towels, the remittance would be:

$$12 \times \$3.45 = \$41.40$$

The last kind of discount is the **cash discount**. The retailer must earn this discount by paying an invoice on or before a stipulated date. It may be coupled with quantity or trade discounts; however, the dollar amount of the cash discount is computed last, after any applicable quantity or trade discounts have been deducted. The latter two discounts are taken and deducted whether or not the cash discount is earned.

The cash discount is usually shown on the invoice in a space labeled, "terms," and it takes the form "8/10," for example; the "8" represents an 8 percent discount, and the "10" represents 10 days, or the time period (examine the invoice in Figure 6-3; disregard "E.O.M."; this applies to "time," which will be covered in the next section).

The first rule for checking invoices, other than determining if the styles shipped were ordered and if the quantities and cost price are as they should be, is to check the extensions. That is, to verify that four dozen shirts at $108.00 per dozen extend to or total $432.00 and similarly that three dozen shirts at $120.00 per dozen equal $360.00; and that the addition of these two extensions plus the freight equals $798.45. Once this calculation has been done, if there are no notations for either quantity or trade discounts, we can calculate the cash discount. Remember that discounts of any kind are applied only to merchandise costs and cannot be deducted from either the freight or insurance charges. Depending upon the shipping terms—for example, F.O.B.—the freight or insurance charges, or both, may or may not be added to the remittance. We discuss this in another section.

• *EXAMPLE 6-8*

To compute the cash discount obtainable on the invoice in Figure 6-3, we must first deduct the freight and insurance charges to determine the pure merchandise costs. Thus

$798.45 − $6.45 = $792.00 Merchandise cost
$Merchandise cost × Discount% = $Discount amount
$792.00 × .08 = $63.36 Discount amount
$Merchandise cost − $Discount amount = $Remittance
$792.00 − $63.36 = $728.64 Remittance

If the remittance amount is the only figure desired, it can be obtained rapidly as follows:

Merchandise cost × Complement of the discount% = $Remittance
$792.00 × (100% − 8%) = $Remittance amount
$792.00 × .92   = $728.64 Remittance amount

• *PROBLEM 6-8*

An invoice has terms of 6/15 and a total of $967.83 as charges, of which $12.69 is for freight and insurance. Determine the amount of discount and the remittance amount if the bill is paid on time.

DATING.   We now discuss the *time* factor, or *when* an invoice has to be paid. The time period during which a cash discount can be taken is determined by a variety of expressions included under the terms in an invoice. Note, however, that after the cash discount period has expired the full amount of the invoice is due.

A phrase that requires little explanation is **cash on delivery (C.O.D.)**. It means that the goods have to be paid for at the time of delivery. Sometimes vendors insist on payment when the merchandise is ordered, although this is obviously a poor way for you to have to do business. It does, however, afford access to merchandise for the novice retailer who has not yet been able to establish a credit base. But if the retailer has a short supply of cash, it also means that the retailer must enter the marketplace frequently, buying merchandise, selling it, and then returning with cash to purchase more goods. Also note that C.O.D. payment does not invalidate eligibility for any of the discounts discussed earlier.

We next discuss two terms simultaneously, **date of invoice (D.O.I.)** and **regular** or **ordinary dating**. It is necessary to know the precise date from which you begin to compute the time period during which you can pay an invoice and still deduct the cash discount. In most cases the discount period begins with the date of the invoice (D.O.I.), which is known as regular or ordinary dating. No notation is made on the invoice to indicate that ordinary dating is in effect.

SHAPELY LEGS 1410 Broadway New York, NY		INVOICE		
		NUMBER: 1235		
		DATE: July 14, 198_		
SOLD TO: Pants 'N Things		SHIP TO: Same		
288 Fulton Ave.				
Riverside, NJ				

Our Order No. 1610	Customer Order No. A9714	Salesperson: House Account	Terms: 8/10 E.O.M.	
Date Shipped: 7/14/8_	Shipped Via: U.P.S.	F.O.B. Store		

Quan.		Description	Cost	Extension	
4 doz.		#1831 Shirt	108/doz.	432	00
3 doz.		#1869 Shirt	120/doz.	360	00
		Freight + Ins.		6	45
				798	45

Figure 6-3

• *EXAMPLE 6-9*

If the terms on an invoice were 7/10 and the invoice was dated March 11, what percentage of discount would be allowed and when would be the last date that the retailer could take the cash discount?

The term "7/10" means that a 7-percent cash discount is allowed if the bill is paid by 10 days from the date of the invoice, or no later than March 21.

Receipt-of-goods (R.O.G.) dating means that the date from which the days are counted to the end of the discount period is the date on which merchandise is received by the retailer. Often, however, shipments arrive after the discount period has ended if the distances between the vendor's shipping point and the retailer are great, weather conditions are severe, the shipment is transferred from one carrier to another to reduce shipping costs, or any combination of these and other factors exists. Whenever possible, the alert buyer therefore attempts to hedge against the possibility of losing the cash discount, by stipulating on the order form that the terms be made R.O.G.

Figure 6-4

	INVOICE	
CRAZY LEGS 1410 Broadway New York, NY	NUMBER: 1929	
	DATE: February 28, 198_	
SOLD TO: Pants 'N Things	SHIP TO: Same	
288 Fulton Ave.		
Riverside, NJ		

Our Order No. 1611	Customer Order No. A9714	Salesperson: House Account	Terms: 3/10 R.O.G.
Date Shipped: 2/28/8_	Shipped Via: U.P.S.	F.O.B. Store	

Quan.		Description	Cost	Extension	
3 doz.		#4721 Shirts	81/doz.	243	00

• *EXAMPLE 6-10 (see Fig. 6-4 for data)*

(1) Determine the last date the retailer can pay the invoice and take the cash discount if the goods are received on March 15.
(2) Determine the discount amount.
(3) Determine the remittance amount if the discount is taken.

The terms are R.O.G., and therefore the date of the invoice, February 28, 198___, has no significance. The merchandise was received on March 15, and the terms are 3/10, or 3 percent within 10 days; thus the bill must be paid no later than 10 days after March 15, or by March 25, to obtain the cash discount. We check first to see that three dozen shirts at $81 per dozen extend to $243 and compute the discount and the remittance as follows:

$$\$Cost \times Discount\% = \$Discount$$
$$\$243.00 \times .03 = \$7.29$$
$$\$Cost - \$Discount = \$Remittance$$
$$\$243.00 - \$7.29 = \$235.71$$

• *PROBLEM 6-9 (see Fig. 6-5 for data)*

(1) Determine the last date the invoice can be paid with the discount still in effect if the merchandise is received on September 19, 198___.
(2) Determine the discount amount.
(3) Determine the remittance amount if the discount is taken.

We now consider **end-of-month (E.O.M.)** dating, which means that the discount period begins at the end of the month.

• *EXAMPLE 6-11*

Terms—3/10 E.O.M., invoice dated June 6. This phrase means that a 3-percent discount can be taken if the invoice is paid within 10 days of the end of June, or by July 10.

• *EXAMPLE 6-12*

Terms—8/10 E.O.M., R.O.G., invoice dated October 20, merchandise received November 5. This means that an 8-percent discount can be deducted if the invoice is paid within 10 days of the end of November, or by December 10.

Advance or **post dating** and **extra dating (X)** can be considered together, because both of them produce the effect of moving the discount period ahead on the calendar.

Among the reasons why these forms of dating are agreed to by vendors and buyers are

1. Vendors may have heavy inventories on hand and would rather show a larger figure in "Accounts Receivable" on their balance sheet than in "Inventory." Therefore they offer this form of dating to induce buyers to accept merchandise early.
2. Vendors with seasonal demand for their goods—for example, manufacturers of snow blowers or lawn mowers—may offer extra dating to provide year-round production.
3. Vendors may consider certain retailers as predictors of trends and hence wish to

		INVOICE				
SIDE SADDLE 1384 Broadway New York, NY		NUMBER: 1929				
		DATE: August 20, 198_				
SOLD TO: Pants 'N Things		SHIP TO: Same				
288 Fulton Ave.						
Riverside, NJ						
Our Order No. 16169	Customer Order No. A9837	Salesperson: House Account		Terms: 7/10 R.O.G.		
Date Shipped: 8/20/8_	Shipped Via: Empire	F.O.B. Store				
Quan.		Description		Cost	Extension	
54 sets		#8347 2 pc. sets		143 ea	7668	00

Figure 6-5

ship merchandise to these merchants early to determine which items will become trend leaders.

4. Retailers may be temporarily overbought and therefore need the extra time to push the purchases officially forward into a more "cash liquid" period.

• *EXAMPLE 6-13*

Invoice dated February 8, terms 8/10 E.O.M., a/o 4/1.

This means that an 8-percent discount can be taken 10 days from the end of the month of April, or until May 10. The term "a/o 4/1" means as of April 1, which is the advance invoice date.

• PROBLEM 6-10

Invoice dated January 12, terms 7/10, a/o 3/1. Determine the last date of the discount period.

Another illustration of advance dating, which is practiced in many markets almost automatically, is to consider any invoice dated the 25th of the month or thereafter as if it were dated the 1st of the following month.

• EXAMPLE 6-14

A retailer with an invoice dated August 25 with terms of 8/10 E.O.M. has until October 10 to pay the bill and take the cash discount. August 25 really means September 1, and 8/10 E.O.M. means an 8-percent discount can be taken if the bill is paid within 10 days of the end of the month of September.

The 25th-of-the-month rule can be used in another way as well. The terms on the invoice may read "8/10 E.O.M., a/o 10/25." Thus, regardless of the actual date on the invoice, the retailer can take an 8-percent discount within 10 days of the end of the month of November, or up to and including December 10. Why? Because "a/o 10/25" means as of October 25, which converts to November 1.

• PROBLEM 6-11

Determine the last payment date on which you can take the cash discount if the date of the invoice is August 19 and the terms are 3/10 E.O.M., a/o 9/25.

Extra dating (X) is included in the terms on the invoice and appears as "3/10, 30X," which means that a 3-percent discount can be taken within 10 days plus 30 days (or a total of 40 days) from the invoice date.

• EXAMPLE 6-15

Determine the last date that the cash discount can be taken if the invoice is dated January 16 and terms are 8/10, 60X.

January 16 plus 10 days is January 26, which would be the last regular date for the discount period; however, with 60X (60 extra days) the last date is then moved to March 26. (Remember that the business calendar has 30-day months.)

The 25th-of-the month rule is also applicable if the invoice date is appropriate.

• EXAMPLE 6-15 (cont.)

Determine the last date that the cash discount can be taken if the invoice is dated February 25 and the terms are 6/10, 30X.

As an invoice date February 25 converts to March 1; to this date we add 10 days plus 30 days extra, with April 10 then becoming the last date of the discount period.

• PROBLEM 6-12

Determine the last date of the discount period for an invoice dated January 28, with terms of 7/10 E.O.M., 30X.

An example which illustrates how several terms are combined is

8/10, net/30 or 8/10, n/30

This means that an 8-percent discount can be taken if the invoice is paid within 10 days; however, the net amount (as discussed on page 100) is due within 30 days, or 20 days after the discount period has expired. The "net" term could also be written as "8/10, n/E.O.M.," indicating that the bill must be paid by the end of the month; or as: "8/10, n/30 E.O.M.," which means that after the 10-day discount period has expired, the bill must be paid within 30 days of the end of the month.

The next payment term, **anticipation**, is a hybrid, for it has to do with both time and money. Anticipation is a discount computed from the original invoice amount (similar to the cash discount) for payment of the invoice earlier than the last date of the discount period. In effect, anticipation is interest charged by retailers to vendors for money the vendors receive prematurely. This additional discount can be taken only with the consent of the vendor. The percentage rate of anticipation varies with business conditions, and for illustrative purposes we used an annual rate of 6 percent. Anticipation is especially advantageous for retailers who have obtained advanced or extra dating and are able to pay for the merchandise very early in the discount period.

• *EXAMPLE 6-16*

An invoice for $3486, which is dated August 15, has terms of 8/10 E.O.M., a/o 9/25, anticipation allowed. If the invoice is paid on August 28, determine the amount of remittance.

The terms indicate that an 8-percent discount can be taken if the invoice is paid within 10 days of the end of the month, whereas "as of September 25" actually means October 1; 10 days from the end of October is November 10.

If the bill is paid on August 28 instead of November 10, the difference in days is (remember you are dealing with 30-day months):

August 28 to August 30	=	2 days
September 1 to September 30	=	30 days
October 1 to October 30	=	30 days
November 1 to November 10	=	10 days
Total	=	72 days

Anticipation is calculated as follows:

$$\text{\$Billed cost} \times \text{Interest rate} \times \text{Days early}/360 = \text{\$Anticipation}$$

Inserting values and a 6% (6/100) interest rate:

$$\$3486.00 \times 6/100 \times 72/360 = \$41.83$$

Cash discount is calculated as before:

$$\text{\$Billed cost} \times \text{Discount\%} = \text{\$Discount}$$

and

$$\$3486.00 \times .08 = \$278.88$$

The remittance amount is then

$$\$3486.00 - \$41.83 - \$278.88 = \$3165.29$$

• *PROBLEM 6-13*

An invoice totaling $4987, which is dated April 1, has terms of 7/10 E.O.M., a/o 5/25, anticipation allowed. If the invoice is paid April 15, determine the amount of remittance.

The last topic related to payments is **loading**. Loading is a practice dictated by the top management in a retail organization that assures that all invoices reflect exactly the same cash discount percentage.

The reasons for establishing this rule vary, but one rationale may be the desire of management to establish a large cash discount reserve which later becomes a critical factor in determining gross margin (see Chapter Twelve). Another reason may be to permit rapid computation of the net merchandise indebtedness of the store.

Loading an invoice, then, has the effect of increasing (or decreasing) the gross amount of the invoice without changing the net amount that has to be remitted to the vendor. The first step in loading, therefore, is to determine the net amount to be remitted to the vendor under the normal terms. After this is done, you can determine the loaded cost.

• *EXAMPLE 6-17*

An invoice for $400 has terms of 3/10. You would like the invoice loaded to reflect an 8-percent cash discount. Find the loaded cost.

Determine the net cost with a 3-percent discount:

$$\$\text{Cost} \times \text{Complement of discount percent} = \$\text{Remittance}$$
$$\$400 \times (100\% - 3\%) = \$388$$

$$\$\text{Loaded cost} = \$\text{Remittance} \div \text{Complement of loaded discount percent}$$
$$= \$388.00 \div (100\% - 8\%)$$
$$= \$388.00 \div .92$$
$$= \$421.74$$

Proof of this calculation can be shown by taking the loaded cost value, $421.74, and treating it as the invoice value for determining a remittance amount with a cash discount of 8 percent:

$$\$\text{Cost} \times \text{Complement of discount percent} = \$\text{Remittance}$$
$$\$421.74 \times (100\% - 8\%) = \$388.00$$

Comparing the figures from the first step with the figure above proves that the loaded value, $421.74, will generate the correct amount of remittance to the vendor.

• *PROBLEM 6-14*

An invoice for $650 shows terms of 4/10. You would like the invoice loaded to reflect a 7-percent cash discount. Find the loaded cost.

Shipping terms.   Shipping terms are important to both vendors and retailers because they not only identify who pays the cost of moving the merchandise to the retailer, but they also ascertain at what point the title or ownership of the merchandise is transferred.

The phrase **free-on-board (F.O.B.)** followed by either *factory* or *store* is the most common shipping term. "F.O.B. factory" means that the vendor transfers merchandise title to the retailer at the factory and that the retailer pays the freight charges from the factory to the store. Conversely, "F.O.B. store" indicates that title to the goods changes at the store and that the vendor pays the transportation expenses to the store.

Between the two conditions (freight payment and title transfer), the retailer should be more concerned about the transfer of title. If this exchange takes place at the vendor's shipping point (F.O.B. factory) the retailer then becomes the legal owner of the goods before taking physical possession of them. The problem with this procedure is that any damage or loss to the shipment on the way to the store is the financial responsibility of the retailer, and the retailer must attempt to obtain compensation from the freight carrier. This process can be long and drawn out and in no way helps to provide the retailer with the full assortment of merchandise that was ordered.

Although the retailer should seek to reduce expenses by stipulating "F.O.B. store," it is actually more important to insure that any losses incurred during shipping be pursued by the manufacturer, who can in turn replace the damaged or lost merchandise.

If the shipping terms are "F.O.B. store—charges reversed," the title to the merchandise is transferred at the store; however, the retailer is obligated to pay for the freight charges.

Shipping terms can also be indicated as

"F.O.B. factory (or store), charges shared: _____% factory, _____% store"

Here the transportation expense is distributed between the manufacturer and the retailer in accordance with the indicated percentages.

This information is summarized in Table 6-1.

While the payment of freight charges may be solely the responsibility of the vendor, often invoices arrive with freight charges added on. Or sometimes delivery of the merchandise from a trucker is accompanied by a demand for

Table 6-1

TERMS	POINT AT WHICH TITLE TRANSFERS	PAYER OF FREIGHT CHARGES
F.O.B. factory	Factory	Retailer
F.O.B. store	Store	Vendor
F.O.B. factory (or store) charges reversed	As indicated	As indicated
F.O.B. factory (or store) charges shared _____ % factory, _____% store	As indicated	Shared

freight payment. If this happens you should deduct the freight charges from your remittance, after subtracting any discounts. (Remember that discounts are taken only on the merchandise charges, not on freight charges.)

- *EXAMPLE 6-18 (see Fig. 6-6 for data)*

Compute the remittance amount and also the last date for payment within the discount period. Your first step is to verify the extension amount for the merchandise:

Figure 6-6

				INVOICE	
SERI PRINTS 1407 Broadway New York, NY			NUMBER:	1968	
			DATE:	April 1, 198_	
SOLD TO: SHEILA BOUTIQUE			SHIP TO:	Same	
2024 Maplewood Dr.					
Racoon Park, PA					
Our Order No. 9742	Customer Order No. 4930	Salesperson: House Account		Terms: 7/10 E.O.M.	
Date Shipped: 4/1/8_	Shipped Via: United	F.O.B. Store			

Quan.		Description	Cost	Extension	
36		#6973, Shirts	42 ea	1512	00
		Freight + Ins.		16	43
				1528	43

$$36 \times \$42 = \$1512$$

You can now calculate the remittance amount:

$$\$Cost \times Complement\ of\ discount\% = \$Remittance$$
$$\$1512.00 \times (100\% - 7\%) = \$1406.16$$

As the terms indicate the discount period is 10 days from the end of the month, you have until May 10 to pay the invoice; and as the shipment is "F.O.B. store," you do not need to include the freight and insurance charges with your payment.

Figure 6-7

			INVOICE			
ACME PET SUPPLY Poodle Park, MD						
			NUMBER:	492		
			DATE:	March 16, 198_		
SOLD TO: Jersey Dog House			SHIP TO:	Same		
Farmhouse Rd.						
Smithtown, GA						
Our Order No. 0492		Customer Order No. 8324	Salesperson: House		Terms: 2/10	
Date Shipped: 3/16/8_		Shipped Via: Fast Freight	F.O.B. Factory			
Quan.		Description		Cost	Extension	
400	lbs	Puppy Chow #3		18/lb	72	00
1200	lbs	Adult Chow #6		20/lb	240	00
		Freight + Ins.			36	85
					348	85

- *PROBLEM 6-15 (see Fig. 6-7 for data)*

Compute the remittance amount and the last date for payment within the discount period.

- *EXAMPLE 6-19 (see Fig. 6-8 for data)*

Compute the remittance amount and the last date for payment within the discount period. As the vendor offers no cash discount (net terms), the merchandise amount remains as $180.00.

The freight and insurance charges are shared, with the retailer paying 80 percent which is

Figure 6-8

POTTERY SUPPLIES 1712 Edgehill Rd. Christine, NM		INVOICE			
		NUMBER: 437H			
		DATE: July 6, 198_			
SOLD TO: The Potting Wheel		SHIP TO: Same			
84 Water Street					
San Jose, CA					
Our Order No. Z642	Customer Order No. 381	Salesperson: Gail		Terms: Net, E.O.M.	
Date Shipped: July 6, 198_	Shipped Via: American Freight	F.O.B. Store, charges shared 20% factory 80% store			
Quan.		Description	Cost	Extension	
30 lbs		Heavy wheel clay, Style H	6/lb	180	00
		Freight + Ins.		28	16
				208	16

$$\$28.16 \times .80 = \$22.528 \text{ or } \$22.53$$

The remittance amount is

$$\$180.00 + \$22.53 = \$202.53$$

With terms of E.O.M., the payment must be made by July 31.

Figure 6-9

	INVOICE	
CUSTOM GLASSWARE 479 Sand Street Mountain View, TX		
	NUMBER: Q1841	
	DATE: August 15, 198_	
SOLD TO: The Glass House	SHIP TO: Same	
419 C Street		
Toledo, OH		

Our Order No. 8493	Customer Order No. G359	Salesperson: House Account	Terms: 2%, 30 days
Date Shipped: 8/15/8_	Shipped Via: Fast Freight Ways	F.O.B. Store, charges shared 35% factory 65% store	

Quan.		Description	Cost	Extension	
24		Long stemmed tulip glasses,	6 ea	144	00
		Style 371			
		Freight + Ins.		37	19
				181	19

• *PROBLEM 6-16 (see Fig. 6-9 for data)*

Compute the remittance amount and the last date for payment within the discount period.

SUMMARY PROBLEMS

• *PROBLEM 6-1 (S)*

A buyer is offered a straight line quantity discount on cases of canned vegetables as follows:

50–100 cases	2.0%
50–250 cases but more than 100 cases	3.0
50 to more than 250 cases	4.5

If the buyer orders 300 cases at $7.50 per case, determine the discount amount and net dollar value for this purchase.

• *PROBLEM 6-2 (S)*

A buyer places an order for stereo units amounting to $8000 and is offered straight line quantity discounts as follows:

For orders between $2500 and $4000	3.0%
For orders between $2500 and $6000 but greater than $4000	4.5
For orders of at least $2500 and over $6000	6.0

Determine the discount amount and net cost of this order.

• *PROBLEM 6-3 (S)*

You have been offered stepped quantity discounts for your purchase of umbrellas as follows:

1–120	6.0%
121–240	6.5
241 and over	7.0

If you order 25 dozen umbrellas and they cost $4.75 each, determine the discount amount and the total net amount.

• *PROBLEM 6-4 (S)*

A vendor is offering you the following stepped quantity discounts:

$1–$250	3.0%
$251–$500	4.0
$501 and over	5.5

Your order amounts to $837. Calculate the net amount you must remit.

- *PROBLEM 6-5 (S)*

A customer in your catalog showroom chooses two items: a refrigerator that lists for $895 and a garbage disposer for $149. Your discount is 37.5 percent on the refrigerator and 25.0 percent on the disposer. Determine your payment to the vendor for this merchandise.

Figure 6-10

			INVOICE		
SANTA CLOTHES 1409 Broadway New York, NY					
			NUMBER: 1647		
			DATE: August 30, 198_		
SOLD TO: The Clothes Pole			SHIP TO: Same		
2975 Bristol Turnpike					
Denver, CO					
Our Order No. P4500	Customer Order No. 4712		Salesperson: Simmons	Terms: 6/10, Net 30 days	
Date Shipped: 9/1/8_	Shipped Via: U.P.S.		F.O.B. Store		

Quan.		Description	Cost	Extension	
9 pcs		#1413, L.S. Dress, Solid	14.75 ea	177	00
12 pcs		#1424, L.S. Dress, Print	14.75 ea	177	00
9 pcs		#1632, L.S. Dress, Stripe	16.75 ea	150	75
				504	75

• *PROBLEM 6-6 (S)*

You are purchasing goods from a vendor who offers trade discounts as a series, 35.0 percent, 24.0 percent, 16.5 percent. Your order is as follows: 6 television sets at $495 each; 8 stereo systems at $630 each; and 5 portable AM/FM radios at $136 each. Determine the net amount you must pay for this order.

Figure 6-11

			INVOICE			
ABBY JANE TOGS 1419 Broadway New York, NY			NUMBER: 9956			
			DATE: June 16, 198_			
SOLD TO: C.A. Hide			SHIP TO: Same			
16 Theater Rd.						
Santa Fe, NM						

Our Order No. P4600	Customer Order No. 861	Salesperson: Sherman	Terms: 6/10, Net 30, R.O.G.
Date Shipped: 6/16/8_	Shipped Via: A.D.S.	F.O.B. Store	

Quan.		Description	Cost	Extension	
15 pcs		#439, Jumpsuit	47.50 ea	712	50

- *PROBLEM 6-7 (S)*

Refer to Figure 6-10 and compute the remittance amount.

- *PROBLEM 6-8 (S)*

Refer to Figure 6-11 and compute the remittance amount and also the last date by which the invoice must be paid to take the discount. The merchandise was received on June 23.

Figure 6-12

	INVOICE		
DEE JAY WHOLESALERS 47 Houston St. Chicago, IL	NUMBER: 9157		
	DATE: April 27, 198_		
SOLD TO: Lancia Luggage	SHIP TO: Same		
37 4th St.			
Fort Hill Springs, OK			

Our Order No. P4839	Customer Order No. 9421	Salesperson: Martin	Terms: 4/10 E.O.M. a/o 5/25
Date Shipped: 4/27/8_	Shipped Via: P.I.	F.O.B. Store	Less 40.0%, 10.0%

Quan.		Description	Cost	Extension	
9		SC 14, Overnight Case	33.75 ea	303	75
15		JC 14, Jewelry Case	24.50 ea	357	50
12		TS 14, Two Suiter Case	38.25 ea	459	00
				1110	25

• *PROBLEM 6-9 (S)*

Refer to Figure 6-12 and compute the remittance amount and also the last date by which the invoice must be paid to take the discounts. The merchandise was received on May 4.

Figure 6-13

		INVOICE			
DOWN EAST PET SUPPLY 4 East St. Lawton, OK					
		NUMBER: 6531			
		DATE: November 25, 198_			
SOLD TO: Bristol's Petland		SHIP TO: Same			
The Barn					
Tuscaloosa, AL					

Our Order No. G8400	Customer Order No. 621	Salesperson: McGinnity	Terms: 4/10 E.O.M. 30 X
Date Shipped: 11/25/8_	Shipped Via: Overland Exp.	F.O.B. Store	Ant. Allowed: 6% per annum

Quan.		Description	Cost	Extension	
400	bags	Pet Food	1.35/bag	540	00
40	pcs	Leashes, assorted sizes	1.20 ea	48	00
50	pcs	Animal Containers	37.50 ea	1875	00
				2463	00

• *PROBLEM 6-10 (S)*

Refer to Figure 6-13 and compute the remittance amount; the merchandise was received on November 30 and will be paid for on December 8.

• *PROBLEM 6-11 (S)*

A vendor offers you cash discount terms of 3 percent, but you want your purchases loaded

Figure 6-14

INVOICE			
CRANSTON CORP. 575 Seventh Ave. New York, NY			
	NUMBER:	7391	
	DATE:	February 20, 198_	
SOLD TO: Nan Grey Dress Shop	SHIP TO:	Same	
1432 Fulton Ave.			
Newton, CA			

Our Order No. P4100	Customer Order No. 431	Salesperson: House Account	Terms: 8/10 E.O.M. a/o 3/25 Ant. Allowed: 6% per annum
Date Shipped: 2/21/8_	Shipped Via: Empire	F.O.B. Store, charges reversed	

Quan.		Description	Cost	Extension	
12 doz		Assorted Styles, Dresses	10.75ea	1548	00
		Freight + Ins.		27	50
				1575	50

to reflect a discount of 8 percent. Calculate the loaded amount for an invoice of $4397 that has a discount of 8 percent rather than 3 percent.

- *PROBLEM 6-12 (S)*

Refer to Figure 6-14 and compute the amount to be remitted if the bill is paid on March 2.

- *PROBLEM 6-13 (S)*

Complete the table on p. 120.

CASE STUDY_____

SIGHT AND SOUND

As the owner of a small electronics store, you have been very careful to stock only those radios, television sets, and stereo components that appeal to your core customers.

Today you were approached by a customer who wanted to buy a video-VCR-stereo unit which you do not normally stock but is within the price range of equipment you carry. Your trade catalog lists the retail price as $1800, which is fine with your customer, who wants you to order it.

A call to your supplier results in the following information: The unit can be delivered to you in time to satisfy your customer; your trade discount is 20 percent; due to an overstocked condition in the supplier's warehouse, the supplier is willing to offer straight line quantity discounts if you will take more than one unit, as follows:

3–5 units	6%
3–10 units but more than 5 units	8
3–20 units but more than 10 units	12
3 to more than 20 units	17

You have enough warehouse space to accommodate 25 units; however, you estimate the rate of sale to be no more than two per month, and you would have to borrow money at 8% interest to pay any invoice unless you had six months or more to send in your remittance.

The vendor is willing to negotiate an initial payment of at least half and the balance to be arranged.

What will be your negotiating points to make payments?

	INVOICE DATE	RECEIPT DATE	TERMS	F.O.B.	FREIGHT AND INSURANCE AMOUNT	MERCHANDISE AMOUNT	PAID DATE	LAST DATE FOR DISCOUNT	REMITTANCE AMOUNT
A	4/16/8_	4/20/8_	4/10 E.O.M., no anticipation	Factory	$ 8.32	$ 114.93	May 10		
B	6/20/8_	6/27/8_	8/10 E.O.M., R.O.G., no anticipation	Store	$16.27	$ 384.24	Aug. 15		
C	5/19/8_	5/21/8_	Net 10 days, less 35%, 20%, no anticipation	Store	—	$ 463.19	May 29		
D	8/13/8_	8/14/8_	8/10 E.O.M., a/o 10/25, anticipation at 6%	Factory	$43.19	$3649.24	Sept. 9		
E	11/25/8_	11/28/8_	7/10, E.O.M., no anticipation	Store Charges Reversed	$34.65	$ 690.00	Jan. 8		
F	2/18/8_	2/27/8_	Net 10 days, E.O.M. no anticipation	Factory	$12.79	$ 597.12	Mar. 10		

Pricing

7

In a society where goods and services are furnished without charge or at their actual cost, pricing is not difficult. However, within our free enterprise social order, goods and services are commonly sold at prices higher than their producer's cost, permitting sellers a profit for their efforts. The resulting problem from this system is to determine the retail price for merchandise and services.

A selling, or retail, price is determined after considering a wide variety of factors. Some of these factors—for example, competition, store location, and the nature of the merchandise (unique, exclusive, or common)—are intangibles. Other factors, such as expenses, profit, and reductions (markdowns, discounts to employees and customers, and shortages), are more perceptible, although in most instances they are only "guesstimates." Consequently, a retailer is very much a cross between an artist and a scientist, blending what is known with what is little known. Primarily, you, the retailer, must set the prices for your merchandise so that they will satisfy the wants and needs of your core customer, serve as a competitive tool against your core competitiors, and, when the merchandise is sold, generate a profit. If you were without competition, you could establish retail prices at whatever level your customers would pay and could maximally afford.

In a highly competitive environment, a decision might be made to use "loss leaders" (selling goods below their actual cost) to attract customers to a store. Other situations may require "traditional" pricing (merchandise priced at customer-anticipated levels) or the use of "keystone" markup (the practice of doubling the actual cost).

Naturally, in pricing you must consider the people who frequent your store, because the selection of a particular location for the shop is usually determined by the customers in the area. Knowledge of their tastes, habits, and spending level will dictate, to a large extent, the prices you can charge. There are exceptions, of course, such as stores that are able to discount high-fashion merchandise because they are located in factory areas with low rentals. They must make their presence known to their prospective clientele, however, which may take some time and require high advertising expenditures.

Rent and advertising costs are expense items and are more easily and accurately assessed than are the spending levels of customers. For these reasons retailers should be able to assign dollar or percentage-of-sale values to these expenses, as well as to other similar expenditures.

The importance of making reasonable estimates of expenses, markdowns, and anticipated sales is twofold: first, to use them to compute the initial markup and second, to serve as standards against which the actual activity of your business can be measured. The latter application requires no explanation; however, **initial markup** deserves attention. Initial markup (IM) is an amount added to the cost of the merchandise in the beginning, which includes the elements of expense, profit, and reductions.

INITIAL MARKUP

The formula for Initial Markup (IM) is*

$$IM\% = \frac{\text{Expenses} + \text{Profit} + \text{Reductions} - \text{Cash discounts}}{\text{Sales} + \text{Reductions}}$$

The individual elements of this formula are explained as follows:

Expenses contain all fixed expenses such as rent and utilities and variable expenses, which include payroll and advertising.

Profit is the anticipated amount you want to see your business produce.

Reductions encompass markdowns (which are explained in detail in Chapter Eight); employee discounts, which are discounts given to employees on their purchases from the store; customer discounts, which are price reductions given to customers on an individual basis for, as examples, purchasing an item which is minimally defective, or as discounts to clubs or religious groups; and stock shortages, which cover both employee and customer theft, as well as "paper" errors resulting from incorrect or poor calculation of inventory.

Cash Discounts are discounts earned by the retailer for on-time payment to vendors (explained in Chapter Six).

Sales are the net value derived from dollar sales minus customer returns.

*Alteration expense is occasionally included as a separate item in the numerator of the initial markup formula. It is excluded here, as the issue of charging women for alterations, while providing this service to men shoppers at no additional fee, is being discussed as a questionable practice both by the retailers and in the courts.

In the initial markup formula, you will note that **reductions** are included in both the numerator and the denominator. They are added to the other elements in the numerator because they are values to be compensated for through the sales of merchandise. The presence of **reductions** in the denominator is to bring the **sales** level up to a point so that enough merchandise will be purchased to cover all types of reductions. As an example, if an employee were to purchase a set of china ticketed at $100 and receive a $20 discount, the store would receive $80. However, the china buyer would still have to have $100 worth of merchandise to cover the $20 discount.

The most basic formula in retailing is:

$$Cost \; + \; Markup \; = \; Retail$$

or

$$C \; + \; MU \; = \; R$$

where cost is the cost of the goods to the retailer; markup the aggregate of expenses, profit, and reductions, as explained; and retail the selling price of the merchandise to the customer.

You can easily find the cost of an item by asking a vendor, "How much is this hat?" If the response is $3, you have found C. But without MU, you are unable to determine R.

• EXAMPLE 7-1

Assume that you know the following from estimates, past experience, lease information, your accountant, or trade sources:

	Cash discounts		$ 3000
Expenses	Annual rent	$18,000	
	Utilities	8000	
	Miscellaneous expenses	5000	
	Payroll	40,000	
			$71,000
Profit	Anticipated profit		$25,000
Reductions	Markdowns	$25,000	
	Employee discounts	3000	
	Customer discounts	2000	
	Stock shortages	5000	
			$35,000

This list, by definition, contains all the components of markup. The problem, however, is to determine how much of those amounts has to be added to the $3 cost of the hat so that you can attach a retail price to it.

The only other item of estimated data you need at this point is sales. Assume, then, that you plan to have $250,000 in sales for the year. The formula for the IM percentage is

$$\text{IM\%} = \frac{\text{Expenses} + \text{Profit} + \text{Reductions} - \text{Cash discounts}}{\text{Sales} + \text{Reductions}}$$

Substituting the dollar values,

$$\text{IM\%} = \frac{\$71{,}000 + \$25{,}000 + \$35{,}000 - \$3000}{\$250{,}000 + \$35{,}000}$$

$$\text{IM\%} = \frac{\$128{,}000}{\$285{,}000}$$

$$\text{IM\%} = 44.9\%$$

Initial markup can also be computed when the value for each element is given a percentage, or when some values are expressed in dollars and others are given as percentages. The latter is more typically the case, because expenses such as rent are known in percentage terms, whereas estimated sales for a given period are expressed as a dollar figure.

When the amounts for certain items, such as markdowns, profit, or payroll, are given as a percentage value, they are percentages or parts of the sales figure.† You would probably not want to reveal actual dollar figures to anyone not entitled to know them, but you could indicate, for example, that your profit for a particular period was 14.7 percent or that your payroll expense was 18.3 percent.

The percentages are derived by forming a fraction in which the numerator is the dollar amount of the category in question and the denominator is the sales figure.

• EXAMPLE 7-2

Referring to the values for each category in Example 7-1, determine their percentage values and calculate your IM percentage.

(1) Compute percentage values:

	Cash discounts	$	3000	÷	$250,000	=	1.2%
Expenses	Annual rent		18,000	÷	250,000	=	7.2%
	Utilities		8000	÷	250,000	=	3.2%
	Miscellaneous expenses		5000	÷	250,000	=	2.0%
	Payroll		40,000	÷	250,000	=	16.0%
Profit	Anticipated profit		25,000	÷	250,000	=	10.0%
Reductions	Markdowns		25,000	÷	250,000	=	10.0%
	Employee discounts		3000	÷	250,000	=	1.2%
	Customer discounts		2000	÷	250,000	=	0.8%
	Stock shortages		5000	÷	250,000	=	2.0%

†Basic to most areas of retailing, the practice is to consider the retail price, or sales, as the base number to which all other figures are related. It is the foundation, or reference, value and is numerically equal to 100 percent. In some limited instances, cost values are used as the base value, but this application is diminishing.

(2) Substitute the values in the IM formula:

$$IM\% = \frac{\text{Expenses} + \text{Profit} + \text{Reductions} - \text{Cash discounts}}{\text{Sales} + \text{Reductions}}$$

$$= \frac{(7.2\% + 3.2\% + 2.0\% + 16.0\%) + 10.0\% + (10.0\% + 1.2\% + 0.8\% + 2.0\%) - 1.2\%}{100.0\% + (10.0\% + 3.2\% + 0.8\%)}$$

$$= \frac{28.4\% + 10.0\% + 14.0\% - 1.2\%}{100.0\% + 14\%}$$

$$= \frac{51.2\%}{114.0\%} \text{ or } \frac{.512}{1.14}$$

$$= .4491 \text{ or } 44.9\%$$

Clearly, the IM percentage obtained by using percentage values is identical to that in Example 7-1, in which dollar values were applied.

If the problem were stated with some values in dollars and others in percentages you could convert percentage values to dollars by multiplying the dollar value for sales (it would always be available in a problem such as this) by the percentage value of the category.

If the payroll expense was estimated at 19.2 percent and sales were estimated at $327,000, the computation would be as follows:

$$\$327,000 \times .192 = \$62,784$$

• *PROBLEM 7-1*

Determine your IM percentage given the following information:

Annual rent	$ 36,000
Utilities	17,500
Miscellaneous expenses	9000
Payroll	19.0%
Profit	11.5%
Markdowns	8.6%
Employee discounts	7.5%
Customer discounts	2.0%
Sales	$480,000
Cash discounts	4000
Stock shortages	4.6%

INDIVIDUAL MARKUP

After completing the IM percentage computation, you are able to calculate the retail price for your merchandise. The following two concepts are used throughout this process: The algebraic truism that "values equal to the same value are equal to each other," and the fact that sales at the retail price are equal to 100.0 percent. That is, $R = 100\%. By combining the two theories, we have R% = $R and C% = $C and MU% = $MU.

The following example illustrates both points:

• *EXAMPLE 7-3*

Determine the retail price for a hat that costs $3 and requires a markup of 44.9 percent. (In general, the matrix format illustrated below is extremely useful in finding solutions involving markup. This format, as well as modifications to it, will be used throughout this text.)

	C	+ MU	= R
%			100.0
$			

Now insert the other known values, C = $3; MU% = 44.9%:

	C	+ MU	= R
%		44.9	100.0
$	3		

Transposing the basic retailing formula:

$$C = R - MU$$

And substituting the known values:

$$C = 100.0\% - 44.9\%$$

$$C = 55.1\%$$

Inserting the value of C into the matrix:

	C	+ MU	= R
%	55.1	44.9	100.0
$	3		

Algebraically it is

$$C\% = \$C$$

or

$$55.1\% = \$3$$

Solve for the value of 1.0% by dividing both sides of the equation by 55.1:

$$\frac{55.1\%}{55.1} = \frac{\$3}{55.1}$$

$$1.0\% = \$.05444$$

As R = 100.0%, its dollar value is determined by multiplying the value of 1.0% by 100

$$R = 100 \times \$.05444$$
$$R = \$5.444$$
$$R = \$5.44$$

The value for R can be put into the matrix, and if it is desirable or necessary, the dollar markup can be computed by transposing the basic retailing formula:

$$MU = R - C$$
$$MU = \$5.44 - \$3.00$$
$$MU = \$2.44$$

	C	+ MU	= R
%	55.1	44.9	100.0
$	3.00	2.44	5.44

The R value, $5.44, represents a 44.9 percent initial markup for an item that cost $3.00. If it is sold for the price of $5.44, it will contribute its share toward payment of its own cost, and of expenses, reductions, and profit.

• *PROBLEM 7-2*

From the following information, determine the IM percentage and the retail price of a toothbrush that costs $.18:

Cash discount	$ 5000
Rent	12,000
Utilities	7500
Miscellaneous expenses	2500
Payroll	6000
Profit	16,000
Reductions	2400
Planned sales	150,000

It is often necessary for you to be able to compute the markup percentage you can obtain on an item when a vendor quotes you both the cost price and a "suggested" retail price. Thus you can see if the product is of any value to your department.

• *EXAMPLE 7-4*

A vendor offers you a handbag that costs $47.50 and has a suggested retail price of $100.00. Determine the markup percentage you can obtain on this item.
(1) Determine the dollar markup:

$$\$MU = \$R - \$C$$
$$= \$100.00 - \$47.50$$
$$= \$52.50$$

(2) Determine the percentage markup:

$$MU\% = \$MU \div \$R$$
$$= \$52.50 \div \$100.00$$
$$= 52.5\%$$

• *PROBLEM 7-3*

Calculate the markup percentage for a book with a cost price of $14 and a suggested retail price of $22.

Determining the price of merchandise, as you have just done, is considered the scientific side of retailing. Pricing as a strategy requires that you decide in advance how you would like your store and merchandise to be perceived. Three alternatives are available: **above the market, at the market,** or **below the market**. Your rationale for selecting a particular strategy, other than your need to cover the cost of the goods, meet your expenses, and generate a profit, can be based upon four pressures: the store and merchandise image, your core competition, your vendors, and your core customers' income. The interaction of these elements is illustrated in Figure 7-1, in which an exclusive or high-fashion shop with prices above the market, for example, would encounter medium-to-light pressure from core competitors and light stress from vendors and cater to core customers in the high-to-medium income range.

The force exerted upon the retailer from the pressure of the store and merchandise image is internal, a stress that is self-imposed. The remaining three pressures, however, are external stresses and have a heavy impact on the shop owner's decisions about goods and their presentation.

Pressure from competition can be generated in ways other than price, such as location, service, and advertising, to mention only a few factors. These pressures can be attacked head-on, though, by offering more or better service or by increasing or changing the focus of the promotional budget. These factors will have been addressed and planned for during the strategic planning process.

A similar approach cannot be offered for countering vendor pressures that result from exclusivity of merchandise where the vendor may control distribution, insuring adherence to high prices, or where there are only a few manufacturers for a particular classification of merchandise, compelling you to make your selections from a limited number of suppliers. Conversely, vendor pressure will be relatively light when there are many suppliers in the marketplace and the merchandise is reasonably commonplace.

Developing responsive tactics for changes in your customers' income include altering your **price points**, and reducing or increasing customer services to affect initial markup, which would change your retail prices without modifying your profit.

In the final analysis, you will find that price strategy is a common solution attempted by retailers. Note, however, that shifting your prices may produce a commensurate move in your market position—for example, from at the market to above the market. This move in turn generates different conditions regarding the other stress factors.

Figure 7-1

PRESSURES	STORE AND MERCHANDISE IMAGE			CORE COMPETITION			VENDOR			CORE CUSTOMERS' INCOME		
Prices	Exclusive	Medium	Discount	Heavy	Medium	Light	Heavy	Medium	Light	High	Medium	Low
Above the Market	X				X	X			X	X	X	
At the Market		X		X	X		X	X		X	X	X
Below the Market			X	X					X		X	X

129

AVERAGING MARKUP

One of the most effective ways to use pricing as a strategy is by developing **price lines, price zones**, and **price ranges** for the different classifications of merchandise in your store. Figure 7-2 illustrates the price range zones and lines for dresses in a shop with prices below the market.

Figure 7-2

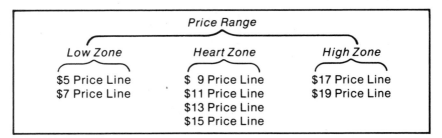

The strategy has many advantages. For the consumer it simplifies the selection process because of the limited number of price lines available and the clear-cut dollar definition between the lines, at the same time providing an adequate assortment. For the retailer the benefits include facilitation of planning and buying, for as the **heart zone** (shown in Fig. 7-2) reveals, certain priced merchandise must be bought heavily to assure adequate assortments and, similarly, other price lines require lighter buying. Another by-product of this strategy is that buyers must segment their purchases into specific price lines, which compels them to think about gaining additional markup when prepricing their merchandise, or similarly passing up purchases that produce marginal markups. This is not to say that an order for attractive merchandise should not be written because of reduced markup, but the buyer must be aware that other purchases must be made with a high markup to compensate for any made with a "short" markup. The process is called averaging markup.

- *EXAMPLE 7-5*

The first situation to be examined is one in which the planned IM percentage and the required number of merchandise units within a particular price line have been determined, and you (the buyer) have already purchased some of the merchandise needed. Your problem is that the merchandise purchased will not generate the necessary IM percentage, and you must determine the average cost for each of the additional merchandise units in your open-to-buy (O.T.B.). The data you have follow:

IM percentage (planned)	48.6%
Price line	$19.00
Total merchandise units needed	300
Merchandise units purchased	75
Cost of each merchandise unit purchased	$12.75

Begin by constructing the matrix used in the earlier example, and insert the values that are given. (Note that the values in boldface are values given in the problem, whereas derived values are accompanied by a number in parentheses to identify the step in which they were computed.)

	C	+ MU	= R	Units
Merchandise needed %	(1) 51.4	**48.6**	**100.0**	
Merchandise needed $	(3) 2929.80		(2) 5700.00	**300**
Merchandise purchased $	(4) 956.25			**75**
O.T.B. $	(5) 1973.55			(6) 225

$$(1)\ C\% = R\% - MU\%$$
$$= 100.0\% - 48.6\%$$
$$= 51.4\%$$

(2) Find the total retail dollar value of the merchandise needed:

$$\$R = \$R \text{ per unit} \times \text{Units needed}$$
$$= \$19.00 \times 300$$
$$= \$5700.00$$

(3) Find the dollar cost of merchandise needed:

$$\$C = \$R \times C\%$$
$$= \$5700.00 \times .514$$
$$= \$2929.80$$

(4) Find the total cost value of the merchandise purchased:

$$\$C = \$C \text{ per unit} \times \text{Units purchased}$$
$$= \$12.75 \times 75$$
$$= \$956.25$$

(5) Find O.T.B. dollars:

$$\$O.T.B. = \$\text{Merchandise needed} - \$\text{Merchandise purchased}$$
$$= \$2929.80 - \$956.25$$
$$= \$1973.55$$

(6) Find O.T.B. merchandise units needed:

$$O.T.B. \text{ units} = O.T.B. \text{ units needed} - O.T.B. \text{ units purchased}$$
$$= 300 - 75$$
$$= 225$$

(7) Find the average cost for the merchandise units open-to-buy:

$$O.T.B. \text{ cost} = \$O.T.B. \div O.T.B. \text{ units}$$
$$= \$1973.55 \div 225$$
$$= \$8.77$$

You could easily compute the markup percentage needed for the open-to-buy as follows:

$$\$MU = \$R - \$C$$
$$= \$19.00 - \$8.77$$
$$= \$10.23$$

and

$$MU\% = \$MU \div \$R$$
$$= \$10.23 \div \$19.00$$
$$= 53.8\%$$

also find the markup percentage on the merchandise purchased:

$$\$MU = \$R - \$C$$
$$= \$19.00 - \$12.75$$
$$= \$6.25$$

and

$$MU\% = \$MU \div \$R$$
$$= \$6.25 \div \$19.00$$
$$= 32.9\%$$

The impact should be clear: The balance of the merchandise you have left to buy must generate a greater IM percentage (53.8%) than that of your first purchase (32.9%). Or else you may have to try to cancel some of the orders from your first purchase in order to bring your markup into line with your IM of 48.6%.

• *PROBLEM 7-4*

Determine the average unit cost for your open-to-buy given the following data:

IM%	53.2
Price line	$40
Total merchandise units needed	350
Merchandise units purchased	60
Cost of each merchandise unit purchased	$22

Another example of averaging markup with which you will be confronted is for merchandise in job lots or closeouts. Vendors offer a variety of styles of this kind of merchandise at the conclusion of a season or as special promotional packages during the year. The items in these assortments may very well have various costs, and you must decide the retail prices for each.

• *EXAMPLE 7-6*

A manufacturer has offered you a special purchase consisting of 30 pairs of figure ice skates at $16.75 each and 42 pairs of hockey ice skates at $12.75 each. You must attain a markup of 52.4 percent. If the figure skates are to be retailed for $36.00, what price should be placed on the hockey skates so that you can reach your markup? (Note that the values in boldface are values given in the problem, whereas derived values are accompanied by a number in parentheses to identify the step in which they were computed.)

		C	+ MU	= R	Units
	%	(2) 47.6	**52.4**	**100.0**	
Total merchandise $		(1) 1038.00		(2) 2180.67	(1) 72
Figure skates $				(3) 1080.00	**30**
Hockey skates $				(4) 1100.67	**42**

(1) Determine the numbers of units purchased and the total cost of the merchandise:

$$30 \times \$16.75 = \$502.50$$
$$42 \times \$12.75 = \$535.50$$
$$\overline{72} \qquad\qquad \overline{\$1038.00}$$

(2) Determine the total retail amount:

$$C\% \quad = R\% \ - \ MU\%$$
$$47.6\% = 100.0\% \ - \ 52.4\%$$
$$C\% \quad = \$C$$
$$47.6\% = \$1038.00$$

$$\frac{47.6\%}{47.6} = \frac{\$1038.00}{47.6}$$

$$1\% \ = \$21.80672$$

$$100\% \ = \$2180.67$$

(3) Determine the total retail amount for figure skates:

$$30 \times \$36 = \$1080.00$$

(4) Determine the balance of the retail amount for hockey skates:

$$= \$2180.67 \ - \ \$1080.00$$
$$= \$1100.67$$

(5) Determine the average retail amount for hockey skates:

$$= \text{Total \$Retail for hockey skates} \div \text{Total units of hockey skates}$$
$$= \$1100.67 \div 42$$
$$= \$26.21$$

• *PROBLEM 7-5*

You have been offered a closeout on two groups of end tables: 60 assorted contemporary styles for $38.50 each, which you are certain can be retailed for no more than $75.00 each, and a group of 80 modern tables, at $32.50 each. What would be the retail price you would have to place on the modern group to attain an average markup of 62.4 percent?

AVERAGING MARKUP ON ALL PURCHASES

The final illustration involves an ongoing problem for buyers, that is, averaging markups on all purchases. For example, you have determined or been given your dollar open-to-buy at retail, broken this figure down by merchandise classification and price line, and obtained your markup percentage. Armed with this information, you travel to the market and begin to buy.

Through prior knowledge and practice you have learned that different vendors have varying cost prices for their goods that you must squeeze into a single price line. Consider the following information:

Figure 7-3

Desired MU% — 50.0%					
$10 Price Line					
Vendor A		Vendor B		Vendor C	
Cost	MU%	Cost	MU%	Cost	MU%
$4.75	52.5%	$5.00	50.0%	$5.25	47.5%

If you were able either to purchase equal quantities from vendors A and C (this would produce an average markup of 50 percent) or to buy merchandise only from vendor B, you would meet your MU% objectives. This is hardly possible, as you will undoubtedly buy from more vendors. Furthermore, your purchases will usually be in unbalanced amounts from each supplier. The problem is to determine what proportion of merchandise you can order at each of the various cost prices in order to obtain the goal of your planned markup.

- EXAMPLE 7-7

As the buyer for better women's blouses you have determined an **open-to-buy** for your $60 price line of $4200 (retail) with a markup of 52 percent. You write an order for 18 blouses that cost $31.50 each. Determine the new O.T.B. dollars at cost and at retail and the MU percentage necessary to meet your planned percentage.

Construct a matrix and write in the appropriate known values. (Note that the values in boldface are the values given in the problem, whereas derived values are accompanied by a number in parentheses to identify the step in which they were computed.)

		$60 Price Line		
		C	+ MU	= R
O.T.B.	%	(1) 48.0	**52.0**	**100.0**
	$	(2) 2016		**4200**
Purchases	$	(4) 567		(3) 1080
New O.T.B.	%		(8) 53.6	
	$	(5) 1449	(7) 1671	(6) 3120

(1) Determine the cost percentage of the open-to-buy:

$$C\% = R\% - MU\%$$
$$= 100\% - 52\%$$
$$= 48\%$$

(2) Determine the dollar cost of the open-to-buy:

$$\$C = C\% \times \$R$$
$$= .48 \times \$4200$$
$$= \$2016$$

(3) Determine the total retail dollars for purchases:

$$\text{Total } \$R = \$\text{Unit retail} \times \text{Number of units}$$
$$= \$60 \times 18$$
$$= \$1080$$

(4) Determine the total dollar cost for purchases:

$$\text{Total } \$C = \$\text{Unit cost} \times \text{Number of units}$$
$$= \$31.50 \times 18$$
$$= \$567.00$$

(5) Determine the new open-to-buy at dollar cost:

$$\text{New O.T.B. } \$C = \text{O.T.B. } \$C - \text{Purchases } \$C$$
$$= \$2016 - \$567$$
$$= \$1449$$

(6) Determine the new open-to-buy at retail value:

$$\text{New O.T.B. } \$R = \text{O.T.B. } \$R - \text{Purchases } \$R$$
$$= \$4200 - \$1080$$
$$= \$3120$$

(7) Determine the new O.T.B. dollar markup:

$$\text{New O.T.B. } \$MU = \text{New O.T.B. } \$R - \text{New O.T.B. } \$C$$
$$= \$3120 - \$1449$$
$$= \$1671$$

(8) Determine the new O.T.B. markup percentage:

$$\text{New O.T.B. MU\%} = \text{New O.T.B. } \$MU \div \text{New O.T.B. } \$R$$
$$= \$1671 \div \$3120$$
$$= 53.6\%$$

At this point we could also determine the quantity of blouses still to be purchased by first finding the number we needed originally:

$$\text{Total original unit O.T.B.} = \$R \div \text{Unit } \$R$$
$$= \$4200 \div \$60$$
$$= 70 \text{ blouses}$$

Then we can determine that

70 blouses − 18 blouses purchased = 52 blouses O.T.B.

Now we can calculate the average cost for these blouses using the new O.T.B. dollar cost:

$1449.00 ÷ 52 = $27.87

• PROBLEM 7-6

If the open-to-buy for your $25.00 lamp line is $3200.00 (retail) and the desired markup percentage is 47 percent, determine the new O.T.B. dollar cost, retail value, and markup percentage after purchasing 30 lamps that cost $14.25 each.

Averaging markup on purchases and adhering to price lines you have established within the price range for each classification of merchandise (see Fig. 7-2) presents another problem. Many times, particularly with job lots and closeout purchases, you will find that the computed retail price does not fall into one of your price lines, and you will have to adjust this price up (producing increased markup) or down (resulting in decreased markup). The "up" or "down" decision will be based upon answers to a variety of questions such as will your core customers see enough value (up) or view the item as a real bargain (down); if your core competitors carry the same merchandise, will your pricing undercut theirs (down) or will you be overpriced (up); will the reduced markup negatively affect your overall markup goal (down) or provide you with additional markup (up)?

• EXAMPLE 7-8

During your overview market visits, you saw men's slacks which cost $42.50 each that you would like to include in your department. Your IM is 52.1 percent; calculate the retail price for this merchandise.

Construct a matrix and write in the appropriate known values. (Note that the values in bold-face are the values given in the problem, whereas derived values are accompanied by a number in parentheses to identify the step in which they were computed.)

	C	+MU	= R
%	(1) 47.9	52.1	100.0
$	42.50		(2) 88.73

(1) Determine the cost percentage:

$$C\% = R\% - MU\%$$
$$= 100.0\% - 52.1\%$$
$$= 47.9\%$$

(2) Solve for the value of 1%:

$$C\% = \$C$$
$$47.9\% = \$42.50$$
$$1.0\% = \$42.50 \div 47.9$$
$$= \$.88727$$

$$100.0\% = \$.88727 \times 100$$
$$= \$88.73$$

If your price lines are $80 and $95, determine the MU% you could obtain at each level: For the $80 price line

$$\$MU = \$R - \$C$$
$$= \$80.00 - \$42.50$$
$$= \$37.50$$

and

$$MU\% = \$MU \div \$R$$
$$= \$37.50 \div \$80.00$$
$$= .46875, \text{ or } 46.9\%$$

For the $95 price line

$$\$MU = \$R - \$C$$
$$= \$95.00 - \$42.50$$
$$= \$52.50$$

and

$$MU\% = \$MU \div \$R$$
$$= \$52.50 \div \$95.00$$
$$= .5526, \text{ or } 55.3\%$$

If the answer were one which simply depended upon rounding off (up or down) to the nearest price line, the decision would be arithmetically made for you to go to $95.00, as $88.73 is only $6.27 away from $95.00 while it is $8.73 from the $80.00 price line.

As you read earlier, however, pricing is a decision, not a mathematically determined value, and your expertise as a retailer will be your guide.

• PROBLEM 7-7

You have decided to purchase picnic tables which cost $38.25 each; your IM is 58.7 percent. Determine

(1) The retail price to meet your IM.
(2) The markup percentage you would obtain if these tables were included in either your $80 or $100 price lines.

CUMULATIVE MARKUP

You must reconcile yourself to the fact that there has never been a perfect buyer. For to attain true perfection, a buyer would always have to have the exact amount of merchandise on hand so that a sale is never lost, markdowns never exceed the amount planned, and goods are sold to the last piece. Although all of this is impossible, it does not mean that you should not try to come as close to perfection as you can.

Two of the key factors of success are the dollar control of inventory and continuous attention to markups. These objectives can be accomplished to a large extent by calculating cumulative markups and cumulative dollar values at cost and at retail for purchases and inventory.

Assume now that you are at the beginning of the buying season for your department. You have received your initial markup and the dollar open-to-buy at retail.

- *EXAMPLE 7-9*

The initial markup for your department on February 1, 198___, is 47.5 percent, and the open-to-buy at retail is $46,000. Determine the dollar open-to-buy at cost and the dollar markup. (Note that the values in boldface are the values given in the problem, whereas derived values are accompanied by a number in parentheses to identify the step in which they were computed.)

		C	+ MU	= R
O.T.B. 2/1/8_	%	(1) 52.5	**47.5**	**100.0**
	$	(2) 24,150	(3) 21,850	**46,000**

(1) Determine the cost percentage:

$$C\% = R\% - MU\%$$
$$= 100.0\% - 47.5\%$$
$$= 52.5\%$$

(2) Determine the cost dollars:

$$*\$C = \$R \times C\%$$
$$= \$46,000 \times .525$$
$$= \$24,150$$

(3) Determine the markup dollars:

$$\$MU = \$R - \$C$$
$$= \$46,000 - \$24,150$$
$$= \$21,850$$

- *PROBLEM 7-8*

Determine the dollar open-to-buy at cost and the dollar markup for your department with an initial markup of 52.3 percent and an open-to-buy at retail of $28,500.

Now that you have determined your O.T.B. dollar values you may proceed to the market to buy merchandise. But if you have carried over salable merchandise from the previous year or season, the value of this merchandise must be subtracted from your open-to-buy to give you the revised open-to-buy (rev. O.T.B.). Obviously, the best situation is one in which you carry over the smallest possible inventory, thus enabling you to bring in fresh stock.

*If there is no use for the cost percentage in future computational work, steps 1 and 2 can be combined to find $C, as follows: $C = $R × (100% − MU%)

• *EXAMPLE 7-10*

Your department, as of February 1, 198___, has an inventory **on hand** (OH) from last year of $4700 at cost, which has a retail value of $7200. Using the values from the matrix in Example 7-9 determine the revised O.T.B. dollar values and the markup percentage needed. (Note that the values in boldface are the values given in the problem, whereas derived values are accompanied by a number in parentheses to identify the step in which they were computed.)

		C	+ MU	= R
O.T.B.	%	**52.5**	**47.5**	**100**
	$	**24,150**	21,850	46,000
OH	%		(6) 34.7	**100.0**
	$	**4700**	(5) 2500	**7200**
Rev: O.T.B. 2/1/8__	%		(4) 49.9	**100.0**
	$	(1) 19,450	(3) 19,350	(2) 38,800

(1) Determine the dollar cost of your revised open-to-buy:

$$\$C \text{ of rev. O.T.B.} = \$C \text{ of O.T.B.} - \$C \text{ of OH}$$
$$= \$24{,}150 - \$4700$$
$$= \$19{,}450$$

(2) Determine the retail value of your revised open-to-buy:

$$\$R \text{ of rev. O.T.B.} = \$R \text{ of O.T.B.} - \$R \text{ of OH}$$
$$= \$46{,}000 - \$7200$$
$$= \$38{,}800$$

(3) Determine the dollar markup of your revised open-to-buy:

$$\$MU \text{ of rev. O.T.B.} = \$R \text{ of rev. O.T.B.} - \$C \text{ of rev. O.T.B.}$$
$$= \$38{,}800 - \$19{,}450$$
$$= \$19{,}350$$

(4) Determine the markup percentage of your revised open-to-buy:

$$MU\% \text{ of rev. O.T.B.} = \$MU \text{ of rev. O.T.B.} \div \$R \text{ of rev. O.T.B.}$$
$$= 49.9\%$$

(5) Determine the markup value of your inventory on hand:

$$\$MU \text{ of OH} = \$R \text{ of OH} - \$C \text{ of OH}$$
$$= \$7200 - \$4700$$
$$= \$2500$$

(6) Determine the markup percentage of your inventory on hand:

$$MU\% \text{ of OH} = \$MU \text{ of OH} \div \$R \text{ of OH}$$
$$= \$2500 \div \$7200$$
$$= 34.7\%$$

• *PROBLEM 7-9*

Your department has merchandise on hand amounting to $9000 at cost and $14,000 at retail; the open-to-buy at retail is $39,500 with a desired markup of 46.4 percent. Determine the dollar values at cost and at retail and the needed markup percentage for the revised open-to-buy.

The next step, after your revised open-to-buy has been determined, is to actually begin to buy. As you proceed through the market you will be writing orders with different vendors. See Fig. 7-4, which is a typical vendor's order form upon which you have written an order.

Your attention now should be directed toward determining the cost and retail values for this order and the markup percentage the sale of this merchandise will generate. This information will permit you to calculate a revised open-to-buy and serve as a check against your planned purchases and planned markup percentage.

• *EXAMPLE 7-11*

Using the values in the completed matrix in Example 7-10 and in the matrix shown below, determine the following factors. (Note that the values in boldface are the values given in the problem, whereas derived values are accompanied by a number in parentheses to identify the step in which they were computed.)

(1) Cost and retail dollar values for the order.
(2) Markup percentage for the order.
(3) Cost and retail dollar values for your revised open-to-buy.
(4) Markup percentage for the revised open-to-buy.

Department IM = 47.5%		C	+ MU	= R
O.T.B. 2/1/8_	%		**49.9**	**100.0**
	$	**19,450.00**	**19,350.00**	**38,800.00**
Purchases 2/10/8_	%		(4) 50.5	
	$	(1) 277.50	(3) 283.50	(2) 561.00
Rev. O.T.B. 2/10/8_	%		(8) 49.9	
	$	(5) 19,172.50	(7) 19,066.50	(6) 38,239.00

(1) Compute the total cost value for your purchases by finding the total cost for each style and summing these costs:

$$12 \times \$3.75 = \$\ 45.00$$
$$12 \times \$4.75 = \$\ 57.00$$
$$18 \times \$4.50 = \$\ 81.00$$
$$18 \times \$5.25 = \$\ 94.50$$

$$\text{Total cost} \quad \$277.50$$

(2) Compute the total retail value for your purchases by finding total retail for each style and summing these retails:

Jeans by Christine
1407 Avenue of the Americas
New York, NY 10001
(212) 555-0007

	SOLD TO		SHIP TO
	Pants N Things		Pants N Things
	288 Fulton Avenue		288 Fulton Avenue
	Riverside, New Jersey		Riverside, New Jersey

OUR ORDER NO.	ORDER DATE	DISTRIBUTION TO FOLLOW ☒ / HOLD FOR CONFIRMATION ☐	SHIPPING DATE	TERMS: 1% - ¹⁄₁₀30 DAYS BALANCE 15 DAYS NO ANTICIPATION ALLOWED F.O.B. RULEVILLE, MISS.
GA 3217	8 / 18 / 8-		As Ready, a/o 9/25	

SHIP VIA	SLMN NO.	DEPT NO.	CUSTOMER ORDER NO.	SPECIAL INSTRUCTIONS
Best	37	0940	1622	Ship Colors and Sizes Complete

CUSTOMER ACCT. NO.	SHIP CODE	S.S.D.	C.D.	
85		/ /	/ /	

	OUR STYLE NUMBER	COLOR NO.	COLOR DESC.	6	7	8	10	12	14	TOTAL NO. OF UNITS	UNIT PRICE	•	STORE NO. / Retail	STYLE NUMBER	UNITS
1	1812	2	Blk.	2	4	4	2			12	3.75		$7.50		
2	1814	3	Fad. Blue	2	4	4	2			12	4.75		$10.00		
3	1937	1	White	3	6	6	3			18	4.50		$8.50		
4	1939	4	Red	3	6	6	3			18	5.25		$11.00		
5															
6															
7															
8															
9															
10															
11															
12															
13															
14															
15															
16															
17															
18															
19															
20															
21															
22															
23															

ALL RETURNS REFUSED WITHOUT PRIOR WRITTEN CONSENT

TOTAL UNITS	TOTAL AMOUNT		TOTAL UNITS	TOTAL AMOUNT

BUYER _____

ORIGINAL

Figure 7-4

$$12 \times \$ \ 7.50 = \$ \ 90.00$$
$$12 \times \$10.00 = \$120.00$$
$$18 \times \$ \ 8.50 = \$153.00$$
$$18 \times \$11.00 = \$198.00$$

Total retail $561.00

(3) Determine the dollar markup for this order:

$$\$MU = \$R - \$C$$
$$= \$561.00 - \$277.50$$
$$= \$283.50$$

(4) Determine the markup percentage for this order:

$$MU\% = \$MU \div \$R$$
$$= \$283.50 \div \$561.00$$
$$= 50.5\%$$

(5) Determine the revised O.T.B. dollar cost:

$$\text{Rev. O.T.B. } \$C = \$C \text{ O.T.B. } 2/1/8\_\_ - \$C \text{ purchases}$$
$$= \$19,450.00 - \$277.50$$
$$= \$19,172.50$$

(6) Determine the revised open-to-buy retail values:

$$\text{Rev. O.T.B. } \$R = \$R \text{ O.T.B. } 2/1/8\_\_ - \$R \text{ purchases}$$
$$= \$38,800 - \$561$$
$$= \$38,239$$

(7) Determine the revised open-to-buy dollar markup:

$$\text{Rev. O.T.B. } \$MU = \text{Rev. O.T.B. } \$R - \text{Rev. O.T.B. } \$C$$
$$= \$38,239.00 - \$19,172.50$$
$$= \$19,066.50$$

(8) Determine the revised open-to-buy markup percentage:

$$\text{Rev. O.T.B. } MU\% = \text{Rev. O.T.B. } \$MU \div \text{Rev. O.T.B. } \$R$$
$$= \$19,066.50 \div \$38,239.00$$
$$= 49.9\%$$

You will notice that although you were able to obtain a markup of 50.5 percent on this order it had no perceptible influence on the overall markup percentage you had to obtain as of February 1, 198__. This is because of the small dollar amount of your order relative to the total open-to-buy.

Your next purchases must be able to generate a markup of 49.9 percent to bring your total markup percentage in line with the overall need of 47.5 percent. Remember that you are behind in markup percentage because you carried over merchandise with a markup of 34.7 percent (see Example 7-10). To illustrate, it is more difficult to buy merchandise for $5 and sell it for $12 (58.3% markup) than it is to buy merchandise for $5 and sell it for $8 (37.5% markup).

• *PROBLEM 7-10*

The revised open-to-buy for your department on September 1, 198___, is presented in the table below. You have purchased merchandise as indicated by the purchase order in Fig. 7-5. Calculate the revised open-to-buy as of September 9, 198___. Construct a matrix to show your final answers.

Department IM = 48.7%		C	+ MU	= R
Rev. O.T.B. 9/1/8_	%		49.9	
	$	41,300	41,190	82,490

While it is always necessary to obtain the cumulative totals for cost and retail dollars and the cumulative markup percentage for each order as a check against your overall goals, it is seldom necessary to compute a revised open-to-buy after writing a single order. If the order is so large, in dollars, however, that you believe it will have a noticeable effect on the remaining open-to-buy, you should calculate a revised open-to-buy. The usual practice for revising your purchases is to determine the cumulative totals of cost and retail dollars for several orders (perhaps the orders you wrote on a particular day) and then amend your open-to-buy.

• *EXAMPLE 7-12*

Using the revised open-to-buy as of February 10, 198___, in Example 7-11 and the following data, determine the revised O.T.B. dollars at cost and at retail and the markup percentage as of February 15, 198___. (Note that the values in boldface are the values given in the problem, whereas derived values are accompanied by a number in parentheses to identify the step in which they were computed.)

PURCHASES FROM:	COST	RETAIL
Vendor A	$3620	$8297
Vendor B	$2389	$4586
Vendor C	$3964	$8004

Department IM = 47.5%		C	+ MU	= R
O.T.B. 2/10/8_	%		**49.9**	**100.0**
	$	**19,172.50**	**19,066.50**	**38,239.00**
Purchases 2/25/8_	%			
	$	(1) 9973.00		(1) 20,887.00
Rev. O.T.B. 2/25/8_	%		(5) 47.0	
	$	(2) 9199.50	(4) 8152.50	(3) 17,352.00

(1) Determine the total dollar value at cost and at retail for the three orders placed through February 25, 198___:

Jeans by Christine
1407 Avenue of the Americas
New York, NY 10001
(212) 555-0007

SOLD TO	SHIP TO
Pants N Things	Pants N Things
288 Fulton Avenue	288 Fulton Avenue
Riverside, New Jersey	Riverside, New Jersey

OUR ORDER NO.	ORDER DATE	DISTRIBUTION TO FOLLOW ☒ HOLD FOR CONFIRMATION ☐	SHIPPING DATE	TERMS: 1% - 1/30 DAYS BALANCE 15 DAYS NO ANTICIPATION ALLOWED F.O.B. RULEVILLE, MISS.
GA 3218	7 / 14 / 8-		As Ready, a/o 8/25	

SHIP VIA	SLMN NO.	DEPT NO.	CUSTOMER ORDER NO.	SPECIAL INSTRUCTIONS
BEST	37	0940	1613	Ship Colors and Sizes Complete

CUSTOMER ACCT. NO.	SHIP CODE	S.S.D.	C.D.
85		/ /	/ /

	OUR STYLE NUMBER	COLOR NO.	COLOR DESC.	6	8	10	12	14	16	TOTAL NO. OF UNITS	UNIT PRICE	•	STORE NO.	STYLE NUMBER	UNITS
1	1014	2	Blk.	3	6	6	3			18	10.75		$19.00		
2		4	Red	3	6	6	3			18					
3	1183	3N	Navy	3	6	6	3			18	11.75		$23.00		
4		1	White	2	4	4	2			12					
5		3	Fad. Blue	2	4	4	2			12					
6	1247	1	White	3	6	6	3			18	12.75		$26.00		
7		3N	Navy	3	6	6	3			18					
8		3	Fad. Blue	2	4	4	2			12					
9															
10															
11															
12															
13															
14															
15															
16															
17															
18															
19															
20															
21															
22															
23															

ALL RETURNS REFUSED WITHOUT PRIOR WRITTEN CONSENT

TOTAL UNITS	TOTAL AMOUNT	TOTAL UNITS	TOTAL AMOUNT

BUYER _____

ORIGINAL

Figure 7-5

VENDOR	COST	RETAIL
A	$3620	$ 8297
B	$2389	$ 4586
C	$3964	$ 8004
	$9973	$20,887

(2) Determine the revised O.T.B. dollar cost:

$$\begin{aligned}
\text{Rev. O.T.B. \$C} &= \text{O.T.B. \$C} - \text{Purchases \$C} \\
&= \$19{,}172.50 - \$9973.00 \\
&= \$9199.50
\end{aligned}$$

(3) Determine the revised O.T.B. dollar retail:

$$\begin{aligned}
\text{Rev. O.T.B. \$R} &= \text{O.T.B. \$R} - \text{Purchases \$R} \\
&= \$38{,}239 - \$20{,}887 \\
&= \$17{,}352
\end{aligned}$$

(4) Determine the revised O.T.B. dollar markup:

$$\begin{aligned}
\text{Rev. O.T.B. \$MU} &= \text{Rev. O.T.B. \$R} - \text{Rev. O.T.B. \$C} \\
&= \$17{,}352.00 - \$9199.50 \\
&= \$8152.50
\end{aligned}$$

(5) Determine the revised O.T.B. markup percentage:

$$\begin{aligned}
\text{Rev. O.T.B. MU\%} &= \text{Rev. O.T.B. \$MU} \div \text{Rev. O.T.B. \$R} \\
&= \$8152.50 \div \$17{,}352.00 \\
&= 47.0\%
\end{aligned}$$

You can see now that your recent purchases have had an impact on aligning the markup percentage of your merchandise with the desired markup. The balance of your buying must still bring in a high markup if you hope to meet your plan, however.

• *PROBLEM 7-11*

Given the following data, determine your revised open-to-buy at cost and at retail and the needed markup percentage on the balance of your purchases:

Open-to-buy as of May 12, 198___, was $16,432 at cost and $34,983 at retail; purchases were made on May 23 from vendor X amounting to $3693 at cost and $7146 at retail and from vendor Y amounting to $5921 at cost and $12,004 at retail.

SUMMARY PROBLEMS

• *PROBLEM 7-1 (S)*

Compute your initial markup percentage from the following data for situations A, B, and C:

	SITUATION A	SITUATION B	SITUATION C
Annual rent	$ 37,000	8.5%	$ 18,000
Cash discounts	11,000	6.0	7.0%
Customer discounts	3200	1.5	1.0%
Employee discounts	8900	2.75	1.5%
Markdowns	40,000	12.0	$ 4000
Miscellaneous expenses	8000	2.0	2.0%
Payroll	90,000	30.5	24.0%
Profit	45,000	12.0	10.0%
Sales	450,000	100.0	$200,000
Stock shortages	20,000	2.6	3.2%
Utilities	19,000	4.5	$ 9500
IM%			

- PROBLEM 7-2 (S)

Calculate the missing data:

	C %	C $	MU %	MU $	R $
A			48.6	8.00	
B		6.25			18.50
C	45.4				24.95
D				37.50	80.00

- PROBLEM 7-3 (S)

Your open-to-buy in the $45.00 price line of sweaters is $12,000.00 at cost, with an initial markup of 52.4 percent. You have already purchased 22 dozen sweaters that cost $22.50 each. Determine the average cost for each additional sweater.

- PROBLEM 7-4 (S)

You have located several new lamp resources and have decided to buy a lamp for $28.75 from one of these vendors. The IM in your department is 62.4% and your price lines are at $70.00 and $80.00. Determine

(1) The retail price to meet your IM.

(2) The markup percentage you would obtain if these lamps were included in either price line.

- PROBLEM 7-5 (S)

An applicance vendor has offered you two styles of hair dryers at a closeout price of $9. One style will fit into your $21 price line, and you plan to buy four dozen of them. If you purchase six dozen of the other style, what price (rounded to the nearest dollar) will generate an average markup of 51.7 percent for the entire order?

- PROBLEM 7-6 (S)

The open-to-buy for your $18.00 children's dress line is 90 units. You have purchased 33 pieces that cost $9.75 each. If your initial markup percentage is 48.9 percent, determine your new open-to-buy at cost and at retail and the markup percentage.

- • *PROBLEM 7-7 (S)*

Your dollar open-to-buy at the beginning of the season is $37,500. Determine the dollar value at cost and the dollar markup with an initial markup of 52.4 percent.

- • *PROBLEM 7-8 (S)*

You have just been moved to the Housewares Department, and in preparation for your first buying trip you have had your stock inventoried. You find merchandise on hand with a retail value of $26,000 that cost $14,500. The open-to-buy for the season is $47,900, with a desired initial markup of 54.8 percent. Calculate the dollar amounts at cost and retail for your purchases and the markup percentage you will need.

- • *PROBLEM 7-9 (S)*

The open-to-buy for the Handbag Department on July 10 was $19,840 at cost and $49,630 at retail. The department's initial markup was 60.4 percent. Purchases for the week totaled $13,567 at cost and $33,984 at retail. Calculate the revised open-to-buy, dollar amounts at cost and at retail, and the needed markup percentage for the balance of the purchases.

- • *PROBLEM 7-10 (S)*

The original open-to-buy for your department was $39,632 at cost and $85,491 at retail. Your initial markup for these purchases was 53.6 percent. You have ordered merchandise as follows:

	COST	RETAIL
Vendor A	$2497	$ 4972
Vendor B	$4924	$10,619
Vendor C	$7693	$14,211

Determine the revised O.T.B. dollars at cost and at retail and the markup percentage needed.

CASE STUDY_____

PLASTICS UNLIMITED

This was a problem you saw coming, and now it is time to address it. When you opened Plastics Unlimited as a gift shop three years ago, you pretty much had the customers to yourself. Although you were on the main business street, your nearest competitor, Nifty Gifties, was four blocks away. That store carried less-expensive merchandise (some of which was discounted) with many items in each category and little depth in stock. Nifty Gifties had merchandise constructed from a variety of materials. In your estimation, you had developed a definite image, but your competitor had not.

Even though you felt you were unique, you had priced your merchandise at the market (keystone markup). To assess your position better, you had assembled the following essential information about your business:

	1ST YEAR	2ND YEAR	3RD YEAR
Sales	$140,000	$160,000	$185,000
Fixed expenses	8000	9000	11,000
Variable expenses	28,000	33,000	40,000
Markdowns	8500	10,400	12,600
Profit	21,000	23,000	26,000

You also reviewed your merchandise classifications and listed the categories: lamps, tables, picture frames, mirrors, dining accessories, napkin rings, serving implements, serving dishes, trays, and so on.

The problem, as you see it, is that the empty store across the street will soon be occupied by a competitor carrying the same price lines and some similar merchandise. Your sources for this information are several vendors whom you consider reputable and reliable.

This news is disconcerting to you and also to two of your recently hired salespeople.

What do you do?

CASE STUDY

CARROT TOP SHOE BOUTIQUE

You have been successfully operating a shoe boutique for several years, with a nice profit each year as a result of your ability to make advantageous purchases on job lots and manufacturers' closeouts.

One of your sales representatives came in this morning and offered you a closeout on one hundred pairs of shoes, separated into two assortments. Assortment one contains 60 pairs at a cost of $24.90 each; assortment two consists of 40 pairs at a cost of $32.90 each. The shoes in assortment one will fit nicely into your $60.00 price line; those in assortment two could fit into your $70.00 price line; however, you must first determine what the average retail price would be for this lot to assure your attaining a 53.9% IM.

If the 40 pairs in assortment two can be priced at $70.00, you will consider purchasing this closeout if, after you've revised your O.T.B., the total purchase is advantageous and you will not be overspent. Your current O.T.B. position shows that you can spend $6500.00 at cost and generate a retail of $13,500.00.

You will have to determine the following:

1. Average dollar retail per pair of shoes for assortment two.
2. Total markup percentage for the purchase if the shoes in assortment two are priced at $70.00.
3. Revised dollar cost and retail and markup percentage of your O.T.B. if you decide to purchase this closeout.

Repricing

8

Changing the price of merchandise from an original retail price to a new selling price is an ongoing and critical function you will perform as a buyer. These adjustments may either increase or decrease the retail price of your goods. The most common change is the downward alteration known as a **markdown**. If you reverse a markdown, that is, return the goods to its original or premarkdown price, this is known as a **markdown cancellation**.

It is also likely that you will encounter other forms of price changes which will either increase or decrease the retail price that was first listed. These revisions may occur as the result of clerical or marking errors, or due to changes by your vendors in the cost of the goods.

MARKDOWNS

Price reductions should not be viewed as if they were a plague. You should remember that you planned for reductions when your initial markup was computed, and they are expected much as the rent expense is expected. However, markdowns should not be considered as an unlimited cure for all forms of merchandise mismanagement. If you use them beyond their projected level, you will effectively reduce your profit margin, very possibly eliminating it completely. Conversely, if markdowns can be decreased, the extra dollars will increase your profit or offset excessive expenses.

Reasons why.   As markdowns are part of your repricing strategy, it is important that you recognize the circumstances that account for them. Prime among the causes of price reductions is customer rejection of the merchandise. This may happen for a variety of reasons:

1. Price—Obviously, if customers do not see adequate value in the merchandise, they will not purchase it; if your price is higher than your core competitor's, the inventory will not move; and conversely, if your price is too low, the merchandise may be suspect and not sell.
2. Merchandise—Customers may find fault with the style, size, or color assortment available (this is typical at the end of a season); the quality of the merchandise may discourage purchasing; and the timing of the merchandise presentation, if it is either too early or too late, will also lead to shopper rejection.

From your viewpoint, you know goods will be left over because of broken sizes and colors and as shopworn merchandise. You may also have overbought, purchased merchandise not to your core customers' liking, bought goods at a "special price" which you expected to generate extra markup, or you may have been caught in the **fashion cycle** with a **fad** item that "died," leaving you with merchandise you are unable to sell at cost. Any or all of the foregoing factors will lead you and your customers to expect a sale, whether it is on specific items, on classifications of merchandise, or as a department or store-wide promotion.

Benefits of markdowns.   Generally speaking, a well-conceived sale is a highly beneficial event for the following reasons:

1. It provides a stimulus for your business during what might be a slack period. This extra volume helps to offset your expenses and keeps your sales force occupied and useful.
2. A sale will help you to clear the slow-moving stock and at the same time give exposure to newer merchandise that is not being sold at reduced prices.
3. Your customers will recognize and appreciate that you are interested in giving them the opportunity to make advantageous purchases.
4. Finally, the vendors from whom you normally buy are essentially in a situation similar to yours with regard to overstocks and poor assortments of styles, colors, and sizes. They need you to help them clear their stock. In the same way that you give your customers a price reduction, the manufacturers will offer you their inventory at discounted prices.

Markdown computation.   The computational work that has to be done for markdowns is relatively simple, but it must be done accurately to insure that the value of your inventory is correct, as well as to keep you informed of your total markdown position.

Physically changing ticket prices should be done prior to the promotion via new price tags, placing a gummed label with the marked-down price on the ticket, crossing out the original price and writing in the sale price, and so on. Remember that the reduced price should be clearly visible to your customers and cashiers, in a form that cannot be altered. An accurate count must be taken, at this time, of how many units are being reduced and from and to what prices. Performing this task before the sale begins is far more accurate than attempting to record markdowns at the cash desk.

• *EXAMPLE 8-1*

An assistant buyer's sale is scheduled for the end of the week. For this event you have planned to reduce a group of 350 bath towels from $10.00 to $6.79, and 600 hand towels from $6.00 to $3.79. Determine the dollar value of the markdowns.

(1) Determine the unit dollar markdown for each item:

$$\text{Unit } \$MD = \text{Original price} - \text{Markdown price}$$

For the bath towels:

$$= \$10.00 - \$6.79$$
$$= \$3.21$$

For the hand towels:

$$= \$6.00 - \$3.79$$
$$= \$2.21$$

(2) Determine the total dollar markdown for each item:

$$\text{Total unit } \$MD = \text{Unit } \$MD \times \text{Numbers of units}$$

For the bath towels:

$$= \$3.21 \times 350$$
$$= \$1123.50$$

For the hand towels:

$$= \$2.21 \times 600$$
$$= \$1326.00$$

(3) Determine the total dollar markdown:

$$\text{Total } \$MD = \$MD \text{ for bath towels} + \$MD \text{ for hand towels}$$
$$= \$1123.50 + \$1326.00$$
$$= \$2449.50$$

• *PROBLEM 8-1*

For the annual "light-up" sale, all table lamps in your department are to be reduced according to the following schedule:

REGULAR PRICE	SALE PRICE
$50.00	$33.35
35.00	23.35
28.00	18.68

Your inventory consists of 130 lamps at $50, 370 lamps at $35, and 243 lamps at $28. Determine the total dollar markdown you have to take in anticipation of this sale.

You have undoubtedly seen sales promoted as illustrated in the preceding problem with a regular, or original, price and a sale price. It is also a common practice to promote merchandise with a percentage discounted from the regular price.

• *EXAMPLE 8-2*

Selected china place settings are to be promoted this weekend at one third off the regular price. Determine the total markdown for 18 settings with an original price of $114 and 37 settings priced at $163.

(1) Unit $MD = Regular price $\times$ MD%
For the $114.00 settings:

$$= \$114.00 \times 1/3$$
$$= \$37.96$$

For the $163.00 settings:

$$= \$163.00 \times 1/3$$
$$= \$54.28$$

(2) Determine the total dollar markdown for each item:

$$\text{Total unit } \$MD = \text{Unit } \$MD \times \text{Numbers of units}$$

For the $114.00 settings:

$$= \$37.96 \times 18$$
$$= \$683.28$$

For the $163.00 settings:

$$= \$54.28 \times 37$$
$$= \$2008.36$$

(3) Determine the total dollar markdown:

$$\text{Total } \$MD = \$MD \text{ for } \$114.00 \text{ settings} + \$MD \text{ for } \$163.00 \text{ settings}$$
$$= \$683.28 + \$2008.36$$
$$= \$2691.64$$

• *PROBLEM 8-2*

Some small electric appliances in your department are being promoted at 40 percent off their original price. Your inventory for the sale is as follows:

QUANTITY	ORIGINAL PRICE
118	$34
63	42
24	50

Determine the total dollar markdown you will have to record before this sale.

As is typical with high-fashion merchandise, you will probably decide to begin to close out your inventory with a drastic price reduction and follow this markdown with others. The number of markdowns you take will vary with the amount of goods, the season, your competitors, and your customers' expectations. However you decide to run your sales, each time you reduce your prices you must perform new calculations.

• *EXAMPLE 8-3*

The promotions you have planned for the swimsuits in your department require the following reductions on the $60.00 price line:

• First reduction, $60.00 to $34.99
• Second reduction, $34.99 to $17.99
• Third reduction, $17.99 to $5.00
• All leftovers given to charity

At the time of the first reduction you had 114 garments; for the second 61 remained; for the third there were 22 swimsuits; and 4 pieces were left to be given to charity. Determine the total markdown.

(1) Determine the unit dollar markdown for the first reduction:

$$\text{Unit } \$MD = \text{Original price} - \text{MD price}$$
$$= \$60.00 - \$34.99$$
$$= \$25.01$$

(2) Determine the total unit dollar markdown for the first reduction:

$$\text{Total units } \$MD = \text{Unit } \$MD \times \text{Number of units}$$
$$= \$25.01 \times 114$$
$$= \$2851.14$$

Repeat steps 1 and 2 for each reduction, as follows:

$$\text{Unit } \$MD = \$34.99 - 17.99$$
$$= \$17.00$$
$$\text{Total unit } \$MD = \$17.00 \times 61$$
$$= \$1037.00$$
$$\text{Unit } \$MD = \$17.99 - \$5.00$$
$$= \$12.99$$
$$\text{Total unit } \$MD = \$12.99 \times 22$$
$$= \$285.78$$
$$\text{Unit } \$MD = \$5.00 - \$0$$
$$= \$5.00$$
$$\text{Total unit } \$MD = \$5.00 \times 4$$
$$= \$20.00$$

(3) Determine total dollar markdown:

$$\text{Total } \$MD = \text{Sum of total unit } \$MDs$$
$$= \$2851.14 + \$1037.00 + \$285.78 + 20.00$$
$$= \$4193.92$$

It should be evident from the above illustration that markdowns must be planned for, in the sense that they should not be unexpected. Thus they can be beneficial, and if you have been able to "buy into your markdowns," you will fare better than buyers who have not anticipated reductions.

• *PROBLEM 8-3*

The planned schedule of markdowns for winter coats is as follows for the $250.00 price line:

December 10	$250.00	to	$149.95
January 2	149.95	to	119.95
January 25	119.95	to	99.00

If your stock was 193 coats on December 10, 87 coats on January 2, and 33 coats on January 25, with the balance being carried over at $99, what will be your total markdown?

Buying for markdowns (**"Buying into your Markdowns"**).   You should never be without some open-to-buy. This is particularly true if you are a promotional retailer or if you are aware of special upcoming sales events, for there are generally many opportunities to purchase goods off price from your vendors. This merchandise often arrives early enough before the special sale to be placed in stock at regular prices, thereby generating considerable extra profit by the additional markup. To illustrate:

• *EXAMPLE 8-4*

You have purchased merchandise from a vendor who has now put its line on sale. One of the styles that did well in your store is A402, which cost $24.75 for each item and retailed at $50.00. The vendor is now willing to sell this item for 40 percent off the original cost. You would be able to have this merchandise in stock for about two weeks before your own promotion. What dollar and percentage markup could you obtain now, and what would they be if you bought this offering? (Note that the values in boldface are the values given in the problem; whereas derived values are accompanied by a number in parentheses to identify the step in which they were computed.)

		C	+ MU	= R
Original	%		(2) 50.5	**100.0**
	$	**24.75**	(1) 25.25	**50.00**
New	%		(5) 70.3	**100.0**
	$	(3) 14.85	(4) 35.15	**50.00**

(1) Determine the original dollar markup:

$$\$MU = \$R - \$C$$
$$= \$50.00 - \$24.75$$
$$= \$25.25$$

(2) Determine the original markup percentage:

$$MU\% = \$MU \div \$R$$
$$= \$25.25 \div \$50.00$$
$$= 50.5\%$$

(3) Determine the new cost price:

$$\text{New cost price} = \text{Old cost price} \times (100.0\% - \text{Discount}\%)$$
$$= \$24.75 \times (100.0\% - 40.0\%)$$
$$= \$14.85$$

(4) Determine the new dollar markup:

$$\$MU = \$R - \$C$$
$$= \$50.00 - \$14.85$$
$$= \$35.15$$

(5) Determine the new markup percentage:

$$MU\% = \$MU \div \$R$$
$$= \$35.15 \div \$50.00$$
$$= 70.3\%$$

It is clear that money can be made with this item if you buy and sell it in advance of your sale. This practice is known as "buying into your markdown," because you buy merchandise for promotional purposes and sell it with an extra markup before ultimately reducing the price. It should also be apparent that you must have a "need" for this type of goods, and this determination requires careful planning.

• *PROBLEM 8-4*

Determine the old and new dollar markups and the old and new markup percentages for a swimsuit that originally cost $14.25 with a retail price of $30.00 that can now be purchased from the manufacturer at 39 percent off the original cost.

In other instances, you may be able to gain the cooperation of vendors to support your special sales by negotiating with them for markdown money, that is, asking them if they can give you either a dollar or a percentage discount on purchases you have already made and received. Although this discussion is occasionally held at the time of the original purchase, it can also be accomplished in conjunction with off-price buying or as an issue by itself.

The reasons you would ask for markdown money range from needing markdown dollars to offset buying errors on your part; to requiring monetary assistance due to circumstances beyond anyone's control, such as weather; to your having received assurances from the vendor that "your best interests are our best interests."

Timing your markdowns.   When do you reduce your merchandise? If you do it too soon you will take unnecessary markdowns without the desired positive effects, whereas if you do it too late you will be an "also ran."

First consider the individual item that looks like a good candidate for a markdown. If it has not been selling, or not selling as well as comparable merchandise, you should do some fast investigating. Ask yourself and everyone else concerned if it has been displayed, advertised, coordinated, and priced properly. Does the fault lie with what you bought? Do your competitors have this item, and if so, what is their price and how have they displayed and advertised it, and so forth? Has it been "sold" correctly? Have you adequately assisted the sales associates with product knowledge?

After you have satisfied yourself that the item has been handled properly and that you have done everything that you can do, mark it down at once. Above all, remember that the first markdown should be the best markdown. Reduce the price sufficiently to clear it out of your inventory quickly. Sale-priced merchandise tends to become shopworn rapidly, and the longer you have it the worse it looks, thus the more it has to be subsequently reduced to sell.

Now think about the regular promotions held in your store: the seasonal sales, anniversary promotions, buyers' days, and so on. These events have very definite beginning and ending dates, advertising and other kinds of sales promotion have been arranged, your sales staff has been appropriately educated, and the size of the staff planned for. Your responsibility here is to make sure that your goods are on hand, priced correctly to sell, and displayed to their best advantage.

The last illustration to consider for promotional timing is a situation in which weather, political events, or circumstances beyond your control have conspired against you and your inventory. Again, take your markdowns quickly. If you are a rainwear buyer and there has been no rain, develop a rain promotion; invest in advertising and move your inventory out.

Filene's Automatic Bargain Basement, which originated in Boston, has solved the problem of both "when" and "how much" by establishing a fixed schedule: a 25-percent reduction after 14 days; a 50-percent reduction after 21 days; a 75-percent reduction after 28 days; and after 35 days, the remaining items are given to charity. The success of Filene's Automatic Bargain Basement is almost legendary. Many stores have attempted to emulate the system; some have been very successful, and others have not fared so well.

For most buyers, there are no hard-and-fast principles governing the size of a markdown because there are many factors to consider. You have to consider the nature of the merchandise (fashion or staple), the original price, seasonal influences, competition, the traditional record of the merchandise (such as white sales), and other store promotions, to mention only a few.

It will be your judgment as to the size of the markdown, and the deciding factors will change in relative importance from season to season. More than one buyer has memorized the following adages: "The first bath is the cleanest" and "Only wine improves with age."

MARKDOWN CANCELLATIONS AND NET MARKDOWNS

Markdown cancellations are revocations of markdowns previously taken. Just as a markdown devalues your stock, a markdown cancellation causes an increase in the worth of your inventory. These cancellations generally occur after a special promotion in which merchandise has been reduced in price for the particular event. Computation of a markdown cancellation is very much like that of a markdown and similarly is completed immediately after the sale concludes.

- EXAMPLE 8-5

Your weekend sale on selected china place settings is concluded (see Example 8-2). Remaining in your stock are five of the $114 settings and nine of the $163 settings. Determine the markdown cancellation for this merchandise if all of it is returned to its original price.

(1) Determine the total unit markdown cancellation (using the previously determined unit dollar markdown values):

$$\text{Total unit \$MD cancellation} = \text{Unit \$MD} \times \text{Numbers of units remaining}$$

For the $114 settings:

$$= \$37.96 \times 5$$
$$= \$189.80$$

For the $163 settings:

$$= \$54.28 \times 9$$
$$= \$488.52$$

(2) Determine the total dollar markdown cancellation:

$$\text{Total \$MD cancellation} = \text{\$MD cancellation for \$114 settings}$$
$$+ \text{\$MD cancellation for \$163 settings}$$
$$= \$189.80 + \$488.52$$
$$= \$678.32$$

At this point you can compute the net dollar markdowns that have accumulated for this promotion by subtracting from the total dollar markdown (computed in Example 8-3) the total dollar markdown cancellation (determined above):

$$\text{Net \$MD} = \text{Total \$MD} - \text{Total \$MD cancellation}$$
$$= \$2691.64 - \$678.32$$
$$= \$2013.32$$

- PROBLEM 8-5

Your Sporting Goods Department has just completed a special sale on tennis rackets. Before the sale began your sales staff marked down 38 rackets from $80.00 to $49.50, 42 rackets from $70.00 to $42.50, and 26 rackets from $60.00 to $34.50. You checked your stock and found that you have remaining 9 of the $80.00 rackets, 13 of the $70.00 rackets, and 4 of the $60.00 rackets. Determine the net dollar markdown.

Sometimes when a sale is concluded, the merchandise is not returned to its original price, but to a lesser value that is still higher than the sale price. This allows the buyer either to continue to promote the merchandise while still gaining the advantage of a selected event or to close out odds and ends remaining after a sale.

• *EXAMPLE 8-6*

The $95.00 desk sets in your department were specially priced at $49.99 for a one-day sale. The original inventory was 108 units. After the promotion you have 26 sets left of various styles and colors, and you feel that the assortment is not good enough to be salable at the original price, although not so poor as to be continued at the sale price. You then decide to reprice them to $65.00. Determine the net dollar markdown:

(1) Determine the unit dollar markdown:

$$\text{Unit } \$MD = \text{Original price} - \text{Markdown price}$$
$$= \$95.00 - \$49.99$$
$$= \$45.01$$

(2) Determine the total dollar markdown:

$$\text{Total } \$MD = \$MD \times \text{Numbers of units}$$
$$= \$45.01 \times 108$$
$$= \$4861.08$$

(3) Determine the unit dollar markdown cancellation:

$$\$MD \text{ cancellation} = \text{New price} - \text{Sale price}$$
$$= \$65.00 - \$49.99$$
$$= \$15.01$$

(4) Determine the total dollar markdown cancellation:

$$\text{Total } \$MD \text{ cancellation} = \$MD \text{ cancellation} \times \text{Numbers of units}$$
$$= \$15.01 \times 26$$
$$= \$390.26$$

(5) Determine the net dollar markdowns:

$$\text{Net } \$MD = \text{Total } \$MD - \text{Total } \$MD \text{ cancellations}$$
$$= \$4861.08 - \$390.26$$
$$= \$4470.82$$

• *PROBLEM 8-6*

The $80.00 cookware sets in your department are to be promoted this weekend. Your inventory is 137 sets, and the sale price is $49.95. Your plan is to price the sets remaining after the sale at $69.95. Determine what the net dollar markdown will be if you sell 93 sets.

MAINTAINED MARKUP

In Chapter Seven you saw that the computation of the initial markup contained the elements of expense, profit, and reductions. The calculation produced a percentage or dollar figure that, when added to the cost of the merchandise in the beginning, gave you an original retail value for your inventory.

Maintained markup (MM) is the markup dollar or percentage remaining after you subtract the cost of the merchandise sold from the final selling price; where the cost of merchandise is the actual billed cost before cash discounts are deducted (the reason for this will be explained in the next section); and the final or net retail price is the original selling price minus reductions:

$$\text{Maintained markup} = (\text{Original retail} - \text{Reductions}) - \text{Cost of goods sold}$$

The maintained markup is more important to you than the initial markup because it is an accurate reflection of your actual business. The initial markup is based on planned figures and is therefore only hypothetical.

• EXAMPLE 8-7

Given the following data, compute your initial markup percentage, the planned maintained markup percentage, and the actual maintained markup percentage:

	PLANNED	ACTUAL
Operating expenses	$162,000	$163,000
Operating profit	25,000	
Reductions	45,000	48,000
Net sales	340,000	350,000
Cash discount (CD)	9,000	10,000

(1) Calculate the initial markup percentage:

$$\text{IM\%} = \frac{\text{Expenses} + \text{Profit} + \text{Reductions} - \text{Cash discount}}{\text{Net sales} + \text{Reductions}}$$

$$= \frac{\$162,000 + \$25,000 + \$45,000 - \$9000}{\$340,000 + \$45,000}$$

$$= 57.9\%$$

(2) Set up the markup matrix and find cost percentage, cost dollars, and markup dollars:

	C	+ MU	= R
%	(a) 42.1	57.9	100.0
$	(b) 162,085	(c) 222,915	385,000*

(a) C% = R% − Mu%
   = 100.0% − 57.9%
   = 42.1%

(b) $C = $R × C%
   = $385,000 × .421
   = $162,085

*The retail value used is Net sales + Reductions = Original retail (as indicated in Chapter Seven), to accommodate merchandise purchased to cover markdowns, employee discounts, customer discounts and stock shortages.

(c) $MU = $R - $C
$$= \$385{,}000 - \$162{,}085$$
$$= \$222{,}915$$

(3) Calculate the planned maintained markup dollars:

$$MM = (\$R - \$Reductions) - \$Cost\ of\ goods$$
$$= (\$385{,}000 - \$45{,}000) - \$162{,}085$$
$$= \$177{,}915$$

(4) Calculate the planned maintained markup percentage:

$$MM\% = \$MM \div \$Net\ retail$$
$$= \$177{,}915 \div \$340{,}000$$
$$= 52.3\%$$

(5) Calculate the actual cost of goods sold dollars:

$$\$C = \$R \times C\%$$
$$= (\$350{,}000 + \$48{,}000) \times .421$$
$$= \$167{,}558$$

(6) Calculate the actual maintained markup dollars:

$$MM = (\$R - \$Reductions) - \$Cost\ of\ goods$$
$$= (\$398{,}000 - \$48{,}000) - \$167{,}558$$
$$= \$182{,}442$$

(7) Calculate the actual maintained markup percentage:

$$MM\% = \$MM \div \$Net\ retail$$
$$= \$182{,}442 \div \$350{,}000$$
$$= 52.1\%$$

GROSS MARGIN

The next step is to calculate **gross margin (GM)**, which as a dollar or percentage figure should include a sum adequate to cover your operating expenses and operating profit. If cash discounts have not been taken or are not available, the gross margin is then equal to the maintained markup. This is usually not the case if cash discounts do exist, for then they are added to the maintained markup. That is

*Gross margin = Maintained markup + Cash discounts

*As indicated in Chapter Seven, alteration expense is no longer clearly defined as a separate item. If alteration expenses do exist, however, and they are not passed on to the customer directly, the formula for gross margin would be GM = Maintained markup + Cash discounts − Alteration expense.

The reasons why cash discounts are held as a value to be used now, rather than as means to reduce the cost of merchandise, vary. Some retailers are late in paying invoices and lose the discount. Others receive different discounts from different vendors, and some prefer to "save" this amount for the computation of the gross margin to use as a cushion against excessive reductions and larger-than-anticipated operating expenses.

Compute the dollar gross margin from the data in Example 8-7

$$
\begin{aligned}
GM &= MM + CD \\
&= \$182,442 + \$10,000 \\
&= \$192,442
\end{aligned}
$$

OPERATING PROFIT

Your **operating profit (OP)** can now be found by subtracting operating expenses (OE) from gross margin:

$$
\begin{aligned}
OP &= GM - OE \\
&= \$192,442 - \$163,000 \\
&= \$29,442
\end{aligned}
$$

You can now compare your planned operating profit with your actual operating profit. Clearly, you have done better than you anticipated, even though your expenses and reductions were over the planned amount, because your net sales and cash discounts increased sufficiently.

The operating profit is so labeled because it represents only the profit obtained after expenses directly associated with the department are deducted. Certain general expenses, such as executive salaries and warehouse costs, will reduce profit. Expenses such as these may be apportioned to individual departments according to some formula developed by top management; they could be allocated, as an example, in proportion to the floor space your department occupies relative to the total store. In a boutique where department operating profits are not calculated, all of these general expenses would be included under operating expenses.

The last element to be deducted from operating profit is taxes. This computation will produce net profit.

• *PROBLEM 8-7*

From the following information, determine your initial markup percentage, planned and actual maintained markup percentage, dollar gross margin, and dollar operating profit:

	PLANNED	ACTUAL
Expenses	$187,000	$194,000
Operating profit	30,000	————
Reductions	47,000	44,000
Sales	380,000	380,000
Cash discount	8,000	7,500

SUMMARY PROBLEMS

• *PROBLEM 8-1 (S)*

A manufacturer offers you two styles of handbags (that you previously had in your stock) at a 35-percent reduction from your original cost: Style 1816 was $18.50 at cost and $40.00 at retail, whereas style 2267 was $22.50 at cost and $50.00 at retail.

You buy 10 dozen of style 1816 and 5 dozen of 2267, estimating that 25 percent of this purchase will be sold at the original price before you put the balance on sale. Calculate:

1. The original markup percentage for each style.
2. The markup percentage for each style at the reduced price.
3. The total *extra* dollar markup you will have on both styles if your estimate of sales is correct.

• *PROBLEM 8-2 (S)*

In preparation for the "Run-for-Your-Money" sale, all the jogging suits in your department are to be reduced as follows:

QUANTITY	ORIGINAL RETAIL	SALE PRICE
117	$48.00	$35.99
86	60.00	41.99
31	70.00	44.99

Determine the total dollar markdown you will take in anticipation of this promotion.

• *PROBLEM 8-3 (S)*

As a final clearance in the Men's Winter Outerwear Department, you have decided to reduce all merchandise and advertise that all stock will be reduced by 60 percent. The inventory and price structure is as follows:

QUANTITY	ORIGINAL PRICE
42	$160
57	190
28	225

Determine the total dollar markdown you will record before the sale.

• PROBLEM 8-4 (S)

In preparation for the sale on men's sport shirts in your department, the following is a schedule of markdowns; a decision has been made to donate any balance remaining on September 10 to charity. Determine the total markdown.

DATE	ORIGINAL PRICES	SALE PRICES
July 25	$20.00 and $24.00	$15.79
	$26.00, $28.00, and $30.00	19.79
August 10	$15.79	$10.79
	$19.79	15.79
August 25	$10.79	$ 8.79
	$15.79	12.79

Your inventory for each date:

DATE	PRICE	QUANTITY
July 25	$20.00	147
	24.00	183
	26.00	176
	28.00	133
	30.00	67
August 10	$15.79	237
	19.79	78
August 25	$10.79	112
	15.79	37
September 10	$10.79	16
	15.79	0

• PROBLEM 8-5 (S)

For the annual "Cook-In" sale, you decided to mark down three groups of pots and pans as follows:

QUANTITY	ORIGINAL PRICE	MARKDOWN PRICE
37	$55.00	$34.50
61	78.00	45.50
23	95.00	62.50

At the conclusion of the promotion your inventory was 16 at $34.50, 22 at $45.50, and 4 at $62.50. These sets are to be returned to their original price. Calculate the net dollar markdown.

• *PROBLEM 8-6 (S)*

The two-piece suits in your department were reduced for a weekend sale as follows:

QUANTITY	ORIGINAL PRICE	MARKDOWN PRICE
41	$60.00	$47.89
59	75.00	59.89
34	90.00	69.89

After the sale, you examine the stock and find that the merchandise cannot be returned to the original prices, for they have become shopworn, and in a few cases the sets were separated and the jacket and slacks sizes no longer match.

You have decided to reprice the merchandise which can still be sold as sets according to the following plan:

QUANTITY	MARKDOWN PRICE	NEW PRICE
16	$47.89	$55.00
21	59.89	65.00
6	69.89	75.00

In addition, the sets that were separated will be priced down as follows:

QUANTITY	MARKDOWN PRICE	JACKET PRICE	SLACKS PRICE
4	$47.89	$25.00	$19.00
6	59.89	30.00	25.00
3	69.89	35.00	27.00

Calculate the net dollar markdown if all the merchandise is sold at these prices.

• *PROBLEM 8-7 (S)*

Given the following data, calculate your initial markup percentage, planned and actual maintained markup percentage, dollar gross margin, and dollar operating profit:

	PLANNED	ACTUAL
Expenses	$243,000	$241,000
Operating profit	56,000	_____
Reductions	74,000	89,000
Sales	600,000	627,000
Cash discounts	14,000	16,500

CASE STUDY

WELCOME BACK

It is April 10, and it has been a hectic week. You have just come back from a very successful five-day buying trip, during which you managed to purchase $22,000 of off-price merchandise at cost, which will generate a markup of 68.2 percent before the annual storewide two-for-one clearance sale. You expect to sell almost a third of this stock at the full retail price before the sale. Your estimate is that this inventory should generate a total maintained markup of approximately 47.5 percent, which is just slightly under your initial markup and better than your overall planned maintained markup.

All of this will help you in achieving a healthy operating profit. You are concerned about this since several of your highly styled items have not sold and your markdowns have considerably exceeded the amount planned. Fortunately, you have held back on your open-to-buy and had the money to spend on this specially priced merchandise you just purchased.

As you scan your mail, you see an envelope from the divisional merchandise manager marked "Urgent—Read At Once." The note is dated April 4, and it reads as follows:

Dear _____:

A computer report of your O.T.B. status for this quarter shows a balance of $23,590. Because of excessive expense overruns in the store, I am compelled to reduce this amount to $8,590.

I trust that you will appreciate the urgency of this situation and comply.

Sincerely,

M. L. Markham
Divisional Merchandise Manager

What would you do?

The Merchandise Budget

THE MARKETING CONCEPT AND THE MERCHANDISE BUDGET

The prime objective of retailers is to generate a profit. This is as true for the merchants who operate hospital gift shops staffed by volunteers, in which profits are donated to the institution, as it is for conventional business people. Regardless of the type or size of the store, the pathway to profit is by satisfying the customers' needs and wants.

If you are going to please your clientele in a merchandise sense, you must have an adequate assortment of goods, at an appropriate price, in the correct place, and at the proper time. This is known as the "marketing concept." The key to the marketing concept is the merchandise budget, which will provide you with a plan for your inventory expenditures. This design is not to be considered as ironbound, however. As you undoubtedly know, when dealing with people you are confronted with the vagaries of human nature, and although many facets are predictab.e, there are always levels of uncertainty present. Your thinking in merchandise planning must allow for some flexibility, as conditions can and will change.

Preparation of a merchandise budget is essential, regardless of the size of the retail organization. The dissimilarity between a budget for a large operation and for a small shop (other than dollar amounts) is in the number of people involved in the process; the principles are the same, but the applications are different.

For a store which is owned, operated, and controlled by a single individual, the owner, in consultation with a qualified accountant, should prepare the merchandise budget. In larger organizations, where there are more levels of responsibility, buyers, divisional merchandise managers, vice presidents for merchandising, and controllers are concerned with budget planning. The merchandise budget is, therefore, a strategy for dollar expenditures over a period of time (usually six months) prepared by concerned individuals to produce a profit for the organization (if it is effectively put into action).

CONSTRUCTING THE MERCHANDISE BUDGET

The merchandise budget is composed of several elements, the most important of which is the planned sales figure. Other parts, such as planned reductions and **beginning-of-the-month (B.O.M.) inventories**, are based upon the sales amount. All of these data are later combined to form the buying plan and to determine the open-to-buy.

Sales planning.   The method most commonly accepted by retailers for producing the merchandise budget is **top-down-bottom-up planning**. With this approach, upper-level managers produce master retail sales figures for the total organization and then divide and subdivide the resources for allocation to each buying unit (the top-down component). The bottom-up segment requires that each buying unit produce an estimate of its retail dollar sales. These individual budgets are assembled by groups and then reassembled to form a total organization budget.

There is seldom agreement between the figures generated by top-down and bottom-up projections, and it will be necessary to negotiate the differences. As a rule, the master total figure produced by top management usually remains firm, as this group is in the best position to view the aggregate environment.

The process then requires that individual buying divisions and departments be scrupulously reviewed to ascertain where "give-and-take" can be practiced. Figure 9-1 provides an overly simplified diagram of the procedure.

The reasons why one division or department is increased or decreased during the initial planning process or in the course of reconciliation are myriad. They could include any or all of the following factors:

1. Changes in the competitive environment
2. Changes in the local, state, and national political scene
3. Changes in the consumers' needs and wants in the market area
4. Any alteration in the economic outlook, which could negatively or positively affect employment figures, the import-export position for the store, and so on
5. Management's view toward changing the philosophy of the store: self-service, discount, exclusive or high fashion, and so forth

This list is not completely inclusive, but it does give you some sense of

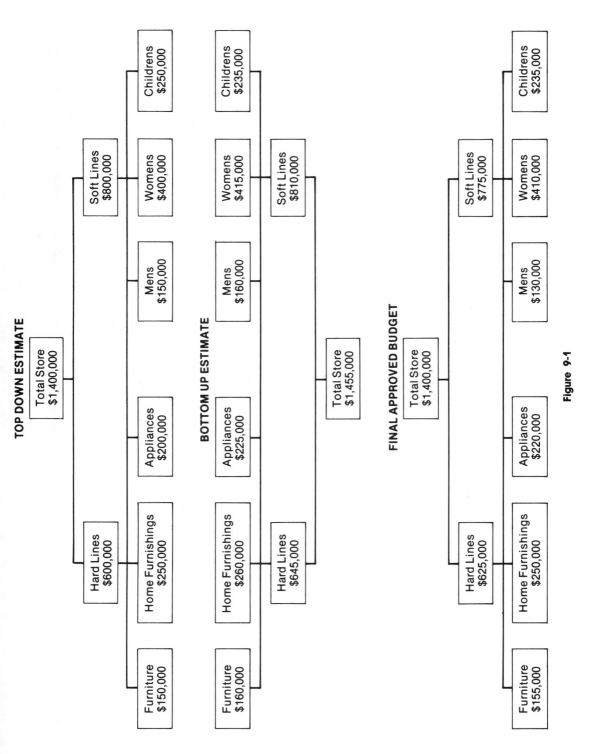

Figure 9-1

the magnitude of the information required to make realistic decisions at the upper management level. The fact that you will not be in a position to make large-scale decisions immediately should not preclude you from developing an awareness of these and other relevant areas.

Of more immediate significance to you in budget preparation is discovering the means by which you can generate bottom-up sales predictions for your department. If the store or department has been in existence for some time, historical data are usually available. By examining the sales figures on a year-to-year basis, you may be able to judge the volume possible in your department. You should, however, review trade publications, consult vendors and your buying office (if one is used), contact trade associations, and analyze the previous year's record for any unusual occurrences, such as strikes, special promotions, weather, changes in floor space, addition or deletion of price lines, and changes in store policies or dates of major holidays, that might have affected your sales.

If you are starting a business from scratch, though, you will have to rely on your knowledge and on information acquired from the resources and publications just mentioned. No matter what kind of store you are buying for, the important point to remember is that your projection and the final approved sales figure should be realistic.

Once the total planned sales figure for the season has been given to you, the next problem is to segment this dollar value into amounts for the individual months. The sales values for each month in the season can be determined in the same manner as your estimate for the total period, that is, referring to the data from prior years and giving weight to any extraordinary events that took place, or that you anticipate will take place, as well as consulting other reliable sources. Whenever possible, it is wise to use at least a three-year overview, as this length of time tends to reduce variations caused by holidays, weather irregularities, and so on.

• *EXAMPLE 9-1*

Given the following data, produce an estimate of the dollar sales value for each month in the spring-summer season with projected sales of $115,300:

	THREE YEARS AGO	TWO YEARS AGO	LAST YEAR
February	$ 12,500	$ 12,650	$ 12,700
March	14,600	14,900	14,700
April	19,700	21,300	21,600
May	24,300	24,600	25,200
June	19,400	20,100	21,300
July	14,400	14,650	15,900
Total	$104,900	$108,200	$111,400

A cursory examination of the data indicates the following: Your department has had consistent annual increases; the slowest month is February; the peak month is May; and the month of March last year experienced a decrease compared with the preceding year.

METHOD 1.   The simplest way to determine the planned sales would be to determine the percentage increase for this year over last year and apply this figure to each month of last year.

(1) Seasonal dollar increase

$$= \text{\$Plan this year} - \text{\$Last year}$$
$$= \$115,300 - \$111,400$$
$$= \$3,900$$

(2) Seasonal percentage increase

$$= \text{\$Increase} \div \text{\$Last year}$$
$$= .035 \text{ or } 3.5\%$$

(3) Apply this percentage increase to each month from last year. Use 103.5 percent as your multiplier, for your dollar figure from last year is the base value, equal to 100.0 percent, and you are adding an increase of 3.5 percent. Hence, your multiplier is 103.5 percent, or 1.035.

February	$\$12,700 \times 1.035 =$	$\$ 13,144.50$
March	$14,700 \times 1.035 =$	$15,214.50$
April	$21,600 \times 1.035 =$	$22,356.00$
May	$25,200 \times 1.035 =$	$26,082.00$
June	$21,300 \times 1.035 =$	$22,045.50$
July	$15,900 \times 1.035 =$	$16,456.50$
	Total $=$	$\$115,299.00$

METHOD 2.   Although the preceding figures may be reasonable, you would be well advised to do other calculations so that your projected monthly sales will be as reliable as possible. The next set of computations to be performed will give you the percentage of the seasonal sales for each month for each year. This is accomplished as follows:

For the month of February, three years ago:

$$= \$12,500 \div \$104,900$$
$$= 11.9\%$$

After these figures are obtained, the next step is to average the figures for each month over the three years and to multiply this answer by the planned dollar seasonal total. The results of these computations are summarized in Table 9-1. You will note minor discrepancies in the totals from rounding-off errors. The differences, however, are too small to have any effect.

Table 9-1

	THREE YEARS AGO	TWO YEARS AGO	LAST YEAR	THREE-YEAR AVERAGE	DOLLAR PLAN THIS YEAR
February	11.9%	11.7%	11.4%	11.7%	$ 13,490.10
March	13.9	13.8	13.2	13.6	15,680.80
April	18.8	19.7	19.4	19.3	22,252.90
May	23.2	22.7	22.6	22.8	26,288.40
June	18.5	18.6	19.1	18.7	21,599.53
July	13.7	13.5	14.3	13.8	15,949.83
Total	100.0%	100.0%	100.0%	99.9%	$115,261.56

METHOD 3.   A summarizing technique for Methods 1 and 2 is to average the monthly plan values determined by each of these methods. Table 9-2 shows the results of this work.

You could indulge in additional computational work and determine each month's increase or decrease over the same month in the preceding year.

Comparing February sales two years ago with February sales three years ago:

Table 9-2

	METHOD 1	METHOD 2	AVERAGE
February	$ 13,144.50	$ 13,490.10	$ 13,317.30
March	15,214.50	15,680.80	15,447.65
April	22,356.00	22,252.90	22,304.45
May	26,082.00	26,288.40	26,185.20
June	22,045.50	21,599.53	21,822.52
July	16,456.50	15,949.83	16,203.17
Total	$115,299.00	$115,261.56	$115,280.29

$$\$\text{Increase (or decrease)} = \text{February two years ago} - \text{February three years ago}$$
$$= \$12,650 - \$12,500$$
$$= +\$150$$

$$\%\text{Increase (or decrease)} = \frac{\$\text{Increase (or decrease)}}{\text{February three years ago}}$$
$$= \frac{+\$150}{\$12,500}$$
$$= +1.2\%$$

And comparing February sales last year with February sales two years ago:

$$\$\text{Increase (or decrease)} = \text{February last year} - \text{February two years ago}$$
$$= \$12,700 - \$12,650$$
$$= +\$50$$

$$\%\text{Increase (or decrease)} = \frac{\$\text{Increase (or decrease)}}{\text{February two years ago}}$$
$$= \frac{+\$50}{\$12,650}$$
$$= +0.3\%$$

This method would be beneficial if there were indications of a definite trend to shift the selling period from one portion of the season to another. For this example, however, neither the original data nor the percentage values derived in Table 9-1 reveal any major alteration in selling pattern; therefore, you may conclude that the planned monthly figures just calculated are adequate. (The next section demonstrates the method to be employed if changes occur.)

Table 9-3

	CALCULATED VALUES	ADD ROUNDING OFF	APPROVED PLANNED SALES
February	$ 13,300		$ 13,300
March	15,400		15,400
April	22,300		22,300
May	26,200	$100	26,300
June	21,800		21,800
July	16,200		16,200
Total	$115,200		$115,300

The final figures should be rounded off to the nearest $100. If the grand total is either over or under because of the rounding off, the difference can be either added to or subtracted from whichever month seems appropriate; in this example, it is added to May, which the data reveals as the strongest month. Table 9-3 shows the final approved sales figures:

- PROBLEM 9-1

The planned sales for fall-winter in your department have been established at $260,000. Develop the monthly figures from the following historical data:

	THREE YEARS AGO	TWO YEARS AGO	LAST YEAR
August	$ 24,100	$ 26,300	$ 28,400
September	26,800	29,100	31,600
October	33,500	36,300	39,700
November	41,200	45,600	47,500
December	47,100	49,800	52,300
January	30,400	32,900	33,900
Total	$203,100	$220,000	$233,400

Reductions planning.   As you learned in Chapter Seven, reductions, which include markdowns, shortages, and employee and customer discounts, must be planned in order to insure an adequate supply of merchandise. You should also recall that the value of this category is usually expressed as a percentage of sales. That is, reductions will be planned as 15.3 percent of sales, for example, or another percentage derived from an analysis of prior years or from reference sources. It is almost never true that the reduction percentage for every, or any, month in a season is equivalent to the reduction percentage for the entire period. The situation is very similar to sales in that each month is different.

The procedure for planning reductions for each month in an upcoming season begins with determining the dollar value of reductions for the entire period as soon as sales and the reduction percentage have been set. Once this has been done, the dollar values can be estimated in a manner similar to that used for estimating planned sales.

- EXAMPLE 9-2

Total planned sales for the spring-summer season have been approved at $400,000, and your planned reductions for the period will be 14.7 percent. The data for reductions in the department for the last three years are as follows:

	THREE YEARS AGO	TWO YEARS AGO	LAST YEAR
February	$ 8400	$ 8700	$ 9200
March	9600	10,100	10,700
April	7300	9300	11,600
May	6700	8900	9300
June	8500	8300	8100
July	9100	7900	6200
Total	$49,600	$53,200	$55,100

(1) Calculate the planned dollar value of the reductions for the season:

$$= \text{Planned sales} \times \text{Planned reductions\%}$$
$$= \$400,000 \times .147$$
$$= \$58,800$$

(2) Compute the monthly reduction percentage for each month in each year:

Monthly reductions% = $Monthly reductions ÷ Total seasonal reductions

For the month of February, three years ago:

$$= \$8400 \div \$49,600$$
$$= .1693, \text{ or } 16.9\%$$

The result of these computations is shown in Table 9-4:

Table 9-4

	THREE YEARS AGO	TWO YEARS AGO	LAST YEAR
February	16.9%	16.4%	16.7%
March	19.4	19.0	19.4
April	14.7	17.5	21.1
May	13.5	16.7	16.9
June	17.1	15.6	14.7
July	18.3	14.8	11.3
Total*	99.9%	100.0%	100.1%

*Totals do not sum to 100% because of rounding-off errors.

An examination of this table reveals a shift in monthly reductions toward April and May, away from June and July. Occurrences of this nature, over a period of several years, are usually explained as changes in promotional policy for the department or the store rather than changes in circumstances in a particular year, such as inclement weather. Obviously, then, there is value to examining figures longitudinally and to converting the dollar values to percentages so that they can be viewed in the proper relationship.

If you wish to confirm your observations further, you can sum the values for February and March, April and May, and June and July for each year. The results are as follows:

	THREE YEARS AGO	TWO YEARS AGO	LAST YEAR
February and March	36.3%	35.4%	36.1%
April and May	28.2	34.2	38.0
June and July	35.4	30.4	26.0
Totals	99.9%	100.0%	100.1%

(3) At this point, the most reliable estimate of your planned reductions would be obtained by using the same percentage values as last year. The computations would be

$Monthly reductions = $Seasonal reductions × Monthly reductions%

February	$58,800 × 16.7% = $ 9819.60 = $ 9800
March	58,800 × 19.4 = 11,407.20 = 11,400
April	58,800 × 21.1 = 12,406.80 = 12,400
May	58,800 × 16.9 = 9937.20 = 9900
June	58,800 × 14.7 = 8643.60 = 8600
July	58,800 × 11.3 = 6644.40 = 6600

Total = $58,700

The rounding-off process has produced an error of $100. This amount can be added to the most appropriate month, and as April has shown the greatest increase, your decision should be to change this figure to $12,500.

- PROBLEM 9-2

The planned sales for the fall-winter season are $200,000 and the planned reductions are 15.8 percent. Research of the past three years shows the following:

	THREE YEARS AGO	TWO YEARS AGO	LAST YEAR
August	$ 4200	$ 4100	$ 4000
September	3700	4000	4600
October	3600	4200	4700
November	3900	4100	4500
December	3800	4100	4300
January	5900	6000	6300
Totals	$25,100	$26,500	$28,400

Calculate and determine your most reliable estimate for the dollar planned reductions for each month of the season.

INVENTORY INVESTMENT PLANNING

You understand, of course, that you must be able to display more than one piece of merchandise to a customer in order to be able to make a sale. No matter if this number is two, ten, or whatever, the point is that your investment in inventory has to be larger than your planned sales. Obviously, the problem is to determine how much higher.

Several strategies have been developed to assist the retailer in attaining a balance between planned sales and planned inventory. These are the **basic stock method**, the **percentage variation method**, the **week's supply method**, and the **stock-to-sales method**.

Regardless of the planning system employed, you should be aware that a measure of the productivity of your investment is essential. The most common standard is **stock turn**, or **turnover**. This value, or rate, is normally an annual rate and is calculated as follows:

Stock turn = Net sales (for the period) ÷ Average retail stock (for the period)

The number that is your answer is an indication of the rate at which your inventory is sold and replaced. To illustrate:

If sales for the misses' dress classification for last year were $280,000 and the average inventory for this period was $75,000, you would calculate stock turn (ST) as follows:

$$ST = \$280,000 \div \$75,000$$
$$= 3.7$$

This answer means that your average stock moved in and out of the department 3.7 times for the year.

On the surface, it would appear that the higher the rate, the greater would be the profit because there is an element of profit in the markup of each garment sold. This argument is true to a certain extent. If you were to subscribe totally to this thinking, you could reduce your average inventory by half, that is, to $37,500. The stock turn would be increased to 7.5, which is calculated as follows:

$$ST = \$280,000 \div \$37,500$$
$$= 7.5$$

The difficulty, however, would be in trying to sustain the sales figure ($280,000) with a greatly decreased stock. Recall from Chapter Eight that one of the reasons for markdowns is customer dissatisfaction with the assortment and quantity of merchandise inventory.

A high stock turn may be an indication that you are "selling out" of merchandise too often and, therefore, are losing sales because of insufficient inventory levels. The result would be lower profits. If you are also buying relatively small numbers of items, you may be negating any advantages available from a quantity discount.

The technique, then, is to attempt to reduce your investment in inventory without affecting your sales. This is not an impossible task and can be accomplished through any combination of the following factors:

1. Study your price zones and ranges, eliminating any that overlap or are unnecessarily close.
2. Build your inventory around a principal theme or item. The slower-moving items will thus be moved out with the "hot" items.
3. Develop key vendors who can supply and quickly resupply you with fast-selling merchandise.
4. Carry reserve stock only for items that you need quickly or constantly.
5. Visit the market frequently (if possible), writing smaller orders. You may have to replace items that vendors no longer have in stock, but it may be to your advantage to have a "fresh" look in your department.
6. Develop and use a unit-control system to weed out slow-moving merchandise rapidly, as well as to pinpoint "runners."
7. Watch and use your dollar controls to regulate your total dollar investment.

   Although a stock turn figure for an entire store is obtainable, it is not nearly so useful as a figure that reflects the activity within individual departments. You should also recognize that the turnover rate for each classification of merchandise within a department may be different, and that you should give your attention to these variances as well as to the combined departmental rate.

   The following example illustrates the computational method used to find average inventory, stock turn for individual classifications of merchandise, and turnover for combined classifications.

• *EXAMPLE 9-3*

   The data for the Audio Department show the following information for the spring-summer season:

Sales of records	$100,000
Sales of tapes	$ 50,000

E.O.M. Inventories

	RECORDS	*TAPES*
January	$27,000	$14,500
February	25,000	13,500
March	31,500	17,700
April	35,000	23,500
May	38,500	27,500
June	41,000	28,500
July	33,000	22,500

   Determine the turnover for each classification and the combined stock turn.

   (1) Average inventory is determined as follows:

Average inventory = (B.O.M. first month + Sum of E.O.M.s for each month in the period) ÷ (Number of months in the period + One)

   (B.O.M. for any month is equal to the E.O.M. for the preceding month).
   Average inventory for records:

   = ($27,000 + $25,000 + $31,500 + $35,000 + $38,500 + $41,000 + $33,000) ÷ 7
   = $33,000

   Average inventory for tapes:

   = ($14,500 + $13,500 + $17,700 + $23,500 + $27,500 + $28,500 + $22,500) ÷ 7
   = $21,100

   (2) Find the stock turn for each classification:

ST = Sales ÷ Average inventory

For records:
= $100,000 ÷ $33,000
= 3.0
For tapes:
= $50,000 ÷ $21,100
= 2.4

(3) Find the stock turn for combined classification:

ST = (Sales for records + Sales for tapes) ÷
(Average inventory for records +
Average inventory for tapes)
= ($100,000 + $50,000) ÷ ($33,000 + $21,100)
= ($150,000 ÷ $54,100)
= 2.8

The resulting stock turn for both classifications of merchandise is clearly not an average of the two individual stock turns, but rather a weighted average that takes into consideration the different contributions made to the combined figure resulting from different sales volumes and average inventories.

• *PROBLEM 9-3*

You are responsible for buying three classifications of merchandise in the Women's Department. From the following data, determine the stock turn for each type of merchandise and the combined turnover for the fall-winter season:

	Sport Shoes	*Rainwear*	*Slippers*
		Sales for the Period	
	$240,000	$180,000	$78,000
		E.O.M. Inventories	
July	$ 16,000	$ 11,000	$ 3800
August	18,000	12,500	5400
September	15,000	14,700	9900
October	14,000	16,600	13,900
November	12,000	19,300	14,800
December	14,500	22,000	9700
January	16,000	19,700	8100

Basic stock method.   The basic stock method of inventory planning is used when the annual rate of stock turn is six or less. (If the turnover for a six-month season has to be determined, the practice is to divide the annual rate by two. Conversely, if the seasonal rate is known, the annual figure may be estimated by multiplying this value by two.)

The rationale for the use of the basic stock method to determine beginning-of-the-month (B.O.M.) inventories is that with slower-moving classifications of merchandise (annual stock turns of six or less), there must be a fixed minimum, or basic amount, of stock on hand at all times, regardless of the sales volume. This concept is expressed in the following formula:

B.O.M. stock = Planned sales for the month + Basic stock,

where

Basic stock = Average inventory − Average monthly sales

- *EXAMPLE 9-4*

You have been given the following approved planned sales figure for the Linens and Domestics Department and the annual rate of stock turn of 2.3. Determine your B.O.M. stocks for each month.

PLANNED SALES	
February	$18,400
March	24,900
April	23,800
May	22,700
June	20,300
July	19,500

(1) Determine the average monthly sales:

= ($18,400 + $24,900 + $23,800 + $22,700 + $20,300 + $19,500) ÷ 6
= $129,600 ÷ 6
= $21,600

(2) Determine the average inventory by using the stock turn equation, which can be restated as

Average inventory = Sales for the season ÷ Seasonal stock turn
= $129,600.00 ÷ (2.3 ÷ 2)
= $112,695.65, or $112,696.00

(3) Determine the basic stock (BS):

BS = Average inventory − Average monthly sales
= $112,696 − $21,600
= $91,096

(4) Determine the B.O.M. stock for each month:

Planned sales + Basic stock = B.O.M. stock

February	$18,400 + $91,096 = $109,496
March	24,900 + 91,096 = 115,996
April	23,800 + 91,096 = 114,896
May	22,700 + 91,096 = 113,796
June	20,300 + 91,096 = 111,396
July	19,500 + 91,096 = 110,596

- *PROBLEM 9-4*

Determine the B.O.M. stock for the Hosiery and Glove Department, which has an annual stock turn of 3.3 and approved planned sales figures as follows:

PLANNED SALES	
August	$36,300
September	39,200
October	41,500
November	43,000
December	48,000
January	33,900

Percentage variation method. The key to understanding this method of B.O.M. stock planning is that it is used in departments that have annual stock turn rates greater than six. This means that with merchandise moving in and out rapidly, the inventory must be very responsive to changes in rates of sale. While minimum amounts must be on hand, it does not follow that the same basic amount must be available during fast-selling months as in slower months. The B.O.M. stock is computed using the following formula:

$$\text{B.O.M.} = \text{Average inventory} \times \tfrac{1}{2}\left(1 + \frac{\text{Sales for month}}{\text{Average monthly sales}}\right)$$

• *EXAMPLE 9-5*

The annual stock turn for your department is 6.3, and the approved planned monthly sales are:

PLANNED SALES	
February	$47,300
March	62,400
April	68,900
May	52,300
June	47,600
July	41,000

Find the B.O.M. stock for each month.
(1) Determine the average monthly sales:

= ($47,300 + $62,400 + $68,900 + $52,300 + $47,600 + $41,000) ÷ 6
= $53,250

(2) Determine the average inventory:

= Sales for season ÷ Seasonal stock turn
= $319,500.00 ÷ (6.3 ÷ 2)
= $101,428.57, or $101,429.00

(3) Determine the B.O.M. stocks:
For February:

$$= \$101{,}429 \times \tfrac{1}{2} \left(1 + \frac{\$47{,}300}{53{,}250} \right)$$

$$= \$95{,}762.31 \text{ or } \$95{,}762.00$$

The other B.O.M. stocks are computed similarly with the following results:

February	$ 95,762
March	110,143
April	116,334
May	100,524
June	96,048
July	89,762

• PROBLEM 9-5

Determine the B.O.M. stocks if the annual stock turn is 8.4 and the approved planned sales are as follows:

PLANNED SALES	
August	$27,400
September	29,600
October	32,900
November	38,300
December	46,200
January	26,100

Week's supply method.   This method is more useful with staple forms of merchandise than with general or fashion goods. The inventory is planned to insure that a supply of stock for a predetermined number of weeks is on hand, rather than stipulating a certain B.O.M. inventory figure.

• EXAMPLE 9-6

You have been told that the Men's Underwear Department basically sells merchandise considered to be staples. The stock turn for the fall-winter season is planned at 4.0, and sales are anticipated to total $78,000 for the period. Determine the stock that must be on hand:

(1) Determine the number of weeks for which a supply has to be in stock:

= Number of weeks in period ÷ Stock turn for period
(according to the business calendar, any six-month period contains 26 weeks)
= 26 ÷ 4.0
= 6.5

(2) Determine the average for weekly sales:

= Sales for the period ÷ Number of weeks in the period
= $78,000 ÷ 26
= $3000

(3) Determine the planned stock:

$$= \text{Average weekly sales} \times \text{Number of weeks' supply}$$
$$= \$3000 \times 6.5$$
$$= \$19,500$$

• *PROBLEM 9-6*

Certain merchandise in the stationery department is considered staples and is reordered by the week's supply method. With planned sales for the spring-summer season at $42,000 and an annual stock turn of nine, determine the value of the inventory that must be on hand.

Stock-to-sales method.   The stock-to-sales method of inventory investment planning requires that a relationship be established between the sales for any given month and the volume of merchandise that must be on hand at the beginning of that month.

As you have learned earlier, the records of your department and store, coupled with your analysis of trends, are undoubtedly the best guide. But, again, you should be aware of the other sources of information that have been referred to previously.

• *EXAMPLE 9-7*

You have been given the following data for the Millinery Department, to determine the B.O.M. stocks:

	SALES LAST YEAR	B.O.M. LAST YEAR	PLANNED SALES
February	$18,500	$27,600	$19,600
March	12,200	26,800	13,500
April	11,700	38,600	12,400
May	10,500	38,800	11,600
June	6300	20,200	7300
July	4100	11,500	5000

(1) Determine the ratio between stock and sales for each month:

$$= \text{B.O.M. stock} \div \text{Sales}$$
For February:
$$= \$27,600 \div \$18,500$$
$$= 1.5$$

The results for the period are summarized below:

	S-S RATIO
February	1.5
March	2.2
April	3.3
May	3.7
June	3.2
July	2.8

(2) Determine the B.O.M. stocks for the planned period:

= B.O.M. S-S ratio × Planned sales

	S-S	PLANNED SALES		B.O.M. STOCK
February	1.5 ×	$19,600	=	$29,400
March	2.2 ×	13,500	=	29,700
April	3.3 ×	12,400	=	40,920
May	3.7 ×	11,600	=	42,920
June	3.2 ×	7300	=	23,360
July	2.8 ×	5000	=	14,000

The foregoing tabulation dramatically illustrates how the stock-to-sales method of planning is responsive to variances in sales in individual months. The other three planning procedures rely on averages of sales, and if the turnover rate is used, you will also be utilizing the figure for average stock. The use of averages dampens the effects of unusual selling periods (either high or low) and may create difficult stock situations. Your experience and constant attention to controls will provide you with the best procedures to follow for inventory planning.

• PROBLEM 9-7

The data for the Better Coat Department follows. Calculate the stock-to-sales ratio and determine the B.O.M. inventory for each month in the season:

	SALES LAST YEAR	B.O.M. LAST YEAR	PLANNED SALES
July	$ 4200	$16,400	$ 6700
August	4800	21,600	7300
September	5900	29,500	8000
October	6800	22,500	8900
November	7900	21,300	10,300
December	10,600	17,000	12,500
January	9700	26,200	11,100

SUMMARY PROBLEMS

• PROBLEM 9-1 (S)

Your planned sales for the Women's Dress Department for the coming spring-summer season are $265,000. The data for the past three years are as follows:

	THREE YEARS AGO	TWO YEARS AGO	LAST YEAR
February	$ 46,600	$ 45,800	$ 47,300
March	55,900	56,500	59,200
April	58,200	64,300	68,700
May	53,100	61,300	62,100
June	42,200	45,200	47,800
July	34,800	36,900	41,900
Totals	$290,800	$310,000	$327,000

You also note that three years ago, Easter occurred toward the end of March, whereas two years ago and last year, the holiday was in April. This year it will be on March 21. Develop the planned monthly sales figures for the planned period.

• PROBLEM 9-2 (S)

Reductions for your department in the forthcoming spring-summer season are planned at 16.7 percent, with planned sales of $435,000. The data for the past three years follow. Determine the planned dollar reductions for each month of the upcoming season.

	THREE YEARS AGO	TWO YEARS AGO	LAST YEAR
February	$ 8600	$ 9200	$ 9800
March	9400	9900	10,700
April	10,300	10,800	11,500
May	11,500	12,400	13,000
June	9200	11,600	12,300
July	8100	9500	10,100
Totals	$57,100	$63,400	$67,400

• PROBLEM 9-3 (S)

You are attempting to evaluate three vendors from whom you have purchased merchandise for the spring-summer season. To facilitate this activity, you have decided to compute the turnover for each vendor. Your records indicate the following:

	Vendor A	Vendor B	Vendor C
		Sales	
	$437,000	$265,000	$397,000
		Inventory	
January	$205,000	$160,000	$171,000
February	274,000	177,000	182,000
March	290,000	183,000	188,000
April	303,000	192,000	199,000
May	315,000	198,000	206,000
June	301,000	191,000	212,000
July	284,000	182,000	197,000

Compute the stock turn and combined turnover for each vendor.

• PROBLEM 9-4 (S)

Determine the B.O.M. inventory for the Jewelry and Watch Department, which has had an annual stock turn of 2.1 and now has approved planned sales as follows:

	PLANNED SALES
February	$27,400
March	30,600
April	35,300
May	39,500
June	46,200
July	32,900

• PROBLEM 9-5 (S)

You have been asked to determine the planned B.O.M. stock for your department from the following data. Your calculations will include using last year's stock turn rate.

	PLANNED SALES	SALES LAST YEAR	E.O.M. LAST YEAR
July	——	——	$58,000
August	$48,000	$45,500	61,000
September	56,000	49,000	63,000
October	59,000	53,000	67,000
November	42,000	40,000	57,000
December	37,000	32,000	52,000
January	39,000	29,000	48,000

• PROBLEM 9-6 (S)

The fasteners (nails, screws, bolts, and staples) in the Hardware Department are stocked according to the week's supply method. The annual turnover rate for this merchandise is 9.6. Given the following planned sales, determine the value of stock to be on hand at any given time.

February	$2200
March	2700
April	2600
May	2500
June	2800
July	2900

• PROBLEM 9-7 (S)

The table below summarizes the data for the Lingerie Department. Use the stock-to-sales method and calculate your B.O.M. stock.

	SALES LAST YEAR	B.O.M. LAST YEAR	PLANNED % INCREASE (+) DECREASE (−) IN SALES	PLANNED B.O.M.
February	$16,300	$ 75,000	+2.0%	
March	18,900	104,000	+5.3	
April	23,400	121,700	+4.6	
May	28,900	109,800	−3.1	
June	27,500	118,300	+3.6	
July	25,100	108,000	+2.2	

STARTING AT THE BOTTOM

The budgeting sequence has begun for the coming fall-winter season, and you are in a different department, thanks to a nice promotion.

In preparation for the bottom-up planning process, you have had your assistant accumulate data on sales, reductions, and B.O.M. stocks, as well as indicate any notations of interest. The assistant produced the table on page 185 and reported that the store's records indicate that two years ago there was a snowstorm in January that forced the store to be closed for four days. A similar weather problem occurred last year in December. Do the bottom-up planning and give your rationale for your decision.

	Three Years Ago			Two Years Ago			Last Year		
	Sales	Reductions	E.O.M. Inventory	Sales	Reductions	E.O.M. Inventory	Sales	Reductions	E.O.M. Inventory
July	$175,000	$26,100	$326,000	$182,000	$29,500	$358,000	$193,000	$31,300	$371,000
August	182,000	23,500	362,000	190,000	28,600	380,000	201,000	30,000	382,000
September	197,000	20,200	375,000	203,000	24,300	393,000	208,000	27,000	390,000
October	205,000	19,700	390,000	209,000	21,300	397,000	214,000	23,000	395,000
November	215,000	16,300	393,000	219,000	14,300	402,000	219,000	18,600	401,000
December	230,000	12,100	410,000	234,000	15,100	430,000	216,000	20,100	460,000
January	195,000	29,500	360,000	168,000	21,200	385,000	203,000	34,600	387,000

Purchase Planning
and Control

10

The six-month merchandise plan. The six-month merchandise plan provides a format for dollar purchasing (as opposed to unit buying) for a season. It brings together the elements of initial markup, sales, reductions, and beginning-of-the-month inventory to produce a dollar open-to-buy figure for each month in the period.

A merchandise plan is as necessary for a department within a chain or department store organization as it is for the individually owned shop or boutique. Although the forms used by different retailers may be as dissimilar as the various types of merchants, the components and preparation are the same. Figure 10-1 is a six-month buying plan form containing the essential planning elements and spaces provided to record data from the prior year and for actual values as they become available. This form then serves you for planning, for "eyeball" evaluation of your inventory's performance, and as a data sheet for the future.

Initially, in planning, you are attempting to provide yourself with a monthly budget that will insure sufficient dollars to cover sales and reductions while leaving an adequate inventory for the opening day of the following month. In managerial terms, this is an example of management by objective (M.B.O.).

The concept can be stated in terms of a formula as

SIX MONTH MERCHANDISE PLAN

Department Name __Men's Furnishings__   Department No. __3100__   Period Covered __Spring-Summer__

	Last Year	Plan		Last Year	Plan
Initial Markup		(1a) 52.9%	Gross Margin		(1c) 52.3%
Reductions		(0) 14.0%	Operating Expense		(D) 44.9%
Maintained Markup		(1b) 46.3%	Operating Profit		(1d) 7.4%
Cash Discount		(0) 6.0%	Season Turnover		(0) 2.9%

Buyer __Shuch__

Date Prepared __Sept. 19, 198__

Spring	Fall	Sales + Last Year	Sales + Plan	Sales + Actual	E.O.M. + Last Year	E.O.M. + Plan	E.O.M. + Actual	Reductions − Last Year	Reductions − Plan	Reductions − Actual	B.O.M. = Last Year	B.O.M. = Plan	B.O.M. = Actual	Retail Purchases Last Year	Retail Purchases Plan	Retail Purchases Actual	Cost Purchases Last Year	Cost Purchases Plan	Cost Purchases Actual
Feb.	Aug.		(2) $67,200			(5) $142,028			(3) $11,172			(4) $142,028			(6) $78,372			(7) $36,913	
Mar.	Sept.		(2) $67,200			(5) $133,628			(3) $12,348			(4) $142,028			(6) $71,148			(7) $33,511	
Apr.	Oct.		(2) $58,800			(5) $150,128			(3) $13,524			(4) $133,628			(6) $89,124			(7) $41,977	
May	Nov.		(2) $75,600			(5) $167,228			(3) $9,996			(4) $150,428			(6) $102,396			(7) $48,129	
June	Dec.		(2) $62,400			(5) $133,628			(3) $6,468			(4) $167,228			(6) $65,268			(7) $30,741	
July	Jan.		(2) $58,800			(5) $144,128			(3) $5,292			(4) $133,628			(6) $75,292			(7) $35,463	
	Total		(0) $420,000			(5) $871,768			(3) $58,700			(4) $865,968			(6) $481,604			(7) $226,834	

Figure 10-1

Planned sales + E.O.M. inventory + Reductions − B.O.M. inventory = Purchases at retail

The preparation of the six-month merchandise plan requires a series of computations, most of which you have already learned in preceding chapters. The individual steps are outlined below.

1. Determine the planned:
   (a) Initial markup (see pages 122–24)
   (b) Maintained markup (see pages 159–61)
   (c) Gross margin (see pages 161–62)
   (d) Operating profit (see pages 162–63)
2. Determine the monthly planned sales.
   These values either will have been generated during the total budget planning process (pages 168–73) or will have been computed from the total seasonal sales and the percentage of sales anticipated for each month, as follows:

   Sales for any month = Total season's sales × Month's percentage of total season's sales

3. Determine the monthly planned reductions.
   These values will have been generated during the total budget planning process (see pages 173–75).
4. Determine the B.O.M. stock levels for each month (see pages 175–83).
5. Determine the E.O.M. stock levels for each month.
   The E.O.M. stock for any month is equal to the B.O.M. stock for the next month. As you cannot plan the B.O.M. inventory for the first month of the next season, however, the E.O.M. inventory for the last month in the period you are planning is assumed to be the average inventory for that season.
6. Determine monthly purchases at retail (see pages 188–90).
7. Determine monthly purchases at cost:

   Cost purchases = Retail purchases × (100% − IM%)

8. Complete the totals for each column of your plan and check your work by calculating the dollar values for retail and cost purchases, using the sums of sales, E.O.M. inventory, reductions, and B.O.M. inventory.

• *EXAMPLE 10-1*

For the Men's Furnishings Department number 3100, complete the six-month merchandise plan from the following planned data:

Planned net sales	$420,000
Operating expenses	44.9%
Planned profit	7.4%
Cash discount	6.0%
Reductions	14.0%
Seasonal stock turn	2.9

MONTH	PERCENTAGE OF SEASON'S SALES	PERCENTAGE OF SEASON'S REDUCTIONS
February	16%	19%
March	16	21
April	14	23
May	18	17
June	22	11
July	14	9

Refer to Figure 10-1. All values given as data in the problem are identified as (D). All derived values are accompanied by a number in parentheses that identifies the step in which that value was calculated.

(1) Determine

(a) IM% $= \dfrac{\text{Expenses} + \text{Profit} + \text{Reductions} - \text{Cash discount}}{\text{Net sales} + \text{Reductions}}$

$= \dfrac{.449 + .074 + .14 - .06}{1.00 + .14}$

$= 52.9\%$

(b) $MM = ($Gross sales $-$ $Reductions$) - $ Cost of goods sold

where

$Gross sales $= $Net sales $+$ $Reductions
                $= $420,000 $+$ (.14 $\times$ $420,000)
                $= $478,800

$Cost of goods sold* $=$ C% $\times$ $Gross sales
                $=$ (1.00 $-$ .529) $\times$ $478,800
                $=$ $225,515

$MM $=$ [$478,800 $-$ (.14 $\times$ $420,000)] $-$ $225,515
    $=$ $194,485

MM% $=$ $MM $\div$ $Net sales
    $=$ $194,485 $\div$ $420,000
    $=$ 46.3%

(c) GM% $=$ MM% $+$ CD%
           $=$ 46.3% $+$ 6.0%
           $=$ 52.3%

(d) OP% $=$ GM% $-$ OE%
           $=$ 52.3% $-$ 44.9%
           $=$ 7.4%

*The cost of goods sold may also be referred to as **gross** cost of goods sold, as it includes all merchandise available for sale during the time period.

(2) Determine the monthly planned sales:

February	16%	× $420,000 =	$ 67,200
March	16	× 420,000 =	67,200
April	14	× 420,000 =	58,800
May	18	× 420,000 =	75,600
June	22	× 420,000 =	92,400
July	14	× 420,000 =	58,800
Total	100%		$420,000

(3) Determine the monthly planned reductions.
Total reductions are planned as 14.0 percent of sales.

$$\$Red = .14 \times \$420,000$$
$$= \$58,800$$

February	19%	× $58,800 =	$ 11,172
March	21	× 58,800 =	12,348
April	23	× 58,800 =	13,524
May	17	× 58,800 =	9996
June	11	× 58,800 =	6468
July	9	× 58,800 =	5292
Total	100%		$58,800

(4) Determine the B.O.M. stock for each month:
As the annual stock turn is less than six (2.9 × 2 = 5.8), you should use the basic stock method to determine the B.O.M. stock for each month.

$$\text{B.O.M.} = \text{Planned sales for the month} + \text{Basic stock}$$

where

$$\text{Basic stock} = \text{Average inventory} - \text{Average monthly sales}$$

and

Average inventory   = Planned sales ÷ Stock turn
  = $420,000 ÷ 2.9
  = $144,828

Average monthly sales = Planned sales ÷ 6
Average monthly sales = $420,000 ÷ 6
  = $70,000

Basic stock   = $144,828 − $70,000
Basic stock   = $74,828

February	$67,200 +	$74,828 =	$142,028
March	67,200 +	74,828 =	142,028
April	58,800 +	74,828 =	133,628
May	75,600 +	74,828 =	150,428

June	92,400 +	74,828 =	167,228
July	58,800 +	74,828 =	133,628
Total			$868,968

(5) Determine the E.O.M. inventory for each month:

The E.O.M. inventory is equal to the B.O.M. inventory of the following month, and the last month's E.O.M. inventory is equal to the average inventory. Sum the E.O.M. inventories:

February	$142,028
March	133,628
April	150,428
May	167,228
June	133,628
July	144,828
Total	$871,768

(6) Determine the monthly retail purchases:

Retail purchases = Sales + E.O.M. + Reductions − B.O.M.

February	$67,200 +	$142,028 +	$ 11,172 −	$142,028 =	$ 78,372
March	67,200 +	133,628 +	12,348 −	142,028 =	71,148
April	58,800 +	150,428 +	13,524 −	133,628 =	89,124
May	75,600 +	167,228 +	9996 −	150,428 =	102,396
June	92,400 +	133,628 +	6468 −	167,228 =	65,268
July	58,800 +	144,828 +	5292 −	133,628 =	75,292
				Total =	$481,600

(7) Determine the monthly cost purchases:

Cost purchases = Retail purchases × (100% − IM%)

February	$ 78,372 × .471 =	$ 36,913
March	71,148 × .471 =	33,511
April	89,124 × .471 =	41,977
May	102,396 × .471 =	48,229
June	65,268 × .471 =	30,741
July	75,292 × .471 =	35,463
	Total =	$226,834

(8) Use the sum of each category to cross check your total:

Sales	$ 420,000
+ E.O.M.	871,768
+ Reductions	58,800
	$1,350,568
− B.O.M.	868,968
Retail purchases	$ 481,600
× C%	.471
Cost purchases	$ 226,834

As the values for cost purchases found in both steps 7 and 8 coincide, you can assume your answer is mathematically correct.

• *PROBLEM 10-1*

You have been given the following planned figures for the fall-winter season in the Art and Print Department number 6150. Prepare the six-month merchandise plan on the accompanying form (Fig. 10-2, p. 195).

Planned net sales	$210,000
Operating expenses	48.8%
Cash discount	4.0%
Planned profit	6.5%
Reductions	12.0%
Seasonal stock turn	3.2

MONTH	PERCENTAGE OF SEASON'S SALES	PERCENTAGE OF SEASON'S REDUCTIONS
August	15%	15%
September	15	10
October	25	15
November	15	20
December	20	15
January	10	25

CONTROL

Dollar open-to-buy.   The six-month merchandise plan you have just learned about generates a purchase value at cost and retail for the beginning of each month in a season. These monthly buying figures are equal to the amount of money you may spend, given the following conditions:

1. It is the beginning of the month
2. You have not placed orders earlier for merchandise to be delivered during the month under consideration
3. Your B.O.M. inventory is as estimated; that is, the sales, reductions, and purchases in the preceding months have balanced out according to the merchandise plan

In most instances the circumstances just described cannot be met at the same time; and, therefore, your purchase figures require modification and control. The term used to express this is **open-to-buy (O.T.B.)**. You worked with this concept in Chapter Seven when you learned about averaging and cumulative markup. Now it is appropriate to view open-to-buy as it relates to the total buying process.

Open-to-buy control is necessary, as it will make available to you information about the balance of purchases remaining in dollars for any given period.

SIX MONTH MERCHANDISE PLAN

Department Name _____ Department No. _____ Period Covered _____

	Last Year	Plan		Last Year	Plan
Initial Markup	_____	_____	Gross Margin	_____	_____
Reductions	_____	_____	Operating Expense	_____	_____
Maintained Markup	_____	_____	Operating Profit	_____	_____
Cash Discount	_____	_____	Season Turnover	_____	_____
Buyer	_____		Date Prepared	_____	

		Sales +			E.O.M. +			Reductions –			B.O.M. =			Retail Purchases			Cost Purchases		
Spring	Fall	Last Year	Plan	Actual	Last Year	Plan	Actual	Last Year	Plan	Actual	Last Year	Plan	Actual	Last Year	Plan	Actual	Last Year	Plan	Actual
Feb.	Aug.																		
Mar.	Sept.																		
Apr.	Oct.																		
May	Nov.																		
June	Dec.																		
July	Jan.																		
Total																			

Figure 10-2

You will need this ongoing information because seldom, if ever, will you use all of your buying money in the beginning of a month.

You should learn to hold back some of your dollars for the following reasons:

1. You may have to reorder fast-selling items and fill in your staple stock
2. Off-price merchandise may become available (see Chapter Eight for a description of buying into your markdowns)
3. You may find a new vendor, or a new line or item may be shown to you that you wish to try

Open-to-buy in its simplest form is computed by subtracting from purchases the value of orders placed for delivery during any given month. You could place several orders for delivery during different months, for example. The value of each order would reduce the purchases for the months in which the merchandise is scheduled for *delivery*, not the month in which the order was placed.

• *EXAMPLE 10-2*

(Refer to the data in Figure 10-1.) In preparation for the coming season, you have gone to the market to place orders. J.C. Accessories has shown you its line, and you have placed orders for delivery in February and March as follows:

Delivery for February 15	$ 8,697 at retail
Delivery for March 15	$12,416 at retail

Determine the balance of open-to-buy for each month:

Retail purchases for February	$78,372
J.C. Accessories order	− 8697
Open-to-buy at retail for February	$69,675
Retail purchases for March	$71,148
J.C. Accessories order	− 12,416
Open-to-buy at retail for March	$58,732

• *PROBLEM 10-2*

Your purchases at retail for October and November are $94,243 and $112,636, respectively. You have placed orders with Iceberg Fashions as follows:

ORDER NUMBER	AMOUNT AT RETAIL	DELIVERY DATE
8140	$ 5327	October 10
8141	6693	October 20
8142	8325	November 10
8143	10,461	November 20

Determine the balance of open-to-buy for each month.

The preceding examples have dealt with relatively static situations in that no consideration has been given to the fact that sales and reductions are taking place concurrently with your buying. The volume of sales and reductions and their distribution throughout the month can have an effect on your open-to-buy.

As an example, if your actual sales or reductions, or both, either exceed your plan or fail to materialize, your open-to-buy will accordingly be either increased or reduced.

- *EXAMPLE 10-3*

(Refer to the month of May in Figure 10-1). On Monday morning, May 19, you are examining your month-to-date figures to verify your open-to-buy, and you see the following figures:

Sales to date	$48,000
Merchandise received	87,500
Reductions to date	6000
Merchandise on order for May	7000

Determine the difference in your open-to-buy.
(1) Determine your open-to-buy according to the six-month merchandise plan:

= B.O.M. purchases at retail − (Merchandise received + Merchandise on order)
= $102,396 − ($87,500 + $7000)
= $7896

You note, however, that the actual sales and reductions for the month appear to be exceeding your original plan. The calendar for May shows 27 business days, and you have completed 15 days by May 19.
(2) Determine the average sales and reductions per day thus far:

Average sales = Sales to date ÷ Number of days
= $48,000 ÷ 15
= $3200

Average reductions = Reductions to date ÷ Number of days
= $6000 ÷ 15
= $400

(3) With 12 business days remaining (27 − 15 = 12), determine the planned sales and reductions for the balance of the month:

Sales = Average sale × Number of days
= $3200 × 12
= $38,400

and

Reductions = Average reductions × Number of days
= $400 × 12
= $4800

(4) Determine your new planned open-to-buy:

Planned sales balance of May	$ 38,400
+ Planned reductions balance of May	+ 4,800
+ Planned E.O.M. inventory	+ 167,228
− Stock on order	− 7,000
− Stock on hand*	− 183,928
New planned O.T.B.	$ 19,500

*Stock on hand = B.O.M. + Merchandise received − (Actual sales + Actual reductions)
= $150,428 + $87,500 − ($48,000 + $6000)
= $183,928

(5) Determine the difference in the open-to-buy (+ or −):

= New O.T.B. − Planned O.T.B.
= $19,500 − $7896
= $11,604

Your computation shows that you will need additional O.T.B. dollars.

• *PROBLEM 10-3*

(Refer to the month of March in Figure 10-1.) On Wednesday, March 18, you have returned to your office and have decided to correlate your planned open-to-buy with the open-to-buy based on the activity to date in the department. The controller's office has generated the following data:

Sales to date	$43,680
Reductions to date	4900
Merchandise received	53,200
Merchandise on order for March	6500

March this year has 26 business days, 14 of which have elapsed by March 18. Determine the difference in your open-to-buy.

It is essential that you conduct a thorough examination of your business as variations occur from your plan. In the preceding example, if you could not find any explainable reason for increases (or decreases) over a period of time, you could conclude that a trend was ensuing and either obtain permission to increase your O.T.B. to support the trend or notify your superior that you would be cutting back on purchases to avoid an overstocked condition.

Another set of circumstances will occur where a known factor can be identified as the cause of unexpected changes in your business; your reaction must be, once again, to examine its impact on your O.T.B.

• *EXAMPLE 10-4*

(Refer to the month of April in Figure 10-1.) On April 10, you are examining your April 1–10 figures to determine a revised O.T.B. after having had a far better than planned promotional event last week. The data are as follows:

	PLANNED (TO DATE)	ACTUAL (TO DATE)
Sales	$20,000	$25,500
Reductions	9000	12,300

(1) Determine the + or − difference in sales:

$$= \text{Actual sales} - \text{Planned sales}$$
$$= \$25,500 - \$20,000$$
$$= \$5500$$

(2) Determine the + or − difference in reductions:

$$= \text{Actual reductions} - \text{planned reductions}$$
$$= \$12,300 - \$9000$$
$$= \$3300$$

(3) Additional O.T.B. at retail needed:

$$= \text{Difference in sales} + \text{Difference in reductions}$$
$$= \$5500 + \$3300$$
$$= \$8800$$

This can be proven by adding the differences found in steps 1 and 2 to the sales and reductions values for April (Figure 10-1) and subtracting the planned retail purchases from the revised O.T.B. retail purchases, as follows:

Planned sales + Difference = $58,800 + $5500	= $ 64,300
+ E.O.M.	= $150,428
+ Planned reductions + Differences ($13,524 + $3300)	= $ 16,824
− B.O.M.	= $133,628
= Revised total retail purchases	= $ 97,924
− Original total retail purchases	= $ 89,124
= Difference in O.T.B.	$ 8,800

• PROBLEM 10-4

(Refer to the month of February in Figure 10-1.) Your core competitor ran an unexpected sale two weeks ago, and you were compelled to run a similar unplanned promotion last week, which was very successful. You have compiled data through February 17 to determine your O.T.B. status, as follows:

	PLANNED: FEB. 1–17	ACTUAL: FEB. 1–17
Sales	$27,600	$35,900
Reductions	6200	7800

Determine the dollar change in your O.T.B. and prove your answer by recomputing the month of February's retail purchases from your six-month plan.

An increased open-to-buy is considered an advantageous position for a buyer. If you have extra funds, however, it does not follow that suitable merchandise will be available to you on short notice, and you may easily find yourself scurrying at a frantic pace throughout the market to accommodate the needs of your department. You might also attempt to bring in merchandise that has been ordered for delivery at a later time, provided that this is appropriate inventory for the current period.

If you find yourself in the position where an increased open-to-buy has not brought in the appropriate amount of stock in the month in which it was first needed, you should attempt to carry over this money into the next month as an aid to restoring the planned E.O.M. inventory for the following month.

Should your mid-month O.T.B. analysis show that you are in an overbought situation, you must act swiftly to avoid overstocking your department. Failure to move promptly will ultimately lead to increased markdowns as a means of reducing inventory and improving your cash position.

Many times you can avoid taking unnecessary markdowns to relieve an overbought status if you have been prudent in your buying and timed the flow of stock into your department so that the merchandise arrives throughout the month rather than in the beginning of the month. If this is not the case, the following steps should help:

1. Review all open orders and determine if there is any marginal merchandise you can either eliminate or reduce in quantity.
2. Depending upon the severity of the situation, cancel as much merchandise ordered as you can. Remember that your order is a legal contract, and vendors need not accept a cancellation (or reduction) if they have met, and are meeting, the terms of the order.
3. If there is merchandise on order that you planned to bring in early, or that will have a long enough selling season if it is brought in later than you had originally planned, attempt to have the vendor deliver this merchandise in the following month.

In any event, you must constantly watch for upward or downward trends in your business, as they will have ramifications for your purchases in future buying periods.

Unit open-to-buy.   Regardless of whether you choose to earn a profit through dollar investment in hard or soft goods or in fashion or staple merchandise, you must know how much to spend and how many units of stock to buy. You have already learned how to calculate how much. You will now learn how many.

For buying purposes, retailers normally categorize merchandise as either being **staple** or **fashion.** Staple merchandise is defined as those classifications that are in regular demand over a period of time. These goods are normally stocked by vendors for quick delivery and reorder to retailers. Fashion merchandise, on the other hand, has an appeal for only a relatively short period of time. When you buy this kind of merchandise, it is normally your responsibility to stock enough goods to carry you through the selling period. Some retailers buy only enough merchandise to last them for short runs and continuously replace their stock with new items. Others attempt to reorder styles to keep a "hot" number in their inventory. Your experience, as well as the store's policies, will help you decide which procedure to pursue for your department.

Individual merchants may consider the same classification of merchandise differently, depending upon their own unique operation. Similarly, items that may be classified as a staple at one time may, through a variety of alterations in the retailing environment, become part of the fashion inventory. An example of this would be domestics, which were once available only in solid white and were considered staples. A walk through any store today would show that this merchandise is available in every color and also in a wide assortment of patterns. Hence this classification of goods has made a transition from staple to fashion merchandise, and this change has had an effect on the methods used to estimate the quantities to be purchased.

The buying of fashion merchandise is accomplished through **model stock planning**, whereas staple goods are ordered by a variation of the **basic stock list**. Model stock planning provides you with an estimate of the dollars and units that should be purchased in specific classifications of merchandise during a period of time. The basic stock list method is used to plan purchases of individual styles within classifications of staple merchandise.

MODEL STOCK PLANNING. To facilitate the use of this method of purchase planning, you must be able to identify certain comparable features of the classification of merchandise. The following items are characteristics that you may use:

1. **Price.** You will have established distinct price zones and price lines (see Chapter Seven), and your merchandise can be grouped in this way.
2. **Color.** This subdivision requires that you identify which are the basic colors, if any, and which colors are the fashion shades for the season. You may also have to develop a category for patterns.
3. **Size.** If the classification of merchandise you are planning to retail is women's sweaters, as an example, you would have to know the proportion of sales made in each size. Similarly, if you are planning to sell towels, you would require information about the percentage of sales for bath-sized towels, hand towels, and washcloths.
4. **Fabrication.** Your knowledge of textiles, as well as of nontextiles, would be essential, in addition to your perception of the market potential for knit fabrics versus woven fabrics, natural materials as opposed to synthetics, metals as opposed to plastics, and so on.

• *EXAMPLE 10-5*

As a buyer in the Small Electric Appliance Department, you are responsible for buying toasters, blenders, and food processors. Your total open-to-buy for the month of April is $36,000. Refer to

Table 10-1

APPLIANCE	TOASTERS			BLENDERS			FOOD PROCESSORS		
Percentage of Total O.T.B.	**45.0**			**30.0**			**25**		
Dollars of Total O.T.B.	(1) 16,200			(1) 10,800			(1) 9000		
Price Line	**$18**	**$22**	**$26**	**$12**	**$15**	**$20**	**$30**	**$40**	**$50**
Percentage of Sales	**30**	**45**	**25**	**20**	**50**	**30**	**20**	**45**	**35**
$O.T.B.	(2) 4860	(2) 7290	(2) 4050	(2) 2160	(2) 5400	(2) 3240	(2) 1800	(2) 4050	(2) 3150
Unit O.T.B.	(3) 270	(3) 331	(3) 156	(3) 180	(3) 360	(3) 162	(3) 60	(3) 101	(3) 63

Table 10-1 for data. (Note that the values in boldface are values given in the problem, whereas derived values are accompanied by a number in parentheses to identify the step in which they were computed.)

(1) Determine the open-to-buy for each classification:

Toasters   = $36,000 × .45
               = $16,200

Blenders   = $36,000 × .30
               = $10,800

Food processors = $36,000 × .25
                = $9000

(2) Determine the open-to-buy for each price line within each classification:

Toasters

For $18 = $16,200 × .30
        = $4860

For $22 = $16,200 × .45
        = $7290

For $26 = $16,200 × .25
        = $4050

Similar computations are performed for blenders and food processors. The results are summarized in Table 10-1.

(3) Determine unit open-to-buy:

Toasters

$18 units = $4860 ÷ $18
          = 270

$22 units = $7290 ÷ $22
          = 331.4 or 331

$26 units = $4050 ÷ $26
          = 155.8 or 156

Similar computations are performed for the price lines in the other classifications. The results are summarized in Table 10-1.

This process could be carried through yet another step if you were required to consider the availability of these appliances in various colors, such as white, avocado, lemon, and brown. You would have to know the percentage of each color for each price line of appliance. To illustrate, if your decision was to purchase 10 percent of the $18 price line of toasters in white

$$= .10 \times 270 \text{ units}$$
$$= 27 \text{ units}$$

• PROBLEM 10-5

Your open-to-buy for the Personal Care Department for December is $43,500. Table 10-2 contains the balance of the data and should be completed to show the unit open-to-buy.

Table 10-2

APPLIANCE	HAIR DRYERS			SHAVERS—MEN			SHAVERS—WOMEN		
Percentage of Total O.T.B.	36			42			22		
Dollars of Total O.T.B.									
Price Line	$15	$20	$25	$27	$34	$39	$22	$26	$30
Percentage of Sales	30	40	30	35	40	25	40	40	20
$O.T.B.									
Unit O.T.B.									

BASIC STOCK LIST PLANNING.   Basic stock list planning is used to maintain levels of merchandise which are classed as staples. Your customers will expect these goods to be in stock in a complete range of sizes and colors at all times.

Although it would appear on the surface that the safest and easiest avenue to success in retailing would be through having a shop in which only staple merchandise was sold, this is not the case, for a number of reasons. Prime among these is the fact that the markup, which contains the element of profit, generated by this kind of merchandise is usually considerably lower than that for fashion goods. Markup, as you have learned, is correlated to risk in the form of markdowns, and staples are relatively free of markdowns. In addition, the competition is far more severe in staples, and prices are often stabilized by what is customary, or by the manufacturer's suggested retail prices.

Buyers of staple goods are confronted with a variety of problems that are in some cases unique to this form of merchandise. For example, you must determine if your staple items are seasonal or nonseasonal in nature. Some merchandise, such as white thread, which has a flat product life cycle, will sell during all months of the year with minor fluctuations. Other items will be sold every year, but only during specific times, having a repetitive product life cycle. An example would be suntan preparations, for which the selling period is essentially during the warmer months of every year. This item would be likely to have a relatively limited demand during other seasons.

Another factor to consider is whether the staples are heterogeneous or homogeneous. If they are heterogeneous, they will perform in the same manner but be different in appearance or properties. Products such as soaps and adhesive bandages fall into this grouping.

Homogeneous items are those that are identical both in performance and properties, differing only in the name of the manufacturer. This category of merchandise would include items such as camera film and electric wall switches.

Furthermore, you must give thought to the decision about whether to purchase branded merchandise, private label goods, or both. If you buy brand names, your decision as to which brand or brands to order will be difficult. You will probably discover that research into core customer preferences is advisable.

The private label discussion is appropriate to staple merchandise as well as to fashion goods, and your decision should take into consideration such factors as specification buying, prestige value, product liability, extra markup, and avoidance of direct competition.

An important factor that will affect your choice of vendors for staple merchandise is the length of time needed for delivery of the merchandise by the vendor after the order has been placed. This is known as the **delivery period (DP)**, and it is an essential item of information needed to calculate the open-to-buy for staple goods. The delivery period is also an element that will affect your turnover rate, which will subsequently have an impact on your profitability.

In order for a department devoted to staple merchandise to be effective in satisfying customers and making a meaningful contribution to profitability, the merchandise assortment must always be complete. To facilitate your stock planning, you must either know the **rate of sale (RS)** for the merchandise stocked previously or develop this rate through trial and error; that is, by carrying the item and performing stock counts at regular intervals to determine the quantity sold over a given period of time. With staple merchandise the rate of sale is generally computed for a one-week period.

The theory in O.T.B. control for staple merchandise is that a **maximum stock (MAX)** and a **minimum stock (MIN)** are calculated. These become the hypothetical upper and lower limits of your inventory. They are computed by combining the following components:

- Rate of sale (RS)—the average number of units sold during a specific time period (usually weekly).
- Delivery period (DP)—the number of time periods between placement of an order and receipt of the goods.
- Reorder period (RP)—the number of time periods allowed to elapse between inventory reviews.
- Reserve (R)—a safety factor, in time periods, to offset delivery problems, labor difficulties, or unusually high sales.
- On-hand stock (OH)—the number of units in your store that are available for sale.

• On-order stock (OO)—the number of units on order from vendors or in transit, as well as any inventory waiting to be processed by your receiving and marking staff.

Stating the preceding concept as formulas:

$$O.T.B. = MAX - (OH + OO)$$

where

$$MAX = RS (RP + DP + R)$$
$$MIN = RS (R + DP)$$

• *EXAMPLE 10-6*

You have the responsibility to reorder light bulbs for your department, and you have the following information for 100-watt, inside-frosted bulbs:

Rate of sale	64 per week
Reorder period	2 weeks
Delivery period	1.4 weeks
Reserve	0.5 weeks
On-hand stock	115 bulbs
On-order stock	50 bulbs

Determine your open-to-buy.
(1) Calculate the maximum stock:

$$MAX = RS (RP + DP + R)$$
$$= 64 (2 + 1.4 + 0.5)$$
$$= 249.6, \text{ or } 250 \text{ uinits}$$

(2) Calculate the minimum stock:

$$MIN = RS (R + DP)$$
$$= 64 (0.5 + 1.4)$$
$$= 121.6, \text{ or } 122 \text{ units}$$

(3) Calculate the open-to-buy:

$$O.T.B. = MAX - (OH + OO)$$
$$= 250 - (115 + 50)$$
$$= 250 - 165$$
$$= 85 \text{ bulbs}$$

It is apparent that your on-hand stock (115 bulbs) is below your MIN (122 bulbs), and you should consider increasing your order to bring your inventory up to the established minimum level.

You will now see how the delivery period affects your stock, in that you must keep inventory on hand for each day and week that the vendor requires for delivery. Similarly, the length of time you take between review periods to write orders will affect your investment in merchandise.

To illustrate, consider that a new vendor has approached you and indicated that your reorders can be delivered in .5 weeks. In addition, you have decided to review your stock position every week. Summarizing this information and the data from the preceding example:

$$
\begin{aligned}
RS &= 64 \\
RP &= 1 \\
DP &= .5 \\
R &= .5 \\
OH &= 115 \text{ bulbs} \\
OO &= 50 \text{ bulbs}
\end{aligned}
$$

$$
\begin{aligned}
(1) \ MAX &= RS \ (RP + DP + R) \\
&= 64 \ (1 + .5 + .5) \\
&= 128
\end{aligned}
$$

$$
\begin{aligned}
(2) \ O.T.B. &= MAX - (OH + OO) \\
&= 128 - (165) \\
&= -37
\end{aligned}
$$

At this point, you have an overbought condition that should be eliminated in less than a week. Of principal importance is that your maximum stock has been reduced from 250 units to 128 units. This reduction in inventory investment will produce an increase in your stock turn, assuming sales remain the same. Improved stock turn, as you learned earlier, will usually be more profitable.

• *PROBLEM 10-6*

Your responsibilities in the Housewares Department include maintaining a basic stock of an open-stock pattern of crystal glassware restricted by the manufacturer to your store. You normally review the inventory every two weeks, and your stock count and records reveal the following information:

	WATER	CHAMPAGNE	OLD-FASHIONED
On hand	31	13	9
On order	24	12	6
Delivery period	1 week	1 week	1 week
Reserve	1 week	1 week	1 week
Rate of sale	36	12	8

The vendor will accept orders for merchandise in half-dozen units. Calculate the quantities to be ordered in each style.

SUMMARY PROBLEMS

• *PROBLEM 10-1 (S)*

The planned data for department 9100, domestics, follow. Prepare the six-month merchandise plan on the accompanying form (Fig. 10-3).

Planned net sales	$375,000
Operating expenses	22.0%
Cash discount	2.5%
Planned profit	$ 20,000
Reductions	$ 30,000
Seasonal stock turn	5.0

SIX MONTH MERCHANDISE PLAN

Department Name _____ Department No. _____ Period Covered _____

	Last Year	Plan			Last Year	Plan
Initial Markup	___	___		Gross Margin	___	___
Reductions	___	___		Operating Expense	___	___
Maintained Markup	___	___		Operating Profit	___	___
Cash Discount	___	___		Season Turnover	___	___

Buyer _____ Date Prepared _____

	Sales +			E.O.M. +			Reductions −			B.O.M. =			Retail Purchases			Cost Purchases		
	Last Year	Plan	Actual	Last Year	Plan	Actual	Last Year	Plan	Actual	Last Year	Plan	Actual	Last Year	Plan	Actual	Last Year	Plan	Actual
Spring / Fall																		
Feb. / Aug.																		
Mar. / Sept.																		
Apr. / Oct.																		
May / Nov.																		
June / Dec.																		
July / Jan.																		
Total																		

Figure 10-3

MONTH	PERCENTAGE OF SEASON'S SALES	PERCENTAGE OF SEASON'S REDUCTIONS
August	11%	14%
September	17	6
October	22	9
November	20	16
December	21	21
January	9	34

• PROBLEM 10-2 (S)

Your six-month merchandise plan shows the following purchase data for the months indicated:

	RETAIL PURCHASES	COST PURCHASES
August	$47,900	$22,226
September	49,800	23,107
October	52,300	24,267

You have placed orders with several vendors for delivery in each of these three months, as follows:

DELIVERY DATE	RETAIL PURCHASES	COST PURCHASES
August 15	$ 6397	$2840
September 15	15,305	7362
October 15	9101	3977

Determine

1. The initial markup percentage on the purchases.
2. The balance of open-to-buy each month.
3. The markup percentage needed on the open-to-buy to attain the initial markup percentage.

• PROBLEM 10-3 (S)

Due to unexpected poor weather the week before Easter Sunday, your inventory is considerably higher than planned. You have obtained permission to run a special post-Easter sale, during which you hope to reduce your stock. Your data are as follows:

	PLANNED: APRIL 1–19	ACTUAL: APRIL 1–19
Sales	$ 64,300	$59,500
Reductions	$ 4800	$ 7700

PLANNED: APRIL 1–19   ACTUAL: APRIL 1–19

Abstract of your six-month plan:

Sales	$112,000
E.O.M.	$220,000
Reductions	$ 8700
B.O.M.	$261,000
Retail purchases	$ 79,700
Cost purchases	$ 38,600

Determine the dollar change in your O.T.B. and prove your answer by recomputing the month of April's retail purchases from your six-month plan.

Colors	% of Total	White/20.0%			Pink/20.0%			Blue/25.0%			Patterns/35.0%		
Size	% of Total	Price Lines/%			Price Lines/%			Price Lines/%			Price Lines/%		
ITEMS / % OF TOTAL — **SHEETS 60.0%** Single	10.0%	$6 35.0%	$8 45.0%	$10 20.0%	$6 30.0%	$8 45.0%	$10 25.0%	$6 30.0%	$8 45.0%	$10 25.0%	$6 25.0%	$8 40.0%	$10 35.0%
Double	15.0%	$8 30.0%	$10 40.0%	$12 30.0%	$8 35.0%	$10 40.0%	$12 25.0%	$8 35.0%	$10 40.0%	$12 25.0%	$8 35.0%	$10 40.0%	$12 25.0%
Fitted Double	15.0%	$12 30.0%	$15 45.0%	$18 25.0%	$12 25.0%	$15 45.0%	$18 30.0%	$12 25.0%	$15 45.0%	$18 30.0%	$12 25.0%	$15 45.0%	$18 30.0%
Fitted Queen	35.0%	$16 25.0%	$20 50.0%	$24 25.0%	$16 25.0%	$20 50.0%	$24 25.0%	$16 25.0%	$20 50.0%	$24 25.0%	$16 25.0%	$20 50.0%	$24 25.0%
Fitted King	25.0%	$25 40.0%	$30 60.0%	$35 0%	$25 30.0%	$30 50.0%	$35 20.0%	$25 30.0%	$30 50.0%	$35 20.0%	$25 15.0%	$30 50.0%	$35 35.0%
CASES 40.0% Reg.	45.0%	$4 50.0%	$6 30.0%	$8 20.0%	$4 30.0%	$6 45.0%	$8 25.0%	$4 30.0%	$6 45.0%	$8 25.0%	$4 25.0%	$6 40.0%	$8 35.0%
Super	55.0%	$6 50.0%	$8 30.0%	$10 20.0%	$6 30.0%	$8 45.0%	$10 25.0%	$6 30.0%	$8 45.0%	$10 25.0%	$6 25.0%	$8 40.0%	$10 35.0%

Figure 10-4

• *PROBLEM 10-4 (S)*

Your six-month merchandise plan for September 198___ shows the following information:

Planned sales	$116,000
E.O.M.	295,000
Reductions	14,000
B.O.M.	275,000
IM%	56.4%

On September 19, you have calculated the following:

Sales to date	$59,500
Reductions to date	7300
Merchandise received	93,000
Merchandise on order for September	36,000

There are 26 selling days in September, of which 10 days remain, including September 19. Determine your open-to-buy.

• *PROBLEM 10-5 (S)*

Your open-to-buy for the Linen Department for June is $56,600. Figure 10-4 on p. 209 contains the balance of the needed data. Compute your unit open-to-buy for each category, rounding off your totals to the nearest quarter dozen.

• *PROBLEM 10-6 (S)*

You are the buyer of scarves for Annette Boutique, Union Square, San Francisco, California, in the Accessories Department. The $10, 24-inch square silk scarf in white and black is ordered according to a basic stock list procedure. The vendor, B & B Neckwear of 15 West 37th Street, New York, New York, offers this merchandise in style 912 white and 913 black at $72 per dozen at cost, for delivery within two weeks, F.O.B., factory; the terms are 8/10 E.O.M., no anticipation.

Today, February 8, you have checked your stock and back orders for this merchandise, as you do every week, and developed the following data:

	912 WHITE	*913 BLACK*
Rate of sale (weekly)	150	80
Reserve supply	1 week	1 week
Stock on hand	297	159
Stock on order	6 dozen	3 dozen

The vendor requires that merchandise be ordered in one-dozen multiples. Calculate the quantities to be bought and write the order on the accompanying form (Fig. 10-5).

Bill to:	ANNETTE BOUTIQUE				DATE ___/___/___									
	UNION SQUARE			ORDERED FROM										
	SAN FRANCISCO, CA													
Ship to:	Annette Boutique													
	1677 Fremont St.													
	San Francisco, CA			RETURNS TO		A	30	32	34	36	38	40	42

| MU% | TOTAL OF ORDER—RET. | ORDER NO. 02492 | SALESMAN | TERMS: AS OF / | | B | 6 | 8 | 10 | 12 | 14 | 16 | 18 |
| | | | | | | C | 5 | 7 | 9 | 11 | 13 | 15 | |

DELIVERY START	COMPLETE	SHIPPING INSTRUCTIONS BEST WAY ☐ AS HAD ☐	SPECIAL SHIPPING INSTRUCTIONS ☐		D	XS	S	M	L	XL		
					E	8½	9	9½	10	10½	11	
					F	6	6½	7	7½	8		

STYLE NO.	QUANTITY	WHOLESALE PRICE	RETAIL PRICE	COST TOTAL	DESCRIPTION	CODE	COLOR	G						
								H						

POSITIVELY NO BROKEN SIZES SHIPPED AND NO SUBSTITUTIONS OF STYLES, SIZES OR COLOR, UNLESS PERMISSION IS OBTAINED. MDSE. RECEIVED AFTER 20th OF MONTH PAYABLE AS OF THE 25th. MDSE.-SHIPPED AFTER COMPLETION DATE, SUBJECT TO RETURN AT BUYER'S DISCRETION.

Figure 10-5

CASE STUDY

SWEATERS UNLIMITED

As the owner of Sweaters Unlimited, your goal has always been to carry a small stock of six attractive basic styles and put the greatest proportion of your investment into fashionable, "trendy" merchandise. You have been quite successful; sales have increased, and your customers have come to know and respect your taste and business practices.

This morning, November 20, you had phone calls from two vendors, both of them offering you off-price merchandise. The first call was from Bristol Woolen Mills, who is in an overstocked position with a basic Shetland pullover in white and black. They are offering this sweater (which you stock 12 months of the year) at $10.75 each at cost, instead of the regular price of $14.75. The regular cash discount will be permitted, and delivery will be in two to three weeks. This sweater retails in your store for $28.00. You must purchase at least ten dozen sweaters to qualify for the special price.

The second phone conversation was with the representative of Margie Carol Knits, who is offering you a 25-dozen "package" of assorted styles, colors, and sizes from the current fall line for $3450 at cost. The representative assured you that the total original retail value for this perfect and new merchandise is $9000 or better; however, you must buy the package as is with no substitutions; you must buy at least 25 dozen sweaters. The regular cash discount will apply, and delivery will be in two to three weeks.

To help you make your decision, you review your records and discover the following information: Bristol Woolen Mills has been a faithful supplier of quality merchandise that has sold well; its delivery period has been consistently 2.5 weeks, and as a result you have kept only a one-week reserve, while reviewing your stock every two weeks. The merchandise on hand and on order for both colors is:

$$OH + OO$$

	S	M	L
White	54	84	27
Black	24	72	57

and the rate of sales is:

	S	M	L
White	10	15	5
Black	5	15	10

Your information about Margie Carol Knits shows that you bought eight styles this past fall, six of which sold extremely well. One was average, and the remaining style sold poorly.

An examination of your merchandise plan shows that your purchases during November were to have been $96,500 at retail and $43,900 at cost. To date you have spent $69,300 at retail and $30,700 at cost on the fashion merchandise and $18,900 at retail and $9790 at cost for your basic stock list inventory. Your plan also provides that 20 percent of your purchases cover basics, while 80 percent should be spent for the fashion lines.

What will you do and why?

Measuring and Evaluating Sales Results

11

Throughout this text, you have been referred to store or department records as sources of data for assistance in planning and decision making. The assumption has been that your superiors, predecessors, or someone has had the foresight to realize that a business cannot be successful in the absence of well organized information regarding its operation, and that this data can be assembled and interpreted to benefit the store.

You will find that regardless of the size (dollar volume, ownership, number of employees, or square footage) of your organization, certain basic knowledge is essential for its operation. Your plan for data collection, organization, and analysis should be accomplished *before* you assume a retailing position or prior to opening your own shop. The type and level of detail of accrued data will be a function of your *anticipated* needs for simple or complex information in order to manage your department or store effectively.

If you are engaged in a unique form of retailing, or if your store is geographically distant from a similar operation, you might assume that your record keeping can be minimal. Nothing could be further from the truth. Your competitive environment will undoubtedly change as others perceive your success, and at this juncture, without appropriate data to assist you to fine-tune your business, you will become history.

Meaningless or trivial data will serve only to clutter your files (and mind). Similarly, information collected and assembled in the absence of very definite plans for its end use will quickly become rubbish and may have the unfortunate effect of deterring you from saving important material.

ARRANGING DATA—CLASSIFYING MERCHANDISE

The bulk of your data will be merchandise information derived from sales and stock reports, both in units and in dollars. As an aid to analysis and planning, you (or your superiors) will decide upon the detail required.

The National Retail Merchants Association (NRMA) developed a **Standard Classification of Merchandise**[1] coding system which provides a hierarchical classification for the full assortment of general merchandise, using a four-digit numeric code. The coding was produced with a logical customer or end-user orientation. It was the hope and expectation of the NRMA that this system would be adopted by retailers, vendors, and equipment manufacturers so that vendors would source-mark merchandise for retailers and these codes could be input via point-of-sale terminal keys or optical scanning devices to provide rapidly prepared, accurate records.

While the system has not yet become universally accepted, the concept of classification of merchandise has great implications for retailers of any scale in terms of arranging data. Table 11-1 lists major merchandise groups; Table 11-2

Table 11-1 Major Merchandise Groupings

CLASSIFICATION NUMBER	MERCHANDISE GROUP
0100	All Shoes
1000	Adult Female Apparel
2000	Adult Female Intimate Apparel and Accessories
3000	Adult Male Apparel
4000	Infants', Boys', Girls' Clothing and Accessories
5000	Personal Needs and Small Wares: Food, Tobaccos
6000	Hobby, Recreation and Transportation
7000	Home Furnishings: Furniture and Decorative Accessories
8000	Home Furnishings: Appliances and Utility Equipment
9000	Domestics, Draperies, and Home Goods Categories

Table 11-2 Subclassifications of Major Merchandise Grouping 1000

1000 ADULT FEMALE APPAREL	
1100	Cloth and All-weather Coats (including rainwear)
1200	Natural and Synthetic Leather and Fur Outerwear
1300	Women's, Misses' and Juniors' Dresses and Suits
1400	Formals
1500	Bridal, Maternity, and Uniforms
1600	Sportswear Tops
1700	Sportswear Bottoms
1800	Coordinates and Related Separates
1900	Swim, Tennis, Snow, Ski, and Other Sports Apparel

Table 11-3 Selected Finite Merchandise Groupings of Subclassification 1600

1600 SPORTSWEAR TOPS

1610 Misses' Knit Tops

1611	Shirts
1612	Blouses
1613	Cut and Sewn Knit Tops (includes T-Shirts)
1614	Sweaters
1615	Jackets
1616	Vests

---

shows how a major group is itself reduced to subclassifications; and Table 11-3 is a more detailed breakdown of a single sub-classification into further subgroups.

To illustrate, the sample ticket shown in Chapter Five in Figure 5-4 for classification code 3231 would be read as follows:

3000	Adult Male Apparel
200	Clothing and Suits
30	Suits—Regular Weight
1	Two-Piece
3231	

While you may not opt to use the NRMA coding system, some method must be adopted, to the level of your needs, which will enable you to accumulate data in an organized and recognizable form.

ASSEMBLING DATA—DOLLARS AND UNITS

Any report that uses sales as a base is useful in two ways: to identify trends, and also for the six-month merchandise plan for the following and comparable season of the next year. Data may be either presented as dollar sales or as unit sales. The unit sales would be recorded as totals within each price line, totals of a major classification, or a finite sum of particular **stock-keeping units (S.K.U.'s)**. The numeric values should, however, be converted to percentages if they are to be meaningful. The procedure for changing either dollar or unit values to percentages is as follows:

1. Determine the total for all classifications or stores:

	DOLLAR SALES	UNIT SALES
Class 1	$ 4900	1546
Class 2	6300	1988
Class 3	3700	1166
Total	$14,900	4700

2. Find the percentage value for each class:

	DATA, AS DOLLARS		DATA, AS UNITS
Class 1	= $4900 ÷ $14,900	or	= 1546 ÷ 4700
	= 32.9%		= 32.9%
Class 2	= $6300 ÷ $14,900	or	= 1988 ÷ 4700
	= 42.3%		= 42.3%
Class 3	= $3700 ÷ $14,900	or	= 1166 ÷ 4700
	= 24.8%		= 24.8%

3. Check your work by summing the percentage values:

$$
\begin{array}{r}
32.9\% \\
42.3 \\
24.8 \\
\hline
100.0\%
\end{array}
$$

• EXAMPLE 11-1

Table 11-4 illustrates monthly data in the China and Glassware Department for a three-store chain. The values have been converted to percentage values and arranged for analysis.

The data in Table 11-4 show the following:

(1) Store 01 has the largest dollar volume, 60.6 percent of the total
(2) China five-piece place settings account for more sales, 40.9 percent, than the other types
(3) Stores 01 and 02 sell more china than earthenware or plastic, 42.1 and 44.1 percent, respectively, while Store 03 sells more earthenware, 39.1 percent of its total
(4) Store 01 ranks earthenware second in sales over plastic, 38.9 to 19.0 percent
(5) Store 02 ranks plastic second over earthenware, 33.9 to 22.0 percent
(6) Store 03 ranks plastic second over china, 34.8 to 26.1 percent

While these conclusions are justified from the information available, you should recognize that sales not only represent customer preferences but are also a function of stock on hand. This will be discussed and illustrated later in the chapter.

You might also find it useful to develop data for sales by price line, which can be used as a planning aid. Refer to Table 11-5.

Given the analysis completed from Table 11-4 and the caveat that you must examine your

Table 11-4 Sales by Class

| Department Number: | 7400 | China and Glassware | | Period Ending: 6/30/8_ |
| Classification: | 30 | Five-Piece Place Settings | | |

DEPARTMENT TOTALS

STORE		01	02	03	TOTAL
$Sales		12,600	5900	2300	20,800
% of Total		60.6	28.4	11.1	100.0

TOTALS BY CLASSIFICATION

China	$ Sales	5300	2600	600	8500
#7431	% of Total	42.1	44.1	26.1	40.9
Earth	$ Sales	4900	1300	900	7100
#7432	% of Total	38.9	22.0	39.1	34.1
Plastic	$ Sales	2400	2000	800	5200
#7433	% of Total	19.0	33.9	34.8	25.0
Store	$ Sales	12,600	5900	2300	20,800
Total	% of Total	100.0	100.0	100.0	100.0

Table 11-5 Sales by Price Line

| Department Number: | 7400 | China and Glassware | | Period Ending: 6/30/8_ |
| Classification: | 7431 | Five-Piece Place Settings | | |

DEPARTMENT TOTALS

STORE		01	02	03	TOTAL
$ Sales		5300	2600	600	8500
% of Total		62.4	30.6	7.1	100.0

TOTALS BY PRICE LINE

$100	$Sales	2100	700	100	2900
	% of Total	39.6	26.9	16.7	34.1
$150	$ Sales	2400	1500	300	4200
	% of Total	45.3	57.7	50.0	49.4
$200	$ Sales	800	400	200	1400
	% of Total	15.1	15.4	33.3	16.5
Store	$ Sales	5300	2600	600	8500
Total	% of Total	100.0	100.0	100.0	100.0

stock on hand, you can now draw inferences from the more detailed information provided in Table 11-5:

1. The best-selling price line in all three stores is $150.
2. Stores 01 and 02 sell the $100 price second best.
3. From the percentage values, it would appear that the $200 price line is better for Store 03 than the $100 line (33.3 to 16.7 percent). By dividing dollar sales by price line, however, you see that Store 03 has sold only one set at $100; two sets at $150; and one set at $200, so there is actually no significant difference between them; therefore, unit sales must be considered as well as dollar sales.

- *PROBLEM 11-1*

You are a fashion jewelry buyer who is responsible for this department in four locations. The accumulated data for the month of April are shown in Table 11-6. Arrange the data from the table in a meaningful fashion and indicate your conclusions.

Table 11-6   Unit Sales by Classification, Price, and Location

		Units				
CLASS	LOCATION/PRICE	1	2	3	4	TOTAL
Necklaces	$10.00	3200	2400	600	1200	7400
	$15.00	1600	2010	800	1100	5510
	$20.00	1700	1900	1200	1700	6500
	$25.00	1400	1850	1100	1800	6150
Bracelets	$ 4.00	1100	1300	280	900	3580
	$ 8.00	1700	1100	375	1150	4325
	$12.00	1200	1050	590	1300	4140
	$15.00	1150	1025	775	1450	4400
Pins	$ 2.50	3620	2900	460	540	7520
	$ 3.00	3400	2750	590	780	7520
	$ 3.50	2800	2400	830	1200	7230
	$ 4.00	2300	2025	1100	1425	6850

Physical profile and the inventory.   Among the many problems confronting buyers is that of determining, as accurately as possible, the physical makeup of their inventory, and questions like the following must be answered:

1. What should be the *breadth* of my merchandise; how many price lines should there be in each classification?
2. What should be the *depth* of my merchandise; how many styles should there be in each price line?
3. What should be the proportion of one classification of merchandise to another?
4. What should be the proportion of sizes (shoes, shirts, dishes, etc.) within each classification?

An alternative that you may have to accept in the absence of accumulated data is to rely on the advice of your vendors. Most manufacturers and their representatives have a sense of the size scales, colors, and style preferences in the marketplace, and they endeavor to produce their merchandise in accordance with this knowledge. You will learn, though, that even the most respected member of this group can make mistakes, and a limited number of them may even advise you incorrectly to relieve the pressure on their own poor assortment. Consequently, you should very carefully assess any and all advice, as the mistakes you buy today become your markdowns tomorrow.

Another possibility to examine is that of shopping your competitors and "eyeballing" their inventory for the proportions of sizes, colors, and styles. Of course, you will see only the *forward* stock, but you can gain much useful insight. The major drawback to this technique is that your department or store may be unique and attract a different clientele from the shop down the street, even though both of you carry the same classifications of merchandise. Thus, shopping your competition could very well cause you to mistrust your own judgment. Obviously, the best and most reliable approach to pursue is to develop your own data base and update and review this information periodically.

The following example illustrates a principle that can be employed to help you determine how to select the proportion of sizes, colors, and styles, as well as the ratio of one item or group of items to another related classification. It is essentially the same process you employed in Example 11-1.

- *EXAMPLE 11-2*

You have accumulated data in the Kitchenware Department in an effort to aid your buying and reduce your markdowns. Your stocks on hand (OH) and unit sales for the last six months, for the items indicated, are listed in Table 11-7. If your open-to-buy for the next buying period is $15,000, determine the amount you will spend for each category, with an explanation for the decisions. In Table 11-7, the sales figures represent unit sales at full price, excluding sales at reduced prices. These numbers are more reliable because they represent purchases made by what is more apt to be your regular customer; when merchandise is available at reduced prices, customers are more willing to make a trade-off between what they really want and what they can get for the marked-down price.

Table 11-7   Cookware

	TOTAL	8" FRYPAN	10" FRYPAN	1-QT. SAUCEPAN	2-QT. SAUCEPAN
Unit OH	1068	164	389	363	152
Unit sales	893	145	361	280	107
Planned E.O.M. for the last month in the period	240	40	80	80	40

(1) Compute the percentage of the total for each item for both OH and unit sales. To illustrate, for 8" frypans:

$$OH\% = 164 \div 1068$$
$$= 15.4\%$$

$$Sales\% = 145 \div 893$$
$$= 16.2\%$$

The completed data are shown in Table 11-8.

(2) Compute the total percentage for both OH and unit sales made by frypans and saucepans. To illustrate, for frypans:

$$Total\ OH\% = 15.4\% + 36.4\%$$
$$= 51.8\%$$

$$Total\ sales\% = 16.2\% + 40.4\%$$
$$= 56.6\%$$

The completed data are shown in Table 11-9.

(3) Compute the percentage of the total for each item. To illustrate, for 8" frypans:

$$OH\% = 15.4\% \div 51.8\%$$
$$= 29.7\%$$

$$Sales\% = 16.2\% \div 56.6\%$$
$$= 28.6\%$$

The completed data are shown in Table 11-10.

(4) Compute the percentage of OH stock that was sold for each item. To illustrate, for 8" frypans:

$$Sales\% = 145 \div 164$$
$$= 88.4\%$$

Table 11-8

	8" FRYPANS	10" FRYPANS	1-QT. SAUCEPANS	2-QT. SAUCEPANS
OH%	15.4	36.4	34.0	14.2
Sales %	16.2	40.4	31.4	12.0

Table 11-9

	FRYPANS	SAUCEPANS
Total OH%	51.8	48.2
Total sales %	56.6	43.4

Table 11-10

	8" FRYPANS	10" FRYPANS	1-QT. SAUCEPANS	2-QT. SAUCEPANS
OH%	29.7	70.3	70.5	29.5
Sales%	28.6	71.4	72.3	27.6

The completed data are shown in Table 11-11.

(5) Compute the actual remaining E.O.M. inventory for each item. To illustrate, for 8″ frypans:

$$
\begin{aligned}
\text{Actual E.O.M.} &= \text{Unit OH} - \text{Unit Sales} \\
&= 164 - 145 \\
&= 19
\end{aligned}
$$

The results for the balance of this computational work and a summary of the data developed in the other steps are presented in Table 11-12.

From observing the information in Table 11-12, you should be able to arrive at certain conclusions about data collection. While you are primarily concerned with profit, in terms of dollars, it is nevertheless wiser to examine unit information segmented into appropriate categories. Viewing unit data in this manner gives you the opportunity to analyze your sales in terms of specific types of classifications of merchandise, which might not be possible if your analyses were confined only to dollar amounts.

Proceeding to the summarized data in Table 11-12, you can see that 16.2 percent of the sales in the department were accounted for by 8-inch frypans, while the stock of this item was only 15.4 percent. A similar but larger gap is shown for the 10-inch frypans, for which sales were 40.4 percent of the department total and the OH stock was 36.4 percent. The reverse situation holds true for 1-quart and 2-quart saucepans, both contributing less to sales than the value of their inventory.

Under most circumstances, the volume of sales for an item carried in a department should be very close to the amount of stock on hand. The data above, therefore, are an indication of an understocked condition for frypans generally and the 10-inch size in particular, and an overstocked position for saucepans as a group, with both sizes almost equally overstocked. This same analysis of stock on hand and sales can be done on a broader scale if you have to compare performance for identical departments in a number of branch stores.

The data carried over from Table 11-11 (percentage of OH stock sold by type) show the percentage of stock on hand that was sold for each item. For example, in the 8-inch frypan category, 88.4 percent of the inventory was sold, while only 70.4 percent of the stock on hand was sold in the 2-quart saucepan category. You can conclude that you were probably overstocked with both sizes of saucepans, while being understocked for both sizes of frypans.

This situation can be further emphasized by examining the actual E.O.M. inventories remaining and comparing them to the planned E.O.M. inventories. Frypans should total 120 pieces, but you actually have only 47; while saucepans, which were also planned to have 120 pieces, have 128 units left.

The computations from Table 11-9 (combined percentage total sales for each type) continue to show a weak OH position for frypans relative to sales, with the reverse being true for saucepans.

The data from Table 11-10 (percentage of total sales by size for each type) give you a sense of the balance in stock and sales for frypans and saucepans as separate groups. That is, the 8-inch frypans accounted for 28.6 percent of the total sales of frypans, with 29.7 percent of the total frypan inventory. The information for 10-inch frypans shows the reverse situation, demonstrating a somewhat understocked condition for this category. You should review the data for saucepans in a similar manner.

After completing these steps, you can examine nonquantifiable information, such as altera-

Table 11-11

8″ FRYPANS	10″ FRYPANS	1-QT. SAUCEPANS	2-QT. SAUCEPANS
88.4%	92.8%	77.1%	70.4%

Table 11-12 Cookware Class 8323

Given data		TOTAL	8" FRYPANS	10" FRYPANS	1-QT. SAUCEPANS	2-QT. SAUCEPANS
Given data	Unit OH	1068	164	389	363	152
	Unit sales	893	145	361	280	107
	Planned E.O.M. for last month in the period	240	40	80	80	40
% of totals (Table 11-8)	OH	100.0	15.4	36.4	34.0	14.2
	Sales	100.0	16.2	40.4	31.4	12.0
Combined % of totals for each type (Table 11-9)	OH	100.0		51.8	48.2	
	Sales	100.0		56.6	43.4	
% of total by size for each Type (Table 11-10)	OH	⧖	29.7	70.3	70.5	29.5
	Sales	⧖	28.6	71.4	72.3	27.6
% of OH stock sold by type (Table 11-11)	Sales	⧖	88.4	92.8	77.1	70.4
Actual E.O.M.		175	19	28	83	45

tions in the market for cookware, customer profiles, and store plans for image changes. If there are no significant differences, you can plan your dollar investment. At this point, however, your data (Table 11-12) must be combined with the preceding nonmathematical analysis to produce your open-to-buy:

1. Determine the dollar amount to be spent for frypans and saucepans, recalling from Table 11-9 that your frypans were understocked; by reasoning that sales were probably lost as a result, you would be safe to estimate from the data that 60.0 percent of your purchases should be allocated to frypans. Therefore

$$\$15,000 \times .6 \qquad = \$9000 \text{ for frypans}$$
$$\$15,000 - \$9000 = \$6000 \text{ for saucepans}$$

2. Determine the dollar amount to be spent for each size of frypans and saucepans. The conclusions drawn from the data (Table 11-10) were that 8-inch frypans and 2-quart saucepans were overstocked in their respective categories. You could reasonably estimate the following:

For frypans:

8" should be 27% of purchases
= $9000 × .27
= $2430
10" should be 100% − 27% = 73%
= $9000 × .73
= $6570

For saucepans:

1-Qt. should be 75% of purchases
= $6000 × .75
= $4500
2-Qt. should be 100% − 75% = 25%
= $6000 × .25
= $1500

• PROBLEM 11-2

Your unit sales and stock information for the Women's Sweater Department follow: If your open-to-buy for the two sweater categories is $97,000, determine the amount of your investment for each type and size.

		32	34	36	38	40
Cardigans	OH	87	112	146	199	208
	Sales	34	73	118	162	175
Pullovers	OH	96	137	175	196	153
	Sales	58	85	153	178	97

ANALYZING SALES DATA

Sales data are generally analyzed in three ways: sales for a particular day compared with the same day last year, that is, a Monday this year relative to the same Monday in the month last year, without regard to date; month-to-date (M.T.D.) sales this year as compared with last year; and year-to-date (Y.T.D.) sales this year as compared with last year. This report is commonly known as a **flash report**. It is useful to calculate both the dollar increase or decrease in all cases and the comparable percentage values.

• *EXAMPLE 11-3*

At the conclusion of Saturday, August 8, you are to prepare the comparisons of day-to-day, month-to-date, and year-to-date sales figures. The comparable Saturday last year was August 9. Your data are as follows:

	LAST YEAR - SALES		THIS YEAR - SALES
August 9	$ 2670	August 8	$ 2346
August 1–9	18,347	August 1-8	21,593
February 1–July 31	179,636	February 1–July 31	193,646

The computational work is similar to that which you did previously. Remember that you are making comparisons from the current year to the previous year; therefore, last year is the base year over which you experienced either an increase or decrease. If your figures this year are greater than figures from the prior year, you have experienced an increase. Conversely, if the data from the current period are less than those from last year, you have encountered a decrease in sales.

(1) Calculate the day-to-day comparison:

$$\$Difference = \$This\ year - \$Last\ year$$
$$= \$2346 - \$2670$$
$$= -\$324$$

$$\%Difference = \$Difference \div \$Last\ year$$
$$= -\$324 \div \$2670$$
$$= -12.1\%$$

(2) Calculate the month-to-date comparison:

$$\$Difference = \$This\ year - \$Last\ year$$
$$= \$21,593 - \$18,347$$
$$= \$3246$$

$$\%Difference = \$Difference \div \$Last\ year$$
$$= \$3246 \div \$18,347$$
$$= 17.7\%$$

(3) Calculate the year-to-date comparison:

(a) Combine the volume of February 1 to July 31 with the sales thus far for August for both last year and this year.

$$\text{Last year February 1 to August 9} = \$179{,}636 + \$18{,}347$$
$$= \$197{,}983$$

$$\text{This year February 1 to August 8} = \$193{,}646 + \$21{,}593$$
$$= \$215{,}239$$

(b)

$$\$\text{Difference} = \$\text{This year} - \$\text{Last year}$$
$$= \$215{,}239 - \$197{,}983$$
$$= \$17{,}256$$

$$\%\text{Difference} = \$\text{Difference} \div \$\text{Last year}$$
$$= \$17{,}256 \div \$197{,}983$$
$$= 8.7\%$$

(4) Arrange the data from steps 1, 2, and 3. (See Fig. 11-1)
The data clearly shows that
(a) August 8 was not as good as the comparable day last year, being off by 12.1 percent.
(b) The month of August, thus far, has an increase over August of last year, being 17.7 percent greater.
(c) The percentage increase in August is greater than the percentage increase for the year, 17.7 percent as compared with 8.7 percent.
   Generally, you would conclude that August this year has been better than the preceding August, and the year-to-date figures reflect a similar condition. Some of the reasons why the specific day (August 8) was "off" could be adverse weather or a sale held last year, or possibly the department, for some reason, is in a lower stock position this year.

The amount of inventory, as has been stated, is a critical factor to consider, and your attention to the level of inventory must be constant.
   While comparisons of current sales to data for the preceding year's are important, it is equally, if not more, important to perform identical computations with the planned sales figures.
   To illustrate, using the data in the preceding example for this year, year-to-date (February 1 to August 8) sales of $215,239 [step 3 (a)] and planned sales of $200,000 for this period, determine the dollar and percentage increase or decrease:

$$\$\text{Difference} = \$\text{Actual sales} - \$\text{Planned sales}$$
$$= \$215{,}239 - \$200{,}000$$
$$= \$15{,}239$$

Figure 11-1

DAY TO DAY				MONTH TO DATE				YEAR TO DATE			
LY $2670	TY $2346	+/− $324 −	+/− 12.1% −	LY $18,347	TY $21,593	+/− $3246 +	+/− 17.7% +	LY $197,983	TY $215,239	+/− $17,256 +	+/− 8.7% +

$$\%\text{Difference} = \$15,239 \div \$200,000$$
$$= 7.6\%$$

Now you can conclude that not only have you beaten last year's figures, but you are also ahead of your plan.

As you have done before, examine your stock levels to determine if they will continue to be adequate to support your sales. You should also examine unit sales for comparison purposes, because if the retail prices of your merchandise are higher than anticipated, owing to market conditions or inflationary trends in the economy, your increases could really not be increases at all, and they might even prove to be decreases.

If, for example, sales had been planned to accommodate an inflation rate of 2 percent and the actual inflation rate is 10 percent, your increase of 7.6 percent would not be an increase at all. As the difference of 8 percent (10 − 2 percent) in the inflation is .4 percent greater than your actual sales increase, you are actually somewhat behind.

• *PROBLEM 11-3*

On Saturday evening, September 24, you are supposed to assemble and arrange the data on the day-to-day, month-to-date, and year-to-date figures for your department and prepare an evaluation of the information. Your records show the following data:

	LAST YEAR—SALES		THIS YEAR—SALES
September 25	$ 9427	September 24	$ 10,563
September 1–September 25	176,915	September 1–September 24	210,631
February 1–August 30	849,312	February 1–August 30	1,403,214

In many cases, a flash report may contain a number of other pieces of information, such as weather on the particular date and the number of *transactions*. Weather data may be useful for explaining why sales increased or decreased compared with the preceding year. Transaction information can be used for determining the dollar value of your average sale, which may over time be an indicator of customer spending—a higher average sale indicating that customers are purchasing higher-ticket items or buying multiples, or that money is being spent more easily. The converse would also be true—a lower average sale showing customer acceptance of lower-priced goods or purchasing of fewer items during each shopping trip, or a tight money supply. Transaction data is also used to evaluate the productivity of your sales associates. This topic is addressed in Chapter 13.

• *EXAMPLE 11-4*

Using the sales data from Example 11-3 and the following information, calculate the average sale, day-to-day, month-to-date, and year-to-date, for both last year and this year, and then evaluate the results.

	LAST YEAR—TRANSACTIONS		THIS YEAR—TRANSACTIONS
August 9	72	August 8	54
August 1–9	479	August 1–8	473
February 1–July 31	4876	February 1–July 31	4797

Calculate average sales for each period:

Average sale = Total sales for the period ÷ Number of transactions

For last year, August 9:

$$= \$2670 \div 72$$
$$= \$37.08$$

The results of the balance of the computations are arranged as follows:

	LAST YEAR		THIS YEAR
August 9	$37.08	August 8	$43.44
M.T.D.	38.30	M.T.D.	45.65
Y.T.D.	36.84	Y.T.D.	40.37

The data show that your average sale is greater this year for all periods compared with last year; that is, although you have had fewer transactions, your average sale has been higher. This phenomenon can be analyzed by raising and responding to a variety of questions, such as

1. Are general economic conditions improving?
2. Are the demographics of your trading area changing? Are there more housing units or more affluent customers?
3. Has the price line and price zone emphasis of your buying altered? Is this the same for the entire store? What are the implications if you have changed but the store has not, and conversely? In the first instance, in which you have changed, the overtone would be that perhaps the store should upgrade its merchandising overall. If the store has generally traded up its stock but you have not, it seems to indicate that higher-priced merchandise is selling and, therefore, you should examine your current inventory to determine if your lower-priced lines are selling poorly. If this is the case, you must eliminate the overstocked situation in less expensive goods and revise your open orders to reflect the need for "better" merchandise.
4. Has the productivity of your sales force increased?
5. Have you inadvertently neglected to buy lower-priced merchandise, or have the selections shown to you by vendors been unusually poor?
6. Have prices increased for some merchandise?

• PROBLEM 11-4

You have the data on p. 229 for your department. Arrange the information and explain the results.

Last Year		
PERIOD	SALES	TRANSACTIONS
November 28	$ 3796	47
November 1–November 28	49,381	614
February 1–October 31	780,002	9752

This Year		
PERIOD	SALES	TRANSACTIONS
November 27	$ 3693	48
November 1–November 27	45,961	610
February 1–October 31	712,419	9371

A final factor to consider in analyzing your sales is your B.O.M. merchandise. Previous chapters have dealt with stock planning, both in dollars and in units, demonstrating the relationship between sales and inventory.

The stock-to-sales ratio (S-S), which was previously discussed in Chapter Nine as a planning tool, is also used to evaluate the effectiveness of the actual inventory. The S-S indicates the numbers of S.K.U.'s or dollars which were on hand to produce one S.K.U. or one dollar of sales. As an example, an S-S of 2.9 would mean that 2.9 (dollars or S.K.U.'s) were available to sell one (dollar or S.K.U.) of merchandise.

The formula used to determine the relationship of stock to sales is:

$$\text{S-S} = \text{Stock} \div \text{Sales}$$

A "perfect," but unsatisfactory, relationship of "1" would be obtained if the amount of inventory was equal to the value of sales. As an example, if the B.O.M. stock were $200 and sales for the period were $200, the S-S would be 1. Obviously, this would be unworkable, because it would leave no merchandise for future selling, and you would have to replace the stock on a daily basis.

- *EXAMPLE 11-5*

Examine the stock-to-sales ratio and other data in Figure 11-2 for class 9320 sheets and for the total department, and analyze the effectiveness of the inventory.

The printout reveals the following:

Total class 9320 S-S = 1.59
Total department S-S = 1.63

Figure 11-2

		\-\-\-\-\-\-\-\-\-\- LAST YEAR \-\-\-\-\-\-\-\-\-\-\-\-\-			\-\-\-\-\-\-\-\-\-LAST YEAR \-\-\-\-\-\-\-\-\-\-			
CLASS	DESCRIPTION	198– UNIT SALES	% TOTAL CLASS	% TOTAL DEPT.	198– UNIT PURCH.	% TOTAL CLASS	% TOTAL DEPT.	STOCK-SALES RATIO
9320 SHEETS (TWIN)								
	TOTAL FITTED	56,800	80.17%	45.94%	86,000	76.55%	42.71%	1.51
BRANDED	SOLID	18,500	26.11%	14.96%	40,000	35.60%	19.87%	2.16
PRIVATE LABEL	SOLID	38,300	54.06%	30.97%	46,000	40.94%	22.85%	1.20
	TOTAL FLAT	14,050	19.83%	11.36%	26,350	23.45%	13.09%	1.88
BRANDED	SOLID	9,300	13.13%	7.52%	19,000	16.91%	9.44%	2.04
PRIVATE LABEL	SOLID	4,750	6.70%	3.84%	7,350	6.54%	3.65%	1.55
	TOTAL BRANDED	27,800	39.24%	22.48%	59,000	52.51%	29.30%	2.12
	TOTAL PRIVATE LABEL	43,050	60.76%	34.82%	53,350	47.49%	26.50%	1.24
	TOTAL CLASS 9320	70,850	100.00%	57.30%	112,350	100.00%	55.80%	1.59
9322 SHEETS (QUEEN)								
	TOTAL FITTED	38,300	72.54%	30.97%	61,000	68.54%	30.30%	1.59
BRANDED	SOLID	21,500	40.72%	17.39%	40,000	44.94%	19.87%	1.86
PRIVATE LABEL	SOLID	16,800	31.82%	13.59%	21,000	23.60%	10.43%	1.25
	TOTAL FLAT	14,500	27.46%	11.73%	28,000	31.46%	13.91%	1.93
BRANDED	SOLID	8,300	15.72%	6.71%	17,500	19.66%	8.69%	2.11
PRIVATE LABEL	SOLID	6,200	11.74%	5.01%	10,500	11.80%	5.21%	1.69
	TOTAL BRANDED	29,800	56.44%	24.10%	57,500	64.61%	28.56%	1.93
	TOTAL PRIVATE LABEL	23,000	43.56%	18.60%	31,500	35.39%	15.64%	1.37
	TOTAL CLASS 9322	52,800	100.00%	42.70%	89,000	100.00%	44.20%	1.69
TOTAL DEPARTMENT		123,650	100.00%	100.00%	201,350	100.00%	100.00%	1.63
RECAP	FITTED	95,100	N/A	76.91%	147,000	N/A	73.01%	1.55
	FLAT	28,550	N/A	23.09%	54,350	N/A	26.99%	1.90
	BRANDED	57,600	N/A	46.58%	116,500	N/A	57.86%	2.02
	PRIVATE LABEL	66,050	N/A	53.42%	84,850	N/A	42.14%	1.28

BOUDOIR BOUTIQUE
CLASSES 9320-9322   BUYERS COPY

On the surface, this would appear to be good. Examining within class 9320, a wide range of S-S is apparent: 1.20 for private label solid fitted sheets to 2.16 for branded solid fitted sheets. This wide disparity is further emphasized when comparing percentage of total class sales to percentage of total class purchases, where branded solid fitted sheets accomplished 26.11% of the sales with an investment of 35.60% of the inventory; conversely, private label solid fitted sheets did 54.06% of the business, with only 40.94% of the stock. The relationship between branded and private label flat sheets is much closer; branded's business was 13.13%, compared with an inventory of 16.91%, and private label's sales were 6.70%, with a 6.54% investment.

Without looking further, the buyer should conclude that the S-S ratios have pinpointed a serious problem in inventory investment, which must be rectified. The sales and profitability for class 9320 will be improved when more stock is carried in private label solid fitted sheets, with a commensurate decrease for branded solid fitted sheets.

- *PROBLEM 11-5*

Examine the stock-to-sales ratio and other data in Figure 11-2 for class 9322 and for the total department and analyze the effectiveness of the inventory. Also, make recommendations for the whole department (classes 9320 and 9322).

In a similar fashion to that which you just saw for S.K.U.'s, you can examine the performance of your dollar investment. As indicated earlier, the scale can be as finite as you want (or need), as it was with the previous example, or it can be for a total department.

- *EXAMPLE 11-6*

Refer to Figure 11-3, which is the six-month merchandise plan developed in Chapter Ten; it now reflects the "actual" figures for the first three months. Examine the data, calculate your S-S ratios for planned and actual values, and then evaluate your results.

(1) Initially, you should observe that there have been variations from the plan, as follows:
- (a) Your B.O.M. inventory for February was lower than it should have been; however, your sales were slightly higher and reductions were less, as were your purchases.
- (b) You calculated your E.O.M. inventory for February, which was the B.O.M. inventory for March, and found yourself low on stock. The purchases were increased, although they may not have arrived on time, and your sales for March are down, while reductions are higher.
- (c) The E.O.M. inventory for March (B.O.M. inventory for April) is greater than planned, while sales and reductions in April are down and purchases are up.
- (d) The E.O.M. inventory for April is higher than it should be; hence your B.O.M. inventory for May will be over the amount planned.

(2) Calculate the S-S ratios for planned and actual values:

$$S\text{-}S = B.O.M. \div Sales$$
$$\text{For February plan} = \$142,028 \div \$67,200$$
$$= 2.11$$

The results of the computations are arranged below:

	PLANNED	ACTUAL
February	2.11	2.03
March	2.11	2.04
April	2.27	2.38

SIX MONTH MERCHANDISE PLAN

Department Name __Men's Furnishings__ Department No. __3100__ Period Covered __Spring – Summer__

	Plan	Last Year
Initial Markup	52.9%	
Reductions	14.0%	
Maintained Markup	46.3%	
Cash Discount	6.0%	
Buyer	_Shuch_	

	Plan	Last Year
Gross Margin	52.3%	
Operating Expense	44.9%	
Operating Profit	7.4%	
Season Turnover	2.9	

Date Prepared __Sep. 19, 198___

Spring	Fall	Sales + Last Year	Plan	Actual	E.O.M. + Last Year	Plan	Actual	Reductions − Last Year	Plan	Actual	B.O.M. = Last Year	Plan	Actual	Retail Purchases Last Year	Plan	Actual	Cost Purchases Last Year	Plan	Actual
Feb.	Aug.		67,200	68,360		142,028	135,340		11,172	10,500		142,028	139,000		78,372	75,300		36,913	35,466
Mar.	Sept.		67,200	66,300		133,628	134,040		12,348	13,600		142,028	135,340		71,148	78,500		33,511	36,974
Apr.	Oct.		58,880	56,740		150,428	157,680		13,524	11,420		133,628	134,040		89,124	91,300		41,977	43,002
May	Nov.		75,600			167,228			9,996			150,428			102,396			48,229	
June	Dec.		92,400			133,628			6,460			167,228			65,268			30,741	
July	Jan.		58,800			144,828			5,292			133,628			75,292			35,465	
Total			420,000			871,768			58,800			848,968			481,600			224,834	

Figure 11-3

SIX MONTH MERCHANDISE PLAN

Department Name __Fashion Jewelry__   Department No. __140__   Period Covered __Fall–Winter__

	Plan	Last Year
Initial Markup	55.6 %	
Reductions		
Maintained Markup		
Cash Discount		

	Last Year	Plan
Gross Margin		
Operating Expense		
Operating Profit		
Season Turnover		

Buyer __Sands__   Date Prepared __May 15, 198___

Spring	Fall	Sales +			E.O.M. +			Reductions −			B.O.M. =			Retail Purchases			Cost Purchases		
		Last Year	Plan	Actual	Last Year	Plan	Actual	Last Year	Plan	Actual	Last Year	Plan	Actual	Last Year	Plan	Actual	Last Year	Plan	Actual
Feb.	Aug.		$120,000	$136,300		$252,000	$233,100		$16,500	$18,000		$260,000	$262,000		$121,500	$125,400		$57,054	
Mar.	Sept.		$160,000	$159,200		$236,250	$221,700		$14,300	$16,500		$252,000	$233,100		$151,550	$164,300		$70,396	
Apr.	Oct.		$187,500	$192,300		$241,300	$225,400		$17,100	$19,300		$236,250	$221,700		$210,350	$215,300		$93,395	
May	Nov.																		
June	Dec.																		
July	Jan.																		
	Total																		

Figure 11-4

(3) Comparing the S-S ratios, it appears that for February and March, your inventory was more productive than originally planned, with approximately the same volume of sales and reductions for the two months. The S-S ratio for April, however, is unsatisfactory, and the combined sales for March and April are lower, as are the reductions.

(4) Projecting ahead into May, using the April E.O.M. inventory as the May B.O.M. inventory and using your planned sales for May, the S-S ratio for May will be 2.08, compared with a planned S-S ratio of 1.99.

(5) It is imperative that you increase sales for May. You have approximately $1500 carried over in reduction money from the first three months that could be used to stimulate sales through a special purchase or a clearance sale of existing stock that may need moving.

(6) You should also project your revised planned purchases for May as follows:

Determine the new planned sales for May. If you feel that the downward trend in March and April (-1.3 and -4.4 percent, respectively) may continue, you might estimate a drop in sales for May at a conservative 4.0 percent. Your sales would then be:

$$\$75,600 \times (100.0\% - 4.0\%) = \$72,576$$

The planned E.O.M. inventory should be commensurately lower:

$$\$167,228 \times (100.0\% - 4.0\%) = \$160,539$$

If reductions for the month are increased to absorb the balance from the preceding months as indicated above, reductions would be

$$\$9996 + \$1524 = \$11,520$$

Your revised purchases would then be

$$\$72,576 + \$160,539 + \$11,520 - \$157,680 = \$86,955$$

As you can see by comparing the revised plan with the original plan, you have reduced purchases by $15,441. This action should correct your S-S relationship. Needless to say, the situation for the balance of this season requires your careful attention.

- *PROBLEM 11-6*

Given the data in Figure 11-4, calculate your S-S ratios and any other data you feel necessary, and then analyze your results with implications for future buying and sales.

SUMMARY PROBLEMS

- *PROBLEM 11-1 (S)*

You are attempting to evaluate the "Tabletop" Department, and you have compiled data for the month ending March 31, 198__, for this year (TY) and for last year (LY). Arrange the information and make your analysis.

Unit Sales by Class, Price, and Location									
		1		2		3		4	
CLASS	LOCATION/PRICE	LY	TY	LY	TY	LY	TY	LY	TY
Plastic	$ 5	93	89	116	130	97	112	206	253
	$ 7	114	126	139	153	120	142	214	250
	$ 9	86	94	120	148	89	98	210	240
Wood	$ 3	187	198	201	216	173	192	234	273
	$ 6	193	181	235	261	198	215	269	299
	$10	181	116	210	257	184	199	258	286
Metal	$ 5	174	198	216	243	187	205	291	315
	$ 9	163	190	274	311	206	237	330	360
	$12	170	189	293	306	195	215	320	349

• PROBLEM 11-2 (S)

You have been trying to alter the image at your shop for almost a year, from that of the mature-woman look to a younger fashion appearance. One of the measures you believe to be reliable in helping you determine if your plans are taking effect is an analysis of the sales and OH stock position of certain categories of merchandise, such as slacks. Originally, slacks were stocked in even sizes, 10 through 20, with an emphasis on sizes 14, 16, and 18. This past year, you introduced sizes 4, 6 and 8 and accumulated data every three months.

Analyze the following information and indicate the dollar investment you should make in each size for the coming three-month period:

	4	6	8	10	12	14	16	18	20
February, March, OH	—	—	36	62	87	134	182	116	93
April Sales	—	—	9	37	52	112	159	89	72
May, June, OH	—	36	54	75	113	124	150	103	64
July, Sales	—	7	17	49	93	101	117	81	35
August, September, OH	24	43	78	110	138	102	95	62	43
October, Sales	5	27	58	83	97	71	51	23	14
November, December, OH	37	81	113	148	139	75	50	38	—
January, Sales	16	45	81	129	116	41	21	12	

• PROBLEM 11-3 (S)

You have the following sales data for the Fine and Fashion Jewelry Department. Arrange the information to show day-to-day, month-to-date, and year-to-date figures, and write an analysis of the results.

	Last Year—Sales			This Year—Sales	
PERIOD	FASHION	FINE	PERIOD	FASHION	FINE
April 19	$ 6397	$ 12,462	April 18	$ 6934	$ 14,692
April 1–April 19	76,482	148,379	April 1–April 18	78,372	158,411
February 1–March 31	187,208	201,636	February 1–March 31	175,412	216,312

• *PROBLEM 11-4 (S)*

As the owner of the "Professional Woman," a two-store organization, you are reviewing your sales and transaction data on a day-to-day, month-to-month, and year-to-date basis. On the evening of June 27, you have assembled the following information. Organize the data and explain any results that appear significant (see Fig. 11-5).

Last Year				
Period	**Cicero Street**		**Washington Street**	
	Sales	**Transactions**	**Sales**	**Transactions**
June 29,	$2,492	33	$4,698	59
June 1-29,	$56,375	772	$112,311	1,404
February 1-May 31	$215,014	2,986	$419,862	5,453

This Year				
Period	**Cicero Street**		**Washington Street**	
	Sales	**Transactions**		**Transactions**
June 28,	$3002	40	$5,293	64
June 1-28,	$61,831	838	$136,655	1,627
February 1-May 31	$222,032	2,771	$461,918	5,437

Figure 11-5

• *PROBLEM 11-5 (S)*

Refer to Figure 11-6. Determine S-S ratios and any other data to evaluate the future sales and stock position in your department.

NOTES

[1]*NRMA Standard Classification of Merchandise.* New York City, The Association, 1969.

SIX MONTH MERCHANDISE PLAN

Department Name __Men's Shoes__ Department No. __3110__ Period Covered __Spring-Summer__

	Last Year	Plan			Last Year	Plan
Initial Markup	52.6%	53.1%		Gross Margin	___	___
Reductions	___	___		Operating Expense	___	___
Maintained Markup	___	___		Operating Profit	___	___
Cash Discount	___	___		Season Turnover	___	___
Buyer __David__				Date Prepared __Sept. 15, 198__		

		Sales +			E.O.M. +			Reductions -			B.O.M. =			Retail Purchases			Cost Purchases	
		Last Year	Plan	Actual	Last Year	Plan	Actual	Last Year	Plan	Actual	Last Year	Plan	Actual	Last Year	Plan	Actual	Last Year	Plan	Actual
Fall	Spring																		
Aug.	Feb.	$16,300	$18,400	$19,000	$37,400	$45,000	$46,900	$1,430	$1,600	$1,650	$36,500	$41,200	$40,300	$19,630	$23,800	$27,250			
Sept.	Mar.	$17,900	$21,000	$21,800	$41,300	$48,700	$51,100	$1,390	$1,550	$1,600	$38,400	$45,000	$46,900	$22,190	$26,250	$27,600			
Oct.	Apr.	$19,500	$23,000	$24,600	$39,600	$46,300	$48,200	$1,250	$1,400	$1,550	$41,300	$48,700	$51,100	$19,050	$21,000	$23,250			
Nov.	May																		
Dec.	June																		
Jan.	July																		
Total																			

Figure 11-6

Merchandising
and Sales-Related Reports
12

During your studies in this text, it has been pointed out that one of the major contributors to store profitability is effective inventory management: balancing stock against sales. Discussions have emphasized the use of accurate values for merchandise on hand or planned to support sales.

As the size of a retail organization increases, so too does the need for an inventory management system which can be responsive to the needs of the organization. The retail method meets these requirements. It is a perpetual inventory system which relies on data to supply all levels of management with "book" values for the dollar value of stock on hand at any given time. As the retail method depends upon the premise that the inventory's average markup percentage will approximate the average cumulative markup percentage for the department, it is most effective when applied to relatively homogeneous groups of merchandise. Hence it is particularly useful for departmentalized stores and limited-line stores (see Fig. 1-2, Chapter One).

Producing a retail method merchandise statement requires that an opening inventory value must be accurately established. This is done by taking a physical inventory (an actual unit count), usually twice a year towards the end of January and the end of June, coinciding with the conclusion of six-month buying plans. While doing a stock count is an arduous task, it will accurately update store records for each department and assure that opening B.O.M.'s are neither understated nor overstated, which would reduce the effectiveness of future plans.

The following list reflects the data needed to produce a merchandise statement. Headings which are asterisked (*) are those needed for multi-store operations only.

- Opening inventory
- Purchases (gross)
- Purchase returns (R.T.V.'s) and allowances
- Transportation charges
- Transfers in*
- Transfers out*
- Additional markups
- Markup cancellations
- Sales (gross)
- Customer returns and allowances
- Markdowns (gross)
- Markdown cancellations
- Employee and customer discounts
- Closing physical inventory (if at the end of the season) or

Figure 12-1

RETAIL METHOD MERCHANDISE STATEMENT (MID-SEASON)

		AT RETAIL	AT COST	AT RETAIL	AT COST	AT RETAIL	MARKUP %	% OF NET SALES
1	OPENING INVENTORY: 2/1/8_				$66900.00	$142028.00	52.90%	
2	PURCHASES (GROSS)		$87500.00	$185750.00				
3	PURCHASE RETURNS & ALLOWANCES		$8900.00	$18600.00				
4	NET PURCHASES (3 - 4)*				$78600.00	$167150.00	52.98%	
5	TRANSPORTATION CHARGES				$6725.00			
6	TRANSFERS IN		$2675.00	$5320.00				
7	TRANSFERS OUT		$1160.00	$2310.00				
8	NET TRANSFERS (6 - 7)				$1515.00	$3010.00		
9	ADDITIONAL MARKUPS			$1560.00				
10	MARKUP CANCELLATIONS			$730.00				
11	NET MARKUPS (9 - 10)					$830.00		
12	TOTAL MERCHANDISE HANDLED (C=1+4+5+8); (R=1+4+8+11)				$153740.00	$313018.00	50.88%	
13	SALES (GROSS)			$159000.00				
14	CUSTOMER RETURNS & ALLOWANCES			$2560.00				
15	NET SALES (13 - 14)			$156440.00				
16	MARKDOWNS (GROSS)	$15650.00						
17	MARKDOWN CANCELLATIONS	$3200.00						
18	NET MARKDOWNS (16 - 17)			$12450.00				7.96%
19	EMPLOYEE & CUSTOMER DISCOUNTS			$6000.00				3.84%
20	ESTIMATED STOCK SHORTAGES			$3500.00				
21	TOTAL MERCHANDISE DEDUCTIONS (15 + 18 + 19 + 20)					$178390.00		
22	BOOK INVENTORY (RET.): 4/15/8_ (12 - 21)					$134628.00		
23	BOOK INVENTORY (COST): 4/15/8_ ((100.00% - MU%) * (22))				$66123.06			
24	GROSS COST OF GOODS SOLD (12 - 23)				$87616.94			
25	PURCHASE DISCOUNTS				$5250.00			
26	NET COST OF GOODS SOLD (24 - 25)				$82366.94			
27	GROSS MARGIN (15 - 26)				$74073.06			47.35%
28	OPERATING EXPENSES				$65575.00			41.92%
29	OPERATING PROFIT (27 - 28)				$8498.06			5.43%

* NOTE: NUMBERS IN PARANTHESES INDICATE ROW NUMBERS

SIX MONTH MERCHANDISE PLAN

Department Name __Men's/Furnishings__ Department No. __3100__ Period Covered __Spring - Summer__

	Plan	Last Year
Initial Markup	52.9 %	
Reductions	14.0 %	
Maintained Markup	46.3 %	
Cash Discount	6.0 %	

	Plan	Last Year
Gross Margin	52.3 %	
Operating Expense	44.9 %	
Operating Profit	7.4 %	
Season Turnover	2.9	

Date Prepared __Sep. 19, 198___

Buyer __Shuch__

Spring	Fall	Sales +			E.O.M. +			Reductions –			B.O.M. =			Retail Purchases			Cost Purchases	
		Last Year	Plan	Actual	Last Year	Plan	Actual	Last Year	Plan	Actual	Last Year	Plan	Actual	Last Year	Plan	Actual	Last Year	Plan	Actual
Feb.	Aug.		67,200			142,028			11,172			142,028			78,372			36,913	
Mar.	Sept.		67,200			133,628			12,348			142,028			71,148			33,511	
Apr.	Oct.		58,880			159,428			13,524			133,628			89,124			41,977	
May	Nov.		75,600			167,228			9,996			159,428			102,396			48,229	
June	Dec.		92,400			133,628			6,468			167,228			65,268			30,741	
July	Jan.		58,800			144,828			5,292			133,628			75,292			35,463	
	Total		420,000			871,768			59,800			868,968			481,600			226,834	

Figure 12-2

- Estimated stock shortage (if this is a report for any period less than the full season)
- Purchase discounts

Where operating expenses are known, or can be accurately estimated, the report can be extended to produce a statement of operating profit.

Mid-season report. A mid-season retail method merchandising statement affords a buyer the opportunity to evaluate actual progress against plan during the season and develop strategies for changes if they are required.

- *EXAMPLE 12-1*

Refer to Figures 12-1 and 12-2, on pp. 239 and 240 and evaluate the progress of your department and make recommendations.

This report has been generated as of 4/15/8__ (see rows 22, 23), for the period 2/1/8__ to 4/15/8__ .

The B.O.M. inventory for February 1 and initial markup (row 1) for this stock are as planned ($142,028 and 52.90%); net purchases should be approximately $194,100: $78,372 + $71,148 + .5 ($89,124) = $194,082, but you have only recorded $167,150 (row 4); Gross sales have been $159,000, which is less than plan, [$67,200 + $67,200 + .5 ($58,800)] = $163,800; reductions (net markdowns, employee and customer discounts, estimated stock shortages) total $21,950 (rows 18, 19, 20). This compares favorably with plan, which totals $30,282 for two and one-half months. Your "bottom-line" gross margin is not good, 47.35% (row 27) compared with a planned G.M. of 52.30%, and although your actual operating expenses are good, 41.92% (row 28) against a planned 44.90%, your operating profit is off by almost 2.0% (row 29).

Figure 12-3

```
                    RETAIL METHOD MERCHANDISE STATEMENT (MID-SEASON)

                    AT RETAIL    AT COST    AT RETAIL    AT COST    AT RETAIL  MARKUP %   % OF
                                                                                         NET SALES
 1  OPENING INVENTORY: 2/1/8_                           $201150.00 $401100.00  49.85%
 2  PURCHASES (GROSS)              $274000.00 $536000.00
 3  PURCHASE RETURNS & ALLOWANCES  $10650.00  $21130.00
 4  NET PURCHASES (3 - 4)*                              $263350.00 $514870.00  48.85%
 5  TRANSPORTATION CHARGES                               $9430.00
 6  TRANSFERS IN                   $8540.00   $17235.00
 7  TRANSFERS OUT                  $6500.00   $12890.00
 8  NET TRANSFERS (6 - 7)                                $2040.00   $4345.00
 9  ADDITIONAL MARKUPS                         $3600.00
10  MARKUP CANCELLATIONS                       $2050.00
11  NET MARKUPS (9 - 10)                                           $1550.00
12  TOTAL MERCHANDISE HANDLED                            $475970.00 $921865.00 48.37%
    (C=1+4+5+8); (R=1+4+8+11)
13  SALES (GROSS)                             $485000.00
14  CUSTOMER RETURNS & ALLOWANCES             $22475.00
15  NET SALES (13 - 14)                       $462525.00
16  MARKDOWNS (GROSS)              $36500.00
17  MARKDOWN CANCELLATIONS         $4200.00
18  NET MARKDOWNS (16 - 17)                   $32300.00                         6.98%
19  EMPLOYEE & CUSTOMER DISCOUNTS              $9700.00                          2.10%
20  ESTIMATED STOCK SHORTAGES                 $5000.00
21  TOTAL MERCHANDISE DEDUCTIONS                                    $509525.00
    (15 + 18 + 19 + 20)
22  BOOK INVENTORY (RET.): 4/30/8_                                  $412340.00
    (12 - 21)
23  BOOK INVENTORY (COST): 4/30/8_            $212896.11
    ((100.00% - MU%) * (22))
24  GROSS COST OF GOODS SOLD                  $263073.89
    (12 - 23)
25  PURCHASE DISCOUNTS                        $10050.00
26  NET COST OF GOODS SOLD                    $253023.89
    (24 - 25)
27  GROSS MARGIN                              $209501.11                        45.30%
    (15 - 26)
28  OPERATING EXPENSES                        $186750.00                        40.38%
29  OPERATING PROFIT (27 - 28)                $22751.11                          4.92%

  * NOTE: NUMBERS IN PARANTHESES INDICATE ROW NUMBERS
```

SIX MONTH MERCHANDISE PLAN

Department Name **Junior Dresses** Department No. **1801** Period Covered **Spring-Summer**

	Plan	Last Year
Initial Markup	49.6%	
Reductions	13.4%	
Maintained Markup	42.8%	
Cash Discount	5.8%	

Buyer **Link**

	Plan	Last Year
Gross Margin	48.6%	
Operating Expense	41.2%	
Operating Profit	7.4%	
Season Turnover	2.1	

Date Prepared **8/30/8-**

Spring	Fall	Sales + Last Year	Sales + Plan	Sales + Actual	E.O.M. + Last Year	E.O.M. + Plan	E.O.M. + Actual	Reductions − Last Year	Reductions − Plan	Reductions − Actual	B.O.M. = Last Year	B.O.M. = Plan	B.O.M. = Actual	Retail Purchases Last Year	Retail Purchases Plan	Retail Purchases Actual	Cost Purchases Last Year	Cost Purchases Plan	Cost Purchases Actual
Feb.	Aug.		152000			415619			17152			394619			185182			93392	
Mar.	Sept.		168000			431619			17152			415619			201152			101462	
Apr.	Oct.		184000			383619			15008			431619			151008			76169	
May	Nov.		136000			335619			19296			383619			107296			54121	
June	Dec.		88000			319619			23584			335619			95584			48213	
July	Jan.		72000			380952			15008			319619			148341			74824	
Total			800000			2267050			107200			2285710			888333			448184	

242

		AT RETAIL	AT COST	AT RETAIL	AT COST	AT RETAIL	MARKUP %	% OF NET SALES
		\RETAIL METHOD MERCHANDISE STATEMENT (SIX MONTHS)\						
1	OPENING INVENTORY: 2/1/8_				$60000.00	$122750.00	51.12%	
2	PURCHASES (GROSS)		$33000.00	$67500.00				
3	PURCHASE RETURNS & ALLOWANCES		$2700.00	$5400.00				
4	NET PURCHASES (3 - 4)*				$30300.00	$62100.00	51.21%	
5	TRANSPORTATION CHARGES				$3150.00			
6	TRANSFERS IN		$1250.00	$2475.00				
7	TRANSFERS OUT		$560.00	$1160.00				
8	NET TRANSFERS (6 - 7)				$690.00	$1315.00		
9	ADDITIONAL MARKUPS			$1200.00				
10	MARKUP CANCELLATIONS			$480.00				
11	NET MARKUPS (9 - 10)					$720.00		
12	TOTAL MERCHANDISE HANDLED (C=1+4+5+8); (R=1+4+8+11)				$94140.00	$186885.00	49.63%	
13	SALES (GROSS)			$45000.00				
14	CUSTOMER RETURNS & ALLOWANCES			$2560.00				
15	NET SALES (13 - 14)			$42440.00				
16	MARKDOWNS (GROSS)	$5450.00						
17	MARKDOWN CANCELLATIONS	$1750.00						
18	NET MARKDOWNS (16 - 17)			$3700.00				8.72%
19	EMPLOYEE & CUSTOMER DISCOUNTS			$1630.00				3.84%
20	TOTAL MERCHANDISE DEDUCTIONS (15 + 18 + 19)					$47770.00		
21	BOOK INVENTORY (RET.): 7/31/8_ (12 - 20)			$139115.00				
22	BOOK INVENTORY (COST): 7/31/8_ ((100.00% - MU%) * (21))		$70076.71					
23	PHYSICAL INVENTORY (RET.): 7/31/8_					$138295.00	49.63%	
24	PHYSICAL INVENTORY (COST): ((100.00% - MU%) * (23))				$69663.65			
25	SHORTAGE OR (OVERAGE) (C=22-24; R=21-23)		$413.06	$820.00				1.93%
26	GROSS COST OF GOODS SOLD (12 - 24)				$24476.35			
27	PURCHASE DISCOUNTS				$750.00			
28	NET COST OF GOODS SOLD (26 - 27)				$23726.35			
29	GROSS MARGIN (15 - 28)				$18713.65			44.09%
30	OPERATING EXPENSES				$13250.00			31.22%
31	OPERATING PROFIT (29-30)				$5463.65			12.87%

* NOTE: NUMBERS IN PARANTHESES INDICATE ROW NUMBERS

Figure 12-5

In the absence of any other information, the conclusion is that your sales are suffering owing to lack of merc⋮andise. You are almost 14% behind in stock [($194,100 − $167,150)/$194,100]. If the problem is to be stopped, you should get more merchandise into the store quickly.

• *PROBLEM 12-1*

Refer to Figures 12-3 and 12-4, on pp. 241 and 242 and evaluate the progress of your department for the period indicated. Make recommendations based upon your evaluations.

End-of-season report. An end-of-season report (see Fig. 12-5) is evaluated very much like the mid-season report, with two exceptions: first, you will have had a physical count taken of your inventory; therefore, your stock shortage or overage will be a known factor, not an estimate, and the physical inventory values at cost and retail will conclude the period and become the B.O.M. figures for the next season; second, it is too late to do anything about correcting buying mistakes (if you made any), but it is not too late to do a final evaluation, searching for the positive aspects, as well as those which were negative, to assist you with the coming season.

PRODUCTIVITY RATIOS

There are several pieces of information that are combined to form other data which are considered to be key measures of productivity.

Merchandise and inventory data.   These data are those which are found on the six-month buying plan and the Retail Method Merchandise Statement.

GROSS MARGIN RETURN ON INVESTMENT (G.M.R.O.I.).   This ratio measures the efficiency of the investment in inventory. A dollar invested in inventory can be compared to a dollar purchasing a share of stock. The G.M.R.O.I. is somewhat comparable to the earnings for each share of stock.

This ratio is computed by dividing the dollar gross margin by the average cost of inventory. The latter value is calculated by adding the E.O.M. cost inventory for each month in the period (season or year) plus the first month's B.O.M. and dividing by seven (for a season) or thirteen (for a year).

• EXAMPLE 12-2

From the following data, determine the G.M.R.O.I.:

INVENTORY AT COST

B.O.M. February	$70,000
E.O.M. February	71,000
E.O.M. March	66,000
E.O.M. April	75,000
E.O.M. May	86,000
E.O.M. June	66,000
E.O.M. July	72,000
G.M. = $235,600	

(1) Find the average cost inventory:

($70,000 + $71,000 + $66,000 + $75,000 + $86,000 + $66,000 + $72,000)/7
$506,000 ÷ 7 = $72,286

(2) Divide G.M. by the average cost inventory:

$235,600 ÷ $72,286 = 3.26

• PROBLEM 12-2

Determine your G.M.R.O.I. from the following data:

MONTH	COST
B.O.M. August	$76,500
E.O.M. August	81,000
E.O.M. September	83,000
E.O.M. October	87,000
E.O.M. November	96,000
E.O.M. December	78,000
E.O.M. January	70,000
G.M. = $355,765	

STOCK TURN.   The stock turn ratio measures the rate of reinvestment of dollars into inventory. The more frequently money is converted into inventory, which is then turned into sales and subsequently into gross margin, the higher will be the return per dollar. Therefore, the stock turn is the greatest influence on the G.M.R.O.I. (The topic of stock turn was discussed in Chapter Nine, relating it to inventory investment planning, and should be reviewed for the computational procedures required, as well as to better understand its importance for the buyer.)

• *EXAMPLE 12-3*

Determine the stock turn and G.M.R.O.I. from the following data for the February 1–July 31 period:

MONTH	E.O.M. (RETAIL)
January	$108,000
February	100,000
March	125,000
April	145,000
May	156,000
June	162,000
July	134,000
Sales: $385,000 G.M.: $157,850	I.M.: 52.4%

(1) Determine average inventory (000's omitted):

$$= (\$108 + \$100 + \$125 + \$145 + \$156 + \$162 + \$134) \div 7$$
$$= \$132.857 \times 1000 = \$132,857$$

(2) S. T. = Sales ÷ Average inventory
$$= \$385,000 \div \$132,857$$
$$= 2.9$$

(3) Determine cost value of average inventory:

$$= (100.0\% - 52.4\%) \times \$132,857$$
$$= \$63,240$$

(4) Determine G.M.R.O.I.:

$$= \$157,850 \div \$63,240$$
$$= 2.5$$

• *PROBLEM 12-3*

From the following data, determine seasonal stock turn and G.M.R.O.I.:

MONTH	E.O.M. (RETAIL)
July	$134,000
August	147,000
September	160,000
October	158,000
November	168,000
December	154,000
January	131,000
Sales: $510,900 G.M.: $215,700	I.M.: 53.7%

Sales data.   While many ratios can be developed using sales as a base, three are more prevalent as gauges of productivity.

SALES (CUSTOMER) RETURNS PERCENT OF GROSS SALES.   There are two inferences which can be drawn from this ratio: customers' acceptance or rejection of the quality of the merchandise they have purchased and the quality of the effort to "sell well" by your sales associates. The ratio is calculated by dividing dollar customer returns ($8,650), by dollar gross sales ($87,500), as follows:

$$\text{Customer returns} \div \text{Gross sales}$$
$$\$8650 \div \$87{,}500 = .099 \text{ or } 9.9\%$$

SALES PER SQUARE FOOT OF SELLING SPACE.   Sales per square foot of selling space produces a dollar value indicating the productivity of each square foot. The implications of this ratio can be to either increase space allotments for some merchandise classifications or conversely to reduce the square footage. This measure of productivity is obtained by dividing net sales ($364,800) by the square footage of the department (2250 sq. ft.).

$$\text{Net sales} \div \text{Square feet}$$
$$\$364{,}800 \div 2250 = \$162.13 \text{ per square foot}$$

SELLING SALARIES PERCENT OF NET SALES.   This percent reveals the average cost to sell one dollar's worth of merchandise. It is computed by dividing selling expense ($27,350), which includes wages, commissions, P.M.'s, bonuses, and benefits to sales associates, cashiers, and stock-keeping personnel, by net sales ($547,000), as follows:

$$\text{Selling expense} \div \text{Net sales}$$
$$\$27{,}350 \div \$547{,}000 = .05 = 5.0\%$$

• *EXAMPLE 12-4*

Given the following data, compute

(1) Sales returns percent of gross sales.
(2) Sales per square foot.
(3) Selling salaries percent of net sales.

Gross sales:	$485,000
Customer returns:	$ 22,475
Square feet of selling space:	5200
Selling expense:	$ 28,900

(1) Determine sales returns percent of gross sales:

$$= \text{Customer Returns} \div \text{Gross sales}$$
$$= \$22{,}475 \div \$485{,}000$$
$$= .046, \text{ or } 4.6\%$$

(2) Determine sales per square foot:

$$= \text{Net Sales} \div \text{Square feet}$$
$$= (\$485{,}000 - \$22{,}475) \div 5200$$
$$= \$88.95 \text{ per square foot}$$

(3) Determine selling salaries percent of net sales:

$$= \text{Selling expense} \div \text{Net sales}$$
$$= \$28{,}900 \div (\$485{,}000 - \$22{,}475)$$
$$= .062, \text{ or } 6.2\%$$

• *PROBLEM 12-4*

Your bookkeeper has provided you with the following information, from which you are to calculate

(1) Sales returns percent of gross sales.
(2) Sales per square foot.
(3) Selling salaries percent of net sales.

Gross sales:	$365,000
Customer returns:	$ 18,750
Square feet of selling space:	3800
Selling expense:	$ 21,850

One of the most respected and often-referred-to reports is the annual **Merchandising and Operating Results of Department and Specialty Stores**[1] (*M.O.R.*). See Figures 12-6 and 12-7, which show condensations of several pages

Departmental Merchandising and Operating Results of 1984
Department Stores—Sales Over $100 Million

DEPT. NO. OR DEMAND CENTER OR SUB CENTER	DESCRIPTION	NO. RPTG. COS.	MERCHANDISING AND INVENTORY DATA					
			CUMULATIVE MARKON %		MARKDOWNS (INCL. EMPLOYEE DISCOUNTS)		STOCK SHORTAGE	
					PERCENT OF NET RETAIL SALES			
			MEDIAN	SUPERIOR	MEDIAN	SUPERIOR	MEDIAN	SUPERIOR
	UPSTAIRS DEPARTMENTS							
0100	TOTAL ALL SHOES	24	51.5	52.3	25.0	21.8	1.0	.6
0101	SUMMARY WOMENS, MISSES & JUNIOR SHOES	18	52.6	53.2	27.1	24.0	1.0	.4
0110	WOMENS & MISSES DRESS AND CASUAL SHOES	21	52.1	53.4	27.7	24.7	.8	.7
0130	JUNIOR & TEEN SHOES	20	52.2	53.4	24.7	23.1	1.4	.8
0301	ALL MENS FOOTWEAR	20	47.8	50.1	15.9	14.3	.9	.5
0401	ALL CHILDRENS FOOTWEAR	14	48.1	49.0	25.8	16.3	1.6	1.0
1000	TOTAL ADULT FEMALE APPAREL	41	51.6	52.7	28.0	21.7	3.2	2.3
1101	SUMMARY WOMENS & MISSES COATS & SUITS	36	51.3	53.7	25.1	20.6	2.3	1.8
1110	WOMENS & MISSES DRESSY & TAILORED COATS	33	50.6	52.0	24.1	18.8	1.6	1.1
1210	WOMENS & MISSES JACKETS, CASUAL & ALL WEATHER COATS	32	51.0	53.7	22.0	16.5	2.0	1.4
1310	WOMENS & MISSES SUITS	28	52.2	55.5	34.9	26.4	3.6	2.5
1401	FURS AND FUR GARMENTS	19	45.5	49.4	19.5	9.5	1.9	.9
1501	SUMMARY ALL DRESSES-EXCEPT JUNIORS	40	51.2	52.7	31.9	27.2	4.9	3.4
1510	BRIDAL & FORMAL	16	49.6	51.1	17.2	8.6	1.4	.9
1530	ALL WOMENS DRESSES	37	51.9	52.7	28.0	22.6	4.2	3.3
1540	ALL MISSES DRESSES	37	51.3	52.3	33.3	28.1	5.3	4.0
1570	MATERNITY CLOTHING & ACCESSORIES	31	52.5	53.7	21.5	14.9	2.9	1.9
1601	SUMMARY WOMENS & MISSES SPORTSWEAR	44	51.9	53.1	27.0	20.1	2.9	2.0
1620	WOMENS & MISSES SPECTATOR SPORTSWEAR	27	52.4	53.8	30.3	25.0	3.4	2.8
1630	WOMENS & MISSES ACTIVE SPORTSWEAR	27	52.3	54.0	25.2	19.5	3.2	2.1
1701	SUMMARY JUNIOR COATS & SUITS	35	51.9	54.4	27.9	21.0	2.8	1.8

SOURCE: Reprinted courtesy of the National Retail Merchants Association from *Merchandising and Operating Results, 1985 edition.*

Figure 12-6

Departmental Merchandising and Operating Results of 1984
Department Stores—Sales Over $100 Million

DEPT. NO. OR DEMAND CENTER OR SUB CENTER	MERCHANDISING AND INVENTORY DATA											
	NET WORK ROOM COST		GROSS MARGIN (INCL. CASH DISCOUNTS)		GROSS MARGIN $ RETURN PER $ AVERAGE COST INVENTORY		CASH DISCOUNTS % OF COST PURCHASES		STOCK TURNS (TIMES) AT RETAIL		STOCK AGE % 0-6 MONTHS	
	PERCENT OF NET RETAIL SALES											
	MEDIAN	SUPERIOR	MEDIAN	SUPERIOR	MEDIAN	SUPERIOR	MEDIAN	SUPERIOR	MEDIAN	SUPERIOR	MEDIAN	SUPERIOR
0100			42.4	44.8	2.09	2.55	6.4	8.2	2.1	2.2		
0101			42.8	45.4	2.16	3.24	6.4	8.4	2.3	2.4		
0110			42.4	45.2			7.0	8.8	2.2	2.4		
0130			43.0	45.1			6.7	8.1	2.3	2.4		
0301			42.7	44.1			6.6	8.1	1.5	1.8		
0401			38.6	41.9			6.4	7.7	1.3	1.5		
1000	.3	.2	42.3	44.0	3.73	5.76	8.5	10.4	3.7	4.0	78.5	90.8
1101	.6	.3	43.0	45.7	3.72	5.11	8.9	10.3	3.8	4.5	78.4	95.8
1110	.9	.5	41.3	44.9			8.6	10.6	3.7	4.3	83.4	97.2
1210	.7	.4	44.9	47.2	4.26	4.89	8.5	10.2	3.9	4.6	79.0	100.0
1310	1.0	1.0	39.5	42.8	3.51	3.91	9.4	10.4	3.5	4.2	81.5	100.0
1401	2.0	.6	36.7	43.7			7.6	10.2	1.8	2.6		
1501	.9	.7	38.7	41.4	3.29	5.23	8.3	10.4	3.4	3.6	69.8	87.3
1510	10.0	4.2	36.7	43.1			8.0	10.3	2.4	2.9		
1530	1.0	.4	39.3	45.3	2.64	3.70	8.2	10.0	3.4	3.8	71.0	100.0
1540	.8	.6	37.9	40.3	3.10	3.51	8.3	10.3	3.3	3.6	79.6	89.0
1570	.2	.1	45.1	49.1			8.4	10.1	3.0	3.8	51.0	79.3
1601	.2	.1	42.8	44.6	3.95	5.95	8.4	10.2	3.8	4.3	75.8	88.8
1620	.2	.1	41.9	44.3	3.96	3.99	10.1	10.4	3.7	4.0		
1630			45.6	47.2	4.13	5.61	9.9	10.5	3.7	4.1		
1701	.3	.2	42.2	44.0			9.2	10.8	3.5	4.1	75.0	100.0

DEPT. NO. OR DEMAND CENTER OR SUB CENTER	DESCRIPTION	NO. RPTG. CO'S.	SALES DATA					
			NET SALES % CHANGE FROM LAST YEAR		NET SALES % OF TOTAL CON-SOLIDATED STORE		NET SALES % OF MOR MERCHAN-DISE DIVISION	
			MEDIAN	SUPERIOR	MEDIAN	SUPERIOR	MEDIAN	SUPERIOR
	UPSTAIRS DEPARTMENTS							
0100	TOTAL ALL SHOES	24	8.3	15.5	4.6	5.4		
0101	SUMMARY WOMENS, MISSES & JUNIOR SHOES	18	9.1	16.8	3.8	4.5	84.4	90.3
0110	WOMENS & MISSES DRESS AND CASUAL SHOES	21	9.2	16.7	2.9	3.3	60.9	66.4
0130	JUNIOR & TEEN SHOES	20	11.7	26.1	.9	1.2	19.2	23.5
0301	ALL MENS FOOTWEAR	20	11.6	16.4	.8	1.1	15.9	23.6
0401	ALL CHILDRENS FOOTWEAR	14	2.9-	10.9	.2	.4	5.2	8.5
1000	TOTAL ADULT FEMALE APPAREL	41	9.3	13.2	23.3	30.1	100.0	100.0
1101	SUMMARY WOMENS & MISSES COATS & SUITS	36	3.3	10.0	1.8	2.3	8.0	9.8
1110	WOMENS & MISSES DRESSY & TAILORED COATS	33	3.7	17.9	1.0	1.3	4.0	5.2
1210	WOMENS & MISSES JACKETS, CASUAL & ALL WEATHER COATS	32	5.1	14.3	.8	1.1	3.2	4.0
1310	WOMENS & MISSES SUITS	28	6.2-	24.5	.3	.3	1.1	1.3
1401	FURS AND FUR GARMENTS	19	12.9	23.3	.4	.6	1.5	2.5
1501	SUMMARY ALL DRESSES—EXCEPT JUNIORS	40	9.7	14.6	3.4	4.4	13.5	16.8
1510	BRIDAL & FORMAL	16	1.8-	10.7	.1	.4	.4	1.1
1530	ALL WOMENS DRESSES	37	8.6	27.1	.3	.4	1.1	1.7
1540	ALL MISSES DRESSES	37	8.4	18.2	2.9	3.7	11.1	15.4
1570	MATERNITY CLOTHING & ACCESSORIES	31	6.0	19.3	.1	.2	.6	.8
1601	SUMMARY WOMENS & MISSES SPORTSWEAR	44	10.6	13.8	12.6	16.2	55.6	58.7
1620	WOMENS & MISSES SPECTATOR SPORTSWEAR	27	10.5	14.1	11.0	13.0	49.9	52.6
1630	WOMENS & MISSES ACTIVE SPORTSWEAR	27	14.9	25.3	1.0	1.5	4.4	5.8
1701	SUMMARY JUNIOR COATS & SUITS	35	5.5-	6.0	.3	.5	1.3	1.7

SOURCE: Reprinted courtesy of the National Retail Merchants Association
from *Merchandising and Operating Results, 1985 edition.*

Figure 12-7

DEPT. NO. OR DEMAND CENTER OR SUB CENTER	SALES DATA				EXPENSES				NOTES
	SALES RETURNS % OF GROSS SALES		$ SALES PER SQ. FT. OF SELLING SPACE (MAIN OR LARGEST SELLING UNIT)		SALES PROMOTION COSTS (NET) % OF SALES		SELLING SALARIES % OF SALES (MAIN OR LARGEST SELLING UNIT)		
	MEDIAN	SUPERIOR	MEDIAN	SUPERIOR	MEDIAN	SUPERIOR	MEDIAN	SUPERIOR	
	13.5	12.0	200.5	213.8	3.8	3.7			
	14.4	12.2	200.7	228.5	3.8	3.5			
0110									
0130									
0301									
0401									
1000	14.0	12.5	159.1	351.8	4.2	2.7	6.4	5.2	
1101	15.2	13.4	192.8	247.9	4.7	4.0	5.7	4.9	
1110	15.2	14.4	163.5	262.2	4.5	3.5	5.9	4.9	
1210	15.2	12.7	165.0	291.5	4.6	3.1	6.1	4.9	
1310	17.3	14.1			7.0	3.3	6.7	5.5	
1401					6.1	5.2	8.1	6.1	
1501	16.9	16.0	146.4	236.6	4.3	2.4	7.6	6.3	
1510			144.6	239.4	1.9	1.4	13.0	5.2	
1530	19.7	15.5	169.3	246.0	4.3	2.3	7.5	6.5	
1540	17.2	15.4	144.8	186.7	4.4	2.7	7.4	5.7	
1570	10.7	9.2	100.4	140.3	2.1	1.4	7.4	5.0	
1601	12.9	10.3	195.5	296.1	3.7	2.6	7.0	4.8	
1620	16.1	13.4	179.7	602.7	4.0	3.9	6.8	5.2	
1630	9.2	4.5	156.4	259.6	3.7	2.2	7.1	4.1	
1701	12.5	10.6	145.0	229.2	5.8	3.3	6.2	4.9	

from this publication and the types of data, productivity and otherwise, which are assembled—invaluable assists to seasoned and novice buyers working in stores of all sizes.

COMPUTERIZATION AND RECORD KEEPING

Sometime in the very distant past, a merchant began recording information about a business. This first data was undoubtedly simple; perhaps a record of sales which could be used to compare with subsequent figures as evidence of progress. As the business developed, so too did the amount and complexity of data.

More recently, with the growth of retailing, information became a necessity, not only as an evaluating and planning base but as a competitive tool, with the resulting need for speed with which raw data could be assembled and converted to meaningful statistics. One problem was (and still is) cost effectiveness: saving, recording, producing, and delivering reports requiring time, people, and physical space.

As pencil and paper have largely been replaced for computational work by hand-held calculators, so too have simple price tickets been supplanted by sophisticated tags. This merchandise data base contains, as you have learned, in a relatively small area, a wide variety of information, in addition to selling price, which must be assembled and made into usable statistics.

Many retailers, both large and small, continue to rely on the traditional method of having a unit control stub removed from merchandise at the time of sale and then beginning the cycle of manual entry onto inventory cards, concluding with a physical examination of these records. Besides the time factor of this procedure, the retailer is still without many forms of reports which are essential for a successful operation.

Point of sale (P.O.S.) terminals. As retailing becomes more competitive through the introduction into the marketplace of more stores, each with a slightly different approach to attract core customers, the pressure to increase sales and gross margin while maintaining or reducing expenses increases. Recognizing that better inventory control and higher productivity are critical, improved methods of data collection and statistical management have been developed by many equipment manufacturers through computerization.

The familiar cash register, with its classic ring, is being replaced by relatively small machines with cash drawers, keyboards and electronic displays. These devices, **point-of-sale terminals**, are connected via cable to a central computer which retrieves and saves data. Sales associates either "key in" S.K.U. information from price tickets or pass a wand over the **alpha-numeric** characters or draw the merchandise over a limited-beam laser scanning device which reads the U.P.C. bar code. The information is transmitted to the store's central computer or controller, which may be no larger than a desk-top personal computer, and saved with the data from other sales, or in a large store from other terminals, for analysis at a later time.

Sophisticated systems such as the IBM 4680 can be used to run point-of-sale programs coupled with price management (returning to the terminal's electronic display the current price for the merchandise, reflecting markdowns or additional markups) and transfers. The store controller can also furnish timely reports about the impact of fast sellers, slow movers, and price reductions. Through their programming, checkout at the close of business is accomplished quickly with the assistance of printed-out totals of the day's transactions.

Highlights of the 4680[2] P.O.S. terminal systems include

1. Reduced checkout errors through item price look-up, item validation, automatic tax calculation, discount calculations, multiple tender processing, and void validation
2. Increased checkout through suspended transaction capabilities
3. Verification of customer credit status for charge or check transactions
4. Assistance with accounting operations and improved cash control
5. Recording and reporting of item movement information
6. Recording and reporting of operator performance terminal (cashier) productivity.

Figure 12-8 An Executive Reviewing Data Generated by a Company-Owned Mainframe Computer.

SOURCE: Courtesy of James Stone, Jordan Marsh.

In-house systems.   With the rapidly declining cost of personal computers and the increasing trust of the computer as a tool as opposed to a "brain substitute," many retailers, large and small, have developed their own in-house systems. These are programs designed to meet the specific needs of the individual merchant. In most cases, the *software* has been written by experienced programmers. With growth of evening computer language classes, however, and the commensurate increase in the numbers of clearly written books on programming, independent store owners and individuals working for retailers at the department manager and buyer levels have begun to develop their own programs to assist them with work which is ideally suited for computer application and is not available through the store's system.

Other in-house systems are those marketed to large-scale retailers by corporations like NCR (formerly National Cash Register Company) and IBM. The latter company is offering retailers with *mainframe* capability license to use its Planning Aid for Retail Information System (P.A.R.I.S.), which is a series of systems: Purchase Order and Merchandise Information, Receiving Checking and Distribution, and Invoice Processing. Each of these systems contains sub-

Figure 12-9

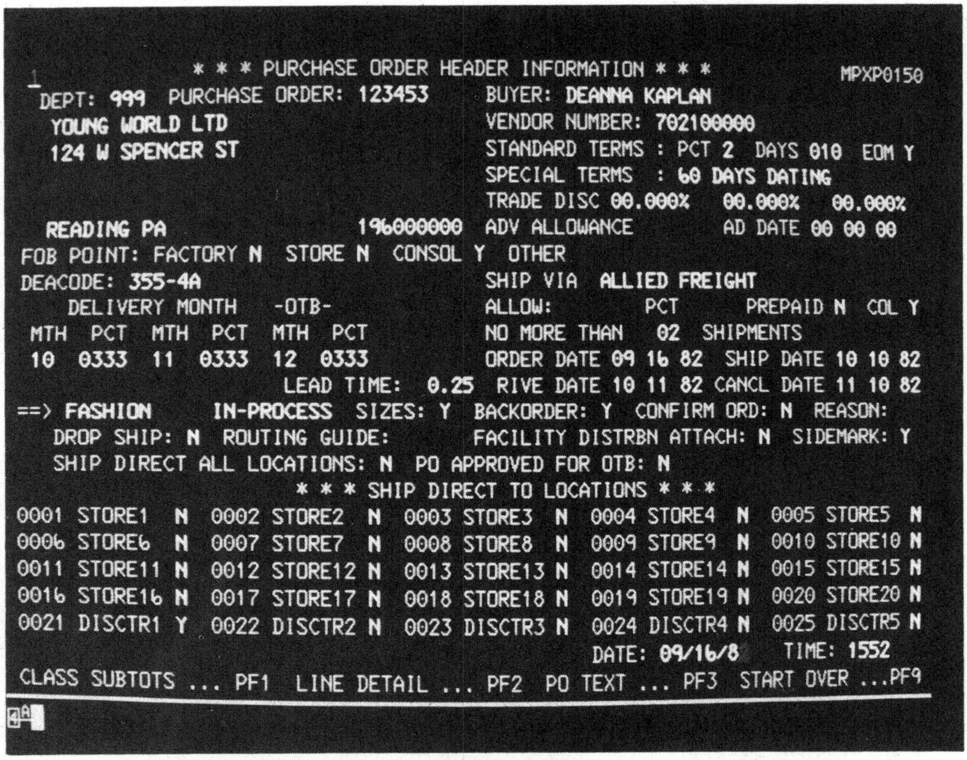

SOURCE: Courtesy of International Business Machines Corporation.

systems, and within these are other subsystems. The Purchase Order and Merchandise Information System, as an example, is composed of the following:

1.0 Purchase Order Entry (see Fig. 12-9)
    1.1 Active Purchase Order Inquiry
    1.2 Active Purchase Order Maintenance (Update)
2.0 Merchandise Inventory Management
    2.1 Unit Control Sales Update
        2.11 Multiple Years of Weekly Unit Sales per Store by S.K.U.
        2.12 Two Weeks of Daily Unit Sales per store (see Fig. 12-10)
    2.2 Merchandise Inventory and Unit Control (S.K.U.) Reporting
        2.21 Unit Control Activity Store Detail Report
        2.22 Unit Control Activity Recap
        2.23 Analysis of Fast/Slow Styles Reports
        2.24 Aged Receipts S.K.U. Analysis
3.0 Department/Class Subsystem

Figure 12-10

SOURCE: Courtesy of International Business Machines Corporation.

4.0 Vendor Subsystem

5.0 S.K.U. Maintenance Subsystem

While the preceding listing does not give specific details regarding each finite system, it is evident that as a buyer working for a retailer committed to accurate record keeping and speedy reporting, you will be well assisted in the performance of your work with computer systems such as P.A.R.I.S.

SUMMARY PROBLEMS

- *PROBLEM 12-1 (S)*

Examine the data in Figures 12-11 and 12-12. Provide an analysis of the discrepancies between your planned values and your mid-season statement, and indicate what measures you will take.

- *PROBLEM 12-2 (S)*

Refer to Figures 12-13 and 12-14, and explain the disparity between planned and actual values for the gross margin and operating profit.

```
                    RETAIL METHOD MERCHANDISE STATEMENT (MID-SEASON)

                    AT RETAIL    AT COST   AT RETAIL    AT COST    AT RETAIL  MARKUP %   % OF
                                                                                         NET SALES

 1  OPENING INVENTORY: 8/1/8_                            $59900.00  $125075.00  52.11%
 2  PURCHASES (GROSS)            $78450.00  $163750.00
 3  PURCHASE RETURNS & ALLOWANCES $1750.00  $3850.00
 4  NET PURCHASES (3 - 4)*                               $76700.00  $159900.00  52.03%
 5  TRANSPORTATION CHARGES                               $2500.00
 6  TRANSFERS IN                  $890.00   $1875.00
 7  TRANSFERS OUT                 $625.00   $1500.00
 8  NET TRANSFERS (6 - 7)                                $265.00    $375.00
 9  ADDITIONAL MARKUPS                      $1395.00
10  MARKUP CANCELLATIONS                    $545.00
11  NET MARKUPS (9 - 10)                                            $850.00
12  TOTAL MERCHANDISE HANDLED                            $139365.00 $286200.00  51.31%
    (C=1+4+5+8);  (R=1+4+8+11)
13  SALES (GROSS)                           $146750.00
14  CUSTOMER RETURNS & ALLOWANCES           $5470.00
15  NET SALES (13 - 14)                     $141280.00
16  MARKDOWNS (GROSS)            $16300.00
17  MARKDOWN CANCELLATIONS       $2300.00
18  NET MARKDOWNS (16 - 17)                 $14000.00                           9.91%
19  EMPLOYEE & CUSTOMER DISCOUNTS           $4100.00                            2.90%
20  ESTIMATED STOCK SHORTAGES               $6050.00                            4.28%
21  TOTAL MERCHANDISE DEDUCTIONS                         $165430.00             17.09%
    (15 + 18 + 19 + 20)
22  BOOK INVENTORY (RET.): 10/15/8                       $120770.00
    (12 - 21)
23  BOOK INVENTORY (COST): 10/15/8          $58808.91
    ((100.00% - MU%) * (22))
24  GROSS COST OF GOODS SOLD                $80556.09
    (12 - 23)
25  PURCHASE DISCOUNTS                      $4800.00
26  NET COST OF GOODS SOLD                  $75756.09
    (24 - 25)
27  GROSS MARGIN                            $65523.91                           46.38%
    (15 - 26)
28  OPERATING EXPENSES                      $55650.00                           39.39%
29  OPERATING PROFIT (27 - 28)              $9873.91                            6.99%


   * NOTE: NUMBERS IN PARANTHESES INDICATE ROW NUMBERS
```

Figure 12-11

```
                    Six-Month and Operating Profit Plan
                          8/1/8_ - 1/31/8_

YOUR PLANNED VALUES ARE:

NET SALES                   =       $375,000.00

OPERATING EXPENSES          =       $162,750.00

OPERATING EXPENSES          =            43.40%

REDUCTIONS                  =        $53,250.00

REDUCTIONS                  =            14.20%

CASH DISCOUNTS              =        $25,500.00

CASH DISCOUNTS              =             6.80%

MAINTAINED MARKUP           =       $165,750.00

MAINTAINED MARKUP           =            44.20%

GROSS MARGIN/PROFIT         =       $191,250.00

GROSS MARGIN/PROFIT         =            51.00%

OPERATING PROFIT            =        $28,500.00

OPERATING PROFIT            =             7.60%

INITIAL MARKUP PERCENT      =            51.14%


STOCK TURN                  =             3.4


                       SIX MONTH BUYING PLAN

                   (PERCENTAGE VARIATION METHOD)
```

	AUG	SEP	OCT	NOV	DEC	JAN	TOTALS
SALES	$ 60000	$ 60000	$ 52500	$ 67500	$ 82500	$ 52500	$ 375000
EOM STOCK	$ 108088	$ 101470	$ 114705	$ 127941	$ 101470	$ 110294	$ 663970
RED.	$ 10117	$ 11182	$ 12247	$ 9052	$ 5857	$ 4792	$ 53250
BOM STOCK	$ 108088	$ 108088	$ 101470	$ 114705	$ 127941	$ 101470	$ 661764
RET.OTB	$ 70117	$ 64564	$ 77982	$ 89787	$ 61886	$ 66116	$ 430455
COST OTB	$ 34260	$ 31547	$ 38103	$ 43871	$ 30238	$ 32305	$ 210327

Figure 12-12

• *PROBLEM 12-3 (S)*

From the data listed in the middle of p. 258, determine the following productivity values:

- Stock turn
- G.M.R.O.I.
- Sales return percent of gross sales
- Sales per square foot
- Selling salaries percent of net sales

MONTH	E.O.M. (RETAIL)
January	$147,000
February	153,000
March	162,000
April	171,000
May	161,000
June	157,000
July	155,000
Gross sales:	$438,800
Customer returns:	$ 28,000
Gross margin:	$271,523
Initial markup:	50.9%
Square feet of selling space:	4770
Selling salaries:	$ 35,300

RETAIL METHOD MERCHANDISE STATEMENT (SIX MONTHS)

		AT RETAIL	AT COST	AT RETAIL	AT COST	AT RETAIL	MARKUP %	% OF NET SALES
1	OPENING INVENTORY: 2/1/8_				$33975.00	$76390.00	55.52%	
2	PURCHASES (GROSS)		$108000.00	$242000.00				
3	PURCHASE RETURNS & ALLOWANCES		$3050.00	$6300.00				
4	NET PURCHASES (3 - 4)*				$104950.00	$235700.00	55.47%	
5	TRANSPORTATION CHARGES				$780.00			
6	TRANSFERS IN		$1760.00	$3750.00				
7	TRANSFERS OUT		$290.00	$630.00				
8	NET TRANSFERS (6 - 7)				$1470.00	$3120.00		
9	ADDITIONAL MARKUPS			$970.00				
10	MARKUP CANCELLATIONS			$450.00				
11	NET MARKUPS (9 - 10)					$520.00		
12	TOTAL MERCHANDISE HANDLED (C=1+4+5+8); (R=1+4+8+11)				$141175.00	$315730.00	55.29%	
13	SALES (GROSS)			$218500.00				
14	CUSTOMER RETURNS & ALLOWANCES			$9590.00				
15	NET SALES (13 - 14)			$208910.00				
16	MARKDOWNS (GROSS)	$18450.00						
17	MARKDOWN CANCELLATIONS	$3700.00						
18	NET MARKDOWNS (16 - 17)			$14750.00				7.06%
19	EMPLOYEE & CUSTOMER DISCOUNTS			$4100.00				1.96%
20	TOTAL MERCHANDISE DEDUCTIONS (15 + 18 + 19)					$227760.00		
21	BOOK INVENTORY (RET.): 7/31/8_ (12 - 20)			$87970.00				
22	BOOK INVENTORY (COST): 7/31/8_ ((100.00% - MUX) * (21))		$39334.76					
23	PHYSICAL INVENTORY (RET): 7/31/8					$84300.00	55.29%	
24	PHYSICAL INVENTORY (COST): 7/31/8_ ((100.00% - MUX) * (23))				$37693.77			
25	SHORTAGE OR (OVERAGE) (C=22-24; R=21-23)		$1641.00	$3670.00				1.76%
26	GROSS COST OF GOODS SOLD (12 - 24)				$103481.23			
27	PURCHASE DISCOUNTS				$5900.00			
28	NET COST OF GOODS SOLD (26 - 27)				$97581.23			
29	GROSS MARGIN (15 - 28)				$111328.77			53.29%
30	OPERATING EXPENSES				$102000.00			48.82%
31	OPERATING PROFIT (29-30)				$9328.77			4.47%

* NOTE: NUMBERS IN PARENTHESES INDICATE ROW NUMBERS

Figure 12-13

```
                    Six-Month and Operating Profit Plan
                           2/1/8_  -  7/31/8_

YOUR PLANNED VALUES ARE:

NET SALES                   =      $210,000.00

OPERATING EXPENSES          =      $102,480.00

OPERATING EXPENSES          =          48.80%

REDUCTIONS                  =       $25,200.00

REDUCTIONS                  =          12.00%

CASH DISCOUNTS              =       $11,760.00

CASH DISCOUNTS              =           5.60%

MAINTAINED MARKUP           =      $105,840.00

MAINTAINED MARKUP           =          50.40%

GROSS MARGIN/PROFIT         =      $117,600.00

GROSS MARGIN/PROFIT         =          56.00%

OPERATING PROFIT            =       $15,120.00

OPERATING PROFIT            =           7.20%

INITIAL MARKUP PERCENT      =          55.71%


STOCK TURN                  =           2.7


                         SIX MONTH BUYING PLAN

                         (BASIC STOCK METHOD)
```

	FEB	MAR	APR	MAY	JUN	JUL	TOTALS
SALES	$ 31500	$ 31500	$ 52500	$ 35700	$ 37800	$ 21000	$ 210000
EOM STOCK	$ 74277	$ 95277	$ 78477	$ 80577	$ 63777	$ 77777	$ 470166
RED.	$ 3276	$ 3024	$ 4284	$ 4536	$ 3780	$ 6300	$ 25200
BOM STOCK	$ 74277	$ 74277	$ 95277	$ 78477	$ 80577	$ 63777	$ 466666
RET.OTB	$ 34776	$ 55524	$ 39984	$ 42336	$ 24780	$ 41300	$ 238700
COST OTB	$ 15400	$ 24589	$ 17707	$ 18748	$ 10974	$ 18290	$ 105710

Figure 12-14

NOTES_____

[1]*M.O.R. Results 1984.* New York: National Retail Merchants Association, 1985.
[2]*The IBM 4680 Store System*, White Plains, New York: January, 1986.

Sales Associate Scheduling and Productivity Analysis

13

With the exception of automatic vending retailing, no serious study of buying and merchandising practices would overlook the impact of sales force management and control on profit.

The store's sales associates are the final connecting link of a chain that begins with the development of a product and concludes with a sale to a customer. Your efforts to buy and control merchandise properly will be wasted unless the people who are on the selling floor have been scheduled appropriately and can be satisfactorily evaluated.

SCHEDULING SALES ASSOCIATES

Payroll disbursement for the sales force is probably one of the largest expense items you will encounter other than merchandise costs. It is also an area that has flexibility in terms of the number of salespeople on the floor at any given time and the wages paid to each salesperson.

Obviously, you cannot open the doors to a shop or allow customers into a department without a salesperson. In addition, if the merchandise is such that a customer and the salesperson may become involved in a situation in which the goods require demonstration or trying on, you may need a second person on hand to back up the first, unless the first employee is extremely competent and can watch for, and be attentive to, more than one customer at one time. The process of determining the number of salespeople required on your selling floor involves the reconciliation of three factors: your planned sales volume, the sum of money allocated for the sales force payroll, and the minimum number of salespeople with whom you can "work" your selling floor.

• EXAMPLE 13-1

The planned sales for the month of April are $58,800, and the percentage of sales for each week follows. In some organizations, the actual calendar month is used for planning purposes, while in others the calendar is modified as in Figure 13-1.

Week 1	16.5%
Week 2	21.6
Week 3	22.3
Week 4	23.7
Week 5	15.9

If your planned monthly selling expense is 11.6 percent, determine the maximum expenditure for each week to cover your selling floor.

(1) Determine the dollar amount equal to the allowable selling expense for the month:

$$= \text{\$Planned sales} \times \text{Selling expense \%}$$
$$= \text{\$58,800.00} \times 11.6\%$$
$$= \text{\$6820.80}$$

(2) Determine the dollar amount you may spend for each week:

$$= \text{\$Monthly selling expense} \times \text{Weekly selling expense \%}$$
$$\text{Week 1} = \text{\$6820.80} \times 16.5\%$$
$$= \text{\$1125.43}$$

Weeks 2, 3, 4, and 5 are computed similarly, with the following results:

Week 2	$1473.29
Week 3	1521.04
Week 4	1616.53
Week 5	1084.51

• PROBLEM 13-1

Your planned selling expense for the coming season is 8.4 percent, and the planned sales for your department in March are

Week 1	$27,910
Week 2	28,490
Week 3	31,150
Week 4	29,040

Determine the planned dollar selling expense.

Once you have the planned weekly expense values, you could in a similar manner plan your daily sales expenses (and hourly, if necessary) if you have

PERIOD ACCOUNTING CALENDAR

SEASON	WEEKS	PERIOD
SPRING	4	FEB
	4	MAR
	5	APR
	5	MAY
	4	JUN
	4	JUL
FALL	4	AUG
	4	SEP
	5	OCT
	4	NOV
	5	DEC
	4	JAN (5 wk. JAN in 1986)

Figure 13-1

A1832 Rev. 12/85

the percentage of the week's sales that were anticipated for each day (and for each hour).

You will usually discover or learn through experience and research which days of the week and hours of each day are the busiest and plan your employees' work schedules accordingly. Figure 13-2 represents the planned scheduling needs for a department, whereas Figure 13-3 shows the employee schedules designed to accommodate the needs of the department for floor coverage.

Although the floor coverage worksheet (Fig. 13-2) indicates that one salesperson can minimally cover the department, it is evident from the schedule that there will be at least two people working most of the time. You can conclude from this that the department is projected to have a larger sales volume than can be accomplished by a single salesperson.

The verification procedure that should be used to confirm that an adequate number of sales associates have been scheduled is to multiply the sales rate per hour (obtained either from records or as reasonable approximations based upon your experience) by the total weekly hours. This product should be at, or close to, the planned weekly sales.

Using the data in Figure 13-3:

$$= \$48.00 \text{ per hour} \times 126.5 \text{ hours}$$
$$= \$6072.00$$

With planned weekly sales of $6,000, it appears that the work schedule should accommodate the sales volume.

The discussion thus far has centered on satisfying the floor coverage needs of the store; however, you must also be attuned to the scheduling limitations imposed by your sales associates. These can range from the associate whose schedule can be designed to include any hours during days or evenings—early or late, and your choice for day off—to the associate at the other end of the scale with constraints on numbers of hours; who can (will) work on only certain days and/or evenings and must have specific days off each week.

No formulae exist to simplify the scheduling process; it is a trial-and-error exercise until you develop the ability to "see" how employees and hours of operation of the store can be combined. Seldom will any two people produce the same schedule, but as long as each adheres to the limits imposed by store policies and employee likes and dislikes, one can be as effective as the other.

• *PROBLEM 13-2*

Produce a schedule for your selling floor given *only* the following information (without regard to selling expense).

STORE HOURS OF OPERATION

Monday, Tuesday, Wednesday, Friday	9:30–6:00
Thursday	9:30–9:00
Saturday	9:30–5:00

FLOOR COVERAGE WORKSHEET – Basic Selling Staff

NO. OF SALESPEOPLE		9:30	10-11	11-12	12-1	1-2	2-3	3-4	4-5	5-6	6-7	7-8	8-9	9:30
MONDAY	SCHEDULED	1	2	2	3	3	3	3	2	2				
	OUT – MEALS				1	1								
	OUT – RELIEFS													
	ON SELL. FLOOR	1	2	2	2	2	3	3	2	2				
	PLAN	1	2	2	2	2	3	3	2	2				
TUESDAY	SCHEDULED	1	2	2	3	3	3	3	2	2				
	OUT – MEALS				1									
	OUT – RELIEFS													
	ON SELL. FLOOR	1	2	2	2	3	3	3	2	2				
	PLAN	1	2	2	2	3	3	3	2	2				
WEDNESDAY	SCHEDULED	1	2	2	3	3	3	3	2	2				
	OUT – MEALS				1	1								
	OUT – RELIEFS													
	ON SELL. FLOOR	1	2	2	2	2	3	3	2	2				
	PLAN	1	2	2	2	2	3	3	2	2				
THURSDAY	SCHEDULED	1	2	2	2	2	3	3	2	2	2	2	2	1
	OUT – MEALS				1	1					1			
	OUT – RELIEFS													
	ON SELL. FLOOR	1	2	2	2	2	3	3	2	2	2	2	2	1
	PLAN	1	2	2	2	2	3	3	2	2	2	2	2	1
FRIDAY	SCHEDULED	1	2	2	3	3	3	3	2	2	2	2	2	1
	OUT – MEALS				1	1					1			
	OUT – RELIEFS													
	ON SELL. FLOOR	1	2	2	2	2	3	3	2	2	1	2	2	1
	PLAN	1	2	2	2	2	3	3	2	2	1	2	2	1
SATURDAY	SCHEDULED	2	2	3	3	4	4	4	4	3				
	OUT – MEALS					1		1						
	OUT – RELIEFS													
	ON SELL. FLOOR	2	2	3	3	4	4	3	3	3				
	PLAN	2	2	3	3	4	4	3	3	3				

STORE	DATE	MIN. FLOOR COVERAGE	DEPTS.	SELLING CENTER #
1	5/14	1		6

1310

FORM SE-3   A1906*   ☑ ORIGINAL   REVISED ☐

Figure 13-2

M = MEALTIME STARTS

R = RELIEF STARTS

Sch	NAME		WEEKLY PAYROLL	HRS.	MONDAY SCHED.HRS.	M	R	TUESDAY SCHED.HRS.	M	R	WEDNESDAY SCHED.HRS.	M	R	THURSDAY SCHED.HRS.	M	R	FRIDAY SCHED.HRS.	M	R	SATURDAY SCHED.HRS.	M	R
A.	C. Dempsy	1	$167.50	33.5	1:30|6:00	12					9:30|6:00	12		4:00|9:30	6		9:30|5:00	12		9:30|6:00	12	
B.	L. Singer	2	165.00	33.0	10.00|6:00	1		9:30|6:00	12					9:30|5:00	12		4:00|4:30	6		4:30|6:00	1	
C.	B. Willets	3	75.00	20.0				10:00|2:00			12:00|4:00			12:00|4:00			10:00|2:00			11:00|3:00		
D.	J. Fleck	4	15.00	20.0				12:00|4:00			10:00|2:00			10:00|2:00			12:00|4:00					
E.	T. Johnston	5	75.00	20.0	12:00|4:00			2:00|6:00			2:00|6:00			5:00|9:00			5:00|9:00			1:00|6:00		3
		6																				
		7																				
		8																				
		9																				
		10																				
		11																				
		12																				
		13																				
		14																				
		15																				
		16																				
		17																				
		18																				

			xx		Aver. Wkly. Comm.(if any) $		Weeks SALES		
		0	xx		0		LY	PLAN	
		$557.50	xx		Total Wkly. Payroll $		$5200	$6000	
					$557.50				
			xx	126.5	Total Wkly. Hours				
					Rate per Hour (Sales)	$47.43			

12 MONTH PLAN

Total Selling Payroll $	% to Planned Sales	BASIC SELL. STAFF Annual Payroll $	% to Pl. Sales	Planned for Extras ($)
$557.50	9.3%	$36,860	9.7%	0

DATE 5/4

DEPTS. 1310

SELLING CENTER 6

SCHEDULES

Basic Selling Staff ☐

☑ ORIGINAL   REVISED ☐

FORM ST-2 A2229*

Figure 13-3

Store Policies:

1. Full time means 32 to 38 hours per week; one business day off. Part time means 10 to 32 hours per week; no business day off.
2. Minimum of two sales associates on the selling floor at all times, one of whom must be a full-time associate.
3. Minimum schedule for work is a four-hour block of time.
4. Associates working five or more continuous hours must have a one-hour unpaid meal break.
5. Associates working eight or more continuous hours must receive a half-hour paid relief break.
6. Overtime pay must be authorized, and is paid at the rate of one and one half times regular rate after 38 hours.

Associates Available:

ASSOCIATE	STATUS	WAGES/BENEFITS PER HOUR	PERSONAL LIKES/DISLIKES
A	F/T:32–38 Hours	$8.00	No Saturdays
B	F/T:32–38 Hours	$7.50	No evenings
C	P/T:10–25 Hours	$6.25	No hours before noon
D	P/T:10–25 Hours	$6.25	Flexible

• *PROBLEM 13-3*

Given the data in Problem 13-2 and the following additional information, plan a schedule for your selling floor:

Planned weekly sales: $8500
Selling expense: 10.0%
Heavy customer traffic: every afternoon 1:00–4:00;
  Thursday evening 7:00–8:30; and all day
  Saturday.
Overtime pay will not be authorized.

PRODUCTIVITY OF SALES ASSOCIATES

Refining data.   Measuring productivity serves three purposes:

1. Provides a source of information as a basis for rewarding sales associates with pay increases, promotions and so on.
2. Furnishes data which is used to pinpoint selling deficiencies, with implications for training or retraining
3. Generates guidelines for scheduling

You should be cautioned here to remember that sales associates often perform nonselling tasks such as restocking, price changing, recording inventory counts, and acting as trainers for new associates. These qualitative contributions to the department will not be reflected in their individual sales (quantitative) data; however, these tasks must be performed if the department is to be successful. Therefore, any overall evaluation of sales associates must involve consideration of both qualitative and quantitative information.

The following data are used to provide statistics for each employee:

1. Gross sales—the dollar total of all sales
2. Customer returns—the dollar total of all merchandise returned
3. Number of sales transactions—the number of sales slips written or the number of times the cash drawer is opened
4. Number of hours worked
5. Gross wages and benefits—total wages (including commissions) and the dollar value of all benefits, such as contributions to health plans and life insurance

• *EXAMPLE 13-2*

Refer to Figure 13-3 and the following data for employee C. Dempsy. Compute net sales; customer return rate; average sale per transaction; average sale per hour; and cost rate percentage.

Gross sales:	$1759.11
Customer returns:	$ 105.55
Number of sales transactions:	103

(1) Compute net sales:

$$= \text{Gross sales} - \text{Customer returns}$$
$$= \$1759.11 - \$105.55$$
$$= \$1653.56$$

(2) Compute customer return rate:

$$= \$\text{Returns} \div \$\text{Net sales}$$
$$= \$105.55 \div \$1653.56$$
$$= 6.4\%$$

(3) Compute average sale per transaction:

$$= \$\text{Net sales} \div \text{Number of transactions}$$
$$= \$1653.56 \div 103$$
$$= \$16.05$$

(4) Compute average sale per hour:

$$= \$\text{Net sales} \div \text{Number of hours worked}$$
$$= \$1653.56 \div 33.5$$
$$= \$49.36$$

(5) Compute cost rate percentage of this employee based upon sales made:

$$= \$\text{Wages} \div \$\text{Net sales}$$
$$= \$167.50 \div \$1653.56$$
$$= 10.1\%$$

By themselves, the foregoing data have little meaning other than to show that Dempsy's average sale per hour (step 4), $49.36, is better than the planned rate of sale per hour in Figure 13-3, $47.43.

• *PROBLEM 13-4*

The data for your employee, H. Kaufman, for the week just ended are as follows:

Hours worked	38.5
Gross wages	$ 217.53
Gross sales	$2432.82
Customer returns	$ 376.18
Number of transactions	159

Calculate net sales, customer return rate, average sale per transaction and per hour, and cost rate for this employee.

EVALUATION

There are two levels of evaluation that can be accomplished. The first of these compares each sales associate's record for a short period of time with his or her cumulative data covering a longer time span, and also makes comparisons between different salespeople, using the same time frames and criteria, as an aid to recommendations for salary increases and promotions (or termination).

The criteria used at this first level are

1. Customer Return Rate—an indicator of how well the salesperson determines and responds to customers' expressed wants and needs; that is, providing customers with what it is they want or need. It is also an indicator of how "hard sell" the salesperson is. The higher the customer return rate, the poorer the salesperson's effectiveness. A salesperson with this problem requires retraining in determining customers' needs.
2. Average Sale per Transaction—the dollar value of the average sale indicates the success of the salesperson in selling either higher-priced merchandise or services or multiples to the same customer. The training implication for a declining average sale per transaction is for multiple-sales training.
3. Average Sale per Hour—this is a reflection of the speed with which a sales associate completes a sale and moves on to the next customer, as well as an indication of whether the associate can work well with more than one customer at a time. A drop-off in average sale per hour implies that the salesperson requires training in working efficiently with customers.
4. Cost Percentage—the store's cost for each dollar of net sales made by this employee. The higher the cost percentage, the more expensive is the employee.

• *EXAMPLE 13-3*

Evaluate the performance of M. Moses from the following data:

	NET SALES	CUSTOMER RETURN RATE	AVERAGE SALE PER TRANSACTION	AVERAGE SALE PER HOUR	COST %
Month of November	$18,600	4.0%	$49.12	$96.25	5.0
Year to Date	38,300	3.0	51.16	82.52	6.3

It seems that this employee is relatively new to the department, as the sales for November are almost half of the total. The rate of returns from customers is up, and the average sale for each transaction is down; both of these items are negative features. The average sale per hour is higher, and the cost of this employee is lower, indicating a higher level of sales productivity.

The overall view of Moses is that this person is selling less per customer but is working with more customers per hour. This increased speed with customers is also generating a higher customer return rate, however.

The evaluation for this employee should be positive, for with proper sales training to reduce customer returns, Moses will probably develop into a fine salesperson.

• *PROBLEM 13-5*

Evaluate the work of S. Link from the following data:

	NET SALES	CUSTOMER RETURN RATE	AVERAGE SALE PER TRANSACTION	AVERAGE SALE PER HOUR	COST %
Month of August	$ 20,500	4.2%	$63.19	$82.13	9.6
Year to Date	150,900	4.1	64.87	81.27	8.9

Using the same criteria identified above, you can make comparisons between individuals.

• *EXAMPLE 13-4*

From the following end-of-year data, make comparisons between Douglas and Eli.

		NET SALES	CUSTOMER RETURN RATE	AVERAGE SALE PER TRANSACTION	AVERAGE SALE PER HOUR	COST %
Month of January	S. Douglas	$ 15,800	2.6%	$47.93	$62.58	8.8
	L. Eli	16,900	2.1	38.16	59.36	9.3
Year to Date	S. Douglas	$190,600	2.3%	$51.16	$54.19	8.3
	L. Eli	200,800	2.1	49.26	52.67	8.7

Customer return rate: Eli "sells" better than Douglas; Douglas's rate is increasing, while Eli's has been constant through the year.

Average sale per transaction: Both are lower for January; may be a function of the retail prices (sales). Douglas's average is higher; may be "pushing" too hard, correlating with customer return rate. Eli, however, is considerably off from 12-month average.

Average sale per hour: Douglas clearly moves from one customer to the next and/or handles multiple customers better than Eli.

Cost percent: Both individuals have increased for January and by almost the same amount (.5% for Douglas; .6% for Eli) although overall Douglas is the least expensive.

Conclusions: Douglas needs some retraining to reduce customer returns; Eli may need some help to improve multiple sales and, in the absence of qualitative information regarding floor responsibilities, could use help to improve average sales per hour, particularly since this sales associate is the more expensive of the two. Both should be continued, with recommendation for a salary increase for Douglas.

• *PROBLEM 13-6*

From the following data, evaluate the two employees against their own records and make comparisons between them:

		NET SALES	CUSTOMER RETURN RATE	AVERAGE SALE PER TRANSACTION	AVERAGE SALE PER HOUR	COST %
Month of April	Stans	$ 5100	.2%	$64.19	$69.33	6.0
	Silver	4400	1.2	63.86	69.67	6.3
Year to Date	Stans	15,100	6.1	62.87	63.85	6.9
	Silver	12,100	.8	59.31	55.17	8.0

At the second level, the data you should develop and use to evaluate your employees involves determining the percentage of contribution to total department sales made by each employee. Then, using this information and the comparative values for each salesperson, you will be better able to assess each individual in the selling area.

In theory, a sales associate's developed data relative to the total performance of the department should reveal a state of equilibrium between the following: percent of total wages, percent of total hours, percent of total net sales, and percent of total customer returns. That is, percent of total wages = percent of total hours = percent of total net sales = percent of total customer returns. As an example, a sales associate who receives 40% of total wages should work 40% of total hours, produce 40% of total net sales, and account for 40% of total customer returns. However, in a practical sense, these measures rarely match, nor should they; a long-term employee will undoubtedly earn more than a recent hire, although they may both work an equal number of hours. But it would not be unreasonable to expect that a superior sales associate with longer service should produce a higher percentage of net sales, with a lower percentage of customer returns.

Specifically, the criteria developed previously are expanded, producing department totals with which each individual can be compared. Algebraically, the criteria are evaluated as follows: (Note: the symbol $<=$ means "less than or equal to"; and $>=$ means "greater than or equal to.")

INDIVIDUAL CRITERIA	SUPERIOR OR EQUAL PERFORMANCE	TOTAL DEPARTMENT CRITERIA
Customer return rate	$<=$	Customer return rate
Average sale per transaction	$>=$	Average sale per transaction
Average sale per hour	$>=$	Average sale per hour
Cost rate %	$<=$	Cost rate %
and Percent of total:		
Net sales $>=$ Customer return rate $<=$ Wages $<=$ Hours		

• *EXAMPLE 13-5*

You have accumulated the following data for the month of April and the year to date for the three sales associates in your department. Calculate net sales, customer return rate, average sale per transaction and per hour, cost rate, and percentages of contribution to total department sales, and then evaluate the results (see Fig. 13-4).

The computations will be shown for Samuels and the totals for the month of April. All others will be summarized in Figure 13-5. (Note that the values in boldface will be values given in the problem, whereas derived values are accompanied by a number in parentheses to identify the step in which they were computed.)

(1) Compute net sales:

$$
\begin{aligned}
\text{Samuels} &= \text{Gross sales} - \text{Customer returns} \\
&= \$6914.18 - \$324.97 \\
&= \$6589.21 \\
\text{Totals} &= \$15,436.44 - \$643.87 \\
&= \$14,792.57
\end{aligned}
$$

(2) Compute customer return rate:

$$
\begin{aligned}
\text{Samuels} &= \$\text{Return} \div \text{Net sales} \\
&= \$324.97 \div \$6589.21 \\
&= 4.9\% \\
\text{Totals} &= \$643.87 \div \$14,792.57 \\
&= 4.4\%
\end{aligned}
$$

(3) Compute average sales per transaction:

$$
\begin{aligned}
\text{Samuels} &= \$\text{Net sales} \div \text{Number of transactions} \\
&= \$6589.21 \div 112 \\
&= \$58.83 \\
\text{Totals} &= \$14,792.57 \div 249 \\
&= \$59.41
\end{aligned}
$$

(4) Compute average sale per hour:

		HOURS WORKED	GROSS WAGES	GROSS SALES	CUSTOMER RETURNS	NUMBER OF TRANSACTIONS
Month of April	Samuels	160.0	$ 840.00	$ 6914.18	$ 324.97	112
	Weber	112.5	562.50	4973.26	208.88	79
	Green	84.5	411.94	3549.00	110.02	58
Totals		357.0	$1814.44	$15,436.44	$ 643.87	249
Year to Date	Samuels	495.0	$2475.00	$20,812.47	$1082.25	359
	Weber	286.0	1430.00	12,902.91	593.53	212
	Green	192.5	912.00	7653.24	321.44	134
Totals		973.5	$4817.00	$41,368.62	$1997.22	705

Figure 13-4

EMPLOYEE PRODUCTIVITY DATA

EMPLOYEE (INPUT)	GROSS SALES (INPUT)	CUST. RET. (INPUT)	NET SALES	% OF TOTAL N. SALES	CUST. RET. RATE	% OF TOTAL RETURNS	# OF TRANS. (INPUT)	AV. SALE PER TRANS.	# OF HOURS (INPUT)	% OF TOTAL HOURS	WAGES (INPUT)	% OF TOTAL WAGES	COST RATE	AV. SALE PER HOUR
M O N T H														
SAMUELS	$6914.18	$324.97	(1) $6589.21	(6) 44.54%	(2) 4.93%	(7) 50.47%	112	(3) $58.83	(9) 160	44.82%	(8) $840.00	46.30%	(5) 12.75%	(4) $41.18
HEBER	$4973.26	$208.88	$4764.38	32.21%	4.38%	32.44%	79	$60.31	112.5	31.51%	$562.50	31.00%	11.81%	$42.35
GREEN	$3549.00	$110.02	$3438.98	23.25%	3.20%	17.09%	58	$59.29	84.5	23.67%	$411.94	22.70%	11.98%	$40.70
TOTALS	$15436.44	$643.87	(1) $14792.57	100.00%	(2) 4.35%	100.00%	249	(3) $59.41	357	100.00%	$1814.44	100.00%	(5) 12.27%	(4) $41.44
Y R T O D T E														
SAMUELS	$20812.47	$1082.25	$19730.22	50.11%	5.49%	54.19%	359	$54.96	495	50.85%	$2475.00	51.38%	12.54%	$39.86
HEBER	$12902.91	$593.53	$12309.38	31.26%	4.82%	29.72%	212	$58.06	286	29.38%	$1430.00	29.69%	11.62%	$43.04
GREEN	$7653.24	$321.44	$7331.80	18.62%	4.38%	16.09%	134	$54.71	192.5	19.77%	$912.00	18.93%	12.44%	$38.09
TOTALS	$41368.62	$1997.22	$39371.40	100.00%	5.07%	100.00%	705	$55.85	973.5	100.00%	$4817.00	100.00%	12.23%	$40.44

Figure 13-5

273

SELECTED EVALUATION DATA

		1	2	3	4	5	6	7	8
		% OF TOTAL WAGES	% OF TOTAL HOURS	% OF TOTAL N. SALES	% OF TOTAL RETURNS	CUST. RET. RATE.	AV. SALE PER TRANS.	AV. SALE PER HOUR	COST RATE
MONTH OF APRIL	SAMUELS	46.30%	44.82%	44.54%	50.47%	4.93%	$58.83	$41.18	12.75%
	WEBER	31.00%	31.51%	32.21%	32.44%	4.38%	$60.31	$42.35	11.81%
	GREEN	22.70%	23.67%	23.25%	17.09%	3.20%	$59.29	$40.70	11.98%
TOTALS		N/A	N/A	N/A	N/A	4.35%	$59.41	$41.44	12.27%
YEAR TO DATE	SAMUELS	51.38%	50.85%	50.11%	54.19%	5.49%	$54.96	$39.86	12.54%
	WEBER	29.69%	29.38%	31.26%	29.72%	4.82%	$58.06	$43.04	11.62%
	GREEN	18.93%	19.77%	18.62%	16.09%	4.38%	$54.71	$38.09	12.44%
TOTALS		N/A	N/A	N/A	N/A	5.07%	$55.85	$40.44	12.23%

Figure 13-6

$$\text{Samuels} = \text{\$Net sales} \div \text{Number of hours worked}$$
$$= \$6589.21 \div 160$$
$$= \$41.18$$
$$\text{Totals} = \$14,792.57 \div 357.0$$
$$= \$41.44$$

(5) Compute cost rate percentage:

$$\text{Samuels} = \text{\$Wages} \div \text{\$Net sales}$$
$$= \$840.00 \div \$6589.21$$
$$= 12.7\%$$
$$\text{Totals} = \$1814.44 \div \$14,792.57$$
$$= 12.3\%$$

(6) Compute percentage of total for net sales:

$$\text{Samuels} = \text{\$Net sales} \div \text{Total net sales}$$
$$= \$6589.21 \div \$14,792.57$$
$$= 44.5\%$$

(7) Compute percentage of total for customer returns:

$$\text{Samuels} = \text{\$Customer returns} \div \text{\$Total customer returns}$$
$$= \$324.97 \div \$643.87$$
$$= 50.5\%$$

(8) Compute percentage of total for wages:

$$\text{Samuels} = \text{\$Wages} \div \text{\$Total wages}$$
$$= \$840.00 \div \$1814.44$$
$$= 46.3\%$$

(9) Compute percentage of total for hours:

$$\text{Samuels} = \text{Hours} \div \text{Total hours}$$
$$= 160.0 \div 357.0$$
$$= 44.8\%$$

Figure 13-6 consolidates the data to be examined. The following is an analysis, with summary and recommendations for Samuels.

Analysis for Samuels: Equilibrium does not exist in columns 1–4. Percent of total wages exceeds the other factors, for both April and YTD; this is confirmed by column 8 (cost rate %), which shows a higher value than the department total. Using percent of total hours (column 2) as a bench mark still shows a negative imbalance, but not as great relative to sales (column 3) and customer returns (column 4). The high value in customer returns is consistent for both April and YTD and is reflected in column 5, customer return rate, which is higher than department totals. Columns 5–7 generate the following:

		INDIVIDUAL PERFORMANCE		TOTAL DEPT. PERFORMANCE	IMPLICATION FOR EMPLOYEE
	Customer Ret. Rate	4.9%	>	4.4%	Negative
APRIL:	Av. Sale/Trans.	$58.83	<	$59.41	Negative
	Av. Sale/Hour	41.18	<	41.44	Marginal
	Cost Rate %	12.7	>	12.3	Marginal

		INDIVIDUAL PERFORMANCE		TOTAL DEPT. PERFORMANCE	IMPLICATION FOR EMPLOYEE
YTD:	Customer Ret. Rate	5.5%	>	5.1%	Negative
	Av. Sale/Trans.	$54.96	<	$55.96	Negative
	Av. Sale/Hour	39.86	<	40.84	Marginal
	Cost Rate %	12.5	>	12.2	Marginal

Summary for Samuels: Definitely requires retraining to reduce unsatisfactory volume of customer returns and to increase amount of sale to each customer (average sale per transaction). Samuels must also learn to work more efficiently with customers to improve average sale per hour.

If improvements in the foregoing eventuate, the cost rate percent will drop, and Samuels will become a productive employee; otherwise, recommend termination.

- PROBLEM 13-7

Compute and arrange employee data from the following, and evaluate the results:

		HOURS WORKED	GROSS WAGES	GROSS SALES	CUSTOMER RETURNS	NUMBER OF TRANSACTIONS
Month of November	James	87	$ 474.15	$ 4395.24	$ 197.79	126
	King	136	748.00	6974.73	292.94	189
	Prince	185	1086.88	8812.64	449.44	235
Year to Date	James	840	4620.00	43,913.52	2020.02	1159
	King	1387	7975.25	73,492.97	3160.20	2075
	Prince	.1516	7959.00	69,169.69	3512.96	1894

SUMMARY PROBLEMS

- PROBLEM 13-1 (S)

Given the following information, produce a schedule for your sales associates for next week.

STORE HOURS OF OPERATION

Monday, Tuesday, Wednesday, Friday	9:30–6:00
Thursday	9:30–9:00
Saturday	9:30–5:00

Store Policies:

1. Full time means 32 to 38 hours per week; one business day off. Part time means 10 to 25 hours per week; no business day off.

2. Minimum of two sales associates on the selling floor at all times, one of whom must be a full-time associate.

3. Minimum schedule for work is a four-hour block of time.

4. Associates working five or more continuous hours must have a one-hour unpaid meal break.

5. Associates working eight or more continuous hours must receive a half-hour paid relief break.

6. Overtime pay must be authorized, and is paid at the rate of one and one half times regular rate after 38 hours.

Planned sales for next week:	$18,000
Planned payroll expense:	12%
Sales Per Day:	

Monday	12.5%
Tuesday	10.0
Wednesday	12.0
Thursday	19.5
Friday	22.0
Saturday	24.0

SALES PERSONNEL NAME	NUMBER	RANGE OF HOURS WORKED PER WK.	WAGE RATE PER HR.	BENEFITS FIXED ANNUAL BASIS	PERSONAL LIKES AND DISLIKES
DAVIS, B.	(1)	32–38	$6.20	$1760	LIKES WORKING EVENINGS
EATON, S.	(2)	32–38	$6.20	$1760	NEVER TUES
GILBERT, D.	(3)	32–38	$6.48	$1940	FLEXIBLE
GREEN, D.	(4)	32–38	$6.48	$1940	NEVER MON
HOSLER, H.	(5)	32–38	$6.20	$1880	FLEXIBLE
LANDON, P.	(6)	10–25	$4.35	$ 642	LIKES EVENINGS
MALLARD, S.	(7)	10–25	$4.35	$ 642	LIKES EVENINGS
POLINSKI, E.	(8)	10–25	$4.35	$ 642	PREFERS MORNINGS OPEN
ROSANI, M.	(9)	10–25	$4.55	$ 642	NO SATURDAYS
TAMERA, S.	(10)	32–38	$7.05	$1980	FLEXIBLE
WALKER, C.	(11)	32–38	$7.05	$1980	FLEXIBLE
WILLIAMS, J.	(12)	20–25	$4.55	$ 895	FLEXIBLE

• *PROBLEM 13-2 (S)*

The selling expense percentage for the coming season is 9.4. You estimate, however, that in May you will need a higher percentage for the first three weeks, owing to the nature of the season. The planned sales for May are $75,600, and the percentage of sales for each week is as follows:

Week 1	23.4%
Week 2	28.7
Week 3	32.1
Week 4	9.2
Week 5	6.6

You plan to spend 90 percent of your selling expense budget during the first three weeks in preparation for the sales for this time, with the balance being distributed proportionately in the final two weeks.

Determine the selling expense allocation for each period.

• *PROBLEM 13-3 (S)*

You have to update the sales productivity data for the two employees in your department, E. Miller and R. Becker, for the last week in November. You have the following information:

*Week 4, November, 198_*

	HOURS WORKED	GROSS WAGES	GROSS SALES	CUSTOMER RETURNS	NUMBER OF TRANSACTIONS
E. Miller	34.5	$232.88	$2330.37	$178.60	82
R. Becker	23.0	158.13	1476.14	$109.23	52

Calculate net sales, customer return rate, average sale per transaction and per hour, and cost rate for each employee.

• *PROBLEM 13-4 (S)*

From the following information, develop the net sales, customer return rate, average sale per transaction and per hour, and cost rate for each employee. Evaluate the results.

		HOURS WORKED	GROSS WAGES	GROSS SALES	CUSTOMER RETURNS	NUMBER OF TRANSACTIONS
Month of May	J. Kutler	193	$ 885.60	$11,500	$ 690.00	263
	R. McKenna	150	714.40	7600	132.00	168
Year to Date	J. Kutler	657	3013.20	37,200	1869.00	804
	R. McKenna	500	2535.90	23,700	260.70	537

• *PROBLEM 13-5 (S)*

Perform the necessary computations from the following data and evaluate these sales associates.

		HOURS WORKED	GROSS WAGES	GROSS SALES	CUSTOMER RETURNS	NUMBER OF TRANSACTIONS
Month of June	Singer	160	$ 960.00	$ 8345.60	$ 342.98	132
	Voncey	130	747.50	7035.60	277.91	109
	Wexler	158	829.50	8070.64	326.05	130
	Woo	74	388.50	3993.78	152.56	61
Year to Date	Singer	763	4387.50	40,556.50	1646.59	633
	Voncey	620	3487.50	33,240.68	1319.65	513
	Wexler	722	3700.25	36,872.54	1485.96	523
	Woo	—	—	—	—	—

• *PROBLEM 13-6 (S)*

Your planned selling expense for next month is set at 8.6 percent, with net sales of $38,500. The data on your sales associates follow. Perform the necessary computations and indicate how many hours of work you should allocate for each employee for the month, and why. You can schedule any employee up to 180 hours per month.

		HOURS WORKED	GROSS WAGES	GROSS SALES	CUSTOMER RETURNS	NUMBER OF TRANSACTIONS
Month of May	Ables	180	$1044.00	$12,981.60	$ 501.09	516
	Charney	176	985.60	12,202.08	391.69	610
	Dorr	143	815.10	10,477.61	472.54	439
Year to Date	Ables	713	4099.75	51,229.05	2023.55	2104
	Charney	653	3656.80	49,210.08	1550.12	2090
	Dorr	318	1812.60	22,962.78	1063.18	1022

Quantitative Analysis of Vendor Performance and Productivity Assessment of the Buyer

14

VENDOR PRODUCTIVITY: QUANTITATIVE CONSIDERATIONS

Buying decisions are often difficult to make. You must not only decide how much to purchase in dollars and units, but you are also forced to decide which vendors are appropriate for you.

Many times several resources will offer you comparable merchandise; which one deserves your order? Obviously, you should buy from the best vendor. The problem is to establish which vendor is "the best."

If you have never purchased from a particular manufacturer, or if there is a new face in the marketplace, you will have to rely on what others may say and, to a larger extent, on your own experience and instincts. In many situations, however, you will be ordering from suppliers with whom you have had prior experience. For this group, you should have accumulated data that is coupled with the information mentioned in Chapter Three to produce **vendor profiles**.

Buyers are generally very secretive about the "black book" they have developed to judge resources, as their vendor profiles are keys to their buying habits and hence to their success. The amount of data and subjective information will vary from one buyer to the next, although certain basic material must be considered essential.

As your vendor relationships develop over a period of time, you should maintain records that will provide you with a longitudinal view of a vendor's performance. An overview of two years has usually proved to be a satisfactory measure.

The following categories are excellent **quantitative** gauges of vendor effectiveness:

1. Dollar cost of merchandise ordered.
2. Purchases received at cost and at retail. This value should be the net value of merchandise received after returns to the vendor have been deducted.
3. Markup by dollar and percentage on net purchases.
4. Net markdowns by dollar and percentage of sales.
5. Cash discount and anticipation (if allowed) as a percentage.
6. Transportation expense as a percentage of purchases.

• EXAMPLE 14-1

You are beginning to update your vendor performance records to include the past spring-summer season. The data for past purchases for Jus' Jeans are summarized from your current files as follows:

	COST	RETAIL
Merchandise ordered:	$25,193.00	
Merchandise received:		
Invoice no. 1643	$ 8397.00	$16,919.50
Invoice no. 1832	6416.18	13,626.80
Invoice no. 2016	7314.16	16,419.30
Returns to vendor		
Credit memo no. 321	$ 87.49	$ 169.30
Credit memo no. 418	113.16	243.10
Net Markdowns:		4316.40
Cash discounts: $2035.72		
Transportation expenses: $24.12		

(1) Compute the percentage of the vendor's orders which were received:

Percentage of orders received = Dollar cost of merchandise received ÷ Dollar cost of merchandise ordered
= ($8,397.00 + $6416.18 + $7314.16) ÷ $25,193.00
= 87.8%

Note: You use the cost values rather than retail values to eliminate any disparity owing to different markup which may be planned for individual styles.

(2) Compute net purchases at cost and at retail:

Net purchases = Merchandise received − Returns to vendor
At cost: = ($8397.00 + $6416.18 + $7314.16) − ($87.49 + $113.16)
= $21,926.69
At retail: = ($16,919.50 + $13,626.80 + $16,419.30) − ($169.30 + $243.10)
= $46,553.20

(3) Compute dollar and percentage markup:

$$\begin{aligned}
\$MU &= \$R - \$C \\
&= \$46,553.20 - \$21,926.69 \\
&= \$24,626.51 \\
MU\% &= \$MU \div \$R \\
&= \$24,626.51 \div \$46,553.20 \\
&= 52.9\%
\end{aligned}$$

(4) Compute the markdown percentage:

$$\begin{aligned}
MD\% &= \$MD \div \$R \\
&= \$4316.40 \div \$46,553.20 \\
&= 9.3\%
\end{aligned}$$

(5) Compute cash discount percentage:
(You should recall from Chapter Six that cash discounts are taken on the cost value of the merchandise; therefore, the cash discount percentage is determined by using this value as the base. The transportation percentage is calculated in the same way.)

$$\begin{aligned}
\text{Cash discount \%} &= \$\text{Cash discount} \div \$\text{Net purchases at cost} \\
&= \$2035.72 \div \$21,926.69 \\
&= 9.3\%
\end{aligned}$$

(6) Compute the transportation expense percentage:

$$\begin{aligned}
\text{Transportation \%} &= \$\text{Transportation} \div \$\text{Net purchases at cost} \\
&= \$24.12 \div \$21,926.69 \\
&= .1\%
\end{aligned}$$

• *PROBLEM 14-1*

You have been given the following information relating to "Plain Nuts," one of your vendors.

	COST	RETAIL
Merchandise ordered:	$25,972.18	
Merchandise received:		
Invoice no. 2391	$ 4972.24	$ 9743.62
Invoice no. 2641	8391.69	16,831.95
Invoice no. 2983	10,493.41	21,641.37
Returns to vendor		
Credit memo no. 23	$ 394.18	$ 775.14
Credit memo no. 86	491.27	982.16
Credit memo no. 93	43.16	81.31
Net Markdowns:		5397.00
Cash discounts: $1948.18		
Transportation expenses: 0		

Compute:

1. Percentage of orders received
2. Net purchases at cost and retail
3. Dollar and markup percentage

4. Markdown percentage
5. Cash discount percentage
6. Transportation expense percentage

Your vendors, like your sales associates, are to be evaluated several different ways. These categories are

1. Longitudinally; each vendor measured against its own performance compared with prior seasons or years.
2. Vendor to vendor (current year); each vendor measured against the performance of the other vendors.
3. Vendor to department totals for all purchases (current year).
4. Each vendor measured against its percentage of the department's total orders received (current year). This comparison assumes that a vendor supplying, for example, 25 percent of your merchandise should contribute (all things being equal) like percentages of your markups and markdowns.

Table 14-1 summarizes the criteria and evaluation guide for each category just identified.

While this is a quantitative analysis, your assessment of what is superior performance will be based upon store policy or judgments made by you. In some instances, a difference of 1 percent may be significant, but in others this may be either too small or too great. However, the importance is in knowing the criteria and the direction each must take to provide you with appropriate information for vendor selection.

In most cases, you will find that the bulk of your inventory is purchased from a relatively small number of manufacturers. This fact makes your regular evaluation of vendors an urgent matter, not something to be considered as a task of low-level priority.

The techniques described should also be used to assay the value of any form of buying office or service that you may be using. You would simply group the data together from the resources recommended to you and consider them in

Table 14-1

CRITERIA	CATEGORY 1	CATEGORY 2	CATEGORY 3	CATEGORY 4
% of Orders Received	> =	> =	> =	N/A
Markup %	> =	> =	> =	N/A
% of Total Markup	N/A	N/A	N/A	> =
Markdown %	< =	< =	< =	N/A
% of Total Markdowns	N/A	N/A	N/A	< =
Discount %	> =	> =	> =	N/A
Transportation Expense %	< =	< =	< =	N/A

Note: Each criterion within each category is rated symbolically; < = means "less than or equal to" and > = means "greater than or equal to." An "equal" level of performance reflects achievement similar to the comparable data, while "less than" or "greater than" indicates the direction the values should be moving to show superior activity.

total. This is not to imply that each vendor in the assemblage should lose its identity, for the vendor should still be considered individually, but the sum of all vendors' data will add to your information base in assessing an outside buying agency.

• *EXAMPLE 14-2*

You have finished the spring-summer season and are preparing to evaluate the vendors. Your buying office suggested two new resources, "Eye Ties" and "Chatterbox," and you placed small orders with them. Refer to the data in Figure 14-1, which was prepared by your assistant. Compute the missing values and review the results.

(The computations will be illustrated only for Rockport Casuals.)

(1) Compute the percentage of each vendor's orders which were received:

$$= \$21{,}647 \div \$23{,}597$$
$$= 91.7\%$$

(2) Compute the percentage of all vendors' orders which were received:

$$= \$72{,}824 \div \$82{,}764$$
$$= 88.0\%$$

(3) Compute the percentage of the total merchandise purchased that was obtained from each vendor:

$$= \$43{,}004 \div \$145{,}459$$
$$= 29.6\%$$

(4) Compute the dollar and percentage markup for each vendor and the cumulative markup for all purchases:

$$\$MU \quad = \$43{,}004 - \$21{,}647$$
$$= \$21{,}357$$
$$MU\% \quad = \$21{,}357 \div \$43{,}004$$
$$= 49.7\%$$
$$\$CMU \quad = \text{Total retail} - \text{Total cost}$$
$$= \$145{,}459 - \$72{,}824$$
$$= \$72{,}635$$
$$CMU\% = \$72{,}635 \div \$145{,}459$$
$$= 49.9\%$$

(5) Compute the percentage of your total markup for the season attributed to the purchases from each vendor:

$$= \$21{,}357 \div \$72{,}635$$
$$= 29.4\%$$

(6) Compute the percentage of markdowns for each vendor and the overall markdown percentage:

$$= \$3295 \div \$43{,}004$$
$$= 7.7\%$$

$$\text{Overall MD\%} = \$12{,}417 \div \$145{,}459$$
$$= 8.5\%$$

CURRENT YEAR

BUYERS COPY - VENDOR ANALYSIS

VENDORS	MERCHANDISE RECEIVED					MARKUP			MARKDOWN			DISC. & ANTIC.		TRANSP. P.	
NAME OR NUMBER	$ COST OF ORDERS (INPUT)	$ COST OF VEN RCVD. (INPUT)	% OF VEN ORDERS RCVD.	$ RETAIL OF RCVD. (INPUT)	% OF TOTAL ORDERS	$	%	% OF TOTAL MARKUP	$ (INPUT)	%	% OF TOTAL MDS.	$ (INPUT)	%	$ (INPUT)	%
ROCKPORT	$23597.00	$21647.00		$43004.00					$3295.00			$1241.00		$0.00	
SEAGULL	$18329.00	$15962.00		$32001.00					$3200.00			$960.00		$0.00	
TOADSTOOL	$25769.00	$20652.00		$41375.00					$2796.00			$1236.00		$20.10	
GREAT KNITS	$6592.00	$6592.00		$13497.00					$1650.00			$410.00		$0.00	
EYE TIES	$3765.00	$3652.00		$7341.00					$651.00			$216.00		$6.35	
CHATTERBOX	$4712.00	$4319.00		$8241.00					$825.00			$235.00		$0.00	
TOTALS															
BUYING OFFICE:															
LAST YEAR															
ROCKPORT	$19867.00	$18341.00		$37915.00					$2764.00			$750.00		$0.00	
SEAGULL	$14633.00	$14297.00		$29648.00					$2431.00			$840.00		$0.00	
TOAD STOOL	$19534.00	$19438.00		$38954.00					$3002.00			$1476.00		$14.00	
GREAT KNITS	$4587.00	$4320.00		$8949.00					$675.00			$295.00		$7.80	
TOTALS															
TWO YRS. AGO															
ROCKPORT	$16978.00	$16350.00		$35960.00					$2100.00			$1192.00		$0.00	
SEAGULL	$15495.00	$15495.00		$32486.00					$1276.00			$1145.00		$0.00	
TOAD STOOL	$18937.00	$18670.00		$37491.00					$1593.00			$1322.00		$0.00	
TOTALS															

Figure 14-1

(7) Compute the percentage of the total markdowns caused by each vendor:

$$= \$3295 \div \$12,417$$
$$= 26.5\%$$

(8) Compute the discount percentage for each vendor and the overall discount percentage:

$$= \$1241 \div \$21,647$$
$$= 5.7\%$$

$$\text{Overall} = \$4298 \div \$72,824$$
$$= 5.9\%$$

(9) Compute the transportation expense percentage:
(illustrated for Toadstool)

$$= \$20.10 \div \$20,652.00$$
$$= .1\%$$

To evaluate the buying office, sum the values for Eye Ties and Chatterbox and perform the necessary computations. The results are summarized below the "Totals" line, current year, in Figure 14-2 and labeled "Buying Office."

(10) Compute the markup percentage for the vendors you used two years ago and last year.

For Rockport two years ago:

$$\$MU = \$Retail - \$Cost$$
$$= \$35,960 - \$16,350$$
$$= \$19,610$$

$$MU\% = \$MU \div \$R$$
$$= \$19,610 \div \$35,960$$
$$= 54.5\%$$

The results from the balance of the computations are shown in Figure 14-2. Note: The percentage values have been carried out to two decimal places, as is common with reports generated by a computer.

You are now prepared to evaluate your vendors according to the categories previously established. (Only Rockport will be evaluated.)

Category 1: Longitudinal analysis
Arrange the data from Figure 14-2 to be analyzed (refer to the criteria listed in Table 14-1).
Evaluation:

	CURRENT YEAR	LAST YEAR	TWO YEARS AGO
1. Orders received	91.74%	92.32%	96.30%
2. Markup	49.66	51.63	54.53
3. Markdown	7.66	7.29	5.84
4. Discount	5.73	4.09	7.29
5. Transp. Expense	0.00	0.00	0.00

CURRENT YEAR

BUYERS COPY - VENDOR ANALYSIS

VENDORS	MERCHANDISE RECEIVED					MARKUP			MARKDOWN			DISC. & ANTIC.		TRANSP. P.	
NAME OR NUMBER	$ COST OF ORDERS (INPUT)	$ COST OF RCVD. (INPUT)	% OF VEN ORDERS RCVD.	$ RETAIL OF RCVD. (INPUT)	% OF TOTAL ORDERS	$	%	% OF TOTAL MARKUP	$ (INPUT)	%	% OF TOTAL MDS.	$ (INPUT)	%	$ (INPUT)	%
ROCKPORT	$23597.00	$21647.00	91.74%	$43004.00	29.56%	$21357.00	49.66%	29.40%	$3295.00	7.66%	26.54%	$1241.00	5.73%	$0.00	0.00%
SEAGULL	$18329.00	$15962.00	87.09%	$32001.00	22.00%	$16039.00	50.12%	22.08%	$3200.00	10.00%	25.77%	$960.00	6.01%	$0.00	0.00%
TOADSTOOL	$25769.00	$20652.00	80.14%	$41375.00	28.44%	$20723.00	50.09%	28.53%	$2796.00	6.76%	22.52%	$1236.00	5.98%	$20.10	0.10%
GREAT KNITS	$6592.00	$6592.00	100.00%	$13497.00	9.28%	$6905.00	51.16%	9.51%	$1650.00	12.22%	13.29%	$410.00	6.22%	$0.00	0.00%
EYE TIES	$3765.00	$3652.00	97.00%	$7341.00	5.05%	$3689.00	50.25%	5.08%	$651.00	8.87%	5.24%	$216.00	5.91%	$6.35	0.17%
CHATTERBOX	$4712.00	$4319.00	91.66%	$8241.00	5.67%	$3922.00	47.59%	5.40%	$825.00	10.01%	6.64%	$235.00	5.44%	$0.00	0.00%
TOTALS	$82764.00	$72824.00	87.99%	$145459.00	100.00%	$72635.00	49.94%	100.00%	$12417.00	8.54%	100.00%	$4298.00	5.90%	$26.45	0.04%
BUYING OFFICE	$8477.00	$7971.00	94.03%	$15582.00	10.71%	$7611.00	48.84%	10.48%	$1476.00	9.47%	11.89%	$451.00	5.66%	$6.35	0.08%
LAST YEAR															
ROCKPORT	$19967.00	$18341.00	92.32%	$37915.00	32.84%	$19574.00	51.63%	33.14%	$2764.00	7.29%	31.15%	$750.00	4.09%	$0.00	0.00%
SEAGULL	$14633.00	$14297.00	97.70%	$29648.00	25.68%	$15351.00	51.78%	25.99%	$2431.00	8.20%	27.40%	$840.00	5.88%	$0.00	0.00%
TOAD STOOL	$19534.00	$19438.00	99.51%	$38954.00	33.74%	$19516.00	50.10%	33.04%	$3002.00	7.71%	33.84%	$1476.00	7.59%	$14.00	0.07%
GREAT KNITS	$4587.00	$4320.00	94.18%	$8949.00	7.75%	$4629.00	51.73%	7.84%	$675.00	7.54%	7.61%	$295.00	6.83%	$7.80	0.18%
TOTALS	$58621.00	$56396.00	96.20%	$115466.00	100.00%	$59070.00	51.16%	100.00%	$8872.00	7.68%	100.00%	$3361.00	5.96%	$21.80	0.04%
TWO YRS. AGO															
ROCKPORT	$16978.00	$16350.00	96.30%	$35960.00	33.94%	$19610.00	54.53%	35.38%	$2100.00	5.84%	42.26%	$1192.00	7.29%	$0.00	0.00%
SEAGULL	$15495.00	$15495.00	100.00%	$32486.00	30.67%	$16991.00	52.30%	30.66%	$1276.00	3.93%	25.68%	$1145.00	7.39%	$0.00	0.00%
TOAD STOOL	$18937.00	$18670.00	98.59%	$37491.00	35.39%	$18821.00	50.20%	33.96%	$1593.00	4.25%	32.06%	$1322.00	7.08%	$0.00	0.00%
TOTALS	$51410.00	$50515.00	98.26%	$105937.00	100.00%	$55422.00	52.32%	100.00%	$4969.00	4.69%	100.00%	$3659.00	7.24%	$0.00	0.00%

Figure 14-2

1. Poor. Percentages of shipments received are declining.
2. Poor. Percentages of markup are declining.
3. Poor. Percentages of markdowns are increasing.
4. Marginal. Percentages of cash discounts, while lower than two years ago, are better than last year.
5. N/A

Category 2: Vendor to vendor (current year)
Evaluation:

1. Good. Better than, or approximately equal to, three of the other five vendors for percentage of orders received.
2. Marginal. Below or close to most other vendors for markup percentage.
3. Superior. Better than four of the remaining five vendors for markdown percentage.
4. Marginal. Below or close to most of other vendors for cash discounts.
5. N/A

Category 3: Vendor to department totals for all purchases (current year)
Evaluation: Note—As Rockport has been the largest supplier for your department, its impact on department totals will have greater significance than other vendors.

1. Superior. Exceeds department value for percentage of orders received.
2. Poor. Markup percentage is less than department total.
3. Superior. Better than department total for markdown percentage.
4. Fair. Very close to department total for discount percentage.
5. N/A

Category 4: Vendor against its percentage of the department's total orders.
Arrange the data (from Figure 14-2) to be analyzed:

Total orders (base value)	29.56%
Total markups	29.40
Total markdowns	26.54

Evaluation:

1. Even. Percentage of total markups is almost the same as percentage of total orders.
2. Superior. Percentage of total markdowns is considerably better than percentage of total orders.

Summary: Very few superior ratings for Rockport. Best recommendation for them is that their merchandise has high salability, based upon their performance in all categories for markdowns. You should try to restore higher markups for their merchandise unless you are compelled to follow price lines comparable to your core competitor's. Certainly continue purchasing from Rockport.

• *PROBLEM 14-2*

At the conclusion of the season, you have assembled the data to begin the analysis of your vendors (see Fig. 14-3). Your buying service has introduced you to See Thru and Band R Fashion. Complete the computational work and provide a vendor analysis.

CURRENT YEAR

BUYERS COPY — VENDOR ANALYSIS

VENDORS	MERCHANDISE RECEIVED					MARKUP			MARKDOWN			DISC. & ANTIC.		TRANSP. P.	
NAME OR NUMBER	$ COST OF ORDERS (INPUT)	$ COST OF RCVD. (INPUT)	% OF VEN ORDERS RCVD.	$ RETAIL OF RCVD. (INPUT)	% OF TOTAL ORDERS	$	%	% OF TOTAL MARKUP	$ (INPUT)	%	% OF TOTAL MDS.	$ (INPUT)	%	$ (INPUT)	%
BLUE SKY	$43758.00	$42986.00		$86491.00					$9432.00			$2316.00		$0.00	
LE PAGE	$43675.00	$40956.00		$81030.00					$8247.00			$2137.00		$0.00	
SYNCO	$32674.00	$32674.00		$63941.00					$4893.00			$1755.00		$0.00	
PEACOCK	$11435.00	$10474.00		$21595.00					$2241.00			$597.00		$8.13	
SEE THRU	$8615.00	$8535.00		$17419.00					$1635.00			$475.00		$8.16	
BRAND R FASHIONS	$5425.00	$5212.00		$10836.00					$963.00			$316.00		$0.00	
TOTALS															
BUYING OFFICE															
LAST YEAR															
BLUE SKY	$43841.00	$42546.00		$85952.00					$8763.00			$2435.00		$0.00	
LE PAGE	$41200.00	$39060.00		$80372.00					$7990.00			$1987.00		$0.00	
SYNCO	$30647.00	$30647.00		$61416.00					$4200.00			$1574.00		$7.65	
PEACOCK	$10300.00	$9929.00		$20347.00					$2075.00			$485.00		$4.90	
TOTALS															
TWO YRS. AGO															
BLUE SKY	$42675.00	$40970.00		$82600.00					$8130.00			$2345.00		$0.00	
LE PAGE	$39750.00	$38485.00		$79350.00					$7690.00			$2165.00		$0.00	
SYNCO	$31900.00	$31529.00		$62932.00					$4830.00			$1564.00		$0.00	
TOTALS															

Figure 14-3

BUYER PRODUCTIVITY[1]

An evaluation of your productivity as a buyer is important to both you and the company. It reveals how well you have done your job and will serve as a basis for increases in compensation and for increased responsibility and promotion.

In many large organizations the appraisal process is formal and is based on documentation; smaller retailers may use a more informal approach; an independent store owner will often use the store's end-of-year profit and loss statement as the sole measure of success.

While the formal process appears to be more burdensome than simply viewing the bottom line of a profit and loss statement, it provides for serious consideration of other ambitions for the organization. Key to the formal process is a statement of performance goals which is a personal by-product of the strategic planning process discussed in Chapter One.

Performance planning. Performance planning or goal setting sets out clearly, in writing, well defined objectives: *what* you expect to accomplish during the following year; *how* these things will be done; and *when* you expect to complete the goals. Within a large organization, these will be discussed with your superior before they become your commitment.

Figure 14-4 Goal Setting Meeting Between Supervisor and Manager

Source: Courtesy of Darryl Ford, Manager Executive Recruitment, and Michele Friedman, Filene's.

ESTABLISHING GOALS. Goal setting requires that you produce plans that will be measurable; that is, that you and your superiors (where appropriate) will be able to review your performance objectively, not subjectively, eliminating bias. As an example, statements such as "increase gross margin" or, if your responsibilities include supervision of the selling floor, "reduce shortages" or "upgrade appearance of department" are nebulous. These phrases are as broad as they are long and do not provide any gauges for comparison. Properly stated, they would be "increase gross margin by 1.3 percent over plan," "reduce shortages by .3 percent over last season," and "upgrade appearance of department by having stock on shelves with largest sizes on lower shelves; colors together with those that are fashion forward on right and all colors arranged brights on top, darks to bottom." The latter statements are clear and well defined. There can be no doubt, in assessing your performance, whether your goals have been met. As a general rule, whenever a verb such as "increase," "reduce" or "upgrade" is used, you must define the base, or reference point, and/or stipulate precisely the alteration to the base you intend to accomplish.

Other than providing subjective, unbiased criteria for assessment, planning in this way gives you precise goals to work towards, which you can review later in the season without causing questions to be raised in your mind about what you might have meant by "upgrade appearance of department."

Goal setting is also another form of management by objective (M.B.O.) and is far preferable to "management by crisis," which is a reactive, rather than a planned, process that allows an executive little, if any, time to thoroughly think through a problem and evaluate the consequences of the reaction.

When goal setting is an organizational requirement, it becomes the yardstick against which an executive's performance is measured. Establishing criteria and assessing your performance against them has many benefits both for you and the organization:

1. As both you (and your superior) have been involved in the performance planning process, the goals have a far better chance of being attained than if they had been established in a dictatorial fashion
2. By clearly defining each goal, both you and your superior know what is expected of you
3. Communication between you and upper management is improved, as you are working toward company goals, and your role in the process is known and can be discussed

ACTION STEPS. Action steps indicate *how* you plan to achieve each individual goal. Referring to the previously stated objective to "increase gross margin by 1.3 percent over plan," you would go back to your Retail Method End-of-Season Report and analyze those items which have added or subtracted from your G.M. and explain which of these would be altered and *how*. As examples,

1. Reduce customer returns (*what*) through sales training, by generating fact sheets about new merchandise highlighting features and benefits (*how*)
2. Improve cash discounts on purchases (*what*) through more active negotiations before orders are placed (*how*)

To summarize goal and action step planning, these should be

1. *Realistic*: neither too easy, nor too difficult
2. *Attainable*: consideration shown for budget, human, and physical resources; the marketplace; and the economy
3. *Specific*: what will be done; where it will be done; how it will be done; and when it will be accomplished
4. *Measurable*: results to be assessed by either quantitative or unbiased qualitative review
5. *Understandable*: concise statements avoiding unnecessary verbiage and jargon

QUANTITATIVE CONSIDERATIONS. The following list of quantitative goals contains measures which have been explained and illustrated earlier in this text and will not, therefore, be further elaborated on.

- Net sales: dollars
- Net sales: percent change
- Markup: percent
- Markdowns: percent
- Shortage: percent
- Gross margin: dollars
- Gross margin: percent
- Departmental operating profit: dollars
- Departmental operating profit: percent
- Stock turn

QUALITATIVE CONSIDERATIONS. Qualitative evaluation of your work will, to a large extent, hinge on the broad criteria established by the organization you work for and be an analysis of the goals you have set. The two general areas of concern are

1. Managerial skills such as interpersonal relationships between you, subordinates, peers, and supervisors; oral and written communication ability; prioritizing work; and follow-through.
2. Merchandising skills, which include selection of appropriate merchandise for your core customer; knowledge of market trends; knowledge of core competitors' merchandise and services; effective use of buying office personnel, information and services; and vendor relationships.

Assessment.   The assessment, or review, procedure is normally an annual event. Pre-reviews may occur at selected intervals, such as every three or six months, so as to be certain that you and your superviors are regularly apprised of your progress.

The end-of-year review will be a formal process and as such will be a meeting at which you, your supervisor, and senior executives may be present. Your superior will present the results of your goals, both quantitative and qualitative; provide a narrative report as an overall appraisal, and finally make a salary recommendation. You and your supervisor will undoubtedly have to respond to questions before the meeting adjourns.

Nothing unexpected happens at an annual review. Long before it occurs, you will know from your own statement of goals how well you have done, so that this meeting should conclude with the company's verbal reaffirmation of your worth to the organization, coupled with a suitable increase in compensation.

SUMMARY PROBLEMS

• *PROBLEM 14-1 (S)*

Prepare the summary data for one of your vendors, "Bobcat Tools," from the following information:

	COST	RETAIL
Merchandise ordered:	$18,641.12	
Merchandise received:		
Invoice no. A693	$ 3494.18	$ 7249.63
Invoice no. A781	3681.24	5624.11
Invoice no. B031	4935.96	10,412.55
Invoice no. B164	5249.63	11,619.76
Returns to vendor:		
Credit memo no. 121	$ 394.22	$ 812.94
Credit memo no. 126	1345.18	2769.07
Credit memo no. 149	632.14	1114.81
Net Markdowns:		5697.48
Cash discounts: $1141.23		
Transportation expense: $86.52		

• *PROBLEM 14-2 (S)*

Your divisional merchandise manager has asked you to prepare a vendor analysis for the past season. The data in Figure 14-5 have been brought together by your assistant. Complete the computational work and write the report.

CASE STUDY

THE NUMBERS GAME

The store you are working for has been rapidly growing in terms of numbers of branches for the past three years. This was one of the reasons you chose to become a member of its buying staff.

As is the case with other organizations that have undergone expansion,

BUYERS COPY - VENDOR ANALYSIS

VENDORS	MERCHANDISE RECEIVED						MARKUP			MARKDOWN			DISC. & ANTIC.		TRANSP. P.	
NAME OR NUMBER	$ COST OF ORDERS (INPUT)	$ COST OF RCVD. (INPUT)	% OF ORDERS RCVD.	$ OF VEN ORDERS RCVD. (INPUT)	$ RETAIL OF RCVD. (INPUT)	% OF TOTAL ORDERS	$	%	% OF TOTAL MARKUP	$ (INPUT)	%	% OF TOTAL MDS.	$ (INPUT)	%	$ (INPUT)	%
HANDLERS	$14560.00	$11347.00			$22831.00					$1895.00			$227.00		$0.00	
CROCKS & PUB	$12545.00	$10162.00			$20162.00					$2056.00			$173.00		$26.00	
KOOKERY	$8150.00	$7913.00			$15826.00					$1519.00			$87.00		$10.00	
THE KILN	$7265.00	$6838.00			$13595.00					$1210.00			$0.00		$18.00	
EARTHEN., INC.	$4975.00	$4880.00			$9859.00					$897.00			$0.00		$0.00	
ENID ORIGINALS	$3250.00	$3145.00			$6328.00					$576.00			$79.00		$0.00	
TOTALS																
BUYING OFFICE																
LAST YEAR																
HANDLERS	$12500.00	$11375.00			$22841.00					$1850.00			$215.00		$0.00	
CROCKS & PUB	$10025.00	$9897.00			$19637.00					$2150.00			$156.50		$18.00	
KOOKERY	$7500.00	$7343.00			$14715.00					$1357.00			$78.20		$7.50	
THE KILN	$6135.00	$6047.00			$12118.00					$1165.00			$0.00		$7.50	
TOTALS																
TWO YRS. AGO																
HANDLERS	$11250.00	$10697.00			$21351.00					$1690.00			$196.00		$0.00	
CROCKS & PUB	$9576.00	$9497.00			$18918.00					$1790.00			$149.50		$14.50	
KOOKERY	$7385.00	$7330.00			$14593.00					$1395.00			$64.90		$6.25	
TOTALS																

Figure 14-5

however, certain problems have surfaced. The merchandise division has had its share of difficulties, and the vice president has scheduled a meeting with all buyers to exchange ideas and recommendations.

Specifically, you and the other buyers are supposed to be prepared to discuss the types of reports and records you keep relating to sales, merchandise, and vendors; how useful these documents are; and any suggestions you can make for changes, additions, or deletions.

A final factor to consider is that the organization is seriously considering changing over to computerized record keeping.

What recommendations would you make?

NOTES

[1]See Appendix B for forms used for buyer evaluation.

Major Federal Legislation Affecting Buyers

LAW	PURPOSE	BASIC EXPLANATION
Sherman Anti-trust Act of 1890	Promote competition	Prohibits establishment of contracts and combinations in restraint of trade. As an example, unrelated stores cannot get together to maintain the price of the *same* article all of them sell.
Federal Meat Inspection Act of 1907	Protect consumers	Requires inspection and labeling of meats.
Clayton Act of 1914	Promote competition	Prohibits vendors from price discrimination to different buyers; or requiring buyers to not buy competing merchandise. Prohibits firms from forming larger organizations through interlocking directorates, if this practice diminishes competition; or acquiring the capital stock of competitors practicing the same form of business.

LAW	PURPOSE	BASIC EXPLANATION
Federal Trade Commission Act of 1914	Promote competition and protect consumers	Created the Federal Trade Commission (F.T.C.) to prevent unfair methods of business. This act covers misleading and misrepresentations in advertising and selling practices.
Federal Communications Act of 1936	Protect consumers	Established the Federal Communications Commission (F.C.C.), which controls licensing of television and radio stations. This agency has come to serve as a check against the broadcasting of deceptive advertising.
Robinson-Patman Act of 1936	Promote competition	Amended the Clayton Act to more clearly define vendor discriminatory practices in pricing.
Wheeler-Lea Act of 1936	Protect consumers	Gives broader powers to the F.T.C. empowering it to examine charges of deceptive acts and practices and to issue temporary injunctions.
Federal Food, Drug, and Cosmetic Act of 1938	Protect consumers	Created the Federal Food and Drug Administration (F.D.A.) to prevent the sale of merchandise that has been adulterated, misbranded, or deceptively packaged. The F.D.A. may require that "warning" labels be affixed to dangerous items.
Wool Products Labeling Act of 1939	Protect consumers and new buyers	Requires a label for fiber content on all products containing wool, indicating percentage of virgin, reprocessed, or reused wool as well as other fibers.
Fur Products Labeling Act of 1951	Protect consumers and new buyers	Requires that the English name of the fur be used; that a statement must be made if the fur is reused; that the name of another animal may not be used, such as "mink-dyed squirrel."
Flammable Fabrics Act of 1953, amended in 1964	Protect consumers	Prohibits the sale, in interstate commerce, of apparel and other items so highly

LAW	PURPOSE	BASIC EXPLANATION
		flammable as to be dangerous.
Textile Fiber Products Identification Act of 1959	Protect consumers	Requires that textile products be labeled with the generic name of each fiber in the article, by percentage of weight in descending order, and the country of origin, where applicable.
Hazardous Substance Act of 1961	Protect consumers	Requires that products used in the home (other than foods, drugs, and cosmetics, which are already covered by law) be labeled to show any substances that may cause injury.
Cigarette Labeling and Advertising Act of 1965	Protect consumers	Requires health warning on cigarette packages and in advertising.
Fair Packaging and Labeling Act of 1966	Protect consumers	Requires that containers show the weight or volume of the contents; that if "servings" are referred to, the weight of single serving be stated; that the package have limited air space and no misleading statements.
Consumer Products Safety Act of 1967	Protect consumers	Established the Consumer Products Safety Commission to prohibit the sale of nonfood and nondrug products that are unsafe
Poison Prevention Act of 1970	Protect consumers	Requires "child-resistant" packages for items that might poison children if the substances could be reached by them.
Magnusen-Moss Improvement Act of 1974	Protect consumers and promote competition	The warranty section of this act requires that guarantees on products be clear and dependable to the consumer. The act empowers the F.T.C. to conduct industry hearings and then develop and adopt legally enforceable, binding trade regulations for an entire industry.
Consumer Goods Pricing Act of 1975	Protect consumers	Eliminates "fair trade" in interstate commerce.

Buyer Evaluation Forms

FILENE'S

APPRAISAL FOR
198_
PERFORMANCE

Name _____

Supervisor _____

Position _____

Position Date _____

APPRAISAL COVERS:

□ FULL YEAR

□ PARTIAL YEAR (Check one below)

　□ New to Filene's

　□ New to this position

　□ Promoted within last 3 months

　To _____
　　New position　　　　　Date

* An Executive who has moved to a new position within a three month period prior to performance appraisal should be appraised by his/her previous supervisor.

PERFORMANCE CODES

Outstanding (O)
This rating represents exceptional performance. Objectives and expectations are consistently surpassed.

Above Average (AA)
This rating represents a highly effective performance. Objectives and expectations are fully met and occasionally exceeded.

Good/Satisfactory (G/S)
This rating represents good solid performance. Objectives and expectations are met.

Marginal (M)
This rating represents less than satisfactory performance. Objectives and expectations are not consistently met.

Unsatisfactory (U)
This rating represents unacceptable performance. Objectives and expectations are not met. The executive should be placed on Substandard.

Learning Curve (LC)
This rating is to be used only as an Overall Performance Rating for an Executive who is new to position, and whose performance has not yet reached full effectiveness. (Executive may not exceed 6 months in position.)

Too New To Rate (N)
In position less than three months.

EXECUTIVE'S PERFORMANCE RATING:

JOB RESPONSIBILITIES _____

GOALS _____

STATISTICAL GOALS (if appropriate) _____

OVERALL RATING _____

SUPERVISOR'S PERFORMANCE RATING:

JOB RESPONSIBILITIES _____

GOALS _____

STATISTICAL GOALS (if appropriate) _____

OVERALL RATING _____

TO BE COMPLETED AT APPRAISAL MEETING

Executive's Comments After Appraisal: _____

_____

_____

Executive's Signature (indicates copy of review received) _____ Date _____

Supervisor's Signature _____ Date _____

VP Divisional's Signature _____ Date _____

SOURCE (for pp.301–313): Reprinted with permission of Filene's, Boston, MA.

THIS IS YOUR PERSONAL CHECKLIST

PERFORMANCE APPRAISAL PROCESS

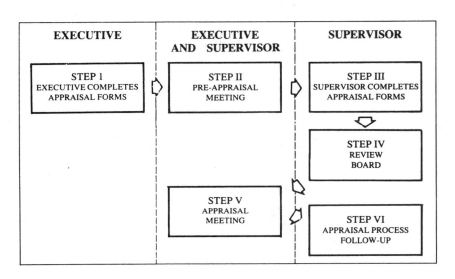

STEP I   **EXECUTIVE COMPLETES APPRAISAL FORMS IN THE FOLLOWING ORDER:**

February

- ☐ Results Against Goals and Major Job Responsibilities
- ☐ Statistical Goals (Sr. Assistant Buyers, Buyers, DSM/GSMs, General Managers, Division Level Executives)
- ☐ Skills and Abilities Analysis
- ☐ Narrative Appraisal
- ☐ Professional Development Plan (Strengths, Areas For Development, Ideas For Development, and Placement Code only)
- ☐ Performance Rating (located on cover)

STEP II   **PRE-APPRAISAL MEETING**

February

- ☐ During the Pre-Appraisal Meeting, the Executive reviews completed Appraisal forms with Supervisor. Executive discusses and supports his/her appraisal of 198 performance. Supervisor listens and clarifies but does not share assessment or evaluation.

STEP III   **SUPERVISOR COMPLETES APPRAISAL FORMS**

February-
March

- ☐ Supervisor completes the designated sections of the Appraisal Forms listed above in Step I.

STEP IV   **REVIEW BOARD**

March-
April

- ☐ Supervisor presents appraisal of Executive's performance to a Review Board, consisting of Filene's Division-Level Managers, Pyramid Head, and a Personnel Official.

STEP V   **APPRAISAL MEETING**

March-
April

- ☐ During the Appraisal Meeting, the Supervisor appraises the Executive's performance. He/she explains the Executive's Performance Rating, Placement Status, compensation, and answers any questions posed by the Executive. Executive and Supervisor review the Professional Development Plan. The Appraisal Packet is signed.

STEP VI   **APPRAISAL PROCESS FOLLOW-UP**

Within 2
Weeks of
Review
Board

- ☐ Supervisor completes Comments on Performance Appraisal Meeting form.
- ☐ Supervisor ensures that Professional Development Plan is inserted into Executive's Goal Packet.
- ☐ Supervisor submits all Appraisal Packets (originals), Professional Development Plans, and Comment Forms to Training and Development. (Supervisor retains copies.)

GOALS FOR 198_

Name _____

Supervisor _____

Complete Now

GOAL # ____

	Completion Date

EXPECTED RESULTS: What measurable change will occur as a result of achieving this goal?

ACTION STEPS/DEADLINES:

Complete Mid-Year

PROGRESS REVIEW: Brief narrative description of progress toward goals. Discuss any obstacles to achievement. May be completed by either Executive or Supervisor, but both must initial.

INITIAL

Exec.	Spvsr.
Date	

RESULTS AGAINST GOALS • **Complete At End of Appraisal Period** • RESULTS AGAINST GOALS

EXECUTIVE'S ASSESSMENT: Were expected results received?
Comments:

RATING

SUPERVISOR'S ASSESSMENT: Were expected results achieved?
Comments:

RATING

Performance Rating Code:

O	AA	G/S	M	U	N
Outstanding	Above Average	Good/Satisfactory	Marginal	Unsatisfactory	Too New to Rate

Replace this page with your copy of Goals for 198 from your 198 Goal-Setting Packet,
and complete assessment. Use this only if you did not retain a copy.

Name _____

GOALS FOR 198

Supervisor _____

Complete Now

GOAL # _____

	Completion Date

EXPECTED RESULTS: What measurable change will occur as a result of achieving this goal?

ACTION STEPS/DEADLINES:

Complete Mid-Year

PROGRESS REVIEW: Brief narrative description of progress toward goals. Discuss any obstacles to achievement. May be completed by either Executive or Supervisor, but both must initial.

INITIAL

Exec.	Spvsr.
Date _____	

RESULTS AGAINST GOALS   •   **Complete At End of Appraisal Period**   •   RESULTS AGAINST GOALS

EXECUTIVE'S ASSESSMENT: Were expected results received?
  Comments:

RATING

SUPERVISOR'S ASSESSMENT: Were expected results achieved?
  Comments:

RATING

Performance Rating Code:

O	AA	G/S	M	U	N
Outstanding	Above Average	Good/Satisfactory	Marginal	Unsatisfactory	Too New to Rate

Replace this page with your copy of Major Job Responsibilities for 198 from your 198 Goal-Setting Packet, and complete assessment of performance. Use this only if you did not retain a copy.

MAJOR JOB RESPONSIBILITIES FOR 198

Name _____

Supervisor _____

List Major Job Responsibilities
in order of priority (#1 = Highest Priority).

Complete Now

JOB RESPONSIBILITY PRIORITY ____	JOB RESPONSIBILITY PRIORITY ____

Complete Mid-Year

PROGRESS REVIEW: Brief narrative description concerning accomplishment of Major Job Responsibilities. May be completed by either Executive or Supervisor, but both must initial.

INITIAL

Exec.	Spvsr.
Date	

RESULTS AGAINST M.J.R.   ●   **Complete At End of Appraisal Period**   ●   RESULTS AGAINST M.J.R.

EXECUTIVE'S ASSESSMENT	EXECUTIVE'S ASSESSMENT
RATING	RATING

SUPERVISOR'S ASSESSMENT	SUPERVISOR'S ASSESSMENT
RATING	RATING

Performance Rating Code:

O Outstanding	AA Above Average	G/S Good/Satisfactory	M Marginal	U Unsatisfactory	N Too New to Rate

Replace this page with your copy of Major Job Responsibilities for 198_ from your 198_ Goal-Setting Packet, and complete assessment of performance. Use this only if you did not retain a copy.

MAJOR JOB RESPONSIBILITIES FOR 198

(CONT'D)

Name _____

Supervisor _____

List Major Job Responsibilities
in order of priority (#1 = Highest Priority).

Complete Now

JOB RESPONSIBILITY PRIORITY _____	JOB RESPONSIBILITY PRIORITY _____

Complete Mid-Year

PROGRESS REVIEW: Brief narrative description concerning accomplishment of Major Job Responsibilities. May be completed by either Executive or Supervisor, but both must initial.

INITIAL

Exec.	Spvsr.
Date _____	

RESULTS AGAINST M.J.R.   •   **Complete At End of Appraisal Period**   •   RESULTS AGAINST M.J.R.

EXECUTIVE'S ASSESSMENT	EXECUTIVE'S ASSESSMENT
RATING	RATING

SUPERVISOR'S ASSESSMENT	SUPERVISOR'S ASSESSMENT
RATING	RATING

Performance Rating Code:

O Outstanding	AA Above Average	G/S Good/Satisfactory	M Marginal	U Unsatisfactory	N Too New to Rate

198 GROSS MARGIN PERFORMANCE

BUYER NAME _____ DIVISION NAME _____ DMM NAME _____

	DEPT.	SPRING			FALL			ANNUAL		
		1984 ACTUAL	1985 PLAN	1985 ACTUAL	1984 ACTUAL	1985 PLAN	1985 ACTUAL	1984 ACTUAL	1985 PLAN	1985 ACTUAL
SALES $										
	Total									
% CHANGE										
	Total									
MARKUP %										
	Total									
MARKDOWN %										
	Total									
SHORTAGE %										
	Total									
GROSS MARGIN $										
	Total									
GROSS MARGIN %										
	Total									
TURNOVER										
	Total									

DEPT. NOS. _____ DEPT. NAMES _____

_____   _____

_____   _____

198 YEAR-END
NARRATIVE APPRAISAL

Name _____

Supervisor _____

The Narrative Appraisal is an opportunity for you to pull all components of the Appraisal Packet together into a summary of your 198 performance. Therefore complete this page only after completing all other pages in this packet (as detailed on inside back cover).

Include reference to goal attainment, fulfillment of job responsibilities, the Skills & Abilities Analysis, and statistical goal results. Describe any special factors which had an important impact on your 198 performance.

EXECUTIVE'S ASSESSMENT:

SUPERVISOR'S ASSESSMENT:

SKILLS AND ABILITIES
ANALYSIS FOR 198

Name _____

Supervisor _____

The following skills and abilities are critical for effective performance. For each item, use the following scale to rate the degree to which you have actually seen the skill or ability being demonstrated.

3	2	1	N
OUTSTANDING (Consistently shows an advanced level of this skill)	**GOOD** (Often demonstrates this skill)	**NEEDS DEVELOPMENT** (A definite area for improvement)	**HAVE NOT OBSERVED**

The Executive and Supervisor both rate each item below. Supervisor uses note column to comment on specific instances or examples used as a basis for the rating. This assessment is to be used for the design of the Professional Development Plan.

In each area below, use the rating scale to answer the question:

TO WHAT EXTENT DOES THIS EXECUTIVE . . .

. . . ANALYZE, MAKE DECISIONS, ACHIEVE GOALS?

Executive's Assessment	Supervisor's Assessment	HE/SHE . . .	NOTES COLUMN Supervisor notes specific comments or instances.
_____	_____	1. Analyzes and interprets data, reports, or analyses in a logical fashion.	
_____	_____	2. Generates innovative, constructive approaches to solving problems.	
_____	_____	3. Anticipates and plans for consequences (e.g., financial or logistical) of alternative actions.	
_____	_____	4. Decides which issues need to be addressed first by weighing their importance and urgency.	
_____	_____	5. Changes priorities and restrategizes actions as conditions change.	
_____	_____	6. Makes sound, timely decisions on own.	
_____	_____	7. Makes decisions in the context of the total business rather than a single function.	
_____	_____	8. Develops broad or abstract ideas and approaches from details; can conceptualize.	
_____	_____	9. Sets and achieves high performance standards.	
_____	_____	10. Defines objectives, develops plans, and follows through to consistently achieve them.	

. . . COMMUNICATE?

HE/SHE . . .

_____	_____	11. Conveys ideas clearly and effectively both in written and spoken form.	
_____	_____	12. Hears, understands, and evaluates objectively the communication of others.	
_____	_____	13. Confronts and resolves differences of opinion constructively.	
_____	_____	14. Demonstrates an awareness of and respect for others' attitudes, feelings, and concerns.	

(CONT'D)

In each area below, use the rating scale to answer the question:

TO WHAT EXTENT DOES THIS EXECUTIVE . . .

. . . EXHIBIT THESE WORK-RELATED ATTRIBUTES?

Executive's Assessment	Supervisor's Assessment	HE/SHE . . .	NOTES COLUMN Supervisor notes specific comments or instances
_____	_____	15. Believes in own abilities and defends ideas, decisions, or staff when challenged.	
_____	_____	16. Initiates action without prompting, and pursues opportunities or projects aggressively.	
_____	_____	17. Demonstrates the capacity to learn and to grasp complex ideas.	
_____	_____	18. Handles stress effectively.	

(RESPOND BELOW ONLY IF YOU ARE THE DIRECT SUPERVISOR OF OTHERS)
. . . SUPERVISE?

HE/SHE . . .

_____	_____	19. Effectively executes all aspects of the Goal-Setting and Appraisal programs.
_____	_____	20. Clearly defines and communicates roles and responsibilties.
_____	_____	21. Lets go of appropriate tasks and assigns responsibilities to others which will develop them.
_____	_____	22. Encourages staff to take risks and new approaches.
_____	_____	23. Provides both constructive feedback and praise on a consistent basis.
_____	_____	24. Communicates information and issues to staff in such a way that they feel informed and connected to the organization.
_____	_____	25. Develops "esprit de corps" and a results-oriented team, encouraging a feeling of trust and mutual support.
_____	_____	26. Supports and stands behind decisions of staff.
_____	_____	27. Actively sponsors partnerships with other areas of the business.
_____	_____	28. Acts as a role-model of pride, care, and commitment to the Filene's organization and goals.
_____	_____	29. Places a high priority on growing and developing executives for Filene's, and achieves those results.
_____	_____	30. Actively motivates staff to perform on a consistent basis.

PROFESSIONAL DEVELOPMENT
PLAN FOR 198
(NEXT YEAR)

Name _____

Position _____

Supervisor _____

TO BE COMPLETED BEFORE REVIEW BOARD:

To be completed by both Executive and Supervisor:

In assessing strengths and areas for development, be sure to consider all of your responsibilities and roles within Filene's. List at least two of each and <u>be specific.</u>

EXECUTIVE'S ASSESSMENT	**SUPERVISOR'S ASSESSMENT**
Strengths	Strengths
•	•
•	•
•	•
Areas For Development	Areas For Development
•	•
•	•
•	•

Executive completes this section:

What do you feel would be effective in helping you develop these areas? Be specific in your ideas.

☐ It would be helpful for my Supervisor to: ☐ Other ideas:

☐ Filene's classes:

To be completed by both Executive and Supervisor:

EXECUTIVE'S ASSESSMENT	**SUPERVISOR'S ASSESSMENT**
PLACEMENT THIS YEAR (check only one)	**PLACEMENT THIS YEAR (check only one)**
____ Promotion Now (P1) ____ Career Professional (C) To _____	____ Promotion Now (P1) ____ Career Professional (C) To _____
____ Promotion 6-12 Months (P2) ____ Current Placement (CPA) To _____ Appropriate	____ Promotion 6-12 (P2) ____ Current Placement (CPA) To _____ Appropriate
____ Lateral Move Within (L) ____ Too New To Determine (N) 12 Months Promotability (in position To _____ less than 3 months) _____	____ Lateral Move Within (L) ____ Too New To Determine (N) 12 Months Promotability (in position To _____ less than 3 months) _____

TO BE COMPLETED BY SUPERVISOR

PROFESSIONAL DEVELOPMENT
PLAN FOR 198 (NEXT YEAR)(CONT'D)

Supervisor writes a Professional Development Goal and completes this plan for the Executive, prior to Review Board. He/she takes into account strengths and areas for development written by the Executive, as well as those identified in the Skills & Abilities Analysis. The goal will be a focus of discussion in Review Board, and may be changed at this time if necessary. This plan is presented to the Executive during the Appraisal Meeting and becomes an additional goal on which the Executive and Supervisor will be evaluated in 198 .

Professional Development Goal:

Supervisor's Commitment to Executive's Professional Development in 1986:

☐ Feedback to be given by Supervisor:

☐ Developmental Activities to be structured by Supervisor (can be activities in current job or exposure to other areas of business):

☐ On-The-Job Training to be arranged by Supervisor:

☐ Filene's Classroom Training:

☐ Executive's responsibility in his/her professional development:

This plan becomes an important document for the Executive's development in 198 . The original is submitted separately to Training and Development. A copy is placed in the Executive's 198 Goal-Setting Packet and a copy remains in the Appraisal Packet.

Signatures

_____ _____
Supervisor   Executive

PERFORMANCE RATINGS

You will be rated on Job Responsibilities, Goals, Statistical Goals (Buyers, Sales Managers, GSM/DSMs, General Managers, Division Level Executives), and Overall Performance. These are the ratings which will be used to appraise your performance.

PERFORMANCE RATING DESCRIPTIONS	STATISTICAL GOALS	GOALS	JOB RESPONSIBILITIES	OVERALL PERFORMANCE
OUTSTANDING: This rating represents exceptional performance. Objectives and expectations are consistently surpassed. Earned by only a very <u>small percentage</u> of performers, due to the challenging nature of the goals we set at Filene's.	Exceeds goal	Consistently surpasses	Consistently surpasses	Exceptional performance
ABOVE AVERAGE: This rating represents highly effective performance. All objectives are fully met and occasionally exceeded. Reserved for the <u>limited percentage</u> of Executives whose performance truly goes beyond supervisors' expectations.	Makes goal	Fully meets, occasionally exceeds	Fully meets, occasionally exceeds	Highly effective performance
GOOD/SATISFACTORY: This rating represents good solid performance. Objectives and expectations are met. Normally earned by a <u>majority</u> of Executives, this rating represents the attainment of all goals and constitutes a positive contribution to Filene's.	Makes plan	Meets goal	Meets job responsibility	Good solid performance
MARGINAL: This rating represents less than satisfactory performance. Objectives and expectations are not consistently met.	Inconsistently met	Inconsistently met	Inconsistently met	Inconsistent — less than satisfactory performance
UNSATISFACTORY: This rating represents unacceptable performance. Objectives and expectations are not met. The Executive should be placed on substandard.	Not met	Not met	Not met	Unacceptable performance
LEARNING CURVE: This rating is to be used only for an Overall Performance Rating for an Executive who is new to position, and whose performance has not yet reached full effectiveness. (In position less than 6 months.)	NA	NA	NA	Hasn't reached full effectiveness
TOO NEW TO RATE: In position less than 3 months.				

Allied Stores Corporation
Executive Performance Appraisal

MERCHANDISING

Date of This Appraisal

Appraisee's Name

Division Code or Unit Store Code
If Unit Store Executive

Appraisee's Position

Department

| Employment Date | Date Appointed to Present Position | Period Covered by This Appraisal |
| | | Mo/Yr | Mo/Yr |

| Current Salary (annual amount only) | Date of Last Increase | Amount of Last Increase (annual amount only) |

Appraised By

Position of Appraiser

REVIEW CRITERIA

The Executive Performance Appraisal provides the opportunity for the manager and employee to exchange information and ideas, and develop an action plan for the appraisee's development and improved performance. The following major areas will be considered during the review:
- Level of management and merchandising skills
- Analysis of quantitative results
- Specific performance strengths and areas needing improvement
- Developmental action plans and goals for the coming review period
- Recommended actions resulting from the appraisal

The following codes should be used in assessing performance levels:

5. OUTSTANDING: Has far exceeded all performance objectives of the position. Highly skilled in relation to the requirements of the job and has made most exceptional contributions to our organization.

4. EXCELLENT: Has exceeded performance objectives of position. Is well skilled in relation to the requirements of the job and has contributed significantly to the organization.

3. GOOD: Has achieved position performance objectives. Skills meet basic job requirements. Contributions to organization are average.

2. FAIR: Has adequately met some, but not all, performance objectives of position. Has not reached agreed upon standards of quantity and/or quality. Needs to improve to fully qualify for position and meet organizational goals.

1. SUBSTANDARD: Has not successfully performed most tasks of the job. On balance, has not achieved established performance objectives. Employee clearly not qualified for this position.

Check the appropriate box to reflect the employee's skill level. If not applicable, check N/A. Where ratings are exceptionally high or low (e.g. 5 or 1) write specific comments for the rating and give supporting examples, evidence or explanation.

	Outstanding	Excellent	Good	Fair	Substandard	Not Applicable
A. MANAGERIAL SKILLS AS EVIDENCED BY:	5	4	3	2	1	N/A
1. Attitude toward job and company.						

Comments: _____

2. Flexibility and adaptability in handling work.						

Comments: _____

AP9A

SOURCE (for pp. 314–321): Reprinted with permission of Allied Stores Corporation and Jordan Marsh Company, Boston, MA.

	Outstanding	Excellent	Good	Substandard	Fair	Not Applicable

A. MANAGERIAL SKILLS AS EVIDENCED BY: (continued)

	5	4	3	2	1	N/A
3. Sound judgment in day-to-day decisions and relationships.						

Comments: _____

_____

_____

| 4. Recognition of problems and acting decisively under pressure. | | | | | | |

Comments: _____

_____

_____

| 5. Seeking responsibility and professional development. | | | | | | |

Comments: _____

_____

_____

| 6. Resourcefulness and imagination in handling professional responsibilities. | | | | | | |

Comments: _____

_____

_____

| 7. An understanding of how current job fits into overall company structure and objectives. | | | | | | |

Comments: _____

_____

_____

| 8. Clear, effective communication on an interpersonal verbal level. | | | | | | |

Comments: _____

_____

_____

| 9. Clear, effective written communication. | | | | | | |

Comments: _____

_____

_____

| 10. Development of subordinates with challenging work, delegation of authority, training, coaching and follow-through on career growth. | | | | | | |

Comments: _____

_____

_____

| 11. Service as an instructor, meeting leader or training resource in the company's formal training programs. | | | | | | |

Comments: _____

_____

_____

AP9A

		Outstanding	Excellent	Good	Fair	Substandard	Not Applicable

A. MANAGERIAL SKILLS AS EVIDENCED BY: (continued)

	5	4	3	2	1	N/A

12. Setting of realistic goals and planning accordingly.

Comments:_____

_____

_____

13. Organizing work and implementing plans.

Comments:_____

_____

_____

14. Accurate, thorough performance reviews for subordinates and conducting productive appraisal discussions.

Comments:_____

_____

_____

15. Follow-through on improvement action plans for subordinates and monitoring performance to assure greater personal growth and achievement.

Comments:_____

_____

_____

OVERALL EVALUATION OF MANAGERIAL SKILLS

Comments. _____

_____

_____

B. MERCHANDISING SKILLS AS EVIDENCED BY:

	5	4	3	2	1	N/A

1. Ability to select merchandise which is consistent with the character of the department and the store while meeting financial goals and objectives.

Comments:_____

_____

_____

2. Anticipating and keeping informed of market trends.

Comments:_____

_____

_____

3. Shopping competition and knowing what they are doing.

Comments:_____

_____

_____

AP9A

	Outstanding 5	Excellent 4	Good 3	Fair 2	Substandard 1	Not Applicable N/A
B. MERCHANDISING SKILLS AS EVIDENCED BY:(continued)						

4. Effectively working with divisions and Allied's merchandise information systems.

Comments: _____

5. Negotiating with vendors to achieve department and store goals and maintaining good vendor relations.

Comments: _____

6. Effectively working with non-merchandising areas.

Comments: _____

7. Effectively working with Allied Stores Marketing Corporation.

Comments: _____

8. Effective use of Allied Stores International programs where applicable.

Comments: _____

9. Initiative, resourcefulness and imagination in seeking and promoting sales and exploiting opportunities for new business.

Comments: _____

OVERALL EVALUATION OF MERCHANDISING SKILLS

Comments: _____

Additional Comments: _____

AP9A

Department No. _____   Department Description _____

C. ANALYSIS OF QUANTITATIVE RESULTS

Enter departmental operating results below. Where buyer is responsible for more than one department make necessary copies of this form and enter results for each department on separate forms. Evaluate results for each department and rate according to the scale. Include all forms with this appraisal. In addition to providing individual department results, where possible, consolidate results for multiple departments into a single analysis on a separate sheet. Space for additional comments is provided below.

		This Year Actual	This Year Plan	Last Year	Variation From Plan	Variation From L.Y.	5	4	3	2	1	N/A
NET SALES $ ($ in M's)	Spring											
	Fall											
	Year											
NET SALES (% Change)	Spring											
	Fall											
	Year											
MARK-UP %	Spring											
	Fall											
	Year											
MARKDOWN %	Spring											
	Fall											
	Year											
SHORTAGE %	Spring											
	Fall											
	Year											
GROSS MARGIN $ ($ in 000's)	Spring											
	Fall											
	Year											
GROSS MARGIN %	Spring											
	Fall											
	Year											
DEPARTMENTAL OPERATING PROFIT ($ in M's)	Spring											
	Fall											
	Year											
DEPARTMENTAL OPERATING PROFIT (%)	Spring											
	Fall											
	Year											
STOCK TURN	Spring											
	Fall											
	Year											

Comments: _____

_____

_____

AP9A

D. AREAS OF STRENGTH IN KNOWLEDGE, SKILL OR PERFORMANCE

List specific examples of performance strengths. Cite actions and results. Consider also whether appraisee has gained new strengths since last review.

_____

_____

_____

_____

_____

_____

_____

_____

_____

_____

_____

_____

_____

_____

_____

_____

_____

E. AREAS FOR IMPROVEMENT IN KNOWLEDGE, SKILL OR PERFORMANCE

List specific examples of performance which were below expectations. Cite weaknesses which contributed to deficiencies in desired results.

_____

_____

_____

_____

_____

_____

_____

_____

_____

_____

_____

_____

_____

_____

_____

_____

F. SUMMARY APPRAISAL

After reviewing the ratings, results and comments development in Sections A through E, indicate your overall appraisal of the executive.

Outstanding 5	Excellent 4	Good 3	Fair 2	Substandard 1
☐	☐	☐	☐	☐

AP9A

G. PLANS FOR FURTHER DEVELOPMENT

Before filling in this section look back over the entire review for skills or results which need improvement. Look also for patterns in deficient skills and relate them if possible to results so that skill improvements could then influence future results.

DEVELOPMENTAL GOALS: Be specific, provide measurable goals. State how each of the goals will be achieved, what methods will be used, who will follow up and when. These goals should provide for self-development in knowledge, skill and ability, which can lead to achievement of business goals.

Areas For Improvement	Activities Planned

AP9A

H. COMMENTS OF SENIOR EXECUTIVE (OR COMMITTEE) EVALUATING THIS APPRAISAL

Signature of Senior Executive:	Date:

I. ACTIONS RESULTING FROM THIS PERFORMANCE REVIEW

☐ No salary increase

☐ Increase of $_____ per_____ to a new salary of $_____ per_____

Other Actions: _____

J. APPRAISEE'S COMMENTS

Signature of Appraisee:	Date:
Signature of Appraiser:	Date:

AP9A

Glossary of Terms

Above-the-market pricing. A pricing strategy which sets the retail price of merchandise higher than that of others carrying the same or similar goods.

Advanced (post) dating. Establishment of a future date on an invoice different from that which was written originally on the invoice.

Alpha-numeric characters. Letters of the alphabet and Arabic numerals which can be read by scanning equipment.

Anticipation. A form of interest given by vendors to retailers for early payment of invoices. The vendor must agree to permit this practice.

Apron. A form attached to either an invoice or a purchase order alerting accounts payable personnel to check particular items before processing the invoice for payment.

At-the-market pricing. A pricing strategy which sets the retail price of merchandise equal to that charged by others carrying the same or similar goods.

Audited sales report. The verified net sales amounts (gross sales − customer refunds) for any given period.

Automatic open-to-buy. A system of open-to-buy which permits buyers in a central office and store personnel to share buying responsibility. Generally used with opening stock distribution plan.

Average markup. The markup attained on a group of items.

Average sale. The gross dollar amount of sales divided by the number of transactions.

Average sale per hour. A dollar value indicating the average amount produced each hour.

Average sale per transaction. A dollar value indicating the average amount of each transaction.

Basic stock list.   Those items of merchandise in a department which are considered to be staples and are expected by customers to be in stock at all times.

Basic stock method.   A procedure for dollar inventory planning used for merchandise classifications with annual stock turns of six or less.

Beginning-of-the-month (B.O.M.) inventory.   The merchandise on hand on the first day of any month.

Below-the-market pricing.   A pricing strategy which sets the retail price of merchandise lower than that of others carrying the same or similar goods.

Book value (of inventory).   The value of inventory as determined by computations made from data generated by a retailer's records (or books) rather than from actual physical merchandise counts.

Branded merchandise.   Those goods produced by a manufacturer, labeled in some unique way to identify them as a product of that firm.

Buyer.   The individual in a retailing organization involved with, and/or responsible for, all activities involved with purchasing decisions.

Buying-into-your-markdowns.   Purchasing merchandise at reduced costs and selling all or part at regular prices, thereby generating extra markup as an offset against anticipated markdowns.

Buying office.   An organization formed to service noncompeting stores with merchandise and market information.

Buying plan.   The method of converting dollar open-to-buy values into unit amounts.

C.O.D. (cash on delivery).   Payment made by a retailer to a vendor when merchandise is delivered. This is an indication of little or no credit standing for the retailer.

Cash discount.   A reduction in the billed cost of merchandise offered by vendors to retailers for payment during a prescribed time preceding the date when the full amount is due.

Central market.   A market city containing the widest possible range of vendors for a particular type of merchandise.

Classification (of merchandise).   A title and/or numeric designation for a broadly defined type of goods, without regard to size, color, price or individual style.

Closeout.   Merchandise offered to retailers by vendors at lower than the original cost price. The goods may have been discontinued, poorly selling styles, or have incomplete size, color, or style assortments.

Commissionaire.   An individual in an overseas market who has expertise with several merchandise lines and provides his or her services for a fee.

Committee buying.   Purchase decisions made by a number of people from within the same store. These individuals may have related or unrelated merchandise responsibility.

Consignment buying.   Purchasing merchandise where the title to the goods remains with the vendor for a specified period of time, at the end of which the retailer may return the unsold portion.

Core competitor.   A competitor whose merchandise and service offerings match or closely approximate the expectations of a retailer's core customer.

Core customer.   A customer whose characteristics, orientation, and expectations are known and understood by the retailer.

Core merchandise. Any merchandise carried in the proper breadth and depth, and priced appropriately to provide satisfaction for a retailer's core customer.

Cost code. A system of letters or numbers which can be substituted for, and disguise the cost of, an item on a price ticket.

Cost of goods (sold). The net cost of merchandise sold, obtained by adding to the billed cost of goods any transportation expenses (and alteration expenses, if applicable), and subtracting from this sum all cash, trade, and quantity discounts.

Cost percentage (of compensation). A percentage value which indicates the dollar cost for each compensation dollar spent.

Cumulative markup. The dollar or percent of markup obtained over a period of time.

Customer return rate. See Sales (customer) returns percent of gross sales.

Customs broker. An individual licensed by the U.S. Treasury Department who acts as a retailer's agent to facilitate the movement of the retailer's merchandise through Customs. Payment is by fee arrangement with the retailer.

D.O.I. (date of invoice). Refers to the date on an invoice which identifies the beginning of the period during which payment for the merchandise must be made. Also known as ordinary dating.

Dating. A general term which indicates that the time period for invoice payment has been altered.

Delivery period. A specified time period during which ordered merchandise must be delivered.

Disposable income. The amount of money left to an individual after all taxes have been deducted.

Divisional merchandise manager (D.M.M.). The individual who is responsible for overseeing and coordinating the efforts of a number of buyers, who usually purchase related classifications of merchandise.

Drop-shipping. A practice of shipping merchandise directly to individual stores in a chain or group, rather than having the goods delivered to a central receiving point.

End-of-the-month (E.O.M.) dating. A term which indicates that the discount period begins at the end of the month and is dependent on other factors, such as D.O.I., R.O.G., and so on.

End-of-the-month (E.O.M.) inventory. The merchandise on hand on the last day of any month.

Expenses. All nonmerchandise expenditures which must be accounted for by markup.

Extra dating. A general term which indicates an additional period of time for invoice payment.

Eyeball inventory (control). A method of stock management which relies upon the use of the eye as a measuring device, rather than physically counting and identifying merchandise.

F.O.B. (free-on-board). A shipping term which when followed by words such as "factory" or "store" designates the physical location where title to merchandise is transferred and to what point the vendor pays transportation charges.

Fad.   A particular style of merchandise which attains rapid popularity and just as quickly experiences a decline in sales.

Fashion.   A particular style of merchandise which has a relatively long selling life and a gradual weakening of sales.

Flash sales report.   The gross sales for a department, prepared at the close of each business day.

Follow-up market visit.   A visit to the market subsequent to an overview visit. The purpose of the follow-up is to place merchandise commitments.

Foreign markets.   Any location, excluding sites in the United States, containing a representative selection of vendors for particular classifications of merchandise.

Forward stock.   Merchandise situated on the selling floor, as opposed to a stockroom area.

General merchandise retailer.   A retailer whose merchandise offerings include apparel, accessories, furniture, appliances, and food.

Generic merchandise.   Unbranded goods without a label other than identification of the product and other information required by law.

Gross margin.   The dollar value remaining after reductions and cost of goods sold are subtracted from sales plus cash discounts.

Gross margin return on investment (G.M.R.O.I.).   A productivity ratio measuring the efficiency of the investment in inventory.

Group buying.   Purchasing done together by noncompeting buyers. This may be accomplished informally or as a formal arrangement known as a buying office.

Hand-to-mouth buying.   Repeatedly purchasing merchandise in small quantities for immediate sale.

Heart price zone.   The central segment of a price range in a merchandise classification, containing those price lines which account for the bulk of the volume.

High price zone.   The end segment of a price range in a merchandise classification, containing the more expensive price lines.

"Hot" number (item).   A particular style of merchandise which has a rate of sale considerably higher than the average for similar goods.

Individual buying.   That method of purchasing which places the authority and decision-making responsibility with a single person.

Individual markup.   The markup on a single piece of merchandise.

Initial markup.   The markup which is calculated from planned figures for a season and is the goal buyers attempt to meet when pricing merchandise for sale.

Invoice.   A bill from a vendor to a retailer for merchandise. It will show merchandise, payment and shipping information.

Job lot.   The term is used synonymously with "closeout."

Key appeals.   Those elements of a retailer's business which will best satisfy the tangible and intangible aspects of the core customer.

Key receiving sheet (key-rec).   A numbered form indicating receipt of merchandise. May be attached to the appropriate invoice.

Keystone markup. The practice of doubling the cost price of an item to determine its retail price.

Landed cost. Total cost of imported merchandise, including first cost of the goods, fees, and shipping costs.

Letter of Credit. A credit line established by a United States buyer (or store) in a foreign bank. A foreign vendor can draw upon this after presenting a draft and shipping documents.

Limited-line retailer. A retailer whose merchandise offering is generally a single line carried in depth, or who may be a specialty shop with one major classification of merchandise.

Line or merchandise line. An assortment of goods offered by a vendor.

Loading (an invoice). Increasing (or reducing) the gross invoice price of merchandise to reflect a larger (or smaller) cash discount. The net payment to the vendor remains the same.

Local market. The market city close to, or within, which a store is located, containing a limited representation of vendors and merchandise of a particular classification.

Loss leader. A promotional tool used to attract customers whereby merchandise is sold at or below cost.

Low price zone. The end segment of a price range in a merchandise classification, containing the least expensive price lines.

Mainframe (computer). Compared with a personal computer, a mainframe is large in size, works considerably faster, has greater memory storage capacity, and requires sophisticated operators.

Maintained markup. The markup dollar remaining after subtracting the cost of goods sold from the final selling price of the merchandise.

Manufacturer's representative. The individual who acts as an agent of a vendor, displaying and taking orders for the manufacturer's merchandise in a showroom and/or visiting stores.

Markdown. A downward alteration in the retail price.

Markdown cancellation. Revocation of a previously taken markdown.

Markdown money. Money, usually in the form of a merchandise credit given by vendors to retailers, to help offset markdowns on the vendor's merchandise.

Market representative (or merchandiser). An employee of a resident buying office whose primary function is to research the market and act as an advisor to the buyers of the office's member stores.

Market show. An exhibition by a substantial number of vendors of their merchandise, at regular intervals, in hotels, halls or auditoriums.

Marketing concept. Providing the customer with what the customer wants; requires the proper combination of merchandise, pricing, timing, promotion, selling effort, and location.

Markup. The broad term which is used to identify the money or percent difference between the cost of the merchandise (before cash discounts) and the selling price.

Merchandise budget. A strategy for dollar expenditures for goods over a period of time, usually six months, within a multi-store organization.

Merchandise transfer.   The movement of goods within a multi-store organization from one location to another.

Middlemen (wholesalers).   Generally, individuals or organizations who buy merchandise from one or more manufacturers in large quantities and resell the goods in smaller amounts to retailers.
   A. Merchant middlemen. Take title and possession of the goods.
      1. Service, or regular, wholesalers. Provide services such as advertising, storage, transportation, and credit.
      2. Limited function wholesalers. Sell their merchandise for cash; do not offer any service.
      3. Rack jobbers. Wholesalers of nonfood items in food stores; they arrange to stock and maintain an assortment of merchandise on a rack or stand in a selected location in each store.
   B. Nonmerchant middlemen. Do not take title but may take possession of the goods. They act as agents of the manufacturer, receiving a fee for bringing together producer and buyer.
      1. Brokers. These middlemen service food stores with groceries, fruits, and vegetables, as well as handling hardware, furniture, small appliances, jewelry, and clothing for relatively low-volume retailers.
      2. Commission people. Represent vendors by displaying the goods in a central market location. These middlemen are particularly effective in the grocery and fruit-and-vegetable areas. They take possession of the merchandise.
      3. Selling agents. These are agents who assume the sales activities for manufacturers who are too small, or who do not care to organize their own sales forces.
      4. Manufacturer's representatives. (Defined separately.)
      5. Auctioneers. This form of middleman predominates in the fruit-and-vegetable field, catering to supermarket chains and large food wholesalers; the latter group then resells to small food stores.

Model stock plan.   The organization for buying of fashion merchandise delineated by price lines, sizes, colors, materials, or whatever other factors are considered appropriate for the particular classification of goods.

Net billing.   The cost price of merchandise, either quoted to a retailer or listed on an invoice, towards which no discount may be applied.

Net cost of goods.   The retailer's cost of merchandise after all applicable discounts have been deducted.

Net profit.   The income available for distribution as dividends and surplus after merchandise costs, reductions, expenses, and taxes have been deducted from total income.

Nonstaple merchandise.   Any merchandise (style or item) which has a fluctuating, noncontinuous customer demand.

Off-price merchandise.   The phrase is used synonymously with "closeout."

On-hand (merchandise).   The goods already in stock.

On-order (merchandise).   The goods which have been purchased but have not been received.

Open-to-buy (O.T.B.).   The dollar amount which may be spent for additional inventory. The phrase may also refer to units, styles, etc. which would indicate a need to purchase a certain quantity of stock.

Opening stock distribution. A system of merchandise distribution wherein new and continuing styles are rank ordered according to sales potential and distributed to stores relative to their sales volume; higher-volume stores receive all styles in depth, lesser-volume stores are shipped only the better styles. This method is frequently combined with the price agreement and listing system.

Operating profit. The income remaining after subtracting operating expenses from gross margin.

Order form. The document used by purchasers to record the specifics of merchandise selection, payment, and shipping terms. It becomes a legal contract when accepted by the vendor.

Overview market visit. Trip to the market to obtain a broad perspective of vendors' offerings. The intention is to scan the field rather than isolate specific styles or materials.

Packing slip. A list, generated by a vendor at the time when merchandise is packed for shipping, which indicates the contents of the shipment. The packing slip may be a copy of the invoice with the pricing information obliterated.

Percentage variation method. Used for dollar planning of beginning-of-the-month inventories in departments with annual stock turn rates greater than six.

Point-of-purchase displays. Any merchandise stand, rack, or visual material used at or near the cash or wrapping desk to stimulate additional sales.

Post dating. The term is used synonymously with advance dating.

Pre-retailing (pre-pricing). The practice, by a buyer, of indicating the retail prices of the merchandise on the order form at the time of purchase. This facilitates the ticketing process and the computation of markup for that order.

Point-of-sale (P.O.S.) terminal. A device which combines a cash drawer, an electronic display screen, a keyboard, and a wand or limited-beam laser scanning device. This machine saves data for transmission to a central computer or will itself provide detailed reports of sales.

Price agreement and listing. A system of distribution wherein a central buyer provides store managers with approved lists of vendors, styles which can be purchased, and agreed prices for each style. Store managers may then order as needed; this method is commonly used for staple merchandise.

Price line. Identifies a specific retail price which will accommodate items of dissimilar but close cost prices.

Price point. This term is used synonymously with price line.

Price range. The breadth of retail prices for a particular classification of merchandise.

Price zone. Identifies a group of price lines clustered together to provide depth in a pricing structure.

Private brand (label). A name, symbol, or illustration that is the exclusive property of a retailer, manufacturer, wholesaler, or buying office to identify the owner of the name with specific items of merchandise.

Product life cycle. The time period during which a particular item, classification, fabric, color, or style will sell well enough for a retailer to generate a profit.

Quantity discount. A reduction in the billed cost of merchandise, owing to either the numbers of units purchased or the total dollar value.

Receipt-of-goods (R.O.G.) terms. Indicates that the counting period for payment begins when the merchandise is received by the retailer.

Reductions. The dollar or percentage values for markdowns, employee and customer discounts, and stock shortages used for sales and initial markup computations.

Regular (ordinary) dating. This term is used synonymously with D.O.I., date of invoice.

Resident buying office (R.B.O.). An organization in a central market which services noncompeting stores with merchandise and general market information.

Retail method. An accounting system utilizing retail values, which generates "book" values for inventory on hand at any given time.

Returns to vendor (R.T.V.). Merchandise returned to a manufacturer for justifiable reasons.

Runner. This term is used synonymously with hot item.

Sales per square foot. A productivity ratio indicating the net dollar sales generated by each square foot of selling space.

Sales (customer) returns percent of gross sales. A productivity ratio indicating the percentage of customer returns.

Season letter. Letters, numbers, or combinations thereof on price tickets to indicate the date of arrival of the merchandise. The date used may designate a six-month season or a particular month or week. The purpose of this information is to track the age of the stock.

Sell through (sales-to-stock). A percentage value reflecting the amount of merchandise sold relative to the quantity received.

Selling salaries percent of net sales. A productivity ratio indicating the cost per dollar of sales.

Shopping (competitors' market). Using powers of observation to analyze.

Short markup. A markup less than what is desired or needed.

Six-month merchandise (buying) plan. A dollar buying plan for a season which brings together the elements of initial markup, sales, reductions, and beginning-of-the-month inventory.

Software. Computer programs which give specific directions for a computer (hardware).

Source marking. Vendor-affixed tags or labels indicating various data required by the retailer for effective stock management. See Uniform Product Code.

Specific needs market visit. A trip to the market to place reorders, find replacement merchandise, seek solutions to isolated vendor problems, and/or find off-price merchandise.

Standard classification of merchandise. A coding system, developed by the National Retail Merchants Association, which provides a hierarchical classification for the full assortment of general merchandise, using a four-digit numeric code.

Staple merchandise. Merchandise which is in continuous demand by customers.

Stock count. Physical counts of merchandise by style, size, color, price, or whatever subdivision may be necessary.

Stock shortage (shrinkage). The dollar difference revealed by comparing the book value of inventory with a physical count of the stock.

Stepped (quantity) discount. A discount offered for purchases at different dollar or unit quantity levels or plateaus. A lower limit is established to ensure, to the vendor, that a minimum amount will be purchased before the discount is applicable.

Stock-keeping unit (S.K.U.). Identifies the smallest quantity of merchandise available for sale. A shirt could be one S.K.U., as would four bars of soap packaged for sale as a single unit.

Stock-to-sales method of dollar planning. Uses a ratio of beginning-of-the-month inventory to sales, to plan future investment in inventory.

Stock turnover (turnover). The number of times during a year that the average inventory is sold. As a productivity ratio it measures the rate of dollar reinvestment into inventory.

Straight line (quantity) discount. A discount offered for purchases within specified dollar or unit ranges. A lower limit is established to ensure, to the vendor, that a minimum amount will be purchased before the discount is applicable.

Strategic planning. An overall plan which has as its goal the attainment of competitive advantages over core competitors, leading to superior profits.

Terms (order or invoice). An agreement between vendor and buyer for payment of invoices.

Top down–bottom up planning. A method of developing a planned seasonal sales figure for each department, which involves all levels of management separately and mutually working towards an agreeable company goal.

Trade discount. A reduction from a list or retail price, offered to members of the trade, certain buyers, or other middlemen in exchange for the performance of services such as warehousing and distribution.

Traditional pricing. Setting the retail price of merchandise at a level which has become customary.

Transactions. The numbers of sales made during a given period. The figure may be determined by counting the number of sales slips or by recording the number of times the cash drawer has been opened.

Trend. A definite tendency or movement in a particular direction over a period of time.

Turnover. This term is used synonymously with stock turnover.

Uniform (universal) product code. A system of marking merchandise with a series of thick and thin lines.

Unit classification plan. A buying plan concerned with merchandise assortments and quantities.

Unit control. A manual or electronic-mechanical system of merchandise record keeping which renders information by vendor, style, color, size, and price. These data are obtained from tickets or labels attached to merchandise, which are removed or recovered by electronic means such as wands or limited-beam laser readers at the point of sale.

Vendor.   A manufacturer, or any form of middleman, from whom merchandise can be purchased.

Vendor profile.   A concise report about an individual vendor, reflecting both qualitative and quantitative productivity information.

Warehousing and requisition.   A system of distribution which requires buyers to maintain adequate quantities of merchandise which have been listed for store managers who must order frequently enough to maintain suitable levels of inventory in their stores.

Weeks supply method of dollar planning.   A system of inventory planning useful for staple forms of merchandise.

Wholesalers.   This term is used synonymously with middlemen.

Selected Formulae Index

Basic Retailing Formula ($ or %)   123

$$\text{Cost of goods} + \text{Markup} = \text{Retail price}$$
$$\text{Retail price} - \text{Cost of goods} = \text{Markup}$$
$$\text{Retail price} - \text{Markup} = \text{Cost of goods}$$

Basic Stock   179

$$\text{BS} = \text{Average inventory} - \text{Average monthly sales}$$

Beginning-of-the-month Stock—for departments with annual stock turns more than six (percentage variation method)   180

$$\text{B.O.M.} = \text{Average inventory} \times \frac{1}{2} \left(1 + \frac{\text{Sales for the month}}{\text{Average monthly sales}} \right)$$

Beginning-of-the-month Stock—for departments with six or less annual stock turns   179

$$\text{B.O.M.} = \text{Planned sales for the month} + \text{Basic stock}$$

Dollar Discount (cash, quantity, trade) Amount   94-95

$$\$\text{Discount} = \text{Discount \%} \times \$\text{Merchandise value}$$

Gross Margin   161-62

$$\text{GM} = \text{Maintained markup} + \text{Cash discount}$$

Initial Markup   122-24

$$\text{IM\%} = \frac{\text{Expenses} + \text{Profit} + \text{Reductions} - \text{Cash discounts}}{\text{Sales} + \text{Reductions}}$$

Maintained Markup Dollars   159-61

$$\$\text{MM} = (\text{Original retail} - \text{Reductions}) - \text{Cost of goods sold}$$

Maintained Markup Percent   159-61

$$\text{MM\%} = \frac{\$\text{MM}}{\$\text{Net retail}}$$

Markdown Dollar Value from Dollar Cost   155-56

$$\$\text{MD} = \text{Original \$cost} \times \text{MD\%}$$

Markdown Dollar Value from Dollar Retail   153

$$\$\text{MD} = \text{Original \$retail} \times \text{MD\%}$$

Markdown Dollars for Each Unit   152

$$\text{Unit } \$\text{MD} = \text{Original \$unit price} - \$\text{Markdown}$$

Markdown from Cost Price   155-56

$$\text{MD \$cost} = \text{Original \$cost} \times (100.0\% - \text{MD\%})$$

Markdown Total Dollar Cancellations   158

$$\$\text{MD total cancellations} = \text{Unit } \$\text{MD} \times \text{Balance of stock}$$

Markup Percentage Based on Retail   131-32

$$\text{MU\%} = \frac{\$\text{MU}}{\$\text{R}}$$

Maximum Stock (units) 204-6

Maximum stock = Rate of sale (Reorder period + Delivery period + Reserve)

Net Dollar Markdowns 159

$$\text{Net \$MD} = \text{Total \$MD} - \text{\$MD total cancellations}$$

Net Retail Dollars 160-61

$$\text{Net \$R} = \text{\$R} - \text{\$Reductions}$$

Open-to-Buy—for units of staple merchandise 205

$$\text{O.T.B.} = \text{Maximum stock} - (\text{On-hand stock} + \text{On-order stock})$$

Open-to-Buy—retail dollars 197

$$\text{\$R O.T.B.} = \text{\$R B.O.M.} - (\text{\$Merchandise received} + \text{\$Merchandise on order})$$

Operating Profit 162-63

$$\text{OP} = \text{Gross margin} - \text{Operating expense}$$

Purchases at Retail 190

$$\text{\$R Purchases} = \text{Planned sales} + \text{E.O.M. inventory} + \text{Reductions} - \text{B.O.M. inventory}$$

Reductions 122-23

$$\text{Reductions} = \text{Markdowns} + \text{Employee discounts} + \text{Customer discounts} + \text{Stock shortages}$$

Remittance Amount 100

$$\text{\$Remittance} = (100.0\% - \text{Discount\%}) \times \text{\$Merchandise value}$$

Sell Through 329

$$\text{Sell Through} = \frac{\text{Sales for the period}}{\text{Stock for the period}}$$

Stock on Hand 198

$$\text{Stock on hand} = \text{B.O.M.} + \text{Merchandise received} - (\text{Actual sales} + \text{Actual reductions})$$

Stock-to-Sales Ratio 182

$$\text{S-S} = \frac{\text{B.O.M. stock}}{\text{Sales for the month}}$$

Stock turn (Turnover) 175

$$\text{ST} = \frac{\text{Net sales (for the period)}}{\text{Average retail stock (for the period)}}$$

Weeks of Supply for Merchandise (staple) 181

$$\text{Weeks of supply} = \frac{\text{Number of weeks in the period}}{\text{Stock turn for the period}}$$

Index